Linking Literacies

Linking Literacies

Perspectives on L2 Reading-Writing Connections

Edited by Diane Belcher and Alan Hirvela
The Ohio State University

Ann Arbor
THE UNIVERSITY OF MICHIGAN PRESS

Copyright © by the University of Michigan 2001
All rights reserved
Published in the United States of America by
The University of Michigan Press
Manufactured in the United States of America
⊗ Printed on acid-free paper

2004   2003   2002   2001   4   3   2   1

A CIP catalog record for this book is available from the British Library.

U.S. CIP applied for.

ISBN 0-472-09753-9 (cloth)
ISBN 0-472-06753-2 (paper)

Acknowledgments

There are a number of people we would like to thank for their help in the completion of this project. The book grew out of the Ohio State Conference on Second Language Reading/Writing Connections held in Columbus, Ohio, in the summer of 1998, and we want to express our deep appreciation to Louis (Bill) Holschuh, Kathleen Romstedt, Lori Sandholdt, and Jun Liu for the leading roles they played in organizing and managing the conference. We also want to thank the many other teaching and administrative staff in ESL Programs and the graduate students in the Foreign and Second Language Education Program at Ohio State who helped make the conference possible. Peter Brandt provided wonderful technological assistance during the conference and while we were preparing the manuscript, and we want to express our appreciation for his help.

As to the book itself, we are extremely grateful to John Swales, Ilona Leki, and Andrea Lunsford for their interest in the project and for their valuable reflections and perspectives on the volume and on themselves as readers and writers as well as teachers of reading and writing. Likewise, we want to thank the special group of authors whose work appears in the volume for their commitment to the project and for their diverse and meaningful contributions to the book. Thanks, too, to Carol Taylor and the Educational Testing Service (ETS) for allowing us to include Joan Carson's chapter, which is based on a larger study she conducted on behalf of ETS. We are also grateful to the University of Michigan Press for permission to reprint material from *Academic Writing for Graduate Students: Essential Tasks and Skills,* by John M. Swales and Christine B. Feak (1994). Finally, we would like to express our deepest gratitude to Kelly Sippell, our editor at the University of Michigan Press. Her support, patience, and enthusiasm were of invaluable help to us from the moment we first began to think about the book to the days of its completion. We could not have asked for a more helpful and understanding editor.

Contents

Foreword

John M. Swales, University of Michigan

Here I sit writing a foreword to a rich collection with the main title *Linking Literacies.* Inevitably enough, this situation calls up some modest textual and intertextual reflections as I stare at the blinking cursor. I have to front the volume but not encroach on the territory carved out by the editors in their introduction, which I have before me in draft. I am here undertaking this small task (I must suppose) because the editors believe that I might have the linked reading and writing skills to complete it successfully and because I happen to know something about the topic. As it happens, I was also at the conference that acted as the catalyst for this volume, where I heard spoken versions of many of the essays that you will find here. Finally, I know many of the contributors (and their work); indeed, three of them are my colleagues at Michigan. So when people claim today that writing is "situated," I can recognize in this particular case that that situatedness has peculiarly multiple dimensions, including several interpersonal ones.

I also happen to be an ESL writing instructor, and one of the lasting values of the contributions that follow has been to reinforce a feeling that, in that role, I have taken reading skills too much for granted. In excuse, I could observe that I usually teach advanced writing courses for international graduate students who have already spent a number of years at an English-medium university. As a group, they seem to manifest only rarely obvious reading problems, and they certainly *say* that for them reading is much the least problematic of the four skill areas. But when I read Grabe's masterly survey of research into the intricacies of reading-writing relations, or Matsuda's salutary historicizing of the field, or Carson's meticulous analysis of reading-writing tasks at both undergraduate and graduate levels, or Dobson and Feak's dissection of what is actually involved in producing a decent critique, there emerges a renewed sense that academic writing is a tip-of-the-iceberg phenomenon. This feeling is reinforced by the trenchant comments in Barks and Watts's chapter regarding the impoverishment that results when ESL reading and writing are considered separately, despite complementarities in the cognitive processes involved in both. Even more deleterious, Barks and Watts argue, is further division into reading as a passive skill but writing as an active one. As the editors observe, we have not had an ESL/EAP volume committed to "linking literacies" since Carson and Leki's *Reading in the Composition Classroom* was published in 1993, although Johns's *Text, Role, and Context* (1997) comes close. It is time, then, for all of us who teach ESL writing to pay renewed attention to the threads that tie academic reading and writing tasks together.

A remaining obstacle to a conjoined approach to reading and writing comes from the fact that the level of sanction applied to transgression is so different in each case. Crimes of writing are manifest and manifold: false authorship, forgery, libel, plagiarism, and, somewhat less certainly, graffiti and pornography. But what are the crimes of reading? It is not exactly a crime to be undercritical or overcritical, however these should be defined, of somebody's text. It may be morally questionable to approve or disapprove of an academic text just because we very much like or dislike the author, but it is not exactly a crime to react in this way. Unlike writing transgressions, reading ones escape the notice of university ethics committees and honor codes and the like.

Partly because of its salience and partly because it is so obviously socially constructed, the topic of plagiarism attracts considerable attention in this volume, having indeed a section unto itself (part 3). Bloch, in a very substantial contribution, explores Western and Chinese attitudes toward authorship and intellectual property but then argues, in a very interesting development, "If there is a more collaborative voice in Chinese rhetoric, then what may be problematic for Chinese students about plagiarism in regard to printed texts may be less problematic in regard to electronic texts." Next, Pecorari surveys the official policies of universities in three English-speaking countries regarding plagiarism and finds it almost universally condemned as an academic crime, with its accompanying collection of draconian sanctions. Both she and Barks and Watts (in the closing chapter of part 3) argue for some ESL relief from this institutionally imposed misery, while the latter offer some classroom solutions to the often unrecognized dilemmas that confront ESL students.

My own experience of teaching U.S. undergraduates suggests that the plagiarism issue is not simply or even mainly an ESL problem. Rather, the strictures against plagiarism (including the "borrowing of ideas") undermine our more general attempts to encourage linked literacies. My stu-

dents, mostly linguistics majors, having survived the footnoting and cita-
tional rigors of the "researched paper" in composition classes, seem for
the most part unable to make much use of their readings in their subsequent written assignments. When pressed, they claim that it is "too risky"
to refer to or utilize their readings in their papers, that it is "safer" to use
their own thoughts and experiences. As a result, their written assignments
typically strike me as being academically undernourished, starved of the
wider context that reading so notably provides. I very much hope, therefore, that at least this volume's chapters on plagiarism will be read by educators outside the field of ESL, for, as I have tried to argue, the problem
affects undergraduate education in general in the United States.

In this foreword, I have not attempted to address all the topics discussed in this valuable collection. I only give mention here to the chapters
that explore new technological capacities and to those that argue, in various subtle ways, for the use of literary texts in the ESL reading-writing
classroom. However, before finishing, I would like to make a few comments about vocabulary, since this topic is discussed in the first two chapters of the volume's final section. The coming employment of appropriate
academic corpora, indeed already deployed in Jabbour's chapter, should
in fact operate to further strengthen the links between reading and writing
instruction as they are developed in this book. Lexical and phraseological
approaches, deriving from corpus linguistics, not only erode traditional
distinctions between grammar and vocabulary but also facilitate learner
acquisition of "phrasicons" or provide access to them via simple concordance programs. Phrasicons facilitate genre-specific reading and writing
tasks and reinforce for L2 learners the largely prefabricated nature of the
language that they are attempting to comprehend and/or compose.

Overall, *Linking Literacies: Perspectives on L2 Reading-Writing Connections* not only tells us, in its more theoretical sections, what we should be
thinking but also shows us, in its more practical sections, what we might
be doing. It has certainly changed my perspective on the central issue of
the reading-writing connection and sharpened my understanding of that
issue in a number of specific directions. The editors, Diane Belcher and
Alan Hirvela, are greatly to be congratulated both on their important originating conference and on the care and attention they have given to
putting this coherent volume together. It should be read by both experienced and beginning ESL instructors and consulted by those with broader
interests in academic literacy and university education.

So I come to the end of this foreword, my attempt to link this volume
to its context, to link parts of my own experience to various themes out-

lined in it, and, more importantly, to link its writers with its potential readers. The blinking cursor comes to rest. Print. Read on.

References

Carson, J. G., and I. Leki, eds. 1993. *Reading in the composition classroom: Second language perspectives.* Boston: Heinle and Heinle.

Johns, A. M. 1997. *Text, role, and context: Developing academic literacies.* Cambridge: Cambridge University Press.

Introduction

Diane Belcher and Alan Hirvela, Ohio State University

As separate fields of inquiry and practice, second language (L2) reading and writing attracted considerable interest in the 1980s and 1990s and gradually established themselves as viable, dynamic areas of research and pedagogy with identities independent of, though certainly deeply influenced by, their first language (L1) counterparts. Recognizing that, as Robert Scholes (1985) has observed, "reading and writing are complementary acts that remain unfinished until completed by their reciprocals" (20), some L2 researchers and practitioners increasingly found themselves working both sides of the reading and writing fence, as it were, and, inspired in part by developments in L1 reading and writing theory and practice, began to look at connections between the reading and writing skills in the L2 context. As William Grabe's chapter in this volume demonstrates, there has been a steady focus on research into L2 reading-writing relationships over the past decade and a half. There has likewise been increased interest in integrated reading-writing instruction in the L2 classroom. In these regards, there are strong similarities between the L1 and L2 domains.

There is also, however, a perhaps surprising and certainly notable difference between these domains. The L1 world has seen the publication of numerous books examining reading-writing connections, and these connections are routinely explored at major conferences. It would appear that the same cannot be said of the L2 domain. While, as noted earlier, William Grabe's opening chapter reveals an ongoing interest in L2 reading-writing relations, that interest has not coalesced into what might be called a critical mass of L2 reading-writing scholarship. The one notable exception to date is Joan Carson and Ilona Leki's collection of papers, *Reading in the Composition Classroom* (1993). Otherwise, L2 reading-writing scholarship has taken the form of papers published in various journals and occasional conference papers, with no centralized site for that scholarship. Given the importance of literacy skills in the overall development of second language proficiency and the extent to which multilingual writers must rely on such skills in academic settings, there is considerable value, for current and future pedagogy and research, in collecting recent data, insights, and practices generated by those investigating and teaching L2 reading-writing relations.

In recognition of that value, in the summer of 1998 a major conference organized for the sole purpose of bringing together L2 reading-writing researchers and teachers was held. That gathering, the Ohio State Conference on Second Language Reading/Writing Connections, provided several prominent reading-writing scholars and a number of other researchers representing a half dozen countries with an opportunity to address a series of questions related to the general topic of L2 reading-writing relations. Meeting in the spirit of Robert Tierney and Margie Leys's (1986) assertions that "the study of reading-writing connections involves appreciating how reading and writing work together in myriad ways" and that "literacy is at a premium when an individual uses reading and writing in concert" (26) to achieve a number of purposes, the participants examined L2 reading-writing relationships from a wide variety of perspectives. Key questions explored at the conference included: How well are we forging links between reading and writing in our classrooms? In what ways are our L2 and often L1-based pedagogical theories and our use of new technology helping us make reading-writing connections, and how are these connections realized in our syllabi, assignments, and materials and in the minds of our students? Do our students actually become better L2 readers and writers as a result of our integrated reading and writing instruction?

This volume consists mainly of essays based on selected presentations from the conference as well as invited essays intended to address important areas not fully represented at the conference. Discussing theory, research, and pedagogy, these essays allow the volume to examine a wide range of issues and concerns within the general rubrics of L2 reading-writing connections and L2 academic literacy. Indeed, a key organizing principle in our construction of the book was to illustrate the many ways in which L2 reading-writing relations are, or can be, manifested. Furthermore, by choosing the phrase "linking literacies" as the opening words in the volume's title, we hoped to draw attention to both the multiple literacies already possessed by students for whom English is an additional language and the literacies they seek to acquire. It is important to understand, especially among teachers with little or no experience in working with such students, that in a writing classroom where these students are participants, there is not just one literacy (i.e., English academic literacy) at hand. Rather, there are complex movements among literacies. Our job, as teachers and researchers, is to help students learn to link these literacies in ways that are empowering to them as readers and writers and effective within the discourse realms or communities in which they use them.

In their important book cited earlier, Carson and Leki (1993) stated that "the ESL teaching profession is on the brink of an important new understanding of the connections between reading and writing" (1). At the various levels of ESL instruction, reading and writing—whether taught separately or jointly—play central roles in our pedagogy as well as our research. In this volume, as well as during the conference from which it developed, our hope has been to provide ESL (and L1) reading and writing professionals and teachers-in-training with a comprehensive and diverse collection of papers about what has taken place in reading-writing relations research and pedagogy since Carson and Leki offered their assessment of this important area within the ESL domain.

Overview of Contents

Linking Literacies consists of four sections, which move from a consideration of theories, history, and research that have had and likely will have an influence on L2 literacy pedagogy (part 1) to examination of actual classroom practices (parts 2–4). More specifically, the latter three parts of this volume focus on how practitioners can link, and hence help learners link, reading and writing in the L2 classroom (part 2); how practitioners and their institutions address one particularly challenging pedagogical issue that invariably arises when novice writers write about reading, that is, plagiarism (part 3); and, finally, how technology is changing not just the ways students learn and teachers teach L2 literacy but also our understanding of what it means (and takes) to acquire that literacy (part 4), which might be better termed "literacies," given the varied processes entailed in print and on-line reading and writing.

While we, as editors, found it relatively easy to assign the chapters in this volume to each of our four sections, we realize that this taxonomy is somewhat arbitrary. As one would expect in an applied field such as ours, the theorists/historians/researchers in this volume are mindful of practice, and the practitioners' chapters are clearly historically situated in their readings of theory and research. Furthermore, issues discussed in one section may also be seen as relevant to another. For example, Newell, Garriga, and Peterson's "Learning to Assume the Role of Author" in part 2 is certainly germane to the textual ownership focus of part 3, and Bloch's "Plagiarism and the ESL Student: From Printed to Electronic Texts" in part 3 discusses technology-related concerns pertinent to the overarching theme of part 4, computer-assisted language learning (CALL). Nevertheless, our four-part arrangement, with chapters configured in each section to inform and motivate each other (as we will discuss shortly), is meant to be helpful to the reader who wants to peruse the volume in the linear way that any print text encourages, that is, from the first to the last page.

Part 1. Grounding Practice: Theory, Research, and History

Part 1 opens with William Grabe's "Reading-Writing Relations: Theoretical Perspectives and Instructional Practices," a sweeping survey of both L1 and L2 reading and writing theory, with special attention to the connectionist perspective—how reading and writing relate to and enhance each other. While the scope of Grabe's overview of the theoretical foundations of current literacy pedagogy is impressive—and essential to an understanding of why reading and writing have been assumed to be pedagogically synergistic—some readers may find even more interesting his exposure of some serious gaps in L2 reading-writing research and theory. Grabe notes, for example, that despite over two decades of assertions that the two modalities enrich each other, there has been little empirical research on the extent to which popular integrated reading-writing practices actually do enhance reading and writing proficiency and lead to improved language and content learning. Grabe encourages future work in these areas, especially L2 EAP (English for academic purposes) literacy studies, by providing a set of ten guiding principles to keep in mind when contemplating L2 literacy curricular development and action research.

In "A Task Analysis of Reading and Writing in Academic Contexts," Joan Carson reminds us why L2 literacy teaching and learning should be of interest to TESOL teacher trainers, SLA researchers, and others concerned with pedagogical approaches to fostering successful L2 use in academic environments. Carson's thick description of reading and writing tasks in six college courses, representing the natural and social sciences and humanities at both the undergraduate and graduate levels, may be one of the most ambitious and comprehensive L2 literacy needs analyses ever attempted. Few studies have exhibited the breadth and depth of analysis one finds in Carson's, with its broad disciplinary and academic-level coverage and its close examination of task artifacts—not just assignment prompts but student responses to the prompts—as well as of faculty perspectives on task goals and L1 and L2 student perspectives on task strategy use. Carson calls attention to some striking differences in the variety and intensity of literacy demands across disciplines and academic levels but also to some pervasive underlying similarities in these demands (e.g., writing as an effective strategy in almost all academic task preparation and subject-area reading as an essential component in almost all academic writing tasks)—demands that those who teach L2 reading and writing will want to help their students prepare to navigate (whether that entails meeting, resisting, or negotiating faculty-imposed goals).

By taking us to the roots of past and, some would argue, continuing neglect of literacy among second language acquisition (SLA) specialists and others, Paul Kei Matsuda's "Reexamining Audiolingualism: On the Genesis of Reading and Writing in L2 Studies" helps us understand why L2 literacy has not been as thoroughly researched and systematically theorized as Grabe and others would like to see. According to Matsuda, the relatively limited interest in L2 literacy studies that applied linguists have exhibited is not simply the legacy of audiolingualism but can be traced back ideologically to the rise of scientific linguistics and the resulting view of language as speech and of writing as only a secondary representation of speech. Matsuda argues that TESOL specialists will need to do more than simply reject audiolingualism, as most have; they must also examine its historical conditions and problematize its underlying assumptions if L2 reading and writing are to receive the attention that they merit and currently too seldom receive in SLA research, linguistics textbooks, and professional training programs.

Part 2. In the Classroom: Teaching Reading as Writing and Writing as Reading

In the opening chapter of part 2, "Connecting Reading and Writing through Literature," Alan Hirvela suggests a somewhat controversial solution to the problem of how to prepare college-bound English-language learners for the wide and varied array of interrelated reading-writing tasks that Carson's study so clearly indicates awaits them. As both difficult and compelling texts, literary works, Hirvela asserts, provide motivating and challenging opportunities for students, especially undergraduates, to rehearse the recursive reading-writing strategies they will need across the curriculum. As Hirvela notes, literary texts "leave readers with gaps" that can be successfully filled "by active, meaning-making reading," which in turn "is often guided most effectively by writing."

Hirvela does not argue that literary texts should replace nonliterary texts but that a place be made in the L2 literacy syllabus for these powerful, imaginatively engaging means of persuading learners that indeed "reading and writing resemble and sustain each other."

Like Hirvela, Mary Malloy argues for the use of literature, but she has rather different objectives in mind for a very different student population. As is indicated by her title, "The Foreign Language Literacy Classroom 'Translating Event' as Reading and Composing: Eighth Graders Read Cross-Cultural Children's Literature," Malloy is interested in the literacy needs of younger learners in the foreign language, not second language, context. From Malloy's perspective, literary texts seem a natural choice for her Anglophone middle school students of German, who are already literate in their L1 and likely to find "mastery-level" pedagogical materials uninteresting. For Malloy, who is eager to reject the long-standing "hegemony" of the target language, literary translation is not a methodological step backward to traditional grammar/translation but a step forward to community language learning. In a Malloy-style classroom, literary translation, far from the usual tedious mechanical exercise performed in isolation, is a highly interactive activity that invites students to take advantage of all their linguistic resources, in both the L1 and the target language. The students are caught up in the excitement of a translating event, in which they enthusiastically assist each other in co-composing an oral English text from their German reading. Malloy's transcriptions of her students' lively translating sessions provide ample evidence for her claim that a collaborative approach to meaning making with sophisticated high-interest texts can lead to engagement with and desire to understand the target language, "cultivating . . . goodwill not only to the school subject but also to the people and culture" represented.

In "Learning to Assume the Role of Author: A Study of Reading-to-Write One's Own Ideas in an Undergraduate ESL Composition Course," George Newell, Maria Garriga, and Susan Peterson are interested in the use of both literary and nonliterary readings as catalysts for source-based analytic writing. According to these authors, for students to learn to write analytically in an academic context, they must write to develop their own ideas about reading, and they must employ formal academic structures to "shape their own interpretations" of reading "as they advance their own ideas." Thus, the goal of literacy acts in college, according to Newell, Garriga, and Peterson, is neither just to read to write nor to write to display what has been read but for students to be able to restructure "information, ideas, and experiences from source texts to make them their own." In their study, Newell, Garriga, and Peterson found that engagement with a series of reading-to-write tasks seemed to provide novice academic writers with the means and motivation to explore their responses to reading as well as to try out more formal academic thinking and reasoning strategies.

Like Newell, Garriga, and Peterson, Barbara Dobson and Christine Feak see the ability to respond analytically to reading as the hallmark of college-level academic literacy. Dobson and Feak feel strongly, though, that undergraduates are seldom given adequate, if any, preparation for the complexities of reading and writing critically, such as the need to weigh the competing knowledge claims of multiple (usually nonliterary) texts. In "A Cognitive Modeling Approach to Teaching Critique Writing to Nonnative Speakers," Dobson and Feak present a series of steps that simulate expert writers' strategy use and guide undergraduates from simple comprehension and personal reaction to evaluation of a text "vis-à-vis their [own, topic-related] knowledge." With the cognitive scaffolding Dobson and Feak offer, undergraduates should be poised to view texts (perhaps even their introductory subject-area textbooks) not just as "storehouses of facts" but as "subjects for evaluation" and to "position themselves in the role of someone with enough knowledge and experience to challenge the written word."

Part 3. (E)Merging Literacies and the Challenge of Textual Ownership

Constructing one's own meaning from others' texts and assuming authority in one's own texts through the development of one's own perspectives and ideas may be such uncontroversial literate acts (indeed achievements) in Anglophone educational contexts that it may be difficult for those of us immersed in this environment to see them as cultural practices. To outsiders, these same practices may appear strangely ego-driven or excessively capitalistic in their privileging of individual ownership of written products, of the ideas expressed in them, and even of "readings" of others' texts—all of which are often referred to by Anglophones as "intellectual property." All three chapters in part 3 address the cultural situatedness of "textual ownership" and the Anglophone academic response to a lack of appreciation or understanding of "textual borrowing" conventions.

As Joel Bloch points out in the opening chapter of part 3, "Plagiarism and the ESL Student: From Printed to Electronic Texts," the Anglophone cultural situation, like others around the world, is actually rapidly changing, as it moves from print to increasingly digital domination (and resulting increased cross-cultural contact). Bloch observes that L2 users may in some respects be advantaged by this move to cyberspace (if and when they are on-line). Not only do electronic connections improve access to information—topical, linguistic, and cultural—and opportunities for L2 interaction, but the new cybertext world may feel more comfortable to those with less individualistic textual practices than it does to those who see concepts like intellectual property at risk on the Internet, with its cut-and-paste, hypertext capabilities. Bloch notes that Chinese students and others with "long and varied traditions of authorship and intertextuality" may indeed be more at home on the Internet than in "traditional class-rooms." As Bloch remarks, those of us who refuse to view texts and ideas as communal, not just personal, property may have more to learn than many of our L2 students.

In "Plagiarism and International Students: How the English-Speaking University Responds," Diane Pecorari points out that, at present, most universities in the Anglophone "center" still appear to be strongly attached to the traditional Western individual-oriented view of intellectual property ownership and are eager to hold students to this standard no matter what their cultural background or stage of literacy acquisition. In her survey of plagiarism policies and practices in 54 universities in Australia, the United Kingdom, and the United States, Pecorari found that "[w]ith few exceptions, the policies examined appeared to assume a universal view of plagiarism as an academic crime." The institutional data Pecorari collected convinced her, as it no doubt will many readers, that Anglophone universities need to recognize that "conventions for citation are not universal," that "new practices" learners are confronted with are "absorbed gradually," and that students should be allowed "a margin of error as they try to hit a new target."

As language educators, Debbie Barks and Patricia Watts respond to the plagiarism challenge, the perceived need to teach students our intertextual ways, in a manner Pecorari found few (or no) universities to do at the institutional level—that is, not by criminalizing but by educating. In "Textual Borrowing Strategies for Graduate-Level ESL Writers," Barks and Watts present a sequence of tasks designed to teach graduate students borrowing strategies acceptable in English-medium universities. Barks and Watts's focus on graduate students seems especially fitting given the small amount of time these students generally have, compared to undergraduates, to absorb new practices and produce discipline-specific texts in response to reading. Strikingly unlike the common plagiarism scare tactics and uncompelling, uncontextualized paraphrasing/summarizing exercises commonly found in many ESL instructional materials, Barks and Watts's sequenced task approach—moving from cross-cultural consciousness-raising, to building textual borrowing strategies, and finally to ethnographic investigations into disciplinary borrowing practices—is noteworthy for its conspicuous recognition of the cultural knowledge and disciplinary expertise that graduate students bring to an EAP class. As Barks and Watts suggest, the EAP teacher may benefit as much as the students do from the window on borrowing practice diversity that this task sequence opens.

Part 4. Technology-Assisted Reading and Writing

In part 4, we are reminded that literacy education is not totally dependent on teachers. None of the contributors in part 4 has visions of technology replacing teachers, but they do see it supplementing and assisting what teachers do and helping students become more autonomous language learners. Terence Odlin, in the opening chapter, "With the Dictionary and Beyond," calls our attention to a low-tech tool that language students have relied on for centuries but the value of which may often be overlooked in L2 literacy classes today that focus on instilling top-down reading and writing strategies. Odlin praises the often underappreciated power of dictionaries—what they can do when, for instance, context fails to help readers or when lexical factors bog writers down with seemingly impossible morphosyntactic issues. Odlin points out, though, that new computer-generated corpora offer even more information about lexis in context than many specialized "learner" dictionaries. While well aware of the dangers of dictionary (especially bilingual dictionary) dependence, Odlin sees dictionaries and corpora as capable of promoting learner autonomy by helping students become the independent language analysts they need to be to grow as L2 readers and writers outside the language classroom.

While computer-generated corpora should help students become more independent language analysts, they should also encourage learners, and their teachers as well, to view language differently—not in the traditional grammar and vocabulary categories but as lexical chunks. In "Lexis and Grammar in Second Language Reading and Writing," Georgette Jabbour argues that a lexical approach to language, far from miring us in sentence-level concerns, frees us to concentrate on discourse issues, for word collocation (or lexical chunks) is inseparable from consideration of context. With the lexical approach, the teacher can provide, according to Jabbour, a context for language discovery as well as for discovery strategy development. Jabbour presents sample exercises derived from her own medical corpus linguistic research that illustrate the types of tasks that can be constructed to expose students to genuine lexical data, that is, naturally occurring language in authentic academic contexts. In response to those who may be troubled by the apparent local, rather than global, processing strategies that the lexical approach seems to focus on, Jabbour argues, "Lexis provides the basis of the bottom-up linguistic elements that . . . connect to the conceptual framework of the text and allow top-down reading and writing to occur." Without lexis, Jabbour observes, there can be no reading or writing.

While Odlin and Jabbour focus on how technology can contribute to self- (student-) and teacher-directed strategies supportive of learner autonomy, Joel Bloch and Janina Brutt-Griffler look at how technology can promote learner collaboration in support of the same aim. In the final chapter of part 4 and of this volume, "Implementing CommonSpace in the ESL Composition Classroom," Bloch and Brutt-Griffler report that the adoption of collaborative writing software in their ESL program resulted in a number of beneficial outcomes: it facilitated student commentary on fellow student texts, made commentary (from students and teachers) more readable and useful, encouraged collaborative composing, and promoted dialogue between student-authors and respondents. Yet Bloch and Brutt-Griffler also found that the impact of CommonSpace on the students as readers was less than ideal for process-oriented writing classes, as the students had difficulty focusing on discourse-level issues. Intervention strategies had to be developed by the teachers to guide students to consideration of global issues while responding on-line. Interestingly, although the CommonSpace-mediated responses to writing, from both fellow students and teachers, were generally well received by the students, they still felt the need, Bloch and Brutt-Griffler note, for face-to-face contact with their teachers in a writing conference. The findings of this study overall, according to the authors, are more supportive of a view of the computer as "tool," a tool that must be intelligently used, than as "tutor," or surrogate teacher. Bloch and Brutt-Griffler conclude that when deciding how (or whether) to use computer-assisted learning, care must be taken to consider the characteristics not just of hardware and software but also of "humanware."

Foreword, Interlude, and Afterword

In the foreword and afterword, John Swales and Andrea Lunsford, respectively, frame this volume by using their own practices as readers and writers and their own experiences as teachers of writing to comment on many of the perspectives offered herein. Their reflections provide a meaningful entry point (Swales) and a thought-provoking sense of closure (Lunsford) to the volume. Ilona Leki, in the interlude, examines how some of the book's chapters appear to answer one of the key questions from the Ohio State conference—Do our students actually become better readers and writers as a result of our classroom practices? In addition to allowing Leki to share some of her own current perspectives on L2 reading-writing relations, the interlude enables readers to pause and reflect before moving into the second half of the volume.

While this volume reflects to a certain extent on the historical underpinnings of reading-writing relations and shows how L1 influences have impacted on the development of reading-writing theory and pedagogy in the L2 context, it paints an even stronger picture of how scholarship on L2 reading-writing connections has established an identity independent of the L1 domain. Meanwhile, it is increasingly the case that the multilingual student writers who are the focus of this book intermingle in Anglophone classroom settings with students for whom English is the native language. Then there are the ever growing numbers of immigrant students in North America, the United Kingdom, and Australia (to name a few Anglophone sites), many of whom experience multiple contact points with literacy as they move between the language(s) they initially learned in their countries of origin and the language they have learned and used for a number of years in the countries where they have later become residents. We must also acknowledge the evolving, technologically based literacies that our students frequently embrace and that are a necessity to control in today's world of computers, Web sites, and cyberspace. The results, especially for teachers of reading and writing, are (a) that the distinction between the L1 and L2 domains is blurring rapidly and (b) that reading and writing instruction can no longer be centered on just one literacy. We have compiled *Linking Literacies* partly in the belief that today's teachers of such traditional L1 courses as first-year college (i.e., "freshman composition") writing classes will benefit from the insights provided by L2 literacy scholars in the same ways that L2 teachers and researchers have been helped by L1 scholarship (cf. Silva, Leki, and Carson 1997). Our hope is that this book, just as it attempts to link the literacies students already possess and those they pursue, will also help provide new and stronger connections between L1 and L2 literacy scholars and teachers. These connections may be vital in the new and exciting world of multiple literacies that we, as teachers and researchers, engage in our literacy instruction and research.

References

Carson, J. G., and I. Leki, eds. 1993. *Reading in the composition classroom: Second language perspectives.* Boston, MA: Heinle and Heinle.

Scholes, R. 1985. *Textual power: Literary theory and the teaching of English.* New Haven: Yale University Press.

Silva, T., I. Leki, and J. G. Carson. 1997. Broadening the perspective of mainstream composition studies: Some thoughts from the disciplinary margins. *Written Communication* 14:398–428.

Tierney, R. J., and M. Leys. 1986. What is the value of connecting reading and writing? In *Convergences: Transactions in reading and writing,* ed. B. T. Petersen, 15–29. Urbana, IL: National Council of Teachers of English.

Part 1

Grounding Practice:
Theory, Research, and History

Chapter 1

Reading-Writing Relations: Theoretical Perspectives and Instructional Practices

William Grabe, Northern Arizona University

The interaction of reading and writing is a much discussed issue that is central to the development of advanced academic abilities. The concepts involved in discussing reading and writing relationships are also very complex—one must disentangle and examine a number of theoretical positions and supporting research to understand the ways in which these concepts can suggest effective instruction. For example, reading and writing relations and their interacting impact on learning require, at a minimum, a theoretical position on reading abilities and their development, a theory of writing abilities and their development, and a theory of learning that explains how the interaction of the two literacy skills enhances learning. Of course, theory is not enough by itself. There must also be supporting evidence from sound research as well as evidence for the implementation of theory as practice. As this review will reveal, existing evidence for such a set of conditions is not easy to establish, particularly for L2 literacy learning contexts.

There are at least five further complicating factors to address as well. First, the numerous subnotions for reading and writing relations are sometimes combined and at times difficult to separate. However, they must be separated if we are to draw appropriate inferences from the research issues and their implications for practice. These notions include reading to learn, writing to learn, reading to improve writing, writing to improve reading, and reading and writing together for better learning. Second, there is a wide variety of L2 contexts that can be explored for the effective use of reading and writing together. These contexts extend well beyond the range of variation usually encountered in L1 contexts, whether for research or for instruction—they include LEP students, ESL and ESP university students, EFL secondary students, EFL university students, FLES students, FL secondary students, FL university students, ESL and EFL professional writers.

Third, L2 reading and writing contexts involve L1-L2 interactions and L1 influences on L2 literacy performance. L2 contexts also imply a range of learning situations that extend from students' first words and sentences in the L2 to writing dissertations in the L2. Fourth, motivations for learning are extended in L2 contexts to include extrinsic purposes that do not arise generally in L1 literacy contexts. Aside from all of the motivations impacting L1 students are the additional considerations that arise when a student does not feel a need to be fully grammatical in the L2 and does not have native speaker intuitions or a developed written voice in the L2. Fifth and finally, the range of research on these issues and on these student contexts varies considerably (for both L1 and L2 contexts).

A major goal of this chapter is to tease apart certain of the aforementioned issues, to note the relevant research with specific groups of students, and to connect this research to instruction. The other major goal is to outline possible curricular and instructional practices, supported by research, that can lead to better literacy skills and enhanced learning.

Theories in Support of Reading and Writing

To understand the nature of reading and writing relationships, it is not enough to state theoretical positions on reading and writing abilities. One must first establish, at least to a minimal degree, some theoretical assumptions about each of the following:

1. A theory of language
2. A theory of learning
3. A theory of language processing
4. A theory of motivation and affective factors
5. A theory of social-context influences
6. A theory of background knowledge and its role in reading and writing

These theories provide important interpretive insights into research and instruction on reading, writing, and reading-writing interactions. I will not attempt to develop full positions for each theory, although some comments are necessary. A theory of language should be one that allows comment on the social uses of language as well as its formal features. It should also be discourse-oriented in its analysis rather than sentential in its primary orientation. Such criteria rule out certain theories of language and its development; nevertheless, these criteria are essential for discussions of literacy development (Halliday 1993; Wells 1994, 1999a, 1999b).

A theory of learning must recognize that interaction is an essential component as is a supporting framework for learning. These concepts and their applications are discussed by Kucan and Beck (1997), Pressley (1998), and Wells (1999a, 1999b). Extensive practice and much repetition are also components that are needed with ill-defined "problem spaces," such as writing and reading skills (Bereiter and Scardamalia 1993; Ellis and Schmidt 1997; Ericsson 1996). At the same time, there must be room for exploration and experimentation, with appropriate corrective feedback when needed. There must also be a role for strategic learning and metacognitive awareness of the goals and purposes for reading and writing, as well as regulation of processes and the ability to solve problems (Pressley 1998; Snow, Burns, and Griffin 1998). These aspects of learning require some awareness of how language is processed, at least on the part of the teacher. Teachers need to understand how goals are developed, how language and background knowledge are used to comprehend and generate messages, and how various subprocesses are involved in successful reading and writing (Grabe 1999; Grabe and Kaplan 1996; Hayes 1996; Hayes and Gradwohl Nash 1996). This knowledge of language processing should influence a teacher's instructional planning.

Three additional theories for understanding reading and writing interaction include theories of motivation and attitudes, theories of social-context influences, and theories of learner background knowledge. Social-context influences on reading and writing are difficult to isolate, but the research to date demonstrates that supportive social contexts generally lead to better reading and writing abilities (Baker et al. 1996; Morrow 1995; Pressley 1998; Snow, Burns, and Griffin 1998). Similarly, instructional contexts in which students build motivation for learning lead to improved literacy development, though this claim is also difficult to isolate in individual studies (Baker et al. 1996; Guthrie et al. 1999; Hayes 1996; Kellogg 1994; Schumann 1997; Snow, Burns, and Griffin 1998; Wigfield and Guthrie 1997). Finally, it is well recognized that learners improve reading and writing abilities when they have greater background knowledge in the associated tasks. Again, however, a number of studies point out the variable effects of background knowledge on performance (Bernhardt 1991; Clapham 1996; Urquhart and Weir 1998; Waters 1996). The complexity of these issues highlights the need to have some theoretical position that will support learning and instruction in appropriate ways.

These theoretical positions, while in themselves neither theories of reading or writing, underlie any carefully thought-out view on reading and writing and their development. For example, to discuss reading, one must understand how reading is processed, how language knowledge itself contributes, how background knowledge plays a role, how both social contexts and motivation influence abilities, and how learning is best accomplished for such goals. The same is true for writing abilities and for the contexts in which reading and writing interact.

Many discussions of reading-writing interactions, particularly in L2 contexts, focus primarily on writing issues, seeing reading as a spring-board to writing tasks and learning for writing. In this respect, many researchers assume basic reading abilities for their students or see such learning issues for reading as unproblematic. The situation in classrooms, however, is far more complex, and it is essential to give serious consider-ation to the reading side as well as the writing side in any serious analysis of reading-writing relations and their instructional implications.

Theories of Reading and Writing

A Theory of Reading

The ability to read for basic comprehension is the skill that underlies most other purposes for reading. Basic comprehension requires rapid and accu-rate word recognition; fluency in processing words, sentences, and dis-course cues; a large recognition vocabulary; a reasonably strong grasp of the structures of the language; an ability to integrate meanings from the text; an ability to make necessary inferences and connections to back-ground knowledge; an ability to vary processes and goals strategically; and an ability to monitor comprehension (Grabe 1999; Pressley 1998; Snow, Burns, and Griffin 1998). These abilities also represent the founda-tion for reading to learn, critical reading, and reading to synthesize infor-mation, and they cannot be bypassed. Thus, the ability to read a short text carefully and accurately for an academic purpose, with no time con-straints, is not necessarily the best indicator that a student is capable of learning from reading. Rather, it indicates a problem-solving ability some-what separate from fluent comprehension abilities (but one that is never-theless useful for academic settings).

At the same time, good readers, and readers who are able to learn from reading, are certainly capable of going beyond basic comprehension. They can engage in sophisticated search processes. They are strategic in relation to their goals for reading. They have the processing resources to reflect critically on what they read. They can also integrate information from texts with their background knowledge (perhaps the best character-ization of learning from texts) and use this information for later literacy tasks (Grabe 1999; Pressley 1998).

For a student to become such an efficient reader does not require mys-terious transformations. A strong theory of learning, more generally, will highlight the need for extensive exposure to print through reading prac-tice; the learning of a large vocabulary; fluency in reading; practice and assisted learning with more complex and difficult texts and tasks; practice in using strategies to understand the text, establish goals, and monitor comprehension processes; and supportive interaction and discussion around textual meaning (Kucan and Beck 1997; Pressley 1998; Wagner and Stanovich 1996; Wells 1999a). Writing about what is to be read or has been read is also a very good way to develop advanced academic reading abilities.

Being able to comprehend texts effectively implies processing effi-ciency, language knowledge, strategic awareness, extensive practice in reading, cognitive resources in working memory to allow critical reflec-tion, and appropriate purposes for reading. Reading to learn from texts then follows from these core skills. Instructional implications involve the development of these core abilities for reading comprehension. How this is to be accomplished is the topic of many textbooks and research studies.

Recent research in academic reading abilities, and including writing tasks as well, emphasizes the ability to read and integrate (and learn) information across multiple texts. Work by Perfetti and his colleagues has been exploring the cognitive demands of tasks that require reading across multiple texts (Perfetti 1997; Perfetti, Britt, and Georgi 1995; Perfetti, Rouet, and Britt 1999; Rouet et al. 1996). He has proposed that readers develop a complex integration of information that can be learned, depending on the types of texts used and the types of tasks performed. There is, at present, no equivalent work in L2 reading contexts. One of the specific extensions of this work into writing is the ability to summarize complex situations created by multiple texts that represent differing types of information and also to resolve conflicting information across informa-tional resources. Similar work has been reported for reading in academic contexts for middle school children, high school students, and university students (e.g., Wineburg 1991, 1994; Stahl et al. 1996), though not from the cognitive perspective developed by Perfetti.

A Theory of Writing

Much like reading, writing abilities and their development can be seen as an outcome of theories of language, processing, learning, social contexts, motivation, and background knowledge. Two recent views of writing abilities that incorporate many of these concepts are those of Grabe and Kaplan (1996, 1997) and Hayes (1996). While it is quite common to encounter theories of writing that emphasize some combination of social and cognitive factors, a broader view of writing, as outlined here, is still not typical. In most cases, the role of motivation is not recognized, and most L1-based theories of writing development ignore the role of language abilities and language knowledge as important factors in writing development. Many theories of writing do not explicitly address theories of learning that would account for successful development of writing skills. Yet all of these factors play important roles in writing and its development (for both L1 and L2 contexts).

Much like reading, writing, as a literate ability, requires extensive practice, supporting social contexts, opportunities to reflect and receive appropriate feedback, assistance with tasks across a range of genres, motivational support and positive experiences, opportunities to interact over the writing produced, and abilities to adapt and adjust purposes for writing. Teachers need, in addition, knowledge of relevant theories of learning and a clear understanding of the processing demands of various writing tasks. The overlap of reading and writing processes and abilities is not simply a matter of conventional recognition of "two sides of literacy." The approach to writing developed by Hayes (1996) not only incorporates processing parallels with reading but also specifically includes reading abilities themselves as essential components of writing abilities. Perhaps the major difference between reading and writing rests with the greater need for automaticity of subprocesses in reading and the greater need for deliberate awareness in writing. A goal for good writing requires reflection on the language choices made; a goal for good reading requires automaticity routines that free up cognitive space for reflection on the meaning rather than the language itself.

Writing across multiple tasks and genres also requires the ability to adapt purposes for writing as needed. These purposes for writing processes include to plan, organize, comprehend, integrate, learn, and critique. For more general purposes, learners need to recognize differences when writing to explain, report, narrate, persuade, synthesize, critique, entertain, learn, and/or discover. These abilities call for efficient cognitive processes, much like reading. Writers need to balance many processes:

1. Planning for writing
2. Using language resources
3. Using background knowledge
4. Solving rhetorical problems
5. Reading to review text to that point
6. Balancing processes strategically
7. Monitoring outcomes
8. Revising plans and text appropriately.

Implications of this view of writing include the need for extensive practice, curriculum planning for long-term development of skills, consistent exposure to a wide range of texts and tasks, opportunities for appropriate feedback and revision, opportunities to discuss writing and revision in relation to goals for writing, models of written texts that represent reasonable solutions for tasks assigned, and tasks that motivate learners.

Two final areas in writing research that have taken on greater importance in recent years include theories of genres and genre knowledge and theories of writing across the disciplines. Both issues arise out of needs for advanced writing abilities in academic contexts, and both typically involve the interaction of writing with reading abilities as learners engage in tasks in response to a range of texts (Johns 1997; Grabe in press; Martin in press; Swales 1990). These issues also provide a major transition to any discussion of reading and writing interaction.

A Theory of Reading and Writing Together

Any theory of how reading and writing work together in support of each other and for enhanced learning of information needs to draw on the individual theories of reading and writing, as noted earlier. The best case of this, from a writing perspective, is the descriptive model of writing processes developed by Hayes (1996). In his descriptive model, he presents writing processes as a combination of individual cognitive processing, social-context influences, motivation, reading processes, and writer background knowledge. His approach incorporates reading into writing (though it does not incorporate writing into reading development). The converse theory, from a reading perspective, involves the processing carried out when engaged in "reading to write" (Carson 1993; Johns 1997; Leki and Carson 1997; Urquhart and Weir 1998) or when integrating information from multiple reading sources (Perfetti, Rouet, and Britt 1999; Perfetti, Britt, and Georgi 1995). These approaches often include summarizing information from texts and integrating information from texts for longer writing tasks. Reading-to-write also includes the notion that writers go back to texts and read in different ways as they seek specific information and adapt reading strategies to match task expectations for the writing (and to fit with the writing production to that point). These research directions will be explored in some detail shortly. It is important, first, to outline briefly the work over the past 20 years on reading and writing relations to set the stage for current directions, L2 complications, and instructional implications.

In the 1980s, a number of authors began to explore the many ways in which reading and writing could be said to interact. Tierney and Pearson (1983) argued for a transactional view of reading and writing as shared ways of composing. Perfetti and McCutchen (1987) reviewed evidence for the complex and shifting relations between reading and writing as academic literacy, pointing to stages where they converge and other stages where they diverge. Stotsky (1983), in a review of earlier research, argued that reading has a limited impact on improving writing but that writing, through summarizing and text structure analysis, measurably improves reading comprehension abilities. Langer and Applebee (1987) argued that students learned content information from texts in complex and distinct ways depending on productive task types performed (answering questions, summarizing, note taking, writing an analytic essay) (see also Marshall 1987; Newell and Winograd 1989). Bereiter and Scardamalia (1984) argued that most students are not experienced at using text material for their own writing purposes but that they can learn aspects of organizational structure from writing based on brief exposures to reading texts (cf. Carson 1990, 1993; Leki and Carson 1997; Tierney and Shanahan 1991).

In L1 literacy contexts, earlier work by Crowhurst (1991), McGinley and Tierney (1989), Spivey (1990), Spivey and King (1989), Shanahan (1984, 1990), Shanahan and Lomax (1988), and Tierney et al. (1989) argued for a number of more specific ways to understand reading and writing relations. Crowhurst (1991) showed that reading persuasive texts along with direct instruction led to improved persuasive writing; she also showed that writing persuasive texts with direct instruction in persuasion similarly led to improved persuasive writing. Her study failed to show improvements in reading comprehension abilities, much like other studies, reflecting the greater difficulty in demonstrating improvements in reading through relatively short-term treatment studies. Spivey (1990; Spivey and King 1989) focused specifically on integrating information from source texts and found that older students and better readers were better able to integrate information from source texts.

Tierney et al. (1989) examined the impact of reading and writing together on a task, as opposed to reading alone or writing alone. They demonstrated that reading and writing together in specific combinations prompts different reasoning processes and seems to engage students in more sophisticated reasoning operations. McGinley and Tierney (1989) made an interesting argument for the effect of reading and writing together to enhance learning. They noted that when students combine reading and writing tasks, they "traverse the topical landscape": students engage the topic numerous times because of varied reading and writing assignments and crisscross the topic from differing perspectives, thus forming a synthesis map of the terrain. Finally, Shanahan and Lomax (1988) examined the reading and writing connections of elementary students, finding that older students use integrated abilities better than younger students. They also argued that reading and writing abilities together accounted better for task outcomes than did either literacy ability by itself as a predictor of performance in the other skill.

Much of the earlier work has been summarized by Tierney and Shanahan (1991; Shanahan 1990; Shanahan and Tierney 1990) under three headings: reading and writing relations, reading and writing interactions, and reading and writing collaborations for enhanced learning. First, in reviews of studies that measured students' reading abilities and their writing abilities and then analyzed the correlations, they reported that reading and writing abilities overlap in complex ways. In general, reading and writing abilities seem to correlate at .5 to .7. So it is possible to talk about shared variance roughly on the order of 25 to 49 percent. These results argue for many skills in common, but they also point to large areas of independent processing. Second, reading and writing interactions follow from the general idea that readers and writers are engaged in a dialogue (at a distance), one in which writers take readers into account and readers take writers into account. While this view is theoretically appealing, there is relatively little direct evidence that students who are more sensitive to readers or writers are better at reading and writing (cf. McKeown and Beck 1998; Newell 1998; Wineburg 1991, 1994). Finally, reading and writing as a collaborative activity is believed to lead to better learning. Again, this appealing notion is in greater need of empirical evidence, particularly with respect to the impact of writing on learning information (cf. Ackerman 1993; Schumacher and Gradwohl Nash 1991; Tierney and Shanahan 1991).

Perhaps some of the more persuasive evidence for learning from reading and writing together comes from evidence not directly focused on questions of reading and writing relations. Slavin's (1995) research on cooperative learning studies (particularly CIRC—Cooperative Integrated Reading and Composition) points out that reading and writing both improve when they are parts of a focused successful cooperative learning curriculum. Similarly, Guthrie (Guthrie and McCann 1997; Guthrie, McGough, et al. 1996; Guthrie, Van Meter, et al. 1996; Guthrie et al. 1998, 1999) argues that a curriculum based on developing a "community of learners" (CORI—Concept-Oriented Reading Instruction) improves both reading and writing abilities when they are part of such a curriculum. How these research and instructional approaches have a bearing on reading and writing relationships is not straightforward, since their goals are distinct from establishing reading and writing relations, but they deserve more attention in future discussion.

In L2 literacy contexts, much less research has been done, though these issues have received more attention in the past decade. Earlier work is summarized nicely by Carson (1990, 1993), who also integrates the L1 and L2 research literature. One of the earliest discussions of reading and writing interactions was carried out by Krashen (1984), who argued that extensive reading will lead to better writing. This view represents another appealing notion that is in need of additional direct empirical evidence. Crowhurst (1991), considering L1 contexts, argued that there is little evidence for the direct impact of wide reading or pleasure reading on improved writing abilities. At the present, there is evidence for the impact of wide reading, though more is needed in L2 contexts (see "Research Issues and Questions to Explore in Reading-Writing Relations" later in this chapter).

L2 contexts are also heavily influenced by two general debates: the interdependency hypothesis (Cummins 1979, 1981) and the language threshold hypothesis. The former assumes that language and literacy skills and strategies transfer positively across languages; the latter argues that L2 proficiency has a greater impact on language and literacy performance and impedes positive transfer of language and literacy skills until a relatively strong foundation is established in the L2 itself. One could think of these two hypotheses as competing alternatives for promoting the development of language and literacy skills in the L1 versus in the L2.

However, these two views are more productively seen as complementary in nature, and having greater or lesser impact are varying stages of L2 development (though also heavily influenced by numerous other factors).

Three specific L2 efforts to explore reading and writing relations in L2 contexts have been presented by Carson et al. (1990), Johns and Mayes (1990), and Campbell (1990). The Carson et al. study examined reading and writing relationships of L2 students across L1 reading and writing measures and L2 reading and writing measures. A complex set of results indicated that simple and sweeping claims for L1 influences on L2 performance must be interpreted in light of numerous other variables. Further, the relations between reading and writing in the L1 and in the L2 were not straightforward for either L1 group (Japanese and Chinese L1 students). Johns and Mayes examined L2 students' abilities to summarize texts and found that low-level students engaged more in copying than transforming; better students were better able to synthesize main ideas into a coherent summary. They also found that L2 language proficiency played an important role in summarizing abilities. It is clear that much more research still needs to be carried out on L2 students' abilities to summarize information from texts. Campbell examined students' uses of information from a text while writing an essay. Nonnative students made much greater use of information directly from the text than did native speakers, and all students engaged in more copying of text segments than was expected. While students have abilities to paraphrase and synthesize information appropriately, they need to be trained and reminded to use these skills and to limit copying.

One of the most consistent implications of two decades of research on reading and writing relations is that they should be taught together and that the combination of both literacy skills enhances learning in all areas. Despite the strength of these assertions, there has been relatively little empirical evidence from specifically directed studies. Part of the problem is that there are many different contexts in which reading and writing interactions occur—there are many types of tasks used, many types of texts and genres used, and many distinct groups of student learners (varying ages, different ability levels, L1 vs. L2, etc.; see my appendix). Research over the past decade has recognized that sweeping claims cannot be made from isolated studies, and more recent studies have sought to understand better a number of more specific questions and assertions. These more restricted areas of inquiry are still quite large in their own rights, but they, nonetheless, represent efforts toward more controlled and more responsible claims for reading and writing interactions.

Theoretical Views of Reading-Writing Relations: New L1 Research and New Directions

Summarizing L1 research on reading and writing relations in the last five to ten years is more complex. Many studies have continued to explore the issues I have outlined already in this chapter. At the same time, new research directions have opened up, and they suggest additional ways to conceptualize and explore reading and writing relations. The most recent research issues that impact these topics involve work on the use of multiple texts for writing and for learning from texts. This section will examine newer developments under the following headings:

> Reading to write
> Writing to read
> Reading to learn and writing to learn
> Reading multiple texts and writing outcomes

There is considerable overlap among these categories, and they should be seen primarily as a heuristic for discussing this more recent research.

Reading to write. Much work has been carried out recently to explore how texts influence student writing. Three issues appear to play important roles: better readers generally write better, appropriate use of text information can support better writing, and extensive exposure to reading can improve writing. On the first topic, McGinley (1992) has demonstrated that better readers are better able to organize, select, and connect ideas for writing (see also Spivey and King 1989). Better readers are also able to write better summaries (Hare 1992; Johns 1985; Winograd 1984). Students who can read arguments and understand them better will produce better summaries. Good readers use text cues and text structure to form their summaries of longer argument texts (Chambliss 1995). On the second topic, a number of recent studies have shown that models of representative texts are effective supports for writing when used appropriately (Charney and Carlson 1995; Smagorinski 1992; Stolarek 1994). From reading, students can also learn genre information that is useful for writing (Crowhurst 1991). A number of studies involving writing from texts have shown that student writing is strongly influenced by the type of task assigned (Greene 1993; Many et al. 1996; Newell 1996; Newell and Winograd 1995; Rouet et al. 1996). On the third topic, there is now a range of evidence to support the argument that reading extensively leads indirectly to better writing. Students are assisted in writing from extensive exposure to print (Elley 1991, 1996; Stanovich and Cunningham 1993; Wagner and Stanovich 1996).

Writing to read. Some work has been done to examine ways in which writing enhances reading (and indirectly learning). There is some direct evidence that writing leads to better reading (Crowhurst 1991). Responding to short-answer questions that serve as anticipation guides and creating graphic organizers before reading can be effective types of writing for improving reading. There is considerable evidence that writing summaries leads to better text comprehension, and summary writing is a common reading comprehension strategy (Hare 1992; Pearson and Fielding 1991; Pressley and Woloshyn 1995). Similarly, practice with text structure analysis and graphic organizers leads to better reading, though the actual writing involved in these cases is minimal (Pearson and Fielding 1991; Vacca and Vacca 1999). Studies and results on writing to read are heavily dependent on types of texts and types of writing tasks.

Reading to learn and writing to learn. The notion that reading leads to learning is not a difficult point to argue, though how this learning occurs and how it is carried out most effectively is a source of much research (see Mosenthal and Cavallo 1998). Recent research has argued that discussions around texts, extensive exposure to print, motivating tasks, and supportive collaboration is an effective way to teach for reading comprehension (Goldman 1997; Guthrie, McGough, et al. 1996; Guthrie, Van Meter, et al. 1996; Guzzetti et al. 1993; Kucan and Beck 1997; Pressley 1998; Pressley and Woloshyn 1995; Stahl et al. 1996; Wagner and Stanovich 1996). The case for writing to learn is somewhat harder to establish, though recent research does argue for effective learning from writing (most commonly in interaction with multiple texts). Newell and Winograd (1995), for example, show that both answers to study questions and essay writing lead to learning from history texts, though each task promoted different types of learning. Summary task research also typically demonstrates that learning arises from this type of writing.

Reading multiple texts and writing with multiple texts. At least three major issues have been developed over the past decade with respect to reading and writing with multiple texts: the cognitive processing required for such tasks, the interaction of reading and writing as tasks are carried out, and the learning gained from reading and writing with multiple texts. The first of these issues involves recent work in cognitive psychology exploring how a reader creates a mental representation of information across multiple texts. This work is best summed up in Perfetti's Documents Model of Comprehension (Perfetti 1997; Perfetti, Rouet, and Britt

1999): a reader's understanding of information from multiple texts is comprised of an intertext model (the specific network of linkages establishing basic comprehension) and a situations model (the reader's elaborations on the basic information, incorporating background knowledge, attitudes, and goal setting). The key to this work is the research using multiple texts and writing tasks to establish types of learning from texts. In particular, it appears that readers of multiple texts use these documents to summarize and write longer essays in distinct ways depending on their reading abilities, their knowledge of the topic, and the task that is required (Perfetti, Britt, and Georgi 1995; Rouet et al. 1997).

Reading and writing interactions while using multiple texts have been examined in a number of research studies. In the case of summarizing, Gradwohl Nash, Schumacher, and Carlson (1993) found that students use the first text from a set to establish a frame of events; they then build on this frame with information from the other texts. Stahl et al. (1996) found that students reading multiple history texts learned information from the first two texts but not much new information after those two. They also concluded that high school students need much more practice in working with multiple texts. Perfetti, Britt, and Georgi (1995) found that university students added little additional information to summaries after the second version of a summary from texts but that they shifted their summaries to fit new perspectives presented by further sets of texts.

Apart from summary writing abilities, studies have explored student writing from multiple texts for a number of tasks. Stahl et al. (1996) found that multiple texts for writing tasks helped students recognize that written texts are not final authorities. (They also found that students need to become more critical readers.) Greene (1993) found that writing from multiple texts improved learning for students in a college history course and that different writing tasks (report writing vs. problem-based essays) led to different types of learning. Another study, by McCarthy-Young and Leinhardt (1998), showed that high school students, writing from history documents, were able to move beyond general strategies for document use to become more critical readers and writers (cf. Lenski and Johns 1997). Rouet et al. (1996, 1997) found that students used documents differently depending on their background and assigned different informational value to various types of texts depending on their majors (see also Wineburg 1991). In almost all recent studies, authors have noted that task factors strongly influence how students use texts and shape writing from texts in distinct ways. At the same time, many authors note that multiple texts provide foundations for building more complex knowledge (Gradwohl Nash, Schumacher, and Carlson 1993; Lenski and Johns 1997; Rouet et al. 1996, 1997; Stahl et al. 1996).

There has been a substantial growth in L1-based research on reading and writing relations in the past decade, in particular on reading and writing with multiple texts. This research points out important issues and questions for the development of L2 writers in academic settings, particularly in contexts where students are expected to deal with multiple texts in their writing.

Reading and Writing Relations in L2 Contexts

In the past decade, there has also been more research in reading and writing relations in L2 contexts, partly because of the greater role of content-based instruction for academic students, and partly because of the greater emphasis on both EAP and writing in the disciplines by applied linguists. At the same time, it is difficult to generalize across L2 contexts when they are so diverse (e.g., LEP/ESL, EFL, ESP/EAP, FL, professional ESL/EFL). Moreover, L2 students create unique contexts for theories of reading and writing themselves. These specific L2 issues must also be accounted for in discussions of reading and writing relations.

L2 reading issues include wide ranges of student abilities in word recognition skills, vocabulary knowledge, reading rates, syntactic knowledge, and L2 world knowledge and cultural knowledge. Students have widely varying amounts of exposure to L2 print and knowledge of L2 discourse organization and genre expectations. They also vary in flexibility and use of reading strategies, influences of L1 literacy skills and language knowledge, motivations for reading L2 texts, and attitudes toward the L2 (Grabe 1999; Grabe and Stoller forthcoming). Moreover, unique L2 issues play important roles in the development of L2 reading abilities. These issues include the various effects of L1 transfer into L2 processing, the role of a language threshold, the impact of more mature study skills and problem-solving abilities, the attributions from success in L1 literacy abilities, and the roles of mental translation, bilingual dictionaries, and cognates.

Any L2 theory of writing and writing development must, similarly, account for greater variability of knowledge resources and language skills, specific L1 resources, and unique rhetorical aspects of writing in an L2. L2 students, except at very advanced levels, do not have the language resources to express complex ideas with careful nuance; nor can they anticipate those audience expectations that they themselves are not very familiar with. They are also strongly dependent on the level of their productive vocabulary and their knowledge of the syntax used for written genres. Moreover, L2 students simply have less practice in writing in their L2, and this limited exposure constrains understanding of discourse organization, alternative planning in writing, experiences with solving rhetorical problems, and basic writing fluency. These issues all make the development of L2 writing distinct from L1 instructional settings. In addition, the L2 student often brings individual variables that are unique to L2 situations. EAP students, for example, have typically already experienced success with literacy in their L1; they have many resources and strategies for writing in their L1; they have more sophisticated ideas that they know they can express in their L1. They also can rely on mental translations, bilingual dictionaries, and cognates to assist them—specific strategies that are unique to L2 settings.

It is also reasonably clear that we know relatively little about how L2 students go about reading and learning from multiple texts on a topic, how they use texts for writing, and how they develop strategies to work with multiple texts and varied writing tasks. This gap is partly due to the widely varying profiles of L2 students; partly it is the result of other issues taking the forefront (interdependence hypothesis, language threshold hypothesis), and partly it is the result of less emphasis, until recently, on advanced EAP students and L2 writing in different disciplines. However, more work has been emerging in the past decade, and this work offers important insights for learning and instruction.

New Directions for Research on L2 Reading and Writing Relations

New developments in L2 research on reading and writing relations are perhaps best initiated with a discussion of Carson and Leki 1993, the first L2 writing book on reading and writing relations. In their edited book, Carson and Leki provided the first serious set of articles addressing reading and writing in ways similar to L1 discussions. Flahive and Bailey (1993), for example, explored reading and writing correlations and found that the relationships are only modest, accounting for 12 percent of variance among measures used. They noted that L2 students may be much more variable in their reading and writing abilities, so one cannot assume that a good reader is a good writer and vice versa. They also noted, much like Carrell and Connor (1991), that different tasks lead to different profiles of student abilities in reading and writing. Connor and Carrell (1993) examined evaluations of student writing on the parts of the writers themselves and by expert composition raters. Both the L2 students and the expert raters evaluated the essays on content, development, and language. Both groups gave less emphasis to text organization, accuracy of response to prompt, and audience. Regardless of the immediate cause of these preferences, they point out that L2 texts tend to be evaluated in similar ways by experienced L2 readers and expert raters of L2 writing. In a third study, Basham, Ray, and Whalley (1993) found that students sometimes interpret texts from L1 cultural frameworks. They found that their Chinese students studied the text closely and followed the text information very carefully; Latino students used the reading as a jumping-off point for their own personal experiences on the topic; Native American students developed a personal orientation to the information in the text. All of these studies deserve to be replicated to determine the strength of their conclusions.

Most of the other chapters in the Carson and Leki volume review issues or provide practical discussion of how to teach reading and writing skills together and in varying contexts. Of these instructional chapters, the one by Johns (1993) is perhaps most relevant to teaching advanced students to synthesize information from texts in EAP contexts. Her chapter highlights the need to examine academic classes in universities and determine the most genuine academic tasks (through faculty surveys and classroom ethnographies), then deconstruct tasks assigned to students for their reading and writing demands (analyze prompts and develop strategies) and compile resources that will help students complete these reading and writing tasks successfully (collect models and analyze, use peer reviews, work with support groups). This approach is developed much more extensively in Johns 1997.

Reading and writing relations in L2 contexts are still concerned with the notions of transfer (interdependence hypothesis) and L2 language proficiency (the threshold hypothesis). There is relatively little recent work in support of the interdependence hypothesis. Indirect evidence can be marshaled by research on reading strategies and writing strategies that seem to be similar across L1 students and L2 students. However, many of these studies may be heavily influenced by method effects—limitations of data collection may have made it unlikely to find strong differences between L1 and L2 students. There is certainly evidence for transfer effects of various types with differing groups of students in L2 reading research (e.g., Durgunoglu and Verhoeven 1998). However, the effects of transfer are highly variable and quite sensitive to specific L1/L2 groups and to the types of task used (e.g., Carrell and Connor 1991; Carson et al.

1990). Few researchers would deny that transfer of literacy skills from the L1 to the L2 occurs, but many researchers believe that positive transfer occurs consistently only after students have had much practice in the L2, have automatized basic L2 language skills, and have been trained to use these potential transfer effects.

Research on the role of a language threshold that will allow transfer and strategic processing above certain basic proficiency levels has gained considerable support in the past decade for both reading and writing abilities. In the field of L2 reading, there is now strong evidence supporting the language threshold hypothesis (Bernhardt and Kamil 1995; Bossers 1992; Carrell 1991; Geva and Wade-Woolley 1998; Lee and Schallert 1997; Verhoeven and Aarts 1998; as well as many related studies). The conclusion here is not that there is a specific set of language structures or vocabulary that needs to be mastered first—in fact, the threshold is variable depending on task, text, and reader—but that L2 knowledge plays a major role in L2 reading abilities. The role of L2 language knowledge is usually much greater than the role of L1 literacy skills, at least up to relatively advanced levels of L2 reading.

There is also now some evidence that an L2 threshold applies as well to L2 writing abilities. In an earlier study, Johns and Mayes (1990) found that L2 summaries were strongly influenced by students' levels of L2 language proficiency. Mixed evidence for the role of language proficiency was also found by Carrell and Connor (1991), with much variability depending on task and genre type. In a more recent study, Sasaki and Hirose (1996) found that a much greater proportion of expository writing ability was accounted for by the L2 knowledge (52 percent) than by L1 writing ability (18 percent). These results match up well with research reported in L2 reading studies. Overall, then, there is a strong case for some flexible notion of a language threshold that must be achieved to perform well on a range of level-appropriate L2 reading and writing tasks.

A third major issue that has now received more attention for L2 reading and writing relations is the role of wide reading or extensive reading for writing improvement (cf. Carson 1990). A major argument proposed early in the 1980s by Krashen (1984) suggested that L2 students will become better writers by a combination of writing practice and extensive reading. Krashen (1993) has reiterated his arguments for extensive reading, supported by some further research, principally Elley 1991 (see also Elley 1996). At the same time, L1-based research on exposure to print has argued that extensive reading leads to language knowledge that would support better writing abilities (e.g., better vocabulary, better verbal fluency, better syntactic knowledge, better semantic memory, better metalinguistic awareness, better knowledge of the world). These arguments and strong supporting research are given a full treatment by Stanovich and his colleagues (Stanovich and Cunningham 1993; Stanovich et al. 1996; Wagner and Stanovich 1996). Based on a decade of persuasive empirical studies, Stanovich argues that students who have much greater exposure to print over years develop a range of literacy-related skills and abilities. A major implication for reading and writing relations, for both L1 and L2 contexts, is that connections between reading and writing may be variable but can be interconnected more efficiently through extensive reading in combination with writing.

A recent L2 study adds further support to the argument that extensive reading contributes to writing abilities. Tsang (1996) reported on a treatment study involving 144 Hong Kong secondary-level students at four grade levels. Three different groups at each grade level received 24 weeks of instruction: group one received regular instruction plus math; group two received regular instruction plus frequent writing practice; group three received regular instruction plus extensive reading. At the end of the six-month period, the group with extensive reading wrote significantly better essays on a posttreatment task. The extensive reading group also learned significantly more content information. With further replications of studies like this one, it would be possible to make as strong a set of claims about the impact of extensive reading on literacy development as can now be made with respect to the language threshold hypothesis.

Two final topics of concern for L2 reading and writing relations, particularly for EAP concerns, have developed considerably in the past decade. The first involves surveying L2 students, their classes, university content classes, and writing contexts in university EAP settings to understand the reading and writing demands on L2 students. The second involves rethinking and refinements of EAP instruction that requires reading and writing together. The former development concerns efforts to take into account EAP literacy environments, the range of tasks that L2 students need to perform, and the need for both students and faculty to become more aware of L1-L2 differences. Leki and Carson (1994) used student surveys to understand student expectations for EAP performance in university settings. They found that students expected more challenging literacy tasks, a wider range of tasks, tasks that combined reading and writing abilities, and assistance with deconstructing tasks and writing models, as well as assistance with understanding teacher expectations. A second study by Leki and Carson (1997) argued strongly that L2 students need more practice with tasks that involve reader-responsible writing, that is, writing from texts in which the content was considered an important part of evaluation.

Both of the Leki and Carson studies reflect recent work on analyzing EAP settings from the perspectives of language minority students in U.S. universities and deriving appropriate instructional approaches. Johns (1993, 1997) highlights many of the same points noted by Leki and Carson, stressing the need to determine genuine tasks for students to practice, which, in turn, will promote careful analyses of task prompts and models of successful task performance and provide much practice and assistance with texts and genres that students will need to work with. Carson (2000) offers a similar translation to practice through an extensive task-based EAP curriculum. In both cases, instruction is centered around the reading and writing of many texts that fit university expectations. Practical implications of reading and writing interactions have also been a long-standing concern of Swales (1990, 1998) as he has expanded from an ESP perspective into advanced EAP needs of L2 students who are engaged in graduate-level work. Zamel (1992) provides a unique practical perspective on L2 reading and writing relations, adopting the position that these relations can lead to effective learning when students begin from writing tasks rather than from the reading of texts.

Finally, it is important to note the work of Silva (1993) and his colleagues in exploring unique issues for L2 writing and highlighting differences between L1 and L2 writing development, particularly in the EAP context. This research points out the unique situations of EAP students in U.S. universities and the need for L1 writing teachers to recognize the different patterns of strengths and weaknesses that L2 students bring to writing tasks; these include different textual interpretations and different ways of using reading and writing in combination (Silva, Leki, and Carson 1997).

Research Issues and Questions to Explore in Reading-Writing Relations

Regardless of the approaches outlined by various researchers, there are a number of issues for which any relatively complete theory of reading and writing interactions must account. These issues include the coordinated processing demands of reading and writing together; the need for considerable practice in writing from texts and reading to write; appropriate levels of language skills and background knowledge; an awareness of strategic goal setting and strategy use, supporting social contexts and instruction for learning; and appropriate (and motivating) tasks. In addition to these general issues in cognitive processing, a number of specific issues arise in contexts in which reading and writing are used together. For almost all of the issues noted in this section, there is a need for more research with L2 students in a range of EAP contexts. The key idea is that reading and writing relations, as a major focus of EAP instruction, is in search of not only grand theories but also important insights that link theory to practice.

For example, there are large sets of research literature on the roles of summarizing, using text models, note taking and outlining, and using graphic organizers in reading and writing instruction. However, they have seldom been examined in combination for their effectiveness in supporting reading and writing relations in more integrated curricular settings, particularly with L2 student performance. In the same way, issues of motivation and affect, task attributions, and task complexity have not been examined in many settings in which reading and writing were taught in combination for L2 students. In all of these areas, research can be found that individually supports their roles in student learning. The goal is to determine how they support learning when used in combination for purposes of improving academic literacy skills and when embedded in appropriate curricular frameworks.

At a curricular level, relatively little research has been carried out to examine explicitly how various newer approaches to curriculum development lead to enhanced practice with reading and writing or lead to enhanced language and content learning when reading and writing are combined in various ways. These newer approaches offer many opportunities for reading and writing interaction and are typically sites for intensive training of EAP literacy abilities (Carson 2000; Johns 1997; Kasper 1997; Snow 1998). Whether or not such curricular approaches actually do emphasize such issues as reading to write, writing from multiple sources, and reading to learn and writing to learn is an open question that can and should be addressed more explicitly. For example, Johns (1997) describes the integrated language and content curriculum at San Diego State University, which focuses intensely on reading and writing tasks to prepare students for academic success. Snow (1998) describes efforts, in a content-based framework, to prepare university faculty to incorporate language sensitivity and appropriate reading and writing tasks into content classrooms (see also Snow and Brinton 1997). These approaches to task-based instruction, content-based instruction, integrated instruction, and advanced

ESP instruction need to be explored and evaluated not only in terms of what they provide for integration of reading and writing but also for their promise in developing successful L2 students in academic settings.

The role of extensive reading needs to be examined more closely for its potential contributions to student success in advanced EAP settings. At present, interesting research studies, in both L1 and L2 contexts, point to its supporting role in student success. However, extensive reading has a number of limitations associated with it, and these limitations make it difficult to establish its importance for EAP contexts. First, extensive reading involves a long-term curricular commitment to the concept, which makes it difficult to show strong benefits, and many students and programs do not have the time or do not want to commit the time to such an effort. It is not controversial to state that many hours of practice are required for a student to become a fluent reader in a language, and there really are no shortcuts, though many students and curriculum developers continue to hope for miracles. Second, reading extensively and fluent reading are often seen as secondary goals. In fact, however, the careful (perhaps critical) reading of a short text, as a problem-solving skill, is a less important skill than fluent reading for basic comprehension, and careful reading is also easier to teach—perhaps that is why it is more highly valued by teachers who want to feel that they are really doing something with students. In general, extensive reading programs are not popular because they demand resources of time and texts, and there are not many successful models to refer to in the L2 literature.

Finally, there is a need to examine the role of talk and discussion in the development of literacy abilities. It is somewhat fashionable to emphasize dialogue around texts and writing output in both L1 and L2 contexts and to emphasize the role of interaction in L2 contexts in particular. Until recently, these assertions have been argued in general ways and, in many cases, in less than persuasive ways relying on overly general theorizing (cf. Bloome and Green 1992). However, a number of recent research efforts have put new life into these assertions, and they point to real and specific benefits of dialogue around texts. This topic could be the source of its own essay, but I will briefly point out that recent work by Pressley and his colleagues (Pressley 1995, 1997, 1998; Pressley and Woloshyn 1995; Pressley et al. 1992), by Beck and her colleagues (Beck and Kucan 1997; Kucan and Beck 1997; McKeown and Beck 1998), and by Wells (Wells 1994, 1999a, 1999b) all make strong arguments for the facilitating effects of conversation and dialogue around text comprehension and student writing. In some respects, Johns (1997) points out this direction for L2 literacy research. These ideas need to be explored in greater depth in contexts in which L2 students are carrying out tasks that require reading and writing interaction. This is one area in which current research in L1 literacy settings may be directly relevant to L2 research efforts.

Instructional Goals and Practices for Reading-Writing Interactions

So what is a teacher to do? Given all that has been reported in this chapter, how is a teacher to draw implications for instruction? These are good questions, and the research to date can appear to be somewhat confusing in its scope and its results. However, it is possible to draw intelligently, if somewhat cautiously, on the research base to develop a set of working principles for instruction and curriculum planning. Below are ten principles that can act as a set of guidelines—though they are certainly not an explicit blueprint for what to do in every setting or with every group of students. These principles are neither comprehensive nor fully generalizable, but they may provide a good place to start when considering EAP literacy instruction, changes to curricula, or possibilities for action research (see, e.g., Wallace 1998).

First, all curriculum planning should involve ongoing cycles of needs analysis. Teachers, curriculum supervisors, and students should all be involved in exploring the institutional demands and expectations that students face. There are many ways in which teachers and students can learn about the real tasks assigned in various disciplinary areas and the needs that students will have if they are to succeed.

Second, students and teachers need to work with the tasks that are major sources of learning and evaluation in the academic environment. These tasks need to be dissected, successful models need to be analyzed and critiqued, and many opportunities for relevant practice need to be generated. Students are much less likely to be academically successful if they do not continually engage in such tasks.

Third, many activities and skills for combining reading and writing need to be practiced if they are to be strong foundations for the more complex tasks required in academic disciplines. For example, summarizing texts, synthesizing multiple sources, working with graphic organizers for reading comprehension, examining discourse features and genre structure, and building strategies for working with texts and writing are essential skills that are not easily developed by students on their own.

Fourth, instruction should include many opportunities to talk about texts and tasks. These discussions should be focused on the topic, text, and tasks at hand and should not be loose topical discussions and personal anecdotes. Dialogue around texts and tasks needs to include critical inquiry and commentary, awareness of both texts and task organization and content, and reflections on text, author, language, process, and task.

Fifth, the work of students and teachers needs to involve a lot of reading and interaction with text resources. This emphasis will increase both basic comprehension and critical reading, and it will provide complexity and more challenging tasks for integrating information and using information.

Sixth, an effective curriculum will include many opportunities to recycle similar tasks for practice. Students cannot be expected to develop effective problem-solving routines and learn appropriate variations without many opportunities to "traverse the topical landscape."

Seventh, students should have opportunities to work with reading and writing tasks in the contexts of an integrated curriculum. Such curricular support provides extended opportunities to develop topical knowledge, synthesize information, build complexity and motivation, and engage in real academic tasks at a high level of sophistication and demand. Integrated curricula also offer greater support for the reading and writing tasks being assigned, since the instruction is connected and not ever-shifting in topic and task.

Eighth, tasks that are used for reading and writing purposes need to be realistic for the academic context. They need to reflect tasks that students will be expected to carry out as part of their future academic work and that will be sources of evaluation of students' learning, but they should not be so difficult that they generate frustration and failure.

Ninth, instruction in reading and writing needs to provide strong support, assistance, and feedback by teachers as well as relevant and useful feedback from peers. Moreover, students should be exposed regularly to various assessment practices used in content classes that involve integration of reading and writing. Performance under pressure is a real part of student life, and regardless of teacher philosophy on the appropriateness of testing practices, it is unfair to limit student experience and practice on tasks that will be crucial in the formal assessment of learning.

Tenth, students need to be taught to find additional information and to use this information appropriately. In some cases, this search will translate into the "research paper" and the use of the library to find information. In other cases, it may involve the collection of original data through fieldwork, measurement of outcomes, surveys, ethnographies, and interviews. In all cases, students should learn how to work with teachers, other students, and outside resources to gather textual resources and how to write from these resources. Students also need to know how to document and report the sources of information collected.

The ten guidelines suggested here represent one way to find shape and coherence out of the growing set of research studies and reports of practice that center on reading and writing relations. It is possible to extend the issues involved in reading and writing relations almost end-lessly. As a final comment, I would like to note one notion that has struck me repeatedly as I reviewed the literature on reading and writing that has appeared over the past two decades. There are many innovative ideas and practices that we need to explore, and that is part of the excitement of this field. At the same time, many fairly traditional ideas and practices have held up well over time, even when they have seemed to move out of fash-ion. For example, a large number of research studies in the 1980s high-lighted the importance of practice in summary writing for reading com-prehension and for learning from texts: this persuasive research base can be overlooked fifteen years later, but it remains as persuasive now as it was then. The lesson the research of the last two decades brings home to me is that we need to reconsider all our practices in light of students' real needs and that our reconsideration should be based on a realistic assess-ment of the academic environments that students are being prepared to work in. We should not let our own personal preferences and views cut off useful ideas and practices for preparing students to work with texts and write effectively.

Appendix. Contexts of Reading-Writing Relations: Variables That Influence Research Studies and Implications for Instruction

A. Tasks
B. Training (students shown how to do tasks)
C. Topics
D. Teachers (and their training, orientations, interests)
E. Text(s)
F. Time
G. Age
H. Grade

I. Individual style
J. Purposes/goals
K. Resources (teachers, students, aids, other texts, intertexts)
L. Social context
M. Cultural context
N. Affective factors
O. Instructional methodologies

References

Ackerman, J. 1993. The promise of writing to learn. *Written Communication* 10:334–70.

Baker, L., J. Allen, B. Shockley, A. Pellegrini, L. Galda, and S. Stahl. 1996. Connecting school and home: Constructing partnerships to foster reading development. In *Developing engaged readers in school and home communities,* ed. L. Baker, P. Afflerbach, and D. Reinking, 21–41. Mahwah, NJ: Lawrence Erlbaum.

Basham, C., R. Ray, and E. Whalley. 1993. Cross-cultural perspectives on task representation in reading to write. In *Reading in the composition classroom: Second language perspectives,* ed. J. G. Carson and I. Leki, 299–314. Boston: Heinle and Heinle.

Beck, I., and L. Kucan. 1997. *Questioning the author.* Newark, DE: International Reading Association.

Bereiter, C., and M. Scardamalia. 1984. Learning about writing from reading. *Written Communication* 1:163–88.

———. 1993. *Surpassing ourselves: An inquiry into the nature and implications of expertise.* Chicago: Open Court Press.

Bernhardt, E. 1991. *Reading development in a second language.* Norwood, NJ: Ablex.

Bernhardt, E., and M. Kamil. 1995. Interpreting relationships between L1 and L2 reading: Consolidating the linguistic threshold and the linguistic interdependence hypotheses. *Applied Linguistics* 16:15–34.

Bloome, D., and J. Green. 1992. Educational contexts of literacy. In *Annual Review of Applied Linguistics,* vol. 12, *Literacy,* ed. W. Grabe et al., 49–70. New York: Cambridge University Press.

Bossers, B. 1992. *Reading in two languages: A study of reading comprehension in Dutch as a second language and in Turkish as a first language.* Rotterdam: Drukkerij Van Driel.

Campbell, C. 1990. Writing with others' words: Using background reading text in academic compositions. In *Second language writing: Research insights for the classroom,* ed. B. Kroll, 211–30. New York: Cambridge University Press.

Carrell, P. 1991. Second language reading: Reading ability or language proficiency. *Applied Linguistics* 12:159–79.

Carrell, P., and U. Connor. 1991. Reading and writing descriptive and persuasive texts. *Modern Language Journal* 75:314–24.

Carson, J. G. 1990. Reading-writing connections: Toward a description for second language learners. In *Second language writing: Research insights for the classroom,* ed. B. Kroll, 88–107. New York: Cambridge University Press

———. 1993. Reading for writing: Cognitive perspectives. In *Reading in the composition classroom: Second language perspectives,* ed. J. Carson and I. Leki, 299–314. Boston: Heinle and Heinle.

———. 2000. Reading and writing for academic purposes. In M. Pally (Ed.), *Sustained content teaching: Developing academic skills in ESL/EFL writing classes,* ed. M. Pally, 19–34. Boston: Houghton Mifflin.

Carson, J. G., P. Carrell, S. Silberstein, B. Kroll, and P. Kuehn. 1990. Reading-writing relationships in first and second language. *TESOL Quarterly* 24:245–66.

Carson, J. G., and I. Leki, eds. 1993. *Reading in the composition classroom: Second language perspectives.* Boston: Heinle and Heinle.

Chambliss, M. 1995. Text cues and strategies successful readers use to construct the gist of lengthy arguments. *Reading Research Quarterly* 30:778–807.

Charney, D., and R. Carlson. 1995. Learning to write in a genre: What student writers take from model texts. *Research in the Teaching of English* 29:88–125.

Clapham, C. 1996. *The development of IELTS: A study of the effect of background knowledge on reading comprehension.* Cambridge: Cambridge University Press.

Connor, U., and P. Carrell. 1993. The interpretation of tasks by writers and readers in holistically rated direct assessment of writing. In *Reading in the composition classroom: Second language perspectives,* ed. J. G. Carson and I. Leki, 141–60. Boston: Heinle and Heinle.

Crowhurst, M. 1991. Interrelationships between reading and writing persuasive discourse. *Research in the Teaching of English* 25:314–38.

Cummins, J. 1979. Linguistic interdependence and the educational development of bilingual children. *Review of Educational Research* 49:222–51.

———. 1981. The role of primary language development in promoting educational success for language minority students. In *Schooling and language minority students: A theoretical framework,* 3–49. Developed by the Office of Bilingual Bicultural Education, California State Department of Education, Sacramento. Los Angeles: Evaluation, Dissemination, and Assessment Center, California State University.

Durgunoglu, A., and L. Verhoeven, eds. 1998. *Literacy development in a multilingual context.* Mahwah, NJ: Lawrence Erlbaum.

Elley, W. 1991. Acquiring literacy in a second language: The effect of book-based programs. *Language Learning* 41:375–411.

———. 1996. Using book floods to raise literacy levels in developing countries. In *Promoting reading in developing countries,* ed. V. Greaney, 148–62. Newark, DE: International Reading Association.

Ellis, N., and R. Schmidt. 1997. Morphology and longer distance dependencies. *Studies in Second Language Acquisition* 19:145–71.

Ericsson, K. A., ed. 1996. *The road to excellence.* Mahwah, NJ: Lawrence Erlbaum.

Flahive, D., and N. Bailey. 1993. Exploring reading/writing relationships in adult second language learners. In *Reading in the composition classroom: Second language perspectives,* ed. J. G. Carson and I. Leki, 128–40. Boston: Heinle and Heinle.

Geva, E., and L. Wade-Woolley. 1998. Component processes in becoming English-Hebrew biliterate. In *Literacy development in a multilingual context,* ed. A. Durgunoglu and L. Verhoeven, 85–110. Mahwah, NJ: Lawrence Erlbaum.

Goldman, S. 1997. Learning from text: Reflections on the past and suggestions for the future. *Discourse Processes* 23:357–98.

Grabe, W. 1999. Reading research and its implications for reading assessment. In *Language proficiency assessment: Proceedings of the eighth LTRC,* ed. A. Kunnan and M. Milanovich, 227–63. Cambridge: Cambridge University Press.

———. In press. Narrative and expository macro-genres. In *Genre and pedagogy: Research and practice,* ed. A. Johns. Mahwah, NJ: Lawrence Erlbaum.

Grabe, W., and R. B. Kaplan. 1996. *Theory and practice of writing.* New York: Longman.

———. 1997. Teaching the writing course. In *Beyond methods: Components in second language teacher education,* ed. K. Bardovi-Harlig and B. Hartford, 172–97. New York: McGraw-Hill.

Grabe, W., and F. Stoller. Forthcoming. *Applied linguistics in action: Researching reading.* New York: Longman.

Gradwohl Nash, J., G. Schumacher, and B. Carlson. 1993. Writing from sources: A structure mapping model. *Journal of Educational Psychology* 85:159–70.

Greene, S. 1993. The role of task in the development of academic thinking through reading and writing in a college history course. *Research in the Teaching of English* 27:46–75.

Guthrie, J., E. Anderson, S. Alao, and J. Rinehart. 1999. Influences of concept-oriented reading instruction on strategy use and conceptual learning from text. *Elementary School Journal* 99:343–66.

Guthrie, J., and A. McCann. 1997. Characteristics of classrooms that promote motivations and strategies for learning. In *Reading engagement: Motivating readers through integrated instruction,* ed. J. Guthrie and A. Wigfield, 128–48. Newark, DE. International Reading Association.

Guthrie, J., K. McGough, L. Bennett, and M. Rice. 1996. Concept-oriented reading instruction: An integrated curriculum to develop motivations and strategies for reading. In *Developing engaged readers in school and home communities,* ed. L. Baker, P. Afflerbach, and D. Reinking, 165–90. Mahwah, NJ: Lawrence Erlbaum.

Guthrie, J., P. Van Meter, G. Hancock, S. Alao, E. Anderson, and A. McCann.

1998. Does concept-oriented reading instruction increase strategy use and conceptual learning from text? *Journal of Educational Psychology* 90:261–78.

Guthrie, J., P. Van Meter, A. McCann, A. Wigfield, L. Bennett, C. Poundstone, M. Rice, F. Faibisch, B. Hunt, and A. Mitchell. 1996. Growth of literacy engagement: Changes in motivations and strategies during concept-oriented reading instruction. *Reading Research Quarterly* 31:306–32.

Guzzetti, B., T. Snyder, G. Glass, and W. Gamas. (1993). Promoting conceptual change in science: A comparative meta-analysis of instructional interventions from reading education and science education. *Reading Research Quarterly* 28:116–59.

Halliday, M. A. K. 1993. Towards a language-based theory of learning. *Linguistics and Education* 5:93–116.

Hare, V. 1992. Summarizing text. In *Reading/writing connections,* ed. J. Irwin and M. Doyle, 96–118. Newark, DE: International Reading Association.

Hayes, J. 1996. A new framework for understanding cognition and affect in writing. In *The science of writing,* ed. C. M. Levy and S. Ransdell, 1–27. Mahwah, NJ:. Lawrence Erlbaum.

Hayes, J., and J. Gradwohl Nash. 1996. On the nature of planning in writing. In *The science of writing,* ed. C. M. Levy and S. Ransdell, 29–55. Mahwah, NJ: Lawrence Erlbaum.

Johns, A. 1985. Summary protocols of "underprepared" and "adept" university students: Replications and distortions of the original. *Language Learning* 35:495–517.

———. 1993. Reading and writing tasks in English for academic purposes classes: Products, processes, and resources. In *Reading in the composition classroom: Second language perspectives,* ed. J. G. Carson and I. Leki, 274–89. Boston: Heinle and Heinle.

———. 1997. *Text, role, and context.* New York: Cambridge University Press.

Johns, A., and P. Mayes. 1990. An analysis of summary protocols of university ESL students. *Applied Linguistics* 11:253–71.

Kasper, L. 1997. The impact of content based instructional programs on the academic progress of ESL students. *English for Specific Purposes* 16:309–20.

Kellogg, R. 1994. *The psychology of writing.* New York: Oxford University Press.

Krashen, S. 1984. *Writing: Research, theory, and applications.* Torrance, CA: Laredo.

———. 1993. *The power of reading.* Englewood, CO: Libraries Unlimited.

Kucan, L., and I. Beck. 1997. Thinking aloud and reading comprehension research: Inquiry, instruction, and social interaction. *Review of Educational Research* 67:271–99.

Langer, J., and A. Applebee. 1987. *How writing shapes thinking.* Urbana, IL: National Council of Teachers of English.

Lee, J.-W., and D. Schallert. 1997. The relative contribution of L2 language proficiency and L1 reading ability to L2 reading performance: A test of the threshold hypothesis. *TESOL Quarterly* 31:713–39.

Leki, I., and J. G. Carson. 1994. Students' perceptions of EAP writing instruction and writing needs across the disciplines. *TESOL Quarterly* 28:81–101.

———. 1997. "Completely different worlds": EAP and the writing experiences of ESL students in university courses. *TESOL Quarterly* 31:39–69.

Lenski, S., and J. Johns. 1997. Patterns of reading-to-write. *Reading Research and Instruction* 37:15–38.

Many, J., R. Fyfe, G. Lewis, and E. Mitchell. 1996. Traversing the topical landscape: Exploring students' self-directed reading-writing-research processes. *Reading Research Quarterly* 31:12–35.

Marshall, J. 1987. The effects of writing on students' understanding of literary text. *Research in the Teaching of English* 21:31–63.

Martin, J. In press. Genres in literacy instruction. In *Genre and pedagogy: Research and practice,* ed. A. Johns. Mahwah, NJ: Lawrence Erlbaum.

McCarthy-Young, K., and G. Leinhardt. 1998. Writing from primary documents: A way of knowing history. *Written Communication* 15:25–68.

McGinley, W. 1992. The role of reading and writing while composing from sources. *Reading Research Quarterly* 27:226–48.

McGinley, W., and R. Tierney. 1989. Traversing the topical landscape: Reading and writing as ways of knowing. *Written Communication* 6:243–69.

McKeown, M., and I. Beck. 1998. Talking to an author: Readers taking charge of the reading process. In *The reading-writing connection,* ed. N. Nelson and R. Calfee, 112–30. Chicago: National Society for the Study of Education.

Morrow, L., ed. 1995. *Family literacy: Connections in schools and communities.* Newark, DE: International Reading Association.

Mosenthal, P., and A. Cavallo. 1998. Profiling changing states of conceptual knowledge: With designs toward developing a universal knowledge interface system for the twenty-first century. *Peabody Journal of Education* 73, nos. 3–4:145–77.

Newell, G. 1996. Reader-based and teacher-based instructional tasks: Writing and learning about a short story in middle-track classrooms. *Journal of Literacy Research* 28:147–72.

———. 1998. "How much are we the wiser?": Continuity and change in writing and learning in the content areas. In *The reading-writing connection,* ed. N. Nelson and R. Calfee, 178–202. Chicago: National Society for the Study of Education.

Newell, G., and P. Winograd. 1989. The effects of writing on learning from expository text. *Written Communication* 6:196–217.

———. 1995. Writing about and learning from history texts: The effects of task and academic ability. *Research in the Teaching of English* 29:133–63.

Pearson, P. D., and L. Fielding. 1991. Comprehension instruction. In *Handbook of reading research,* ed. R. Barr et al., 2:815–60. New York: Longman.

Perfetti, C. 1997. Sentences, individual differences, and multiple texts: Three issues in text comprehension. *Discourse Processes* 23:37–35.

Perfetti, C., M. Britt, and M. Georgi. 1995. *Text-based learning and reasoning*. Mahwah, NJ: Lawrence Erlbaum.

Perfetti, C., and D. McCutchen. 1987. Schooled language competence: Linguistic abilities in reading and writing. In *Advances in applied psycholinguistics*, vol. 2, *Reading, writing, and language learning*, ed. S. Rosenberg, 105–41. New York: Cambridge University Press.

Perfetti, C., J.-F. Rouet, and M. Britt. 1999. Toward a theory of documents representation. In *The construction of mental representations during reading*, ed. H. van Oostendorp and S. Goldman, 99–122. Mahwah, NJ: Lawrence Erlbaum.

Pressley, M. 1995. A transactional strategies instruction Christmas carol. In *Teaching for transfer: Fostering generalization in learning*, ed. A. McKeough, J. Lupart, and A. Marini, 177–213. Mahwah, NJ: Lawrence Erlbaum.

———. 1997. The cognitive science of reading. *Contemporary Educational Psychology* 22:247–59.

———. 1998. *Reading instruction that works: The case for balanced teaching*. New York: Guilford.

Pressley, M., P. El-Dinary, I. Gaskins, T. Schuder, J. Bergman, J. Almasi, and R. Brown. 1992. Beyond direct explanation: Transactional instruction of reading comprehension strategies. *Elementary School Journal* 92:511–54.

Pressley, M., and V. Woloshyn, eds. 1995. *Cognitive strategy instruction that really works*. 2d ed. Cambridge, MA: Brookline Books.

Rouet, J.-F., M. Britt, R. Mason, and C. Perfetti. 1996. Using multiple sources of evidence to reason about history. *Journal of Educational Psychology* 88:478–93.

Rouet, J.-F., M. Favart, M. Britt, and C. Perfetti. 1997. Studying and using multiple documents in history: Effects of discipline expertise. *Cognition and Instruction* 15:85–106.

Sasaki, M., and K. Hirose. 1996. Explanatory variables for EFL students' expository writing. *Language Learning* 46:137–74.

Schumacher, G., and J. Gradwohl Nash. 1991. Conceptualizing and measuring knowledge change due to writing. *Research in the Teaching of English* 25:67–96.

Schumann, J. 1997. *The neurobiology of affect*. Language Learning Monograph Series, vol. 48, supp. 1. Malden, MA: Blackwell.

Shanahan, T. 1984. The nature of reading-writing relations: An exploratory multivariate analysis. *Journal of Educational Psychology* 76:466–77.

———, ed. 1990. *Reading and writing together: New perspectives for the classroom*. Norwood, MA: Christopher-Gordon.

Shanahan, T., and R. Lomax. 1988. An analysis and comparison of theoretical models of the reading-writing relationship. *Journal of Educational Psychology* 78:116–23.

Shanahan, T., and R. Tierney. 1990. Reading-writing connections: The relations among three perspectives. In *Literacy theory and research: Analyses from multiple paradigms,* ed. J. Zutell and S. McCormick, 13–34. Chicago: National Reading Conference.

Silva, T. 1993. Toward an understanding of the distinct nature of L2 writing. *TESOL Quarterly* 27:757–67.

Silva, T., I. Leki, and J. G. Carson. 1997. Broadening the perspective of mainstream composition studies. *Written Communication* 14:398–428.

Slavin, R. 1995. *Cooperative learning.* 2d ed. Boston: Allyn and Bacon.

Smagorinski, P. 1992. How reading model essays affects writers. In *Reading/writing connections,* ed. J. Irwin and M. Doyle, 160–76. Newark, DE: International Reading Association.

Snow, C., M. S. Burns, and P. Griffin, eds. 1998. *Preventing reading difficulties in young children.* Washington, DC: National Academy Press.

Snow, M. A. 1998. Trends and issues in content-based instruction. In *Annual Review of Applied Linguistics,* vol. 18, *Foundations of second language learning,* ed. W. Grabe et al., 243–67. New York: Cambridge University Press.

Snow, M. A., and D. Brinton, eds. 1997. *The content-based classroom: Perspectives on integrating language and content.* New York: Longman.

Spivey, N. 1990. Transforming texts: Constructive processes in reading and writing. *Written Communication* 7:256–87.

Spivey, N., and J. King. 1989. Readers and writers composing from sources. *Reading Research Quarterly* 24:7–26.

Stahl, S., C. Hynd, S. A. Glynn, and M. Carr. 1996. Beyond reading to learn: Developing content and disciplinary knowledge through texts. In *Developing engaged readers in school and home communities,* ed. L. Baker, P. Afflerbach, and D. Reinking, 139–63. Mahwah, NJ: Lawrence Erlbaum.

Stanovich, K., and A. Cunningham. 1993. Where does knowledge come from? Specific associations between print exposure and information acquisition. *Journal of Educational Psychology* 85:211–29.

Stanovich, K., R. West, A. Cunningham, J. Cipielewski, and S. Siddiqui. 1996. The role of inadequate print exposure as a determinant of reading comprehension problems. In *Reading comprehension difficulties: Processes and intervention,* ed. C. Cornoldi and J. Oakhill, 15–32. Mahwah, NJ: Lawrence Erlbaum.

Stolarek, E. 1994. Prose modeling and metacognition: The effect of modeling on developing a metacognitive stance toward writing. *Research in the Teaching of English* 28:154–74.

Stotsky, J. 1983. Research on reading/writing relationships: A synthesis and suggested directions. *Language Arts* 60:627–42.

Swales, J. 1990. *Genre analysis.* New York: Cambridge University Press.

———. 1998. Teaching the literature review to international graduate students. Paper presented at the Ohio State Conference on Second Language Reading/Writing Connections. Columbus, OH, July.

Tierney, R., and P. D. Pearson. 1983. Toward a composing model of reading. *Language Arts* 60:568–80.

Tierney, R., and T. Shanahan. 1991. Research on the reading-writing relationship: Interactions, transactions, and outcomes. In *Handbook of reading research,* ed. R. Barr et al., 2:246–80. New York: Longman.

Tierney, R., A. Soter, J. O'Flavahan, and W. McGinley. 1989. The effects of reading and writing upon thinking critically. *Reading Research Quarterly* 24:134–73.

Tsang, W.-K. 1996. Comparing the effects of reading and writing on writing proficiency. *Applied Linguistics* 17:210–33.

Urquhart, S., and C. Weir. 1998. *Reading in a second language: Process, product, and practice.* New York: Longman.

Vacca, R., and J. Vacca. 1999. *Content area reading.* 6th ed. New York: Longman.

Verhoeven, L., and R. Aarts. 1998. Attaining functional biliteracy in the Netherlands. In *Literacy development in a multilingual context,* ed. A. Durgunoglu and L. Verhoeven, 111–33. Mahwah, NJ: Lawrence Erlbaum.

Wagner, R., and K. Stanovich. 1996. Expertise in reading. In *The road to excellence,* ed. K. A. Ericsson, 189–225. Mahwah, NJ: Lawrence Erlbaum.

Wallace, M. 1998. *Action research for language teachers.* New York: Cambridge University Press.

Waters, A. 1996. *A review of research into needs in English for academic purposes of relevance to the North American higher education context.* TOEFL Monograph Series, 6. Princeton, NJ: Educational Testing Service.

Wells, G. 1994. The complementary contributions of Halliday and Vygotsky to a "language-based theory of learning." *Linguistics and Education* 6:49–61.

———. 1999a. *Dialogic inquiry: Towards a sociocultural practice and theory of education.* New York: Cambridge University Press.

———. 1999b. Language and education: Reconceptualizing education as dialogue. In *Annual Review of Applied Linguistics,* vol. 19, *A survey of applied linguistics,* ed. W. Grabe et al., 135–55. New York: Cambridge University Press.

Wineburg, S. 1991. Historical problem solving: A study of the cognitive processes used in the evaluation of documentary and pictorial evidence. *Journal of Educational Psychology* 83:73–87.

———. 1994. The cognitive representation of historical texts. In *Teaching and learning in history,* ed. G. Leinhardt, I. Beck, and C. Stainton, 85–135. Hillsdale, NJ: Lawrence Erlbaum.

Wigfield, A., and J. Guthrie, eds. 1997. *Motivation for reading.* Special issue, *Educational Psychologist* 32, no. 2.

Winograd, P. 1984. Strategic difficulties in summarizing texts. *Reading Research Quarterly* 19:404–25.

Zamel, V. 1992. Writing one's way into reading. *TESOL Quarterly* 26:463–85.

Chapter 2

A Task Analysis of Reading and Writing in Academic Contexts

Joan G. Carson, Georgia State University

ESL/EFL instruction in academic settings has been hampered by a lack of meaningful insight into the specific language needs of NNS students across various modalities (i.e., speaking, listening, reading, and writing) relative to their use in different kinds of tasks within particular academic disciplines. The search for such insight has centered on academic needs analysis research. However, much of this research has been limited in nature. Some attempts to address the question (e.g., Behrens 1978; Bridgeman and Carlson 1983; Casanave and Hubbard 1992; Daniels 1983; Jenkins, Jordan, and Weiland 1993; Sherwood 1977) have focused almost exclusively on writing and, to a lesser extent, on reading and concentrate on three areas: faculty perceptions of the importance of reading and writing subskills, students' abilities to perform the identified subskills, and the frequency with which students are required to perform reading and writing tasks. Other studies (e.g., Eblen 1983; Hoey 1986; Sternglass 1986; Vande Kopple 1986, 1991, 1992) have examined either the characteristics of the texts (involving textual linguistics) or the interaction between text and the reader/writer (cognitive analyses). A number of L2 researchers have studied the writing tasks assigned in academic degree programs (Braine 1989; Canseco and Byrd 1989; Hale et al. 1996; Horowitz 1986; Johns and Mayes 1990), and their results reflect those of L1 research in that (1) tasks vary considerably across the surveyed areas and (2) all writing subskills are important.

The L2 studies adopting a four skills approach (e.g., Christison and Krahnke 1986; Johns 1981; Ostler 1980) consistently report that the most frequently needed skills are reading and listening. Despite the fact that reading is routinely identified in L2 studies as an essential skill for NNS

This research was conducted with a grant from Educational Testing Service, Princeton, New Jersey. I would like to acknowledge the assistance of Gita Wilder, April Ginther, and Leslie Grant at ETS and of Harriet Allison, research assistant at Georgia State University.

students, this area of EAP has received the least attention. Furthermore, previous research has not systematically related the language skills, academic tasks, and academic subskills that NNS students must have to perform successfully in academic contexts. Given the differing demands made by university faculty across disciplines and between undergraduate and graduate courses, what is needed is awareness of the broader perspectives that might be offered by analyses of (1) assignments given across levels and disciplines in university settings, (2) the materials that students produce in response to those assignments, and (3) interviews of both faculty and students in direct relation to specific academic tasks. The research reported here, which is derived from a larger academic needs analysis study focusing on reading, writing, listening, and speaking skills, sought to provide that awareness by moving beyond the survey methodology employed in previous studies. It expands the informational base to include multiple sources, among them faculty and student interviews, class "artifacts," descriptions of exams and assignments, and the evaluated student products of these tasks.

Research Questions

The original study from which this chapter is drawn examined a series of research questions relative to such domains of interest as the language demands of the various academic fields studied, the tasks contained within them, and the time constraints under which the tasks are performed. The research questions examined in this chapter, which focuses specifically on reading and writing, include

A. What are the similarities and differences among academic tasks across levels and disciplines?
B. What is the appropriate order of magnitude of an academic task that is most useful for analysis?
C. What is the relative importance of reading and of writing in the performance of academic tasks?
D. To what extent does the performance of academic tasks require integration of reading and writing?

Methods

Design

This study was carried out at Georgia State University, a large, urban, nonresidential institution. Although the data collected in this study do not appear to be atypical in any particular way, it is important to note that information from a single site does not produce generalizable results.

The project examined the academic demands of and the literacy skills needed in entry-level undergraduate and graduate courses in three academic disciplines: biology, history, and psychology. These three disciplines were selected to represent the life sciences, the humanities, and the social sciences and are typically represented in core courses at the undergraduate level. Freshman composition was not included in this pilot because of the wealth of information that is already available about writing demands in first-year composition courses and because previous research suggests that the type of writing that occurs in composition courses is not typical of or generalizable to writing in other academic domains.

The data collection emphasized academic language tasks and subtasks across the disciplines and academic levels. For the purposes of this study, a task was identified as "a piece of work or an activity, usually of a specified objective, undertaken as part of an educational course or at work" (Crookes 1986, 1). A task included both an assignment and a response to an assignment. Thus, the initial focal point of data collection was on the activities and products (exams, graded assignments, oral and written reports, etc.) that were the basis of grades in a course—what I refer to as "evaluated products." Thus, an examination of the academic tasks and associated evaluated products, combined with faculty and student interviews, provided a basis for accessing the language competencies that students might use to carry out those tasks.

A triangulated approach to data collection was used by gathering and analyzing information from three principal sources: (1) artifacts from each of the specified courses, (2) interviews with professors of those courses, and (3) interviews with students in those courses. This approach elicited a richer base of data than an examination of the course artifacts alone. Faculty and student interviews were included to help confirm or refute inferences about the areas of interest in this study.

Selection of Courses and Subjects

The six courses selected for inclusion in the study were Biology 141 (Introductory Biology), History 112 (World History from 1500 to the Present), Psychology 101 (Introductory Psychology), Biology 698 (Eukaryotics), History 890 (Historiography), and Psychology 854 (Cognitive Psychology)—the first three courses undergraduate, the last three graduate. These six courses were selected because they represented entry-level courses in each of the disciplines of interest and at both levels of study (undergraduate and graduate). In other words, these courses were expected to be courses that either undergraduate or graduate students would typically take during their first year of study.

The course section chosen for analysis was from a course that was being taught by a full-time faculty member. Because there was no section of the undergraduate psychology course being taught by full-time faculty at the time, an experienced graduate teaching assistant was selected to participate in the study.

In addition to the professors from each of the specified courses, a maximum of eight students per course were also selected to be interviewed. Student participants were identified through a random stratified sampling procedure. First, the course instructor was asked to differentiate students who were native speakers (NSs) and those who were nonnative speakers (NNSs) from the class roll. Then the instructor was asked to identify "successful" students (those with an A or above-average grade in the course) and "less successful" students (those with a C average or below in the course). The researchers randomly selected from the course roll four successful and four less successful students, two NSs and two NNSs in each category. The students so selected were contacted by phone and invited to participate in the study. However, in some courses there were gaps in these categories to the extent that there were insufficient total numbers of students in a particular category. Table 1 shows the distribution of student interviews by course and by language background.

TABLE 1.   Distribution of Student Interviews by Course and by Language Background

	Native Speakers	Nonnative Speakers	Total
Undergraduate			
Biology	4	4	8
History	4	3	7
Psychology	4	4	8
Graduate			
Biology	3	2	5
History	4	—	4
Psychology	4	2	6
Total	23	15	38

Data Collection

Because the interviews with instructors and students were to be centered around the evaluated products in a course, it was necessary to collect course artifacts prior to the interviews to allow the researchers to focus interview questions on the specific products from that course. Virtually all of the instructors provided the researchers with relevant course artifacts, including student work from the previous or the current term, even though these data were collected shortly after the start of the term.

In the initial phase of data collection, the researchers collected the following artifacts:

1. Course syllabi
2. All course texts (primary texts, secondary texts, study guides, handouts, lab manuals, etc.)
3. All exams and quizzes
4. Instructions for all evaluated assignments
5. Evaluated products, that is, examples of all evaluated products (exams, quizzes, papers, etc.) representing a range of student work from the previous and the present term, as available

Separate interview guides were prepared for each type of evaluated product (e.g., multiple-choice tests, essays, or papers). Collecting and examining the artifacts before the interviews with instructors allowed the interviewers to focus directly on course requirements in relation to the evaluated products. This procedure allowed for a specificity that would not have been possible without the exam, study guide, quiz, and so on, and it invited instructor comments that were rooted in their actual classes and evaluation procedures.

Based on information gathered in the artifact collection and in the instructor interviews, an interview guide was developed for use with students. Students were interviewed only once, for about 45 minutes. Whenever possible, the interviewer brought to each student interview copies of the evaluated products to be discussed. Students were asked about their experiences in preparing for and completing each evaluated product. The interviews were audiotaped, with the students' permission, and the audiotapes were later transcribed.

Data Analyses

Given the amount and the variety of data collected, many different analyses could have been undertaken. For the data analysis, primarily qualitative methods were used for three reasons: (1) the data, for the most part, do not lend themselves to quantitative analysis (except for specific aspects that are reported); (2) the primary goal of the research was to identify, rather than quantify, general parameters that could form the basis of future research; (3) because of the lack of previous research, the focus was on emergent themes in the data that could be used to construct a framework for analysis. In other words, the methodology reflects the goal of examining academic language from a holistic perspective, which entailed considering interrelationships that would not be evident from a quantitative analysis.

The analysis itself focused on three major interpretive categories: objectives, text, and task. "Text" was defined as any part of the content of the course (oral and written), and "task" was defined as the way in which the mastery of the text/course content is measured and/or the course requirements are fulfilled. This definition of task was adopted to provide a coherent and comparable focus of investigation across disciplines and academic levels. The rationale for this focus was that evaluated products constituted not only what the professor valued in the course but also the goal toward which students directed their energy and efforts. As such, evaluated products served as the superordinate categories for the language demands and activities that occurred in each course being examined.

Analyses of the data were done as follows.

1. *Objectives.* Course objectives were understood both as the context within which the course proceeded and the goals toward which the course was directed. These objectives were noted as stated in the course syllabus or in the professor and student interviews.

2. *Texts.* Each course text was ranked as either primary or secondary. Primary texts were those from which the major content for the course was drawn: textbooks, lectures, and laboratory manuals. Secondary texts were those that provided additional course content and information: syllabi, study guides, handouts, references, and individualized read-

ings for presentations and/or reports. Each text was then examined with respect to both its function in the course and its relationship to other course texts. This information was derived from multiple sources: the syllabus, professor interviews, and student interviews.

Texts were individually analyzed for a number of features:[1]

a. *Topics.* The topics covered in the course were organized in the analysis by the groupings in which they were evaluated; that is, topics were understood as constituting an organizational unit as determined by the subject matter that was included in an exam, quiz, or other evaluated product.

b. *Amount.* The amount of assigned text material was calculated by the number of pages for each of the following: the total pages per term, per chapter, per class, and per exam.

c. *Characteristics.* Two major characteristics of texts were examined: prose and graphic information. In the original study, the prose characteristics were subdivided and analyzed within four categories: organization of text, amount of text, content parameters, and language demands. For the purposes of this chapter, two categories were included:

(1) *Organization.* Organization was described at the level of the entire book, the chapter, and the page or paragraph. Description focused on the major features relative to each of these levels.

(2) *Content Parameters.* Content parameters were described in terms of the types and numbers of references (average per page), the types of pedagogical aids provided, the average number of graphics per chapter and their function in relation to the text, and the text's general orientation to the subject matter (e.g., general principles, variety of perspectives, use of examples, predominant themes). Graphic information was included in the aspect of the analysis and in the analysis of graphics

---

1. The examined texts include only written texts. Information about oral texts was gathered in the interviews and is analyzed to the extent possible by topics, functions, and language.

themselves, since this information also needed to be understood as integral to the content parameters.

The characteristics of the graphic information (in addition to the prose information already noted) were additionally analyzed by two categories:

(a) *Types.* The types of graphic information presented in the text included all the ways in which information was presented in a format other than prose. These types included figures, illustrations, photos, drawings, maps, tables, time lines, and typefaces.

(b) *Functions.* The functions of graphic information were determined by examining the relationship of the information to the prose text (e.g., supplemental to text, illustration of text, additional details referred to in text).

3a. *Tasks (In-Class).* Course tasks were defined as evaluated products, and each evaluated product was described separately. Because in-class exams and quizzes (hereafter referred to as "tests") were the most common evaluated product, the analysis of these tasks will be described first.

a. *General Parameters.* The general parameters for each test were determined from the test itself, from the syllabus, and from professor and student interviews. The information noted included the percentage of the grade constituted by the test, the amount of time allowed for the test, whether or not dictionaries were permitted, the average number of words per test, whether or not points for questions or sections of the test were indicated, and the detail (or lack thereof) of the directions given for the text.

b. *Task by Prompt Type.* Tests were further analyzed by prompt type (e.g., multiple choice, true-false, short answer, essay), the average points per item, and the amount of the test constituted by that prompt type.

c. *Response/Demand.* The response to each prompt type (i.e., the demands of the question) for in-class tests was further analyzed. This information was primarily gathered from professor and student interviews. Five categories were used in the analysis:

(1) what the professor expected to learn from a student's response (e.g., evidence of knowledge of basic information or of ability to interpret data);

(2) sources a student needed to draw on to respond to the prompt type (e.g., lecture, text, study guide);

(3) the relative importance of each of these sources;

(4) the relationship among sources (e.g., between lecture and text);

(5) the preparation required by students before attempting a prompt type.

3b. *Tasks (Out-of-Class)*. Out-of-class evaluated products included assignments, such as papers, critical reviews, take-home exams, or classroom presentations.[2] The analysis that was done for these products was much the same as that done for the in-class products, although there were several notable differences:

a. The way in which the task was presented and described for students was described in the "General Parameters" section of the analysis.

b. Because prompt types were irrelevant for these assignments (each out-of-class task typically had a single exemplar), a task analysis, which included primarily the language and cognitive demands, was done instead of an analysis of prompt type.

c. Given the nature of out-of-class tasks, preparation and production were often conflated and difficult to separate. For example, writing a take-home exam might involve reading the text and writing study notes (preparation), writing a response to the exam (production), and then reading specifically while filling in gaps in the response (preparation or production?). However, these distinctions were considered to be trivial for the most part, since the ultimate purpose of the analysis is to describe what students must be able to do to perform successfully in an academic class.

---

2. Class presentations are included here in out-of-class assignments, since what was evaluated in these presentations was primarily the work that students had done out of class, that is, the organization and content of the material presented.

Results and Discussion

Information for each of the primary categories of information (objectives, texts, tasks) was compared across disciplines (biology, history, and psychology) but within levels (undergraduate vs. graduate). Following the category comparison across disciplines are descriptions of similarities and differences across academic levels.

Objectives

Undergraduate

The objectives of the three undergraduate courses were similar: to introduce basic concepts, principles, and facts of the discipline. These courses, then, present the fundamental "building blocks" that are needed for further study in the discipline but also explicitly or implicitly aim to introduce students to relevant themes that unify the course topics as a coherent area of inquiry. The course in world history covered the period from 1450 to the present but was organized into three principle eras, suggesting the connectedness of historical events. The biology class covered five primary topics (e.g., cell structure and function, evolution, genetics) that did not necessarily build on one another, but the five themes of biological study (e.g., unity within diversity, relationship between form and function) were connecting threads that ran throughout each of the topics. In psychology, the individual units appear to be unrelated in a cumulative sense but in fact provide both a historical and methodological overview of the way in which psychological study has been/is done. Thus, it would be simplistic to conclude that introductory undergraduate courses are merely providing students with the basic facts of a discipline.

Graduate

Interestingly, there were no explicit objectives given for the graduate courses in biology and psychology, even though all the graduate courses examined were ones that graduate students would be expected to take in their first year of study. We might assume that this lack is due to the implicit understanding (by both professor and students) that for graduate students the objectives of the course were clear: to learn more about the discipline (or a specific aspect of the discipline—eukaryotics or cognitive psychology) for which their undergraduate studies have prepared them.

Nevertheless, interviews with the biology professor about assigned tasks revealed objectives that were implicit in the course: to learn the basic information; to simulate work that biologists do; and to understand why things are considered to be true, so that later findings can be evaluated in light of new evidence. Although not stated directly either in the syllabus or in the interview, the implicit objectives of the psychology course, considering the types of answers the professor expected on the exams, were to learn the basic information and to be able to evaluate psychological theories with reference to relevant studies.

In the graduate course in historiography, however, the course objectives were spelled out in the syllabus: to provide information on trends and traditions of historical interpretation and to give students an opportunity to do historical research. Historiography, then, is a research methods course for history students, and perhaps the need for explicit objectives results from the fact that graduate students have often not been introduced to research methods in history as undergraduates.

Comparison of Undergraduate and Graduate Objectives

It appears that undergraduate and graduate course objectives are somewhat different. Perhaps introductory courses are much broader in nature (of the overview type) because their goals are different: to provide students with the fundamentals of the field and to introduce students to the ways in which a discipline constructs itself (i.e., how studies in a particular area are done). Thus, students are primarily absorbing knowledge that has been created. Graduate courses assume and build on undergraduate studies in the field and require graduate students to take a more critical stance toward knowledge in the field. Thus, introductory graduate courses include in their objectives that students not only acquire knowledge but also begin doing what disciplinary experts do: evaluate approaches and results.

These differences in objectives, however, are not differences that would be important in a teaching situation that aims to prepare students to begin either undergraduate or graduate studies. The goals of a particular course are goals toward which students are expected to progress; their entry-level abilities are better discerned as those proficiencies that would enable students to cope with the demands of the course and are probably best seen in the analyses of text and task demands that follow.

Texts

Undergraduate

The texts (oral and written) across disciplines were similar in many ways. Each course had a primary course text, with biology and history having two each (including a biology laboratory manual and a history primer that provided mainly geographical material). Each course also had a syllabus and a study guide as secondary texts, although the study guide in psychology was only recommended, not required. In all three undergraduate courses, the lecture was the primary text and the only oral text.

The functions of the texts across disciplines were similar as well, with the primary content provided by the primary texts (both oral and written). The lecture overlapped the reading for the most part, with some additional information (primarily examples) provided in the biology lecture. The function of the lectures was to highlight relevant information in the reading to help students focus on important information in the text. The study guides were the principal secondary texts and were intended to direct students' study focus with review and study questions.

The total amount of reading differed substantially by course, with the reading in biology nearly twice that in psychology, that in history nearly three times that in psychology. These differences affected students' strategies for coping with the reading demands, but the amount of text was offset somewhat by the cognitive difficulty of the biology and psychology texts. In other words, although students reported having more to read in history, the time spent reading was not necessarily longer, since the reading in the other courses was more difficult.

A surprising finding was the relevance of narrative and chronological presentations at the metalevel of the text, although this can be related in the case of psychology and biology to one of the course objectives—to provide students with a sense of how inquiry proceeds and/or has proceeded in the field. At the level of the chapter, analysis and classification predominated across disciplines, whereas at the paragraph level, cause and effect, analysis, and classification were most common. In the laboratory manual, process paragraphs were common, as one might expect. Again, these organizational patterns relate to the objectives of the course and can be understood in that context.

Introductory texts tended to include a large amount of graphic information, ranging from an average of 11 graphics (history) to 30 (psychology) per chapter. The common graphics used were figures and typefaces, with time lines used in history and psychology, photos in biology and psychology. (The lack of photos in the history text is undoubtedly an artifact of the chapters chosen for analysis, since photographs were nonexistent before the 19th century.) The function of the graphic information, however, was not always the same. In biology and psychology, the graphics were used to illustrate, exemplify, and summarize information that was presented in the text—in other words, to allow visual as well as linguistic processing of information. In history, however, the graphic information was more often supplemental and peripheral to the text, although the time lines helped students visualize relationships between and among events in the text. In addition, professors in each of the three courses used the chalkboard extensively, primarily to write terms or draw diagrams of concepts that they wanted to highlight in their lectures.

No references were given within the text itself for biology and history. However, the psychology text averaged 3.4 parenthetical references per page.

Graduate

The texts across disciplines at the graduate level varied considerably. There were three primary written texts in both history and psychology, but there was no assigned primary reading in biology. The finding of no assigned primary reading in biology seems odd, perhaps even idiosyncratic: in this course, the primary content was presented in lecture format, and students were told to read the course text only if they needed additional clarification.

Lectures in psychology were geared toward presenting material that overlapped to a large extent with the readings but that also contained additional information. Given the nature of the evaluated products in the history course, the lectures were not a crucial source of information but tended to expand on assigned readings. In history, class discussions that expanded on the lecture and readings were also a significant part of the course, as were the reading reports that students were asked to do.

For secondary texts, both biology and psychology professors provided students with study guides that were extremely important for students' test preparations. The biology study guide described the test format and gave sample questions for each prompt type. The biology professor liked to "reward" students for working through the study guide by including in some tests one of the questions from the study guide. The psychology study guide was quite different in nature, listing both topics to be included in each test and readings from the three primary texts that were relevant to each topic. In this way, the study guide also served as a kind of syllabus for the course.

Students in biology and history also were required to read additional texts for various assigned tasks, although these were classified as secondary texts. In biology, students had to do a critical review of an article, which entailed reading additional background information, including related journal articles. In history, students had a significant amount of additional reading, since they were required to do original archival research. Since these assignments were individual according to students' interests, no analysis was done of these texts.

The amount of text that students needed to process in graduate courses varied, from no assigned reading (except journal articles for the critical review) in biology to almost 900 pages in cognitive psychology. Although there was less assigned primary reading in history (503 pages), there was probably more total reading required in this course, given the reading demands of the archival research project.

Analysis predominated at the primary-text metalevel for both the biology and psychology texts, but the three primary texts in history were somewhat different (and difficult to characterize). In one of the history texts, the fact that chapters were assigned in an unsequenced order meant that no metalevel organization was obvious. The second primary text was clearly chronological in order, but the third text was a topical anthology and resisted categorization. The metalevel organization of the secondary text in history was classification.

At the level of the chapter, both biology texts and one of the history texts evidenced analysis as the primary organizational pattern, with the history text including exemplification. The two additional texts in history were organized by chronology and analysis (in the form of argument) by chapters. All three texts in psychology were organized at the chapter level by classification and chronological order. Classification and analysis were the patterns used in the secondary history text.

At the paragraph level, all three primary course texts utilized analysis patterns, although there were additional patterns that varied by discipline. Biology included significant process and description patterns. History used classification and exemplification, and psychology focused on problem/solution, definition, and cause and effect, as well as analysis. The secondary text in history was organized primarily by analysis and classification at the paragraph level.

The amount of graphic information varied considerably by discipline, with the biology text averaging 20 figures per chapter while the history texts had few or sometimes no graphics. For the three primary texts in psychology, the averages of graphics per chapter were 3, 6, and 8. It must be kept in mind that although the biology text had a large number of figures per chapter, the text itself was not assigned, so this average is in large part inconsequential. However, the professor drew frequent charts and diagrams on the chalkboard as she lectured, so graphics figured prominently in the oral text.

Graphics functioned as an important part of the course material in biology and psychology only, where they illustrated text information, added detailed information to the prose text, and highlighted important terms and concepts. The predominant forms of graphic information in the biology text (oral and written) were figures and diagrams. In psychology, the predominant form was graphs, both in the written text and in the oral text. The graphs that were drawn on the chalkboard in psychology were those the professor expected students to learn. In history, the few graphics (primarily cartoons) added little to the course content, and the professor in the history course rarely utilized the chalkboard.

Not surprisingly, little pedagogical information was included in the course texts, except for the study guides in biology and psychology. No references were given in the biology text, but the primary history texts averaged between .3 and 1 endnote per page. The psychology texts included parenthetical references that averaged between 1.6 and 3.4 per page.

Comparison of Undergraduate and Graduate Texts

The similarities among undergraduate written course texts and the dissimilarities among graduate written course texts no doubt have to do with the differing objectives of undergraduate and graduate education: to introduce students to a discipline versus to immerse students in the discipline. With the exception of the graduate biology course, in which the lecture, not the written text, served the primary function of information presentation, the lectures served similar functions in both undergraduate and graduate courses: to present and highlight/focus on material that overlapped with the written text. However, the lectures in the graduate courses provided additional or supplementary information more often than did the lectures in the undergraduate courses (although some supplementary information was noted also in undergraduate courses).

While the types of content (overlapping vs. additional or supplemental) of the oral texts/lectures are important to notice, the function of the oral texts/lectures is probably more important: to highlight/focus on important information that students need to attend to. Both professors' and students' interviews confirm that this function was a pivotal one (see the following discussion of task responses), especially given the amount of material that students were asked to read. Lectures provided cues as to what students needed to focus on, and without this focusing, the distinction between trivial and important information from reading would be a much more difficult task (cf. the example given shortly about the role of experiments in the undergraduate vs. the graduate psychology courses). In other words, what was important in reading was not just a function of what appeared to be important in the text. Importance was determined by the professor's focus, not just the reading alone. Thus, while listening and note taking, particularly in the case of overlapping information, could be understood as somewhat less important than reading in terms of accessing content information (or vice versa), these skills are of considerably more importance with respect to the students' need to focus their reading and studying appropriately.

The predominance of study guides across academic levels is also noteworthy, to the extent that professors at both levels were concerned with helping students separate trivial from important information. What constituted trivial information versus important information varied, however, across levels. In the undergraduate psychology course, concepts were the most important, and experimental studies were not a significant focus. In the graduate psychology course, however, students were expected to focus on and learn which experimental studies supported various findings/concepts. In the undergraduate biology course, the professor expected students to be able to understand the examples, or ways in which concepts/theories were exemplified in the real world, but in the graduate biology course, the professor focused on the theories themselves. This finding is no doubt a result of the subject matter as well, since the broad themes introduced in the undergraduate course were more amenable to real-world exemplification, whereas the course in eukaryotics investigated cellular phenomena, which are not so readily demonstrated in this way. For the undergraduate and graduate history courses, the differing topics—learning history versus doing history—meant that the information presentation was not amenable to comparison. Again, though, the graduate history course, like the graduate courses in biology and psychology, was concerned with theoretical underpinnings to an extent that the undergraduate course was not.

Metalevel organizational structure varied for the levels of the courses examined, with chronology predominating at the undergraduate level, analysis at the graduate level. At the chapter level, analysis was the most common organization observed (for five of the six courses), with classification also noted for four of the six courses. Paragraphs were most often organized by analysis patterns that were common across all the courses, with classification evident in four of the six courses.

Graphic information was much more prevalent in undergraduate texts than in graduate texts, and the function of graphics differed by level as well. In the biology and psychology undergraduate courses, graphics were used to illustrate, exemplify, and summarize information presented in prose form. Thus, they could be used to help understand the reading. In the history courses, the graphics were peripheral in that they were not directly related to what had been presented in prose or necessarily important informationally. In the biology and psychology graduate courses, however, the graphic information illustrated information that had been given in prose or lecture format and provided supplemental content that students were expected to learn. As with the undergraduate history course, graphic information in the graduate course was insignificant.

Tasks

The task analysis that follows includes two separate aspects: task description and task response.

Undergraduate

Task Description

Tasks (or evaluated products) across disciplines at the undergraduate level evidenced more similarities than differences. In all three courses, in-class, timed, multiple-choice exams or quizzes constituted the principal form of evaluation. These tests comprised 100 percent of the grade in biology (four exams, including a cumulative final), 66 percent of the grade in history (seven quizzes and a cumulative final), and 92 percent of the grade in psychology (including a cumulative but optional final exam). In the history quizzes, questions were drawn from both the main course text and the primer; the biology exams included questions based on the students' lab work (there were no separate graded lab assignments). For the in-class exams and quizzes, NNSs in all courses were allowed to use dictionaries.

The time allowed for and number of items included on in-class tests varied. For biology exams, the average number of items was 82 (average of 1,546 words), and the students were given one hour and 15 minutes to complete the test. In history, the quizzes averaged 26 items (average of 646 words), and 20–30 minutes were given for completion. The final history exam included 150 items (average of 4,087 words), and students were allowed two hours. The exams in psychology averaged 50 items (average of 1,684 words), with a one-hour time limit.

The cognitive demands of the exam and quizzes reflected the course objectives: to have students acquire basic concepts and principles in the field. Thus, it is not surprising that for all the courses, questions of the recognize/retrieve/identify type predominated, as shown in table 2. Although the percentages of question types varied by discipline, significant similarities are worth noting: the predominance of recognize/retrieve/identify questions and the presence of application/infer questions across disciplines. Although the percentages for the final exam in history are not included in table 2, they were not substantially different from the quiz averages noted there.

In-class tasks represented 86 percent of the evaluated products in undergraduate courses; out-of-class tasks represented 14 percent. Out-of-class requirements included a take-home essay assignment in the history course (33 percent of the grade), and the psychology course required students to participate in the typical experiments assigned to students in entry-level psychology courses (8 percent of the grade). If a student merely showed up to participate in the experiment, she or he was given credit, even though it is conceivable that an NNS might be not be able to perform the experimental task because of inadequate language skills. However, because participation in the experiments was the only requirement (i.e., there was not a quality measure attached to this assignment), there is no analysis of this aspect of the course.

The take-home essay assignment in history consisted of two parts, one of which was due at midterm, with the continuation and final part due at the end of the term. Students were given a total of five prompts (averaging 183 words), from which one was chosen. The essay was a question that

TABLE 2.   Percentages of Question Types in Exams and Quizzes across Undergraduate Disciplines

	Biology	History	Psychology	Average
Recognize/Retrieve/Identify	95%	89%	63%	82%
Definition	3	24	33	20
General Text Info.	37	44	17	33
Synthesized Text Info.	55	22	12	30
Application/Infer	5	11	33	16
Analogy	—	—	4	1

required synthesis and rewarded interpretation of information from the course. Students were directed to not use additional references or quote information; rather, they were expected to synthesize information in their own words.

Task Response

Because of the similarities of the tasks on the in-class tests, task responses to exams and quizzes as reported in student interviews were also similar across undergraduate disciplines. Information sources included the primary texts, lectures, and study guides, although the relative importance of each source differed across courses. In biology, the lecture and reading were the most important, comprising information required for approximately 80 percent of the exam. The other 20 percent of the exam questions came from the lab text, the lab experience, and the study guide. For the history course, the lecture was most important, with the study guide serving as an outline and focus. The text was used principally as a reference, with students using the index to look up topics and terms mentioned in the lecture, while they used the glossary to define terms from the study guide. For psychology, the primary text was the source for 75 to 85 percent of the exam questions, with the lecture providing the bulk of the remaining information, while the study guide provided the focus. In all courses, students used the study guide to help focus the information in the readings and lectures, since the lectures and written texts primarily complemented one another.

Preparation for exams and quizzes was also similar across disciplines, with students needing to memorize information as well as to understand relationships. Students also reported the need to analyze processes, events, and information and to synthesize/integrate text information, especially across written texts and lectures. Students in biology and psychology mentioned the need to apply the information they had learned to real-life situations.

Students mentioned using four skills to prepare for in-class tests. Reading was required to process assigned readings, lecture notes, the study guide, and the students' own study notes. Writing was important for taking lecture, reading, and study notes and to complete answers to the study guide questions. Listening was relevant for lectures and also for understanding students' in-class questions and professors' answers to in-class queries. Finally, speaking was important to students who needed to ask questions to clarify concepts presented in the lecture.

In task production (i.e., actually taking the test), the cognitive demands were again similar across disciplines, as well as considerable for these multiple-choice exams. Students mentioned the need to understand the questions and possible answers, with this comprehension made more difficult by the professors' use of frequent paraphrases. Retrieving information from memory was also important, as was the need to both recognize the correct response and eliminate the incorrect responses. In biology and psychology, students also had to apply information that they had learned to novel situations.

The take-home essay exam in history required somewhat different abilities. The information sources included lecture material, handouts, the primary texts, and a dictionary. Although the professor had instructed students not to use additional source material, most of the students we interviewed mentioned that they had used library sources as well, when they were not satisfied with the amount of content available to them from course materials. Seventy-five percent of the information needed for the essay was included in the lecture and handouts, and students used the primary texts for reference.

To prepare for the essay, students needed to employ a range of cognitive processes: identify relevant information; retrieve information from memory; analyze the relationships of facts and events as well as complex events; organize the information chronologically, topically, and geographically; and interpret the meaning of the events being reported. Both reading (of the primary text, lecture notes, handouts, study notes, and dictionary) and writing (paraphrasing information from the lecture and written text, synthesizing lecture and reading notes, and summarizing) were required in preparing for the task.

In producing the essay, students typically utilized the following cognitive processes: separating trivial from important information; adding additional information; retrieving prepared information; organizing material; making connections among events and facts; and analyzing, synthesizing, and interpreting information. Both reading and writing played valuable roles, although reading was more important in the preparation phase. In terms of writing abilities, students needed to organize information logically, paraphrase, provide appropriate support, and attend to form (mechanics and spelling) and grammar (although the professor indicated that grammatical correctness was not a primary concern as long as incorrectness did not interfere with meaning).

Graduate

Task Description

The tasks across disciplines at the graduate level were varied, as can be seen in table 3.

Of these tasks, 57 percent were in-class assignments (the exams in biology and psychology), and the remaining 43 percent were out-of-class assignments (the critical review in biology and all the history assignments).

For all in-class exams, students were allowed the full class period, which ranged from one to two hours; no dictionaries were allowed. The biology study guide provided explicit descriptions, and the biology test gave full directions for the true-false section but a title only for the short and long essay sections. In the psychology exam, there were sparse directions, often the title only; students were expected to know how to complete each section. For all item types, reading played a central role.

TABLE 3.   Tasks (with Subtasks) Assigned across Graduate Disciplines and Percentage of Total Grade (and of Task Total)

Biology	History	Psychology[a]
Midterm Exam (30% of total grade) True-False (30% of exam)	Research Report (33% of total grade)	Exams (100% of total grade) Multiple Choice (19% of exam) Matching (14% of exam)
Descriptive Essay (40% of exam) Problem-Solving (30% of exam)		Short Answer (43% of exam) Essay (30% of exam)
Final Exam (40% of total grade) Short Essay (60% of exam) Longer Essay (40% of exam)	Final Exam (33% of total grade)	
Critical Review (30% of total grade)	Oral Research Report, Class Discussion, Oral Report on Reading (33% of total grade)	

[a]The percentages of subtypes for psychology exams add up to more than 100 percent because students were often given the choice of answering a smaller number of questions than the exam presented (e.g., selecting two questions out of four). The percentages are of all the possible questions on the exam, however.

In terms of cognitive demands, the in-class exams in biology and psychology were most directly comparable, with comparable types of question, although there were differences in exam format, as shown in table 4.

Both the biology and the psychology exams contained a number of recognize/retrieve/identify question types, but the subtype was predominantly questions that required students to synthesize information from text(s). In addition, although there were few application/infer questions, both disciplines included evaluation/infer questions in their evaluations of student performance.

The 43 percent of evaluated products that were produced out of class were extremely varied, although their common thread is that they were all based on reading. Each assignment will be discussed individually here.

For the critical review in biology, students were asked to choose a scholarly article from a list prepared by the professor. The task was described in the syllabus, and students had one month to complete the assignment. The paper, which was to be a critical review of a recent article in the field, consisted of five pages, and the format was specified: introduction and analysis of the article. The language demand was primarily reading the review and related articles, and the cognitive demands included recognizing and retrieving important information and evaluating the material.

The research report in history also required a significant amount of reading, since students were asked to do archival research and present an original analysis. The topics were selected by the students, based primarily on archival material that was available to them. The report needed to be approximately 40 pages long, and students were given six weeks to complete the assignment. The cognitive demands included recognizing and retrieving important information, evaluating the material, and organizing it into a coherent analysis. Both the professor and the students reported that this task was especially difficult since students needed to "find the story" that linked various pieces of archival data. The students were also required to give a 30-minute presentation of their findings in an oral report to the class.

The final take-home essay was a four-item exam, with no length specified. A brief description of the assignment was given in the syllabus, and, as with the other course assignments, the professor provided additional information orally in class.

Task Response

Task responses varied across disciplines given the different nature of the assignments, although the in-class exam responses in biology and psy-

TABLE 4.   Percentages of Question Types across All Graduate Exams

| | Biology[a] | | | Psychology[b] | | | |
	True-False (15%)	Descriptive Essay (35%)	Essay (35%)	Multiple Choice (19%)	Matching (14%)	Short Answer (43%)	Essay (30%)
Recognize/Retrieve/Identify	15%	33%	20%	16%	14%	43%	22%
Definition	—	—	—	1%	2%	3%	—
General Text Info.	—	—	—	4%	4%	8%	—
Synthesized Text Info.	15%[c]	33%[c]	20%	11%	8%	32%	22%
Application/Infer	—	—	—	—	—	—	—
Analogy	—	—	—	—	—	—	—
Evaluation/Infer	—	—	15%	2%	—	—	14%

[a]The percentages of question types in biology do not equal 100 percent. The missing 15 percent is a sentence–completion question type that resisted categorization.

[b]The percentages of subtypes for psychology exams add up to more than 100 percent because students were often given the choice of answering a smaller number of questions than the exam presented (e.g., selecting two questions out of four). The percentages are of all the possible questions on the exam, however.

[c]These percentages reflect questions that were a combination of synthesis and application/infer question types.

chology shared some features. In biology, the sources of information were primarily the lecture, the study guide, and question-and-answer sessions in class, with the primary text used for reference material. The most important sources were the lecture and the study guide, with the study guide directing students to specific text pages as needed to explain specific concepts or fill in the gaps in students' understanding. In psychology, the information sources included the primary and secondary texts, the lecture, the study guide, and question-and-answer sessions in class. However, the primary written text information was the most important, as the lecture tended to overlap the text with some additional information. The lecture primarily helped guide students' reading and study focus, and the study guide directed students to specific text pages for information on crucial experiments.

In preparing for biology and psychology exams, students were faced with multiple cognitive demands: selecting important concepts and experiments, synthesizing information from texts, analyzing and organizing information according to anticipated exam questions, and memorizing information (including experiments and illustrative diagrams and graphs).

Regarding reading and writing, for both courses, students read the text (selectively according to their lecture notes and study guide questions), their lecture notes, the study guide, their study notes, and their own written-out answers to possible exam questions. Writing demands included taking lecture notes, reading notes, and study notes, as well as writing answers to potential exam questions.

All exam questions in biology required writing, and the students mentioned multiple cognitive tasks: understanding the question and all tasks required, retrieving all relevant facts from memory, synthesizing and evaluating information, applying relevant evidence to novel situations, and justifying answers in terms of class information. Reading was required in the sense of reading the question carefully and recognizing key words/concepts. Writing demands included explaining logically, including main points and appropriate support, using key words, and attending to mechanics and grammar only as necessary for clarity. Students were encouraged to use graphics in their written answers, and diagrams and illustrations often constituted a significant portion of their responses.

Exam questions in psychology were of two types: (1) multiple choice and matching and (2) constructed response. For the multiple-choice and matching items, the cognitive demands included understanding questions and possible answers, retrieving information from memory, and distinguishing between multiple possibly correct answers. The primary language task was reading for these item types and required understanding extremely complex sentence structures and recognizing restatements/ paraphrases of information. Several students also reported using language cues to answer the matching questions—looking for subject-verb matches or analogous language forms (e.g., matching noun phrases).

Answering short-answer and essay questions in psychology exams required multiple cognitive processes: recognizing key words/concepts, retrieving presynthesized memorized information, organizing information, and evaluating/critiquing evidence. The primary language demand for this item type was writing, in which students were required to organize information logically, paraphrase, maintain a focus, include appropriate support, comment critically, and appropriately use cognitive psychology terms and academic language. As in the biology class, there was minimal attention to mechanics and grammar. The professor also encouraged students to embed previously answered questions in subsequent ones, to the extent that the information was relevant. Students could omit part of a response that they had already covered in an earlier question by referring to the question number.

All task responses to out-of-class assignments involved a significant amount of reading and writing, but there were differences among them. For the critical review in biology, information sources included the primary article to be reviewed, the course text (as reference), Medline (a computer database), related journal articles, and class notes. In terms of importance, the primary article and related articles (typically found through the Medline search) were the most relevant, followed by the course text and class notes. Students used the related articles as context for the primary article and referred to the course text for background information.

Task preparation involved multiple cognitive demands: finding the main points of the article, analyzing information critically, synthesizing and evaluating the information, and finding new questions raised by the findings. Language demands included reading the selected article critically; finding the main points and omitting extraneous information; reading related articles, course text information, and class notes; and reading Medline information. Writing preparation included preparing reading notes, defining terms, paraphrasing, quoting selectively, organizing information, and synthesizing notes.

Producing the critical review overlapped with preparing for it. The cognitive demands were identical to those needed for task preparation, as were the reading demands. The writing, however, was somewhat different in that students needed to attend particularly to organization and clarity and were instructed to write for an audience of their peers. They needed to use their own words, which involved significant paraphrasing. Although technical vocabulary needed to be spelled correctly, the professor allowed nonstandard grammar as long as the meaning was clear.

The research report in history required students to use archival materials as their main source of information, with secondary sources and course materials used as context for archival data. Both the conceptual framework needed and the procedures to be used came from the course materials.

The cognitive demands in preparing for the research report required students to select relevant data, keep information in memory, summarize main ideas, organize material, synthesize primary and secondary materials, analyze data and find connections among them, and interpret information. Language demands included reading archival data, secondary sources, and relevant course content. Students reported reading between 500 and 4,000 pages of information, including skimmed material. Writing preparation was primarily note taking, which required summarizing and paraphrasing. Students also mentioned outlining drafts of their reports.

Producing the research report necessarily overlapped with its preparation. Cognitively, students needed to understand the task and to synthesize, analyze, and interpret the data (although these activities were typically complete before the report was produced). In writing the report, students reported reading their notes and primary texts as needed. Writing demands included organizing the information logically with an introduction, body, and conclusion; providing appropriate citations/documentation; and using students' own words. Proper grammar and mechanics were critical.

For the final take-home exam in history, the primary texts, lecture, and class discussion constituted the information sources, although the primary texts were the most important for half of the questions. Lecture information complemented the readings with additional perspectives and interpretations, while class discussions provided expansion of the lectures and depth to the readings.

In preparing for the final exam, students needed to analyze, synthesize, organize, and critically evaluate texts. In addition, they were required to apply concepts to real-world situations, evaluate approaches, and construct interpretive frameworks. Reading demands included understanding main ideas, developing familiarity with primary sources, and reading class notes and lecture notes. Students also needed to write lecture, reading, and class discussion notes.

Production of the final exam overlapped with preparation. The cognitive demands were the same as those required for preparation and were typically completed before the exam was produced. When writing the final exam, students read both their notes from multiple sources and the primary texts as necessary. Writing required organizing information and supporting generalizations with evidence. In addition, students had to use their own words, avoid jargon, and give evidence of "style." As with the research report, correct grammar and mechanics were critical.

The oral report in history was based on an assigned reading, the primary source, and related course materials that provided critical perspectives on the reading. In preparing for the oral report, students needed to select the important points in reading, then organize, synthesize, critically analyze, and interpret the text. Language demands included understanding the main ideas and relating the information to previous knowledge. Writing preparation primarily involved note taking: summarizing and paraphrasing the reading, outlining the presentation, and writing out questions for class discussion.

In giving their oral reports, students had typically completed the cognitive processing necessary before the presentation. Reading involved reading a topic outline or notes as necessary, but there was no writing required during the report. Students needed to present a clear and organized summary of the reading, ask questions, and elicit comments from the class.

Comparison of Undergraduate and Graduate Tasks

For both undergraduate and graduate courses, the majority of the grade was determined by in-class (i.e., timed) exams (86 percent of undergraduate tasks vs. 57 percent of graduate tasks). Both levels included out-of-class evaluated products, and as might be expected, a larger percentage of graduate work needed to be done out of class (14 percent of undergraduate assignments vs. 43 percent of graduate assignments). All out-of-class products, whether undergraduate or graduate, were writing assignments that required synthesizing information, as well as some interpretation, although interpretation/critical thinking was more important at the graduate level than at the undergraduate.

All in-class exams at the undergraduate level were in a multiple-choice format, whereas most of the exams in graduate courses included constructed response (the majority of the psychology exam and virtually all of the biology exam).[3] Given the difference in format, the number of items per exam varied as well, with more items included in undergraduate tests (except for history quizzes, which were by definition shorter than exams) than in graduate tests. Thus, the reading demands of undergraduate exams (i.e., the exam itself) were heavier than those for graduate exams.

Both the undergraduate and the graduate in-class exams required understanding discipline-specific and general academic vocabulary, and there seemed to be little pattern evidenced in the variety of syntactic structures used either across disciplines or across academic levels. Exams at both levels included a majority of questions from the recognize/retrieve/ identify category, although differences in the subtypes were evident. For undergraduate courses, there were more questions requiring definition and general text information; for graduate courses, more questions requiring synthesized text information. The undergraduate courses also included more application/inference questions, while the graduate courses had evaluation/inference questions, which were nonexistent on undergraduate exams.

For both undergraduate and graduate in-class exams, students typically had the class period in which to complete the test (except for the history quizzes). NNSs were allowed to use dictionaries in all three undergraduate courses but in none of the graduate courses.

Task responses for in-class exams also showed some similarities across academic levels. Common sources of information were lectures, primary written texts, and study guides, and in all courses, lectures and written texts tended to overlap, with little supplemental information in either source. The principal function of this overlap at both academic levels was to focus students on important source information.

Student interviews indicated that students tended to rely on their individual strengths (either listening or reading), with the presentation format in which students judged themselves to be weaker serving as the secondary source. For example, NNSs tended to rely more on the text in the graduate biology course than did NSs, even though the entire course content consisted of information from the lecture, with the professor advising the students to use the text as a "reference." At the same time, the reading load was so formidable in the undergraduate history course that

---

3. Even the true-false section of the psychology and biology exams required that students justify their choices in writing.

both NNSs and NSs relied heavily on lectures to guide them in reading selectively.

Because of the overlap, students also reported various note-taking strategies in lectures, including bringing texts to class and highlighting information in their books as the professor lectured. Other students took copious lecture notes and then read their texts selectively on the topics that were focused on in class. Thus, both reading and taking lecture notes appear to be strategies that students used variably and idiosyncratically.

Preparation for in-class quizzes and exams tended to require similar types of cognitive processes, primarily memorizing, analyzing, and synthesizing information from texts (oral and written). Undergraduate students in biology and psychology also needed to be able to apply the information they had learned to real-life situations. Students at both levels noted that memorizing was insufficient and that understanding relationships among concepts was equally important in their preparation.

Language demands were also similar across academic levels in terms of reading (lecture notes, text or reading notes, study notes, and the study guide) and writing (lecture, reading, and study notes, as well as answers to study guide questions).

In test taking, undergraduates and graduates had to deal with somewhat different tasks, with the undergraduate students seeing reading as the primary task; the graduate students, writing. (This difference, of course, had to do with the exam format.) Undergraduates specifically mentioned the need to understand questions and answers that were often paraphrases of information that they had learned. While understanding questions was important for graduate students as well, the paraphrasing and subtle semantic distinctions in vocabulary were not a factor. Nevertheless, the complex sentence structures used in the multiple-choice section of the graduate psychology exams constituted a reading demand for students in this course.

Except for the take-home exam in history, no writing was required for undergraduate exams in the three courses, but writing demands were paramount for graduate students. These students needed to be able to organize information logically, include appropriate support, and use appropriate disciplinary vocabulary. Grammar and mechanics were not a factor in the exam as long as the meaning was clear. Graphic information (diagrams and illustrations) was appropriate in the graduate biology exam and could be used in addition to and in lieu of prose. Paraphrasing was not a significant demand, as the text's or professor's words were equally acceptable.

No common out-of-class assignments were found across the disciplines or academic levels, but task preparation and production can be compared since all the assignments required writing from reading. The undergraduate task (take-home essay) and the reading report and final take-home exam in graduate history were based exclusively on information and reading from the course texts. Two graduate assignments (the critical review in biology and the research report in history) were based primarily on noncourse texts. Nevertheless, these graduate out-of-class assignments were all situated in the context of course content, so the course readings were still required as background information.

As noted earlier, preparation and production are often conflated in out-of-class tasks, so the discussion here does not draw any real distinction in these two phases. The significant cognitive demands of out-of-class assignments included identifying, analyzing, synthesizing, organizing, and interpreting relevant information, as well as recognizing and understanding relationships. Graduate students had to additionally evaluate information critically.

The language demands, as noted earlier, were primarily reading and writing, and the source texts varied with assignments, although the graduate tasks required considerably more reading than did the undergraduate. The writing demands were considerable for all assignments. Summarizing was a critical skill at all stages of the process. Students needed to take reading notes and lecture notes (where appropriate), then organize the information logically, focus on important ideas, and provide appropriate support. In all tasks, paraphrasing—using students' own words—was crucial. Graduate students needed to be able to use quotations and citation/documentation appropriately as well (no quotes were allowed in the undergraduate assignments). The graduate history professor required correct grammar and mechanics in all written assignments, but both the undergraduate history professor and the graduate biology professor allowed nonstandard grammar as long as the meaning was clear.

Summary of Results

Because of the restricted nature of the sample (six courses in one university), the findings here are, of course, not generalizable. Nevertheless, based on these data, the following are responses to the research questions and major categories that the study was designed to explore.

Research Question A

What are the similarities and differences among tasks across levels and disciplines?

The principal similarities and differences in tasks for these three disciplines at the undergraduate and graduate level seem clear. Similarities include the following:

- In-class tasks constitute the majority of evaluated products in all undergraduate courses represented in this database and in two of the three graduate courses represented.
- The principal sources of information for tasks in all courses examined are the primary written text(s) and lectures.
- Reading and listening are the language skills needed across all disciplines and across academic levels.
- The information in written texts and in lectures primarily overlaps in all the courses, and this overlap tends to function to provide a focus on important information.
- The need for note taking (reading and/or lecture) varies with the students' perceived strengths in language processing. Types of note taking vary by individual.
- The recognize/retrieve/identify question type is the most common for all in-class exams.
- All in-class exams across academic levels and in disciplines where they were given require, at least, that students synthesize information from texts.
- Reading and understanding the question (and possible answers where indicated) is an important aspect of successful production for all tasks.
- The cognitive demands of task preparation and production for in-class and out-of-class tasks across disciplines and across academic levels required distinguishing trivial from important information; analyzing, synthesizing, and organizing information; and understanding relationships between and among concepts.
- The language demands of task preparation for in-class and out-of-class tasks across disciplines and academic levels include reading (information sources) and writing (reading and/or lecture and/or study notes).

- All tasks require both general academic and discipline-specific vocabulary comprehension and/or use.
- Recognizing paraphrases is an important skill for all in-class exams.
- Producing paraphrases is an important skill for all out-of-class tasks.
- In-class tasks are not held to a standard of grammatical and mechanical correctness except for comprehensibility.
- Speaking is the least important skill across disciplines and academic levels.

Differences include the following:

- Task differences are more apparent across disciplines at the graduate level than at the undergraduate.
- Writing tasks (papers and exams) are more important at the graduate level than at the undergraduate.
- Graphic information serves different purposes at different academic levels, with graphics in undergraduate texts illustrating and exemplifying prose, while graphics in graduate texts additionally provide supplemental information to prose text.
- Cognitive demands vary by academic level, with retrieval and application of information more important at the undergraduate level, while interpretation and evaluation of information are more important at the graduate level.
- The acceptability of nonstandard language for out-of-class tasks varies with professor and not with discipline or academic level.

Research Question B

What appropriate order of magnitude of a task is most useful for analysis?

While the evaluated product is the organizing category, the level of task preparation seems to be the appropriate level to explore for teaching purposes, since task preparation includes all the cognitive academic language skills that students must be able to perform from the beginning of their academic studies. Successful task preparation leads to the possibility of successful task production and is therefore likely to be indicative of a student's potential to deal with academic language tasks.

Research Question C

What is the relative importance of reading, of writing, of listening, and of speaking in the performance of academic tasks?

Reading and listening, as much of the research has already shown, are clearly the two most important language skills for successful performance of academic tasks—both preparation and production. However, listening and reading interact, given the overlapping nature of information presented in these formats, so it is not necessarily the case that students would perform as successfully in one format or the other as they would when the two are combined. Reading is also an extremely important component of task production to the extent that students need to read exam questions and task directions.

Writing is clearly an important skill, even though it is less represented in the tasks described in these data at the undergraduate level. Nevertheless, the ability to use writing for task preparation (note taking, especially) is evident across disciplines and across academic levels. In addition, writing constitutes a significant portion of graduate task production and is likely to be apparent at the undergraduate level with a broader representation of general education courses and of postsecondary institutions.

In these data, speaking is the least important language skill. Except for the two oral presentations in the graduate history course, there was little speaking evident across disciplines and academic levels. Although asking questions in class was frequently mentioned, it appears that this questioning ability is not crucial to academic success, in the way that the other three language skills are.

Research Question D

To what extent does the performance of academic tasks require integration across skills and levels?

Integration across skills is extremely important: students need to be able to write lecture, reading, and study notes, to write exams and papers based on reading, and to listen for reading focus (or read for subsequent listening comprehension). In this study, there was no evidence of isolated language skills in any of the course tasks that were investigated. As for undergraduate and graduate language demands, as the analysis shows, the demands are remarkably similar across academic levels. What appears to account for differences that do occur is not language demands but cognitive demands.

Conclusions

Clearly, this study was limited in its focus on one large, urban, public university and in its selection of three disciplines. Nevertheless, it offers some valuable pedagogical perspectives for ESL/EFL teachers in general and reading/writing instructors in particular. For example, it suggests that the popular notion that "good readers will be good writers" is of even greater value when applied in a local sense—that is, relative to specific tasks and academic disciplines—than when applied on a global level. The more we understand the specific reading and writing needs and skills accompanying commonly assigned academic tasks, the better we can prepare students to read and write well within those contexts. Furthermore, there is reason to approach with caution the standard pedagogical emphasis on preparing students primarily for task production. The results of this study suggest that an increased emphasis on reading and writing related to task preparation, not just production, is in order. Also, the results lend support to the belief in designing integrated skills courses—in reading and writing especially, but other combinations as well.

Future research needs to consider other types of institutions (dimensions could include private institutions, smaller institutions, and community colleges) and to include other disciplines (general education courses at the undergraduate level, such as English or economics, and NNSs' preferred graduate majors, such as business or computer science). Students and ESL instructors of bridge courses and adjunct courses are likely to be another important source of information. In addition, the NNSs who participated in this study were fairly proficient in English, and students of differing levels of language proficiency need to be included. In the meantime, the results of this study demonstrate the value of conducting task-based reading-writing research drawing on multiple sources of data and investigating task representation and preparation as well as text production in academic settings.

References

Behrens, L. 1978. Writing, reading, and the rest of the faculty: A survey. *English Journal*, September, 54–60.

Braine, G. 1989. Writing in science and technology: An analysis of assignments from ten undergraduate courses. *English for Specific Purposes Journal* 8, no. 1:3–15.

Bridgeman, B., and S. B. Carlson. 1983. Survey of academic writing tasks required of graduate and undergraduate foreign students. TOEFL Research Report 15. Princeton, NJ: Educational Testing Service.

Canseco, G., and P. Byrd. 1989. Writing required in graduate courses in business administration. *TESOL Quarterly* 23, no. 2:305–16.

Casanave, C. P., and P. Hubbard. 1992. The writing assignments and writing problems of doctoral students: Faculty perceptions, pedagogical issues, and needed research. *English for Specific Purposes Journal* 11, no. 1:33–49.

Christison, M. A., and K. J. Krahnke. 1986. Student perceptions of academic language study. *TESOL Quarterly* 20, no. 1:61–81.

Crookes, G. 1986. *Task classification: A cross-disciplinary review.* Technical Report 4. Honolulu: Center for Second Language Classroom Research, Social Science Research Institute, University of Hawaii at Manoa.

Daniels, H. A. 1983. *Famous last words: The American language crisis reconsidered.* Carbondale: Southern Illinois University Press.

Eblen, C. 1983. Writing across the curriculum: A survey of a university faculty's views and classroom practices. *Research in the Teaching of English* 17:343–49.

Hale, G., C. Taylor, J. Bridgeman, J. Carson, B. Kroll, and R. Kantor. 1996. *A study of writing tasks assigned in academic degree programs.* TOEFL Research Report 54. Princeton, NJ: Educational Testing Service.

Hoey, M. 1986. Overlapping patterns of discourse organization and their implications for clause relational analysis in problem-solution texts. In *Studying writing: Linguistic approaches,* ed. C. R. Cooper and S. Greenbaum, 187–214. Beverly Hills: Sage.

Horowitz, D. M. 1986. What professors actually require: Academic tasks for the ESL classroom. *TESOL Quarterly* 20, no. 3:445–62.

Jenkins, S., M. K. Jordan, and P. O. Weiland. 1993. The role of writing in graduate engineering education: A survey of faculty beliefs and practices. *ESP Journal* 12, no. 1:51–67.

Johns, A. M. 1981. Necessary English: A faculty survey. *TESOL Quarterly* 15, no. 1:51–57.

Johns, A. M., and P. Mayes. 1990. An analysis of summary protocols of university ESL students. *Applied Linguistics* 11, no. 3:251–71.

Ostler, S. E. 1980. A survey of academic needs for advanced ESL. *TESOL Quarterly* 14, no. 4:489–502.

Sternglass, M. 1986. The relationship of task demands to cognitive level. *Educational Review* 38:161–68.

Sherwood, R. 1977. A survey of undergraduate reading and writing needs. *College Composition and Communication* 28:145–49.

Vande Kopple, W. J. 1986. Given and new information and some aspects of the structures, semantics, and pragmatics of written texts. In *Studying writing: Linguistic approaches,* ed. C. R. Cooper and S. Greenbaum, 72–111. Beverly Hills: Sage.

———. 1991. Themes, thematic progressions, and some implications for understanding discourse. *Written Communication* 8:311–47.

———. 1992. Noun phrases and the style of scientific discourse. In *A rhetoric of doing: Essays on written discourse in honor of James L. Kinneavy,* ed. S. P. Witte, N. Nakadate, and R. D. Cherry, 328–48. Carbondale: Southern Illinois University Press.

Chapter 3

Reexamining Audiolingualism: On the Genesis of Reading and Writing in L2 Studies

Paul Kei Matsuda, Miami University (Ohio)

Most of the existing historical accounts of second language reading and writing begin with the 1960s because, as many researchers have pointed out, written language was largely neglected in the early years of second language (L2) studies.[1] The neglect of written language in the early years is usually attributed to the dominance of the audiolingual approach, an approach to language teaching that privileges spoken language over written language (Buckingham 1979; Paulston 1972; Raimes 1983, 1991; Saville-Troike 1973).[2] In fact, proponents of the audiolingual approach in the 1960s articulated a number of assumptions that certainly underprivileged written language, including the following:

- Language is speech (Brooks 1960; Finocchiaro 1964; Rivers 1968).
- Writing is a secondary representation of speech (Brooks 1960; Finocchiaro 1964; Lado 1964).

I would like to thank John Swales for allowing me access to the Michigan ELI Library, Joan Morley for her helpful insights, and Patsy Aldridge, former ELI librarian, for her assistance. I also thank Peter H. Fries, Diane Belcher, and Alan Hirvela for their insightful comments.

1. See, e.g., Grabe 1991, Leki 1992, Raimes 1991, Reid 1993, and Silberstein 1987. Cf., however, Silva 1990; Silva starts his history from about 1945.
2. Following the common usage during the 1960s, I refer to this pedagogical approach as the audiolingual "approach," although reference to it as a "method" is more widely accepted today. The terms *approach* and *method* were used almost interchangeably until Anthony (1965) clarified the relationships among approach, method, and technique. This does not mean, however, that Harold E. Palmer's (1921) oral method and Charles C. Fries's (1945) oral approach can be treated as if they were identical, although they are strikingly similar in many ways because of the strong influence of Henry Sweet.

- Speech should be taught before writing (Brooks 1960; Finocchiaro 1964; Lado 1964; Rivers 1964).[3]

Given these assumptions, it would be easy to conclude, as has often been done, that the audiolingual approach was the reason for the neglect of written language and that reading and writing somehow became part of L2 studies because of its demise.

Although this existing explanation regarding the genesis of reading and writing in L2 studies provides a convenient descriptor for our understanding of the history of L2 studies, it seems to oversimplify the complex historical relations that have shaped this particular approach to language teaching as well as the status of written language in contemporary L2 studies. There are at least three reasons to believe that the dominance of the audiolingual approach was not the direct cause of the neglect. First, the rise of the aforementioned assumptions about written language predates the emergence of the audiolingual approach in the mid–20th century. Second, as H. H. Stern (1983) points out, the audiolingual approach in its distinct form became popular only in the late 1950s and the early 1960s—just when the teaching of writing became an important concern in L2 studies. Third, even after the decline of the audiolingual approach, reading and writing, while they have become quite visible in journals and at conferences, have not been fully integrated into professional preparation programs or important subfields of second language studies, such as second language acquisition.

In fact, it was not the audiolingual approach that caused the neglect of written language in the early years; rather, both the neglect of written language and the rise of the audiolingual approach resulted from the dominance of audiolingualism, the ideology in language teaching that began with the rise of scientific linguistics in the 19th century and continued to be influential at least until the fall of the audiolingual approach—the last major pedagogical manifestation of this ideology. Although the terms *audiolingualism* and *audiolingual approach* have often been used interchangeably (e.g., Grabe 1991; Leki 1992; Susser 1994), they need to be distinguished because the failure to do so has led teachers and researchers to disdain this particular pedagogical approach (i.e., the audiolingual approach) without also problematizing its underlying assumptions (i.e., audiolingualism) and the historical conditions that created those assump-

---

3. Note that the term *writing* in these statements does not refer to written discourse in the contemporary sense or even to the act or process of writing, because, prior to the 1960s, linguists usually equated writing with orthography.

tions. To contribute a better understanding of audiolingualism and the audiolingual approach as well as of their impact on the status of reading and writing in L2 studies, I here trace the development of audiolingualism in its historical context and, in the process, consider the place of written language in its various pedagogical manifestations. I then explain how reading and writing became part of L2 studies in the early 1960s despite the popularity of the audiolingual approach.

Such a historical understanding of the genesis of reading and writing issues in L2 studies is important because our theories and practices are, whether we like it or not, always historically situated; that is, what we consider to be important in terms of research and teaching problems is constructed largely by our perceptions of what preceded those problems. Since contemporary L2 reading and writing research and instruction have developed, at least initially, in response to the perceived dominance of audiolingualism, evaluating the significance and limitations of current theories and practices is not possible without a clear understanding of this historical condition.[4] This historical study tries to provide the context in which we can understand and critique current theories and practices of reading and writing in L2 studies.

Henry Sweet and the Origin of Audiolingualism

The origin of audiolingualism can be traced back to the reform movement of the late 19th century, which arose in reaction to the perceived dominance of the traditional, text-based approach to language teaching that was derived from the teaching of Latin.[5] According to Howatt (1984), the three basic principles of the reform movement were "the primacy of speech, the centrality of the connected text as the kernel of the teaching-learning process, and the absolute priority of an oral methodology in the classroom" (171). One of the most influential leaders of this movement was British phonetician Henry Sweet (1845–1912). In his monograph *The Practical Study of Languages* ([1899] 1964), he pointed out that "there are . . . many signs of dissatisfaction" with the "great conservatism in scholastic circles—as shown in the retention of antiquated text-books, in the prejudice against phonetics, and so on" (2). To alleviate this perceived prob-

---

4. The perceived dominance of the audiolingual approach was often mentioned in article introductions as a point of departure (e.g., Buckingham 1979; Paulston 1972; Saville-Troike 1973), which suggests that it was one of the major exigencies for L2 reading and writing specialists.
5. For a discussion of the reform movement, see Howatt 1984.

lem, Sweet articulated a number of key assumptions that established the relationship between linguistics and language teaching and that, consequently, contributed to the rise of audiolingualism.

First, Sweet made the distinction between what he called "'antiquarian' philology" and "living philology" (1). "Antiquarian" philology, as defined by Sweet, is concerned with the study of classic—or "dead" (vi)—languages, such as Greek and Latin, and with written symbols. Living philology, in contrast, dealt with modern languages in their spoken form. Influenced by the view of the study of language as a branch of natural science—a view that was developed by scientific philologists in Germany and popularized in England through the work of Max Müller ([1864] 1873)—Sweet insisted that living philology was a scientific discipline, as opposed to "antiquarian" philology, which was considered more humanistic.[6] Bloomfield (1914, 1925) later referred to this distinction by using the terms *philology* and *linguistics*. According to Bloomfield's definition (1914, 308), philology is the "study of national cultural values, especially as preserved in the writings of a people," while linguistics is defined as "the study of man's function of language [i.e., speech]." He also notes (1925, 4) that "the British use of 'philology' for linguistics leaves no name for the former subject and ought not be imitated" in the United States. The conflation of philology/linguistics and writing/speech binaries—motivated by scientific linguists' desire to establish their own disciplinary domain—is partially responsible for the exclusion of written language from linguistics and applied linguistics in the early years.

Another important assumption Sweet made was about the distinction between theoretical and practical studies of language, which later became the distinction between linguistics and applied linguistics. Sweet ([1899]1964) defined theoretical study of language as the study of "history and etymology" of language, while practical study of language was concerned with "learning to understand, read, speak, [and] write a language" (1). Although the goals for the two studies of language were different, they were, in his view, closely tied to each other by their common foundation: phonetics, or "the science of speech-sounds." Sweet explained that "phonetics is to the science of language generally what mathematics is to astronomy and the physical sciences" (4). Although he defined it "from a practical point of view" as "the art of pronunciation" (4), he also stressed that "the practical study of language is not in any way less scientific than the theoretical" study (1).

---

6. Both Sweet (1877, vii) and Saussure ([1916] 1959, 3) credit Max Müller for popularizing in England the view of linguistics as a natural science.

Although Sweet's definition of the practical studies of language included all four skills, he emphasized the primacy of spoken language in his work. He argued that speech should be taught before writing, because he considered speech to be "the source of the written language" and therefore the basis of "all study of language" (49). He maintained, "by starting from the spoken language we have less to learn, and we learn it accurately" (51). A similar view can be found in Ferdinand de Saussure's posthumous publication, *Course in General Linguistics* ([1916] 1959), which was later praised by Bloomfield ([1923] 1970) for "its clear and rigorous demonstration of fundamental principles" of scientific linguistics (106). In *Course*, written language is defined merely as "a tangible form of [sound] images" (15) that "exists for the sole purpose of representing [speech]" (23). It is there further stated that "the linguistic object is not both the written and the spoken forms of words; the spoken forms alone constitute the object" (24). In other words, writing was there seen not as a "guise for language" but as a "disguise" (30).

Furthermore, Sweet did not recognize what Silva (1993) calls the "distinct nature of L2 writing" (658). Sweet ([1899] 1964) contended that "if . . . we first get a thorough knowledge of the spoken form of the foreign language, and then proceed to learn its literary form, we shall be in exactly the same position as regards relative strength of associations as the natives themselves" (52). Although Sweet clearly recognized that there were spoken and written forms of language, he maintained that it was the spoken language that mattered in second language teaching; to him, there was no significant difference between first and second languages in terms of reading and writing.

Despite those assumptions, Sweet did not dismiss written language entirely. On the contrary, his definition of the practical study of language included all four skills, and the goal of language learning in his approach shifted from spoken language to written language once the student had attained the mastery of spoken language. He wrote: "When the sounds of a language have once been mastered, the main foundation of its study will be connected texts: the reader will henceforth be the centre of study, to which the grammar, dictionary, and other helps must be strictly subordinated" (163). It should also be noted that, in some ways, Sweet's view of written discourse was far more sophisticated than the views of his American followers. For instance, in the chapter "Texts; the Reading-Book," he elaborated on a number of concepts that became salient in the 1970s and 1980s, including cohesion, context, and the classification of texts. He also articulated the importance of the use of limited vocabulary, which was later emulated by Fries.

Sweet also encouraged, for advanced learners, the use of *free composition,* or the production of extended written discourse, as an alternative to exercises and translation. However, he wrote that free composition was to be done only "on subjects taken from the texts already studied, so that the compositions are reproductions of what is already known" (205), because it was based on the principles of the direct method, which emphasized the importance of establishing the association between the learner's second language and external reality without relying on the first language. E. Creagh Kittson (1918) explained in the context of French and German instruction, "If we set [the learner] to write on a subject about which he has never read or spoken in the foreign language, he will obviously be driven to thinking in English" (133–34). In this model of the reading-writing relationship, reading also took the place of invention, providing the content of writing. Although this approach may seem somewhat restrictive, it may have been sensible, especially for students who had little background in writing, because it would allow them to focus on the production of language, which was cognitively demanding in itself.

The Spread of Audiolingualism

In the first half of the 20th century, Sweet's theory of language teaching became influential in many parts of the world (Allen 1973). In Europe, the International Phonetic Association developed a statement about language teaching (Passy 1929) that reflected Sweet's pedagogical work.[7] Danish philologist Otto Jespersen's view of pedagogy was also influenced by Sweet (Jespersen 1904). In Japan, Sweet's follower Harold E. Palmer promulgated what he termed "the oral method" (Palmer 1921), which emphasized the primacy of speech and the importance of oral habit formation. Later, in the United States, these assumptions were transformed into the basis of the audiolingual approach through the work of Charles C. Fries (1887–1967) and Leonard Bloomfield (1887–1949).

If Sweet was one of the world's first influential applied linguists, Bloomfield and Fries were the first U.S. applied linguists, although Robert B. Kaplan (1993) claims the title of the first professor of applied linguistics in the United States. Like Sweet, both Bloomfield and Fries strongly

---

7. For an English translation of the IPA articles, see Stern 1983, 89.

believed that linguistics was a science with practical applications, especially in the realm of language teaching. Bloomfield (1933) claimed, for instance, that "the methods and results of linguistics, in spite of their modest scope, resemble those of natural science, the domain in which science has been most successful." He also wrote that "the study of language may help us toward the understanding and control of human events" (509). Similarly, Fries (1945) argued that "those who deal with language in a practical way, especially those who teach it, must look to the results of linguistic science for the knowledge upon which to base their procedure" (105). In other words, these linguists literally sought to "apply" linguistics to language teaching, whence came the term *applied linguistics*.[8]

That these two individuals developed similar views of language teaching at about the same time is not a mere coincidence. In addition to Sweet's influence, they were mutually influenced by one another's work, particularly in the area of pedagogy. Fries cites *An Introduction to the Study of Language* (Bloomfield 1914) in his early work *The Teaching of the English Language* (1927), which in turn appears in Bloomfield's extensive bibliography in *Language* (1933). Bloomfield's view of linguistics and language teaching was also incorporated into Fries's most influential pedagogical work, *Teaching and Learning English as a Foreign Language* (1945). Their lives also intersected at several crucial points. Both Bloomfield and Fries were founding members of the Linguistic Society of America in 1924. At the invitation of Fries, Bloomfield gave lectures at the LSA Linguistic Institute at the University of Michigan between 1938 and 1940 (Hockett 1970, 541), just when Fries was developing his oral approach.

These two individuals' views of language teaching became influential throughout the United States—Fries's in English and Bloomfield's in foreign languages—because of two related but different developments prompted by U.S. foreign policy. To show how audiolingualism was institutionalized in the United States, I now want to examine each of these developments in some detail.

Fries and the English Language Institute

A student of Fred Newton Scott, who was a renowned rhetorician and linguist at the University of Michigan, Fries had been involved in the teaching of English and rhetoric from the beginning of his career; in 1928, he became the president of the National Council of Teachers of English,

8. As Kaplan (1993) points out, the term *applied linguistics* was "initially nearly inextricably tied to language teaching" (374).

which Scott had helped to found.[9] Although Fries had always been interested in applying the insights from linguistic sciences to the teaching of
English, he did not become involved in the teaching of ESL until the late
1930s. What prompted his involvement in ESL, as well as the creation of
the first intensive English program at the University of Michigan, was a
development in U.S. foreign policy during the 1930s. At the Pan-American
Conference in 1933, President Franklin D. Roosevelt announced what
came to be known as the Good Neighbor Policy, the principle of international cooperation "aimed at countering threats of European totalitarian
influences which were moving into Latin America" (Morley et al. 1984,
177). As a result of this development, the U.S. Department of State became
interested in providing scientific and technological support for Latin
American countries, and the teaching of the English language in Latin
American countries became an important agenda for the federal government. Anticipating the need to develop pedagogical materials for Latin
American students, R. H. Fife of the American Council on Education
invited Fries to join the council's Committee on Modern Languages in
1935. Three years later, the council commissioned Fries to compile a study
of existing vocabulary lists for teaching. The result was Fries's 1940 publication (with Traver) of *English Word Lists,* in which he concluded, "For the
teaching of English as a foreign language . . . we need first a restricted list
of words in a limited range of 'meanings'" (89). Perhaps because of this
experience, along with the influence of Henry Sweet, the use of limited
vocabulary became one of the central features of Fries's intensive English
curriculum.[10]

In 1939, the U.S. Department of State and the Rockefeller Foundation
jointly sponsored an invitational conference to decide on the theoretical
basis for second language pedagogy. The University of Michigan was chosen as the site of this conference because of its reputation in the area of linguistic sciences. At this conference, Fries first proposed his approach to
second language teaching, which he later called the "oral approach" (Fries
1945). His pedagogical approach, in the words of Harold B. Allen (1973),
who was Fries's student at the time, "not only relied heavily upon the
principles of Henry Sweet but also added a significant dimension taken
from current linguistic theory" (299). As a result of this presentation, Fries

---

9. Donald C. Stewart (1979, 1985) has written extensively on the life and work of Fred
Newton Scott. See also Berlin 1984 and Kitzhaber 1990.
10. Allen (1973) notes, however, that the attention to the lexical problems in the ELI
was "inadequate . . . even though Fries, along with his assistant Aileen Traver, had
investigated the history of vocabulary studies" (303).

received a grant from the Rockefeller Foundation, and the English Language Institute (ELI), the first intensive program of its kind, was established at the University of Michigan in 1941.[11]

The goal of the ELI was to develop the mastery of the sound and the structure of spoken language within a limited vocabulary in a short period of time—that is, less than three months (Fries 1945). Written language was not one of the instructional goals, as Fries wrote.

> No matter if the final result desired is only to *read* the foreign language[,] the mastery of the fundamentals of the language—the structure and the sound system with a limited vocabulary—must be through speech. The speech *is* the language. The written record is but a secondary representation of the language. To "master" a language, it is not necessary to read it, but it is extremely doubtful whether one can really read the language without first mastering it orally. (6)

This does not mean that written language was completely excluded from the ELI curriculum. In fact, the first two editions of *An Intensive Course in English for Latin American Students* (English Language Institute 1942, 1943) included a selection of graded reading materials prepared by Virginia French, who was a staff member at the ELI between 1942 and 1944. Soon after French left the ELI to study at Columbia University, however, this feature disappeared from the curriculum almost entirely. When the outline of the materials from the 1943 edition was appended to Fries's *Teaching and Learning English as a Foreign Language* (1945), the section on reading was not included. Furthermore, the reading component was discontinued in later versions of *An Intensive Course in English* (i.e., English Language Institute 1958; Fries and Shen 1946).

The intensive nature of the program was probably one of the reasons for the exclusion of written language as an instructional goal, because few students achieved the "mastery" of language within a few months of instruction for which the ELI was designed. Reading and writing were removed from the ELI curriculum because Fries was increasingly convinced that instruction in reading could be effective "only when one has ... [such] a thorough control of the fundamentals of a language that he can almost automatically produce utterances in accord with the usual patterns of that language" (Fries 1945, 7). Like Sweet, Fries was frustrated by students' tendency to rely on translation when they were given written text to work with. Fries wrote, "Unless one has mastered the fundamentals of

---

11. See Allen 1973 and Morley et al. 1984 for descriptions of the historical origin of the ELI.

the new language *as a language*—that is, as a set of habits for oral production and reception—the process of reading is a process of seeking word equivalents in his own native language" (6).

Although Fries (1945) ruled out reading and writing from the ELI curriculum, he was not arguing for "the arbitrary exclusion of all graphic symbols in connection with the language learning"; he believed "every means" available, including written symbols, should be deployed to achieve the mastery of spoken language. In fact, written symbols were used so that students would be able to use the print materials developed at the ELI, and essay exams were used as a way of testing students' mastery of sentence structures. Fries explained, "Teachers will often use written symbols in the classroom; printed manuals or textbooks will be used by the students; written notes will be taken by the students; and even written exercises may be part of the work" (8). However, Fries saw reading and writing, especially for beginning learners, primarily as the ability to translate spoken sentence patterns into written symbols and vice versa. When writing was used at the ELI, it was employed as a way of practicing and demonstrating previously learned sentence patterns. Once students "mastered" the fundamentals of spoken language at the ELI, they went on to the University of Michigan's freshman composition program, where they were expected to learn reading and writing with their native English-speaking peers without further ESL support.

The ability to speak English did not, however, guarantee that students were ready for freshman composition courses designed primarily for native speakers of English. The Department of English Language and Literature at Michigan came to recognize this problem in the mid-1950s, partly because of the rapid increase of international students after World War II. As a result, the department created in 1954 an ESL section of freshman English (Klinger 1958), which became one of the first of the credit-bearing ESL writing courses that began to appear in the 1950s.[12] However, this development did not necessarily happen at other institutions that adopted the Michigan ELI model, and as a result students at those institutions were likely left on their own in learning to read and write in composition classrooms.

The pedagogy developed at the Michigan ELI became influential throughout the United States for two reasons. First, the ELI provided pro-

---

12. In 1955, the Department of English Language and Literature hired, on a part-time basis, Sarah E. Grollman, a former graduate student of Fries and John H. Muyskens in the Department of Speech, to teach ESL sections of freshman English (Klinger 1958).

fessional preparation for teachers of ESL, who developed intensive language programs as well as teacher preparation programs at other institutions (Allen 1973). Although Darian (1972) notes that special courses in language teaching methods had existed as early as 1910–20, usually in connection with Americanization programs, the teacher preparation program at Michigan was probably the most influential in the professionalization of TESL. Another reason was the ELI's success in producing a series of publications, including professional books (e.g., Fries 1945; Lado 1957); a popular textbook series, which came to be known as the "rainbow series" (Morley et al. 1984, 189); and *Language Learning: A Quarterly Journal of Applied Linguistics*, which was established in 1948 by the Research Club in Language Learning at the University of Michigan. All of these publications were widely circulated both within and outside the United States. Although a few innovative programs were not associated with Michigan (Moulton 1961), most of the intensive programs, as well as some ESL writing courses developed in English departments, continued to use materials and methods developed at the Michigan ELI well into the 1960s and the 1970s. However, as Morley et al. (1984) suggest, "the 'real' Fries program never left the University of Michigan campus, as neither the aura of the charismic personality of Fries himself nor the milieu of the Ann Arbor environment was 'exportable'" (176).[13]

Bloomfield and the Army Specialized Training Program

In the context of foreign language teaching, Fries's oral approach in English language teaching was paralleled by Bloomfield's work. Bloomfield, who began his career as a teacher of German, was also interested from early on in developing an approach to language teaching based on the principles of linguistic science. His 1914 book, *An Introduction to the Study of Language,* already included a chapter, on the teaching of languages, that showed conspicuous influence from the reform movement of the late 19th century, especially through Jespersen's *How to Teach a Foreign Language* (1904). John P. Hughes (1968) also notes that Bloomfield drafted a booklet for the teaching of foreign language in the 1930s, drawing heavily on the work of such reformists as Sweet and Palmer. However, Bloomfield was not able to find a publisher for it, perhaps because the notion of language

---

13. For a detailed account of how the Michigan ELI became influential throughout the United States, see Matsuda 1999.

teaching as an application of linguistic sciences had not become widely accepted in the United States (Hughes 1968). In 1941, his booklet was finally adopted by the Intensive Language Program of the American Council of Learned Societies, which was one of the cosponsors of the Summer Institute on Linguistics at Michigan. The goal of the council's program was to prepare anthropologists for fieldwork by providing instruction in little-known and undescribed languages, such as Native American dialects. In the following year, Bloomfield's booklet was published by the Linguistic Society of America as *Outline Guide for the Practical Study of Foreign Languages* (1942).

Bloomfield's *Outline Guide*, which articulated the principle of mimicry and memorization—or "mim-mem" for short—focused entirely on spoken language, because of his belief that "writing is not language, but merely a way of recording language by means of visible marks" (Bloomfield 1933, 21). To Bloomfield, the notion of written language was an oxymoron, as he wrote in *Linguistic Aspects of Science* (1939).

> For all linguistic study it is of primary importance to know that writing is not the same thing as language. Failure to make this distinction was one of the chief factors that prevented a beginning of linguistic science in the seventeenth and eighteenth centuries. The popular-scholastic contrast of "spoken language" and "written language" is entirely misleading. (6)

Perhaps Bloomfield's exclusive focus on spoken language was appropriate for the purpose of this program, however, because few Native American languages had a written form.

The most significant impetus for the institutionalization of Bloomfield's pedagogical approach came at the beginning of World War II. The U.S. Armed Forces needed a way of developing spoken language proficiency in German, Italian, and Japanese, as well as in other non-Western languages, for which detailed descriptions of linguistic features were unavailable. For this reason, they developed the Army Specialized Training Program (ASTP), a language teaching program modeled after the American Council of Learned Society's Intensive Language Program. Bloomfield's *Outline Guide*—along with its accompanying volume, *Outline of Linguistic Analysis* (Bloch and Trager 1942)—was adopted as one of the textbooks for the program (Hughes 1968; Moulton 1961). The goal of the ASTP was to achieve fluency in spoken language within nine months, but because it also emphasized area studies, especially at the beginning, readings in history, geography, economics, and culture became part of the program. Writing was not an important part of the program, and when it was introduced at all, it was kept to a minimum (Matthew 1947).

Although the ASTP was "surprisingly short-lived" (Hughes 1968, 70), its impact was significant. When the war ended, many colleges and high schools developed language programs modeled after it (Hughes 1968; Matthew 1947), and teachers who taught in this program, as well as some of the students, began to teach in foreign language programs across the United States. Furthermore, the Sputnik crisis of 1957 prompted the U.S. government to pass the National Defense Education Act (NDEA) in 1958, which led to the creation of professional preparation programs in foreign languages, which further promulgated the linguistic approach to language teaching practiced in the ASTP. In 1964, the NDEA was modified to extend the professional preparation opportunities to ESL teachers. However, it became increasingly apparent that this method, which came to be known as the "army method," was not quite appropriate for other educational contexts. In high schools and colleges, foreign language classes tended to be much larger, thus making close supervision of drills difficult. In addition, students were not as disciplined as were military personnel.[14] The most important difference, however, was in the format of these programs. While the ASTP was intensive in nature, foreign language instruction in educational institutions usually took place over an extended period of time. For these reasons, the ASTP approach was gradually modified to suit the new context.

The Audiolingual Approach and the Rise of Written Language

In the 1960s, these two traditions of linguistic approaches to language teaching—the oral approach and the ASTP method—were consolidated and gradually transformed into a new approach. The term *oral approach* was also replaced by a semantically accurate alternative, *aural-oral approach.* Finally, Nelson Brooks, in his *Language and Language Learning* (1960), proposed the use of the term *audiolingual* as an alternative to the phonetically ambiguous term *aural-oral.*[15] Brooks's book became popular

---

14. See Hughes 1968 for a discussion of the ASTP and the Army Method.
15. Following the work of psycholinguists Charles E. Osgood and Thomas A. Sebeok (1954), Brooks (1960) divided language into "three broad bands," including "audio-lingual, gestural-visual, and graphic-material," or "in simpler terms, . . . talk, gesture, and writing" (16). Among the three, he argues, the "audio-lingual" is "central" and the only band that is "on its own"; to him, gestural-visual is "but a faint obbligato in the rendition of speech" (17), and graphic-material is "complete[ly] dependen[t] upon the central audio-lingual band" (18).

partially because, in the following year, a special "A-LM edition" (Brooks 1961), with an introduction by William Riley Parker of Indiana University, was published and distributed for free by Harcourt Brace as background reading for the A-LM Secondary School Audio-Lingual Materials series for teachers of French, German, Italian, Russian, and Spanish. In fact, it became so popular that the second edition (Brooks 1964) appeared only four years later.

Although the audiolingual approach is often referred to as the "audiolingual method," it was not a monolithic set of prescribed pedagogical techniques, as the term *method* seems to imply. Rather, the audiolingual approach consisted of a set of assumptions about language and learning that guided curricular and pedagogical decisions in various pedagogical contexts. In "Linguistics and Language Teaching in the United States, 1940–1960," William G. Moulton (1961) outlined what he considered to be the "slogans of the day" in language teaching: language is speech, not writing; a language is a set of habits; teach the language, not about the language; . . . a language is what its native speakers say, not what someone thinks they ought to say; and languages are different (86–89; see also Lado 1964). Rivers (1964) provided further support for the audiolingual approach by examining these linguistic assumptions in light of psychological theories of learning, making "suggestions and recommendations for the modification or improvement of audio-lingual techniques" (149).[16]

Written language became part of second language studies in the 1960s, just when the term *audiolingual* was gaining currency and books promoting this approach were beginning to appear. In the same year that Brooks's popular book on the audiolingual approach was first published, *Language Learning* printed an article on writing pedagogy by Edward Erazmus, who at the time was a staff member of the Michigan ELI and a contributor to one of Michigan's popular textbooks. In this article, Erazmus (1960) discussed some of the concepts that became popular in composition studies much later—including tagmemic invention (Young, Becker, and Pike 1970) and free writing (Elbow 1973, 1981).[17] Even Fries and Bloomfield—in Bloomfield's case posthumously—began to publish books on reading (Bloomfield and Barnhart 1961; Fries 1964), although

---

16. While it is true that Rivers (1964) scrutinized the linguistic assumptions of the audiolingual approach that also "purports to be soundly based on psychological theory" (7), her goal was not to reject the audiolingual approach but to apply the recent findings of psychological studies.

17. Incidentally, Pike was also a staff member of the Michigan ELI in the academic years 1942–43 and 1947–48. In the fall of 1976, he also served as the interim director of the ELI.

their view of written language as a mere representation of speech had not changed.

Why did proponents of the audiolingual approach, which was supposed to be the reason for the neglect of reading and writing, suddenly begin to consider the teaching of written language? First, the view of language teaching as an application of linguistics came under severe attack toward the end of the 1950s. One of the arguments raised against these linguistics-based approaches was their neglect of writing. In 1960, two articles condemning scientific linguists, particularly Fries, appeared in *College English* (Sherwood 1960; Tibbetts 1960), which prompted Albert H. Marckwardt, the third director of the ELI, to write a defensive response in *Language Learning* in the following year. To justify the role of linguistics in language teaching, Marckwardt (1961) called for more efforts, on the part of linguists, to demonstrate their commitment to written language: "It is by no means enough . . . for us to protest that we are not without interest in the structure of the written language. This must be demonstrated as well by studies which are calculated to show the structural differences between it and spoken English" (17). In Marckwardt's article, however, written language continued to be seen "in terms of its deviations from the spoken pattern" (16).

In the context of foreign language education, where reading had traditionally been the goal of instruction, the audiolingual approach was met by considerable resistance partly because of its emphasis on spoken language. For this reason, proponents of the audiolingual approach emphasized that "reading and writing are not neglected" (Rivers 1968, 45). Rivers (1968) wrote that "writing is a skill which must be taught" (258), although she made it clear that "it should . . . be considered the handmaid of other skills and not take precedence as the major skill to be developed" (241). Brooks, who did not discuss reading and writing in the first edition of his *Language and Language Learning* (1960), responded to the critics of the audiolingual approach by adding a chapter on reading and writing in the second edition (1964).

Another reason for the rise of written language, a reason that applies primarily to the context of ESL writing, is the creation of what I call the disciplinary division of labor between L1 and L2 writing (Matsuda 1998, 1999). As we have seen, written language was not a significant part of TESL before the 1960s; instead, second language writing issues were often addressed by composition specialists. The conclusion of World War II brought a large number of international students to U.S. higher education—by the early 1950s, there were almost 30,000 international students

(Davis 1997, 2). As a result, the ESL student population at some institutions reached critical mass, and the teaching of ESL became a concern at the annual meetings of the Conference on College Composition and Communication (CCCC), which is often described—inaccurately, I hasten to add—as an organization for L1 composition specialists. Since 1955, workshops and panels on ESL issues were presented almost every year, and those sessions were attended not only by ESL specialists but also by teachers and administrators of composition. A number of prominent ESL specialists—including Kenneth Croft and Robert Lado, both of whom were associated with the Michigan ELI—attended CCCC regularly. Harold B. Allen, a student of Fries's and the founding president of TESOL, was a key figure in the formative years of CCCC (Matsuda 1999; Philips, Greenberg, and Gibson 1993).

The situation began to change in the early 1960s, however. Because of the professionalization of ESL, which was prompted primarily by the success of the Michigan ELI, ESL specialists began to argue that ESL students should be taught only by trained specialists with a background in linguistics. As a result, composition teachers who did not see themselves as ESL specialists felt discouraged from participating in ESL sessions at CCCC. By the time Robert B. Kaplan began to attend CCCC at the urging of Allen, the attendance at ESL sessions had become quite small; in 1965, when Kaplan chaired the ESL workshop, no one attended the session. Discouraged by the small attendance, the ESL workshop in 1966, chaired again by Kaplan, decided not to meet again at CCCC. Incidentally, 1966 was the year TESOL became an organization that served the needs of ESL specialists. As a result, writing issues were divided into first language and second language components, and second language writing came to be associated almost exclusively with L2 studies.[18]

Conclusion

As I have described, reading and writing became part of L2 studies in the 1960s not so much because of the demise of the audiolingual approach but because of the effort to justify its place in the second language teaching profession that was emerging during this period. This effort, however, was largely unsuccessful; the audiolingual approach soon began to wane as its theoretical bases—descriptive linguistics and behavioral psychol-

---

18. See Matsuda 1999 for a detailed account of the development of second language writing issues between the 1940s and the 1960s and the creation of the disciplinary division of labor between L1 and L2 writing.

ogy—became discredited and were replaced by more cognitive and social orientations. However, the efforts to replace the audiolingual approach have failed to critique the historical conditions that led to the rise of audiolingualism and the subsequent creation of the audiolingual approach. As a result, the audiolingual approach became an icon that represented the old school of thought to be replaced by new methods or approaches, while the complexity of historical conditions that surrounded its rise and fall were obscured.

Today, few language teachers or theorists openly claim to be proponents of the audiolingual approach. Yet the neglect of written language continues to be apparent in many aspects of L2 studies. In the field of second language acquisition, the amount of attention given to the acquisition of reading and writing competence is rather negligible (e.g., Ellis 1985, 1994; Larsen-Freeman and Long 1991). In linguistics, despite developments in written discourse analysis, popular introductory linguistics textbooks continue to perpetuate the rather limited view of writing that informed various pedagogical approaches during the audiolingual era— that is, the view of writing as an inaccurate orthographic representation of speech (e.g., Fromkin and Rodman 1993; Yule 1985).[19]

Even in TESL, opportunities for professional preparation in teaching second language reading and writing have been severely limited (Kroll 1991, 1993; Reid 1993; Roy 1988). In 1993, Reid lamented that "only within the last five years have entire courses in teaching ESL writing been conceived, designed, and taught" (vii). Ian C. Palmer's 1995 survey of 159 TESL/TEFL master's programs in the United States suggests that only "about 40% of the programs offered combined courses in Reading and Writing or just Reading" (cited in Reid 1995–96, 3). Kroll (1993) also points out that, although prospective teachers may have been introduced to reading and writing issues "through general methodology texts," they "may not have spent much class time discussing or have read all that much about teaching writing and reading at the most advanced level, let alone exploring ways to connect them," because "methodology texts encompass approaches to teaching learners at all levels" (64).

To fully understand the status of reading and writing in L2 contexts,

---

19. Fromkin and Rodman (1993) define writing as "any of the many visual (nongestural) systems for representing language, including handwriting, printing, and electronic displays of these written forms" (364), while maintaining that "spoken language still has primacy" (377). Similarly, Yule (1985) contends that "the written forms provide . . . unreliable clues" to linguistic sounds (14). Although these textbooks provide chapters on writing, they are concerned only with writing systems (i.e., orthography).

then, the scope of our investigation cannot be limited to theoretical or pedagogical concerns but must also include examinations of larger social, political, and historical contexts. As Rivers (1964) aptly points out, "priority of objectives and expected outcomes in foreign-language learning" are "preferences established according to geographical, historical, or contemporary exigencies and not examinable in relation to psychological learning theory" (8). In the same vein, the critique of language pedagogy should not be limited to the examination of theories in linguistics, second language acquisition, or even reading and writing. I hope this historical study serves as a starting point for further investigation of the status of reading and writing in L2 studies, as well as for investigation of many other important historical issues in second language studies.

References

Allen, H. B. 1973. English as a second language. In *Current trends in linguistics: Linguistics in North America,* ed. T. A. Sebeok, 10:295–320. The Hague: Mouton.

Anthony, E. M. 1965. Approach, method, and technique. In *Teaching English as a second language: A book of readings,* ed. H. B. Allen, 93–97. New York: McGraw-Hill.

Berlin, J. 1984. *Writing instruction in nineteenth-century American colleges.* Carbondale: Southern Illinois University Press.

Bloch, B., and G. L. Trager. 1942. *Outline of Linguistic Analysis.* Baltimore: Linguistic Society of America.

Bloomfield, L. 1914. *An introduction to the study of language.* New York: Henry Holt and Company.

———. 1925. Why a linguistic society? *Language* 1:1–5.

———. 1933. *Language.* New York: Holt, Rinehart, and Winston.

———. 1939. *Linguistic aspects of science.* Chicago: University of Chicago Press.

———. 1942. *Outline guide for the practical study of foreign languages.* Baltimore: Linguistic Society of America.

———. [1923] 1970. Review of Saussure. In *A Leonard Bloomfield anthology,* ed. C. F. Hockett, 106–8. Bloomington: Indiana University Press.

Bloomfield, L., and C. L. Barnhart, eds. 1961. *Let's read: A linguistic approach.* Detroit: Wayne State University Press.

Brooks, N. 1960. *Language and language learning: Theory and practice.* New York: Harcourt, Brace, and Company.

———. 1961. *Language and language learning: Theory and practice.* A-LM ed. New York: Harcourt, Brace, and Company.

———. 1964. *Language and language learning: Theory and practice.* 2d ed. New York: Harcourt, Brace, and Company.

Buckingham, T. 1979. The goals of advanced composition instruction. *TESOL Quarterly* 13, no. 2:241–54.

Darian, S. G. 1972. *English as a foreign language: History, development, and methods of teaching.* Norman: University of Oklahoma Press.

Davis, T. M., ed. 1997. *Open doors, 1996/1997: Report on international educational exchange.* New York: Institute of International Education.

Elbow, P. 1973. *Writing without teachers.* New York: Oxford University Press.

———. 1981. *Writing with power: Techniques for mastering the writing process.* New York: Oxford University Press.

Ellis, R. 1985. *Understanding second language acquisition.* Oxford: Oxford University Press.

———. 1994. *The study of second language acquisition.* Oxford: Oxford University Press.

English Language Institute. 1942. *An intensive course in English for Latin American students.* Vols. 1–3. Ann Arbor: University of Michigan, English Language Institute.

———. 1943. *An intensive course in English for Latin American students.* Rev. ed. Vols. 1–4. Ann Arbor: University of Michigan, English Language Institute.

———. 1958. *An intensive course in English.* Rev. ed. Vols. 1–4. Ann Arbor: University of Michigan, English Language Institute.

Erazmus, E. T. 1960. Second language composition teaching at the intermediate level. *Language Learning* 10:25–31.

Finocchiaro, M. 1964. *English as a second language: From theory to practice.* New York: Regents.

Fries, C. C. 1927. *The teaching of the English language.* New York: Thomas Nelson.

———. 1945. *Teaching and learning English as a foreign language.* Ann Arbor: University of Michigan Press.

———. 1964. *Linguistics and reading.* New York: Holt, Rinehart, and Winston.

Fries, C. C., and Y. Shen. 1946. *An intensive course in English for Chinese students.* Vols. 1–4. Ann Arbor: University of Michigan, English Language Institute.

Fries, C. C., with A. A. Traver. 1940. *English word lists: A study of their adaptability for instruction.* Washington, DC: American Council on Education.

Fromkin, V., and R. Rodman. 1993. *An introduction to language.* 5th ed. Fort Worth: Harcourt Brace Jovanovich.

Grabe, W. 1991. Current developments in second language reading research. *TESOL Quarterly* 25, no. 3:375–406.

Hockett, C. F., ed. 1970. *A Leonard Bloomfield anthology.* Bloomington: Indiana University Press.

Howatt, A. P. R. 1984. *A history of English language teaching.* Oxford: Oxford University Press.

Hughes, J. P. 1968. *Linguistics and language teaching.* New York: Random House.

Jespersen, O. 1904. *How to teach a foreign language.* London: Allen and Unwin.

Kaplan, R. B. 1993. TESOL and applied linguistics in North America. In *State of* the art TESOL essays: Celebrating twenty-five years of the discipline, ed. S. Silberstein, 373–81. Alexandria, VA: Teachers of English to Speakers of Other Languages.

Kittson, E. C. 1918. *Theory and practice of language teaching, with special reference to French and German*. London: Oxford University Press.

Kitzhaber, A. R. 1990. *Rhetoric in American colleges, 1850–1900*. Dallas: Southern Methodist University Press.

Klinger, R. B. 1958. The International Center. In *The University of Michigan: An encyclopedic survey in four volumes*, ed. W. A. Donnelly, 4:1843–49. Ann Arbor: University of Michigan Press.

Kroll, B. 1991. Teaching writing in the ESL context. In *Teaching English as a second or foreign language*, ed. M. Celce-Murcia, 2d ed., 245–63. Boston: Heinle and Heinle.

———. 1993. Teaching writing IS teaching reading: Training the new teachers of ESL composition. In *Reading in the composition classroom: Second language perspectives*, ed. J. G. Carson and I. Leki, 61–81. Boston: Heinle and Heinle.

Lado, R. 1957. *Linguistics across cultures: Applied linguistics for language teachers*. Ann Arbor: University of Michigan Press.

———. 1964. *Language teaching: A scientific approach*. New York: McGraw-Hill.

Larsen-Freeman, D., and M. H. Long. 1991. *An introduction to second language acquisition research*. London: Longman.

Leki, I. 1992. *Understanding ESL writers: A guide for teachers*. Portsmouth, NH: Boynton/Cook.

Marckwardt, A. H. 1961. Linguistics and English composition. *Language Learning*, special issue 2:15–28.

Matsuda, P. K. 1998. Situating ESL writing in a cross-disciplinary context. *Written Communication* 15, no. 1:99–121.

———. 1999. Composition studies and ESL writing: A disciplinary division of labor. *College Composition and Communication* 50, no. 4:699–721.

Matthew, R. J. 1947. *Language and area studies in the Armed Services: Their future significance*. Washington, DC: American Council on Education.

Morley, J., B. W. Robinett, L. Selinker, and D. Woods. 1984. ESL theory and the Fries legacy. *JALT Journal* 6, no. 2:171–207.

Moulton, W. G. 1961. Linguistics and language teaching in the United States, 1940–1960. In *Trends in European and American linguistics, 1930–1960*, ed. C. Mohrmann, A. Sommerfelt, and J. Whatmough, 82–109. Utrecht: Spectrum.

Müller, M. [1864] 1873. *Lectures on the science of language*. 2d ser. New York: Scribner, Armstrong, and Company.

Osgood, C. E., and T. A. Sebeok. 1954. *Psycholinguistics: A survey of theory and research problems*. Baltimore: Waverly.

Palmer, H. E. 1921. *The oral method of teaching languages: A monograph on conversa-*

tional methods together with a full description and abundant examples of fifty appropriate forms of work. Cambridge, UK: Heffer.

Palmer, I. C. 1995. Required courses for master's degree in TESOL: A nationwide survey. Paper presented at the annual meeting of TESOL, Long Beach, CA, March. ERIC ED 389171.

Passy, P. 1929. *La phonétique et ses applications.* Cambridge, UK: International Phonetic Association.

Paulston, C. 1972. Teaching writing in the ESL classroom: Techniques of controlled composition. *TESOL Quarterly* 6, no. 1:33–59.

Phillips, D. B., R. Greenberg, and S. Gibson. 1993. *College Composition and Communication:* Chronicling a discipline's genesis. *College Composition and Communication* 44, no. 4:443–65.

Raimes, A. 1983. *Techniques in teaching writing.* New York: Oxford University Press.

———. 1991. Out of the woods: Emerging traditions in the teaching of writing. *TESOL Quarterly* 25, no. 3:407–30.

Reid, J. M. 1993. *Teaching ESL writing.* Englewood Cliffs, NJ: Regents/Prentice-Hall.

———. 1995–96. President's message: Let's put the "T" back in TESL/TEFL programs. *TESOL Matters* 5, no. 6:3.

Rivers, W. M. 1964. *The psychologist and the foreign language teacher.* Chicago: University of Chicago Press.

———. 1968. *Teaching foreign language skills.* Chicago: University of Chicago Press.

Roy, A. M. 1988. ESL concerns for writing program administrators: Problems and policies. *Writing Program Administration* 11:17–28.

Saussure, F. de. [1916] 1959. *Course in general linguistics.* Ed. C. Bally and A. Sechehaye with A. Reidlinger. Trans. W. Baskin. New York: Philosophical Library.

Saville-Troike, M. 1973. Reading and the audiolingual method. *TESOL Quarterly* 7, no. 4:395–405.

Sherwood, J. C. 1960. Dr. Kinsey and Professor Fries. *College English* 21, no. 5:275–80.

Silberstein, S. 1987. Let's take another look at reading: Twenty-five years of reading instruction. *English Teaching Forum* 25:28–35.

Silva, T. 1990. Second language composition instruction: Developments, issues, and directions in ESL. In *Second language writing: Research insights for the classroom,* ed. B. Kroll, 11–23. New York: Cambridge University Press.

———. 1993. Toward an understanding of the distinct nature of L2 writing. *TESOL Quarterly* 27, no. 4:657–77.

Stern, H. H. 1983. *Fundamental concepts of language teaching.* Oxford: Oxford University Press.

Stewart, D. C. 1979. Rediscovering Fred Newton Scott. *College English* 40, no. 5:539–47.

———. 1985. Fred Newton Scott. In *Traditions of Inquiry*, ed. J. Brereton, 26–49. New York: Oxford University Press.

Susser, B. 1994. Process approaches in ESL/EFL writing instruction. *Journal of Second Language Writing* 3, no. 1:31–47.

Sweet, H. 1877. *A handbook of phonetics*. Oxford: Clarendon.

———. [1899] 1964. *The practical study of languages: A guide for teachers and learners*. London: Oxford University Press.

Tibbetts, A. M. 1960. The case against structural linguistics in composition. *College English* 21, no. 5:280–85.

Young, R. E., A. L. Becker, and K. L. Pike. 1970. *Rhetoric: Discovery and change*. New York: Harcourt Brace Jovanovich.

Yule, G. 1985. *The study of language: An introduction*. Cambridge: Cambridge University Press.

Part 2

In the Classroom:
Teaching Reading as Writing
and Writing as Reading

Chapter 4

Connecting Reading and Writing through Literature

Alan Hirvela, Ohio State University

Carson and Leki (1993) have pointed out that "it is chiefly in the thousands of L2 writing classrooms that the question of how reading and writing may interact specifically arises" (2). While many teachers of reading may still focus exclusively on providing students with a repertoire of effective L2 reading strategies, teachers of writing, especially in more advanced courses, are increasingly recognizing that they cannot treat writing as a skill—or set of skills—unto itself. This is mainly because, as Carson and Leki have also noted, "reading can be, and in academic settings nearly always is, the basis for writing" (1). In particular, as Spack (1988) has observed, "[p]erhaps the most important skill English teachers can engage students in is the complex ability to write from other texts, a major part of their academic writing experience" (42). Writing with or from source texts is an act of reading as well as writing, since it is through reading that the required writing material is appropriated. In high school and college settings, then, where most writing is in one way or another related to an act or acts of reading, students' performance as readers is bound to have an important effect on their performance as writers. Students who do not read texts well are not likely to write about them successfully. Nor will they gain the knowledge of writing that effective reading provides through exposure to the ways in which texts are organized by writers.

Because the act of writing in which source texts are involved begins with reading and students' ability to compose as readers, writing instructors must factor reading into their teaching. Attention paid to reading should impact on students' performance as writers, thus necessitating a pedagogical link between reading and writing. However, connecting reading and writing also benefits students as readers. Flynn (1982) explains: "Through writing, students gain a fuller understanding of their reading. . . . In all forms, writing forces readers to define ideas clearly, and so results in fuller comprehension. Writing necessitates rereading and rethinking. Material is not simply ingested; it is digested" (149). Writing, then, draws students' attention to their practices and effectiveness as readers and as such highlights the importance of reading, a point that otherwise may fall by the wayside as students read quickly to complete a writing assignment. Thus, as Bartholomae and Petrosky (1987) have explained, "[t]here is no better place to work on reading than in a writing course" (iii). Furthermore, says Troyka (1986), "[w]riting and reading are reciprocal meaning-making activities; one is diminished without orientation toward the other" (187). This is why, as Andrea Lunsford (1978) has asserted, "[t]he teacher of writing must automatically and always be a teacher of reading as well" (49).

The larger question this chapter addresses is how teachers can account for both reading and writing in their classes. Increasingly, the issue many L2 writing (and reading) teachers confront is not whether to link reading and writing but how to do so meaningfully. Such questions as what texts to use and what to do with those texts are crucial in integrated reading-writing instruction. This chapter examines these more specific questions from a perspective that remains underdeveloped in L2 research and pedagogy, a perspective concerned with the roles literary texts can play in connecting reading and writing and thus developing students' L2 academic literacy skills. For a variety of reasons, literature is generally not associated with L2 academic reading-writing instruction, despite being a rich resource for such pedagogy. After this chapter briefly reviews literature's status in L2 instruction to contextualize its later discussion of literature as a medium for integrated reading-writing instruction, it addresses the central question of why literature merits greater use in the reading-writing classroom. The chapter concludes with a description of major pedagogical perspectives and practices underlying recent literature-based reading-writing instruction in L1 and L2 contexts and offers a framework for future literature-based academic reading-writing instruction.

Literature's Place in L2 Instruction

Literature has a curious history in the teaching of foreign languages. As well-known histories of language teaching by Kelly (1969) and Howatt (1984) show, literary texts have traditionally been a staple of foreign language instruction. There have been three primary reasons for this. One, the emphasis in foreign language teaching until well into this century was on the acquisition of reading and writing skills. Two, literary texts have long been seen as the best examples of a target language in use, as reflected, for example, in Coleridge's famous definition of poetry in *Table Talk* as "the best words in the best order." Third, the ability to read and appreciate literary texts in a foreign language has long been a marker of successful acquisition of a language. Vincent (1986), for example, has observed, "There is a long and honourable tradition of seeing an appreciation of literature as the pinnacle of foreign language achievement" (209), while Marckwardt (1978) explains, "For many years, and indeed until quite recently, the reading of literature was regarded as the capstone of the foreign language learning experience" (3). Also worth noting is the longtime dominance of the grammar-translation approach to language teaching, a method that historically relied heavily on the translation of literary texts because of their elegant and precise use of language.

Modern teaching of English as a second and foreign language has been marked by a rejection of such exalted views of literature. Between the move to the primacy of spoken over written language in the 1940s and the accompanying shift to structurally based pedagogies, literature has been considered by many language teaching professionals in the second half of this century to be ill suited for teaching English to a nonnative speaker (NNS). Syntactically, lexically, and culturally, literary texts have often been depicted as too difficult for NNS learners. This view of literature was compounded in the 1970s by the advent of the English for specific purposes (ESP) movement and its emphasis on matching the type of English taught with the specific target language needs of learners, for example, teaching "hotel English" to workers in hotels catering to English-speaking guests. Literature was seen by most of the early proponents of ESP to have little or no value in such instruction. There was also, as Strevens (1977) pointed out, a strong reaction in ESP against the tradition in which language teaching was seen as a "handmaiden of literary studies" (89). The development of the communicative language teaching methodology and of an interest in stylistics in the 1980s brought literature into a gradually more favorable light, but serious damage had already been done to literature's place in ESL theory and pedagogy. What Rutter (1985, 59) has described as a "generation of neglect" of literature had taken place, leaving many ESL teachers and teacher trainers disposed against literature or at least unaware of its possibilities for ESL instruction.

The move away from literature has been felt not just in general ESL pedagogy but in the teaching of reading and writing as well. For many reading teachers, the "difficulty factor" has once again been a mark against literature, as has been the belief that students cannot easily apply the L2 reading strategies they have been taught to the processing and comprehension of literary texts. In the domain of writing, both L1 and L2 compositionists have been engaged in the past two decades in a literature-composition debate over the role of literary texts in such teaching sites as mandatory first-year university writing courses (see Belcher and Hirvela 2000 for a recent review of this debate). L1 composition theory and research impact significantly on L2 writing theory and practice, and arguments against literature in the L1 literature-composition debates have unquestionably influenced many L2 compositionists to reject or distrust literature, particularly against the backdrop of literature's marginal status in ESL at large. Furthermore, I have elsewhere shown (Hirvela 1993) that ESL teacher training programs offer minimal coverage at best of literature as a device for L2 writing (or general language) instruction, thus communicating the subtle message that literature does not belong in the L2 writing classroom. What L2 writing teachers and teachers-to-be have not encountered in the professional literature and training, they will not be likely to include in their classrooms. To quote a popular saying, "out of sight, out of mind."

Also complicating literature's role in L2 writing (and reading) instruction is the view of literature commonly held in the field of English for academic purposes (EAP). Much L2 writing instruction (at the college level, in particular) occurs within the context of EAP's focus on providing students with the pragmatic composition skills and discourse knowledge necessary to write in and for "the academy." Horowitz (1990), in an often cited critique of literature in EAP, identified two key arguments against literature. One was that writing about literature does not prepare students for the writing required in the most dominant discourse communities, so that students in such situations would not be acquiring the ability to meet the specific needs and expectations of the university discourse communities they would write in. The other was that few ESL students intend to enter a literature-based discourse community, so the majority of students being taught how to write about literature would be acquiring knowledge and skills irrelevant to their needs.

However, strong arguments have also been made in favor of a literature-composition link. Likewise, the general view of the integrated reading-writing classroom that has emerged as scholars and practitioners have explored reading-writing connections offers compelling reasons for the inclusion of literature in a joint reading-writing pedagogy. The next section explores some of these reasons for using literature in the reading-writing classroom.

Why Literature?

Reasons for using literature to make meaningful connections between reading and writing can be grouped in two major categories. One concerns the makeup of the reading-writing classroom: its major components, activities, expectations, and so forth. The other concerns the nature of literature itself and what literary texts, because of their "literariness," can contribute to teaching and building reading-writing relations.

The Reading-Writing Classroom

The writing classroom has undergone dramatic changes since the late 1970s, partly as a result of the significant interest that developed in reading as related to writing. Previously, reading served mainly as a source of rhetorical models from which students could learn to structure their own essays according to carefully articulated guidelines for composing standard kinds of papers, such as comparison-contrast essays. As reading-writing scholarship gained momentum in the 1980s, student writers were no longer regarded strictly within the context of writing activity and skills; their abilities and experiences as readers also began to be examined. Likewise, reading was moved out of the passive language skill category and reconceptualized as more than a means of mechanically acquiring templates for writing through superficial reading of model essays. In a summary of the early reading-writing research, Stotsky (1995) noted a recurring theme: "reading experience seemed to be a consistent correlate of, or influence on, writing ability" (773). The net result of this scholarship was a major transformation of the writing classroom from one that treated writing separately from reading (and in the process paid little or no attention to reading) to one that, to varying degrees, factored reading into the writing equation. The gradual shift to a focus on students as readers as well as writers meant that the dynamics of the writing classroom—the teaching and learning activities conducted, the texts assigned, the teaching strategies employed, and so on—likewise shifted.

Central to the changed writing classroom that emerged from the focus on reading-writing connections was a notion of reading and writing captured by Tierney and Pearson (1983) in an often cited assertion: "at the heart of understanding reading and writing connections one must begin to view reading and writing as essentially similar processes of meaning construction. Both are acts of composing" (568). They went on in the same seminal article, "Toward a Composing Model of Reading," to note: "few would disagree that writers compose meaning. In this paper we argue that readers also compose meaning (that there is no meaning on the page until a reader decides there is)" (569). Whatever different nuances have emerged in various views of reading-writing relations in the years since this conceptualization of reading and writing was published, the notion of both reading and writing as active, meaning-making activities has been a common denominator in reading-writing scholarship and remains a foundation of the transformed reading-writing classroom. Whether in L1 or L2 settings, students in joint reading-writing classrooms are encouraged to look at reading as they do at writing—as an active process of meaning construction in which they have major roles to play beyond passively identifying the intended meaning embedded in the words and sentences of assigned texts. In the integrated reading-writing classroom, students are asked to see all of their productive actions as acts of composing

Another feature of the transformed writing classroom involves seeing reading and writing as recursive processes, as Petersen (1982b) explains.

> The modern composition teacher emphasizes the recursive process of composing—from discovery to first drafts, to revisions and second drafts, to editing. The reader-response critic recognizes the recursive nature of the reading process—of meaning emerging from personal-affective mental functions and of the readers' active composition of the text they read. . . . this common acknowledgement of recursiveness suggests that there is a common mental activity which actively composes and shapes what we read and what we write. (465–66)

In line with this view, students are now taught strategies for recursive reading and writing and are expected to perform reading and writing in this manner. The benefits of rereading a text and composing a new reading of it as well of rewriting one are taught. Reading and writing become more successful when done recursively because, as Bartholomae and Petrosky (1986) point out, "this is one of the lessons that a reader must learn: that reading, like writing, begins in confusion, anxiety, and uncertainty; that it is driven by chance and intuition as well as by deliberate strategy and conscious intent" (21). By learning how to move back and forth through the texts they read and write, students make sense of and construct meaning out of confusion, especially when they are also taught to see reading and writing as joint meaning-making activities. Through recursive reading and writing, they learn to reject, revise, or retain earlier hypotheses formed in their initial contact with the texts they read and write. For L2 writers, combining recursive reading-writing techniques with the meaning-making notion of reading and writing is especially important, and the portrait of confused initial reading and writing supplied by Bartholomae and Petrosky may be even more operative. Confronted with perhaps very different kinds of texts than they read in their L1, and expected to write according to principles and expectations perhaps also quite different than those of their L1, L2 readers and writers are in particular need of the ability to read and write recursively as a means of relieving initial anxiety and confusion over what they have read and written. In this way they are better positioned to make sense of what they read and write and then to gain control of acts of reading and writing.

A third major feature of the transformed reading-writing classroom is the "social-constructivist" view of reading and writing. This model accounts for the social and cultural forces and background knowledge, as well as the cognitive processes, that readers and writers are influenced by as they read and write. Underlying the social-constructivist paradigm is the belief "that 'meaning' does not exist in a text but in readers and the representations they build" (Haas and Flower 1988, 167); that is, while texts contain meanings intended by their authors, readers are not blank slates or objective parties when they read texts. While searching for meaning embedded in a text, readers are influenced not only by the text itself but by their own personal and cultural background, by their general ideas and attitudes as well as by the notions of reading and writing that they carry into the process. Because such a paradigm privileges readers' performances and places less emphasis on the texts they compose from or respond to, a major responsibility of writing teachers is to draw students' attention to this constructivist framework of reading and writing, that is, to help them recognize what they contribute to the acts of reading and writing. For example, a common scenario in many college assignments is one where students are asked to read source texts and to compose papers based on those texts. The teacher's task, in part, is to increase students' understanding of how reading and writing in response to source texts "are hybrid acts of literacy . . . in which writing influences reading and reading influences writing" (Spivey 1990, 259) in the course of the writer's own construction of a representation of meaning. With their already established L1 reading and writing skills and the notions they bring to reading and writing as multilingual individuals, L2 students do not enter the acts of reading and writing in the L2 as unbiased participants. Rather, how they read and write in the L2 will be influenced to varying degrees by the literacy experiences and conceptualizations of reading-writing conventions they bring from their L1 literacy backgrounds into the domain of L2 reading and writing. The social-constructivist paradigm creates space in the reading-writing classroom to account for such knowledge and skills. This is where, for example, contrastive rhetoric can contribute to pedagogy (and research) in the reading-writing field.

Complementing the social-constructivist model in the emerging reading-writing classroom is the notion of text world production. As Kucer (1985) explains, the representation of a reading—while reading and writing—requires that "the reader or writer must attempt to impose an organization on the meanings being constructed" (330). Drawing from the material contained in the source text(s) and from their own literacy knowledge and experiences, readers and writers generate a new text world. In the writing classroom, awareness of reading and writing as constructive acts and of strategies for text world production that enable the writer to communicate clearly and effectively the text world she or he has created have become important focuses of instruction. Students are helped to see how they compose meanings as they read and write and then how they can make the text worlds they have produced clear and meaningful for their audience. They learn to see that they do not simply locate text worlds; they also create them in the course of reading and writing about their reading.

In this kind of writing classroom, there are numerous benefits for students as readers and writers. Bartholomae and Petrosky (1987), for example, note: "writing also, however, gives you a way of going back to work on the text of your own reading. It allows you to be self-critical" (4). Reagan (1986) explains: "teaching reading in the writing classroom is more effective than teaching writing alone. The carry-overs in text knowledge make it easier to learn the conventions of language; the similarities in processing help develop fluency; the focus on meaning teaches writers to become readers and makes them aware of the need to clearly organize and develop their ideas" (184). Furthermore, as Krashen (1984) has asserted, "it is reading that gives writers the 'feel' for the look and texture" of written language and the rhetorical structures commonly found in target language texts (20). And as Carson and Leki (1993) note, "writing provides a way into reading, extends reading, and consolidates understanding of a text just as reading sustains writing and furnishes, for the writer, the counterpart of another voice" (2).

These core reading-writing perspectives illustrate the kind of pedagogical atmosphere that exists in the writing classroom where reading also plays a major role. The question now is what literature has to offer within such an atmosphere. More specifically, how can working with literary texts help students see the joint meaning-making, constructive nature of reading and writing and engage in meaningful, recursive reading and writing that generate successful and appropriate text worlds? How can their ability to participate in effective text world production be enhanced through a literature-based approach? What does literature bring to the reading-writing equation that is not as easily found in other text types? These questions are addressed in the next section of this chapter.

The Benefits of Literature

Literary texts promote reading-writing connections mainly because of (a) the properties they contain as literary texts and (b) the kinds of reading and writing activities students can perform with them as a result of those properties. This is particularly the case with fiction.

Chambers (1984) has observed that "story is the fundamental grammar of all thought and communication" (59). Abbs and Richardson (1990) further explain: "We are all narrative makers. We spend much of our lives telling our own stories and listening to the stories of others. Events happen to us, we put words around them, and—depending on what we can remember, how we feel and who is listening—narrate them in different ways" (9). As texts, then, stories have a universal appeal and cut across all kinds of boundaries in ways that other kinds of texts might not. Furthermore, stories have a powerful effect on people. Because of their imaginative nature and narrative structure, they invite their audience into them, and audiences respond to them. They allow readers and writers to adopt both roles, spectator and participant, that are central to literate acts (Britton 1984). The conventional, information-based texts common in reading and/or writing instruction usually confine students to the more passive spectator role. While reading and writing about literature, students move beyond being spectators to being participants as well, because literature encourages us to empathize with or react against the characters who attract our attention, vicariously experience what they do as we identify with them, and speculate on those aspects of their lives that the authors have not described for us. As the reader-response theorists posit, we fill in gaps that authors deliberately left in their texts to encourage our involvement in and engagement with the texts. We also react emotionally and intellectually to the events of stories. Likewise, literary texts—unlike the information-based texts that dominate L2 academic reading-writing instruction—prompt us to solve mysteries and answer questions, creative activities that foster deeper connections to texts than is often the case with other text types. These connections, in turn, increase the motivation to read and to write about what we have read. Instructors can build on that enhanced engagement and motivation while drawing attention to the ways in which reading and writing interact. This is why, says Costello (1990), "narrative literature seems a natural component of the ESL curriculum" (22), especially, she adds, of its reading and writing portions. As I will explain in detail in the next section of this chapter, this ability to engage readers and to inspire responses makes literary texts especially well suited to integrated reading-writing in both L1 and L2 domains.

It is also important to remember that students in L2 writing courses bring literary backgrounds into such courses. Indeed, in their own cultures, literature is frequently venerated, and the reading of such texts plays a fundamental role in their education. The traditional and commonly held beliefs and attitudes of their culture may have been taught through classic literary texts, and reading and writing may also have been taught at least in part through them. Chinese students, for example, often are taught principles of Chinese composition by having to imitate what they read in Chinese literary classics. Many NNS students, then, have a particular degree of familiarity with literary texts and experiences and may well have an especially deep attraction to such experiences. In addition, their view of literacy acquisition is likely to include literature as an important and natural component of the acts of reading and writing, since literature may well have played a large role in their L1 literacy acquisition. While literary texts in English may prove difficult to read, students may nevertheless associate them with literacy in a way that invites their inclusion in academic literacy instruction.

Widdowson (1979, 1984) and Spack (1985) point out another major benefit of literature: the "deviant language" and rhetorical structures of literary texts, rather than being deterrents to pedagogical use of literature, allow students to make meaningful comparisons between text types. While making such comparisons in their reading of literary and nonliterary texts, they acquire valuable knowledge of text types and of different uses of language—knowledge that can expand their repertoire of writing strategies and resources. In a similar vein, Gajdusek and van Dommelen (1993b) point out that "the classroom process of reading and interpreting a literary text genuinely involves student/readers while modeling the analytical patterns of thought that underlie expository writing" (201).

While performing such acts as writing an analysis of a literary text or constructing an argument concerning a character or theme in a text, students can apply the writing strategies commonly found in academic essays. The advantage of the literary text is that because it draws the reader into its midst through its imaginative qualities, students are provided with additional motivation in the course of constructing their academic essays. They want their interpretations or analyses to be clearly understood and appreciated, thus increasing their incentive to work with the techniques of academic writing being taught. Because their engagement with the literary text may be deeper and more personal than in the case of a nonliterary text, the practice gained in expository writing may have a greater impact on them than is true of more conventional kinds of reading-writing assignments. In short, literature-based reading and writing experiences may resonate more powerfully in their memories and their associations with L2 literacy instruction. In this way, reading and writing are connected at deeper levels than may otherwise be the case.

Gajdusek (1988), Gajdusek and van Dommelen (1993b), Oster (1989b), and Spack (1985) also make the point that reading and writing about literary texts enhances students' critical thinking skills in an L2 context. Literary texts are not meant to be read passively. They demand and encourage judgments and analysis on the parts of readers, and writing is the means by which these judgments take shape. In the process of making these judgments and analyses, students become more critical thinkers. Reading and writing are closely linked as students use writing to explore and make sense of their reading in the course of forming more effective analyses of what they have read.

Still another benefit of literature in the reading-writing classroom is developed in particular by Rosenblatt ([1938] 1976, 1978). Rosenblatt distinguishes between "efferent" and "aesthetic" reading. Efferent reading is that associated with information-based texts and involves the retrieval and later use of information from such texts. As Rosenblatt (1978) explains, the reader's "attention is directed outward . . . toward concepts to be retained, ideas to be tested, actions to be performed after the reading." Aesthetic reading, in contrast, is that associated with literary texts, and in this kind of reading, explains Rosenblatt, "the reader's primary concern is with what happens *during* the actual reading event" (24). Rosenblatt's thesis, which has become a central point in the extensive reading-writing research and pedagogy found in L1 contexts, is that students need both kinds of reading experiences to be fully equipped academic readers and writers. A focus on just one kind of reading (and subsequent writing) limits the range of the reader/writer as she or he encounters the spectrum of reading- and writing-related needs in academic life. Hence, literature in the reading-writing classroom complements the more commonly used nonliterary texts and efferent reading experiences by allowing for rich aesthetic reading and writing encounters. It also prepares students for the aesthetic reading experiences required in some courses in the academic community. Students do not simply read textbooks and information-based texts. Some courses may well require the reading of literary-type texts, for example, historical novels in a history course or ethnographic narratives in sociology or psychology courses.

Literature, then, can play a number of valuable roles in academic literacy instruction—roles not as easily satisfied by an exclusive diet of information-based, nonliterary texts. This is not to say that literature should dominate the reading-writing syllabus or curriculum. But in light of the perspectives just cited, it deserves a place in such a syllabus, because its imaginative properties make possible reading-writing experiences that enhance and enrich students' academic literacy skills and that cannot easily be generated with nonliterary texts.

Applications of Literature in Reading-Writing Instruction

As I noted briefly earlier, uses of literature in reading-writing instruction generally revolve around student responses to literary texts. These responses may be ends in themselves or, as is more often the case, the starting point or means to other forms of reading and writing. The response mode is the most natural for literature-based reading and writing because of the properties of literary texts already described. Literature is written to evoke a response on the part of the reader, and it is in the response process that the most productive and meaningful connections between reading and writing occur.

Pedagogy in the L1 Domain

Most of the theoretical and pedagogical work related to the bridging of literature, reading, and writing has occurred in the L1 domain, and it is generally felt to have begun with the work of the noted scholar of literary and reading theory, I. A. Richards. While teaching poetry at Cambridge University in the early 1920s, Richards was surprised, even distressed, by his students' frequent misreadings of the poems he assigned. This led to his groundbreaking research into the causes of their responses, described in his classic text, *Practical Criticism* (1929). Richards developed the practice of assigning his students groups of poems (four usually), minus the names of the authors of the poems. The students were then asked to write personal commentaries about the poems, that is, "protocols," which Richards later used as the basis for class discussion of the protocols themselves and of the assigned poems. These protocols of readings, constructed through writing, formed a meaningful, though unintended, link between reading and writing. Inspired in part by Richards's work, Louise Rosenblatt engaged, in the 1930s and in succeeding decades, in seminal research into the interaction, or "transaction," between literary texts and their readers as reflected in students' writing about the transaction. Like Richards, Rosenblatt's focus was not explicitly on connections between reading and writing, but her emphasis on readers' responses to literature paved the ground for advocates of reading-writing connections in the 1970s and later to investigate ways in which responses to literature would bring reading and writing together in the composition classroom.

Literature-based reading-writing pedagogy in the past two decades is also heavily indebted to the work of such well-known reader-response theorists as Wolfgang Iser, Norman Holland, and Stanley Fish. As Cai (1997) explains of their work, "reader-response theory shifts the focus of critical attention from the text as the sole locus of meaning to the reader as an important constituent of meaning" (209). This change in focus privileges (a) how students read and (b) the meaning-making nature of the act of reading, with writing playing a key role in the expression of students' readings. Robert Probst (1988), an important proponent of applications inspired by reader-response theory at the high school level, provides additional insight into the increased value placed on how students read and on connections between reading and writing when he points out that "to learn to read more perceptively and intelligently, we must reflect on our own perceptions of a work to see what they reveal both about us and about the text" (15). Writing is the mechanism by which that reflection takes place, and because it is so directly linked to the act of reading, it solidifies the reading-writing connection. Literature's role is to provide maximum opportunities for such reflective and active reading and writing, because of its unique potential, through its imaginative properties, for engaging readers' interest and, consequently, their text-building (i.e., text world production) abilities.

Also playing a central role in literature-based reading-writing pedagogy is David Bleich's (1978) development of a "response heuristic," that is, a system for responding in writing to literary reading experiences. Bleich's approach involves asking students to construct "response statements" in which they describe and analyze, in writing, their initial readings of literary works. These are intended to be informal essays in which students place particular emphasis on identifying the subjective factors that they believe have influenced how they have read a text. Understanding of these factors can then be accounted for in later readings of—and writing about—the assigned text. This notion of response statements and an underlying response heuristic motivates most of the L1 and L2 literary reading-writing pedagogy of the past two decades.

Bruce Petersen's work in the early 1980s captured initial attempts to link literature, reading, and writing. Petersen (1982b), asserting that the "personal matrix at the heart of reading and writing processes implies that reading and writing are connected thinking processes which derive from similar, if not identical, mental structures" (460), proposed that students compose "raw response statements" like those discussed in Bleich's work. The importance of his work rests in how these statements can be used. Because he also believed (1982a) that "we learn largely by using language" (107), he felt that "whatever method is used to generate responses, the class must share them in groups" (115). In his pedagogy, students are urged to compose their individual "raw response statements" and then share them in collaborative settings, such as full class discussions and smaller group analyses of and responses to individual response statements.

Also important in earlier work linking reading, writing, and literature was Elizabeth Flynn, whose pedagogy centers around two major types of writing: expressive and transactional. Flynn (1983) defines expressive writing as "writing close to the self, writing which reveals initial attempts to come to terms with a topic" (342–43). This represents the first stage in the reading of and writing about a literary text, a stage that also focuses on response statements, often in the form of journal entries. In Flynn's approach, "response statements . . . are envisioned as links between texts and students' experiences" (347). After this initial work with a text, argues Flynn, "expressive or writer-based writing is transformed into 'transactional' or 'reader-based' writing." She continues, "This movement from writing which is close to the self to writing which communicates with an audience almost always involves significant re-conceptualization, radical revision of early drafts" (343).This transactional writing, where the emphasis is on what to do with the ideas and insights acquired through expressive writing, takes place in formal essays about the text. "Writing in this last phase," Flynn says, "reflects a reenvisioning of the text, and often students discover a new focus" (343), one that revolves around more formal analysis of the roles of characters in a story, the theme of a story, and so on. Beach and Marshall have provided a highly popular adaptation of Flynn's approach (supplemented by Petersen's emphasis on discussion and the contributions of reader-response theorists) in their well-known textbook, *Teaching Literature in the Secondary School* (1991). In their approach, initial response statements in the form of journal entries are converted into a personal essay about an assigned text. Such essays, Beach and Marshall maintain, "can be extremely valuable in helping students learn the conventions of clear writing and in providing yet another way of knowing about texts" (88) as students attempt to reshape their own reactions to a text into writing that is meaningful for a wider audience—their instructor and their classmates. Later, students write more formal, analytic essays about the same text. In each of these stages, the acts of reading and writing overlap and sustain each other.

More recent literature-reading-writing pedagogy of note has been developed by Mariolina Salvatori. Working once again with Bleich's notions of a response heuristic and response statements, Salvatori (1996) has outlined a pedagogy that involves three stages: (1) the writing of an initial, informal, personal response to a text; (2) a more detailed "reflective commentary on moves made as readers"; (3) a formal paper involving analysis and assessment of the assigned text (446). Salvatori also asks her students to compose a "difficulty paper" early in their reading of a text. While using writing to unravel their complications with the text, they both heighten their awareness of how they read and experience writing as a part of reading. In general terms, Salvatori's approach stresses the value of allowing students to engage in "recursive and self-monitoring readings" of texts (449) through the kinds of writing tasks described earlier.

The work of Kathleen McCormick is also contributing to current literature-based reading-writing pedagogy. Influenced, like the others cited earlier, by reader-response theory as well as major models of reading and recent developments in critical pedagogy, McCormick's (1994) instructional approach revolves around a "variety of assignments—response statement, formal essay, collaborative project, and individual research essay—in which students are required to 'read' in order to write from a critically literate perspective" (10). Where McCormick's work differs from the early work of Petersen and Flynn is in her decreased emphasis on expressivist writing and on what she sees as an undue privileging of the text in their work. She conceptualizes the response statement as more of an analytical tool than an expressivist device. Her form of response statement links reading and writing in the process of asking students to examine how they have been constructed as readers and writers by the established conventions of reading and writing. In the collaborative stage of her pedagogy (where students generally work in groups of three), students engage in a critical analysis of "the text's relationship to the historical and ideological conditions in which it was produced." Here students are asked to read and write "symptomatically," that is, "studying the ways in which a text is culturally constructed" and "analyzing the history of its reception" (162). The students collaborate in the writing of short, group research papers that are distributed to and discussed by the class as a whole. Later, the students write an individual, formal research paper, in which McCormick hopes they will be "able to develop critical positions of their own based on an interrogation of their own repertoires and on symptomatic readings of cultural and historical texts" (168). Ultimately, in McCormick's approach students strive to become more self-aware readers, with writing once again playing the discovery role seen in the other pedagogies described earlier.

Another notable L1 approach to literature-reading-writing pedagogy—perhaps the best-known of all the approaches—is the pedagogy developed by David Bartholomae and Anthony Petrosky at the University of Pittsburgh and described in detail in two influential books: *Facts, Artifacts, and Counterfacts* (1986) and *Ways of Reading* (1987). These books describe a course in reading-writing connections for basic writers in which students complete long, thematically based assignment sequences. Underlying this kind of extended pedagogy is Bartholomae and Petrosky's (1987) assertion that "in academic life, readers seldom read single essays in isolation," that they "read, rather, with a purpose—with a project in mind or a problem to solve" (vi). Students in their course read a variety of text types, with considerable emphasis on literature in the form of short stories, and compose a wide range of papers. Bartholomae and Petrosky describe the pedagogy globally in these terms: "Our students regularly write assignments and work on projects that ask them to read various kinds of texts closely, to study texts for particular purposes, and to work across texts" (19). Students in their course write multiple drafts of essays and are taught such staples of academic writing as paraphrasing, quoting, and techniques for research-based reading and writing. At the heart of the course's design and assignments is their belief in a pedagogy that "presents reading as an action to be completed by writing" (vii).

Bartholomae and Petrosky argue that short stories figure prominently in this pedagogy because "they offer thick, readable slices of life-material rich enough for a reader's time and effort" (vii). They sustain students' interest throughout the assignment sequences and provide meaningful contexts for the significant engagement in the joint acts of reading and writing that Bartholomae and Petrosky believe is essential to the development of literacy skills valued within the academic community.

Bartholomae and Petrosky's approach places less emphasis on reader-response theories and response statements than do the pedagogies already described, although individual responses to texts still play a valuable role in their instruction. Their approach to the use of literature (i.e., short stories) is outlined in their teachers' manual for the course (1996). Basically, they ask students to read and write about stories from a variety of perspectives. One scenario requires asking students to conceptualize a story as a set of arguments constructed by the author in support of the text's theme. As readers and writers, the students identify those arguments, for example, citing evidence in a story to support the idea that a certain character is a hero. They are also asked to use evidence from one story to comment on a theme or character in another, for example, to use the definition of a hero constructed in one text to assess the behavior of a character in another. One of their approaches resembles Richards's work with student protocols, in that students generate responses to texts and then, in the act of comparing their responses with those of other students in class discussion, explore the reasons why different readers of the same text develop different responses. Finally, students may use the stories as prompts for constructing narratives about themselves and their own experiences relative to those described in the story they have read. In all of these tasks, reading serves writing purposes and writing serves reading purposes, hence the tasks cement the link between the two acts.

Pedagogy in the L2 Domain

While there has been, as I noted earlier, increased attention paid to uses of literature in L2 instruction in the 1980s and 1990s, relatively few attempts have been made to forge an explicit link between reading, writing, and literature. Instead, the emphasis has been on discussing ways of using literature to increase students' overall communicative competence. The thesis in this work is that literature's imaginative properties encourage students to respond to texts and that in the process of responding they can develop their communicative abilities as they search for appropriate vocabulary and syntactic structures to express their ideas and feelings about the assigned text. Literature, then, is often seen as a prompt for authentic language practice. While this kind of emphasis is enriching communicative language teaching as well as reclaiming a place for literature in ESL instruction, it has not contributed significantly to a focus on literature in an integrated reading-writing context, because, as I have observed elsewhere (Hirvela 1996), use of students' personal responses for such purposes does not allow for the development of a meaningful response heuristic of the kind that has developed in L1 pedagogy. Indeed, with the exception of the work of a handful of L2 reading-writing specialists, there has been little emphasis on the creation of a substantive literature-reading-writing response heuristic. However, the major work that has been reported thus far has demonstrated in valuable ways how literature can draw L2 reading and writing together.

Ruth Spack's 1985 *TESOL Quarterly* article, "Literature, Reading, Writing, and ESL: Bridging the Gap," was perhaps the first major attempt to make the literature-reading-writing connection in the L2 context. Drawing on the work of a number of the L1 specialists cited earlier as well as on previous attempts to reestablish a place for literature in L2 instruction, Spack described a series of activities that would forge the reading-writing link for students while also expanding their general L2 competence. The approach in that article and in her literature-based textbook, *The International Story* (1994), relies on the use of short stories and novellas and revolves around students eventually writing formal literary analyses of the texts they have read. In the approach she advocated in 1985, materials for these papers are generated through a combination of "class discussions and notes, in-class writing exercises, literary journals, and, occasionally, research" (709). A key element in this approach is "write-before-you read" activities in which students write about and later discuss themes and experiences central to the assigned literary texts before reading the texts. In this way they gain a valuable entry point into the texts and establish some self-confidence as readers. Journal entries serve as response statements and allow students to explore their initial understanding of and reactions to texts. Eventually students write thesis-driven essays in which they support their interpretation of the text.

The approach outlined in *The International Story* operates along similar lines. The movement is from initial response statements, to more involved reflective and analytical writing, and finally to composing essays discussing students' interpretations of the assigned texts. These essays serve as occasions for teaching commonly accepted strategies of academic writing, such as paraphrasing and direct quotation, as well as for teaching reading and writing as joint activities. An interesting addition in this more recent approach is the inclusion of a writing task (like Salvatori's "difficulty paper") in which students, while constructing their initial response statements, can comment on where they encountered problems in reading the text and why.

Underlying Spack's pedagogy in the 1980s and 1990s was a belief in the value of creating opportunities for students to engage in interpretive acts in their reading and writing. As Spack (1985) explained, "by interpreting texts and considering alternative interpretations, students come to understand in a fundamental way how meaning can be created through reading." She went on to point out: "this understanding of reading can help make students aware that when they write texts, they need to consider the reader's point of view. An active exploration of this writer/reader interaction can lead students to realize and internalize the idea that what they write becomes another person's reading and must therefore anticipate a reader's needs and meet a reader's expectations" (706). Through this emphasis on point of view, as in the opportunity to practice paraphrasing and quoting directly from texts while supporting an interpretive thesis, students improve their writing ability while simultaneously strengthening their reading ability.

Point of view plays a much larger role in Judith Oster's (1989a) literature-reading-writing pedagogy. In her approach, students write and discuss initial response statements and are shown the role that point of view played in their first reading of the text. Once they have learned about point view, Oster explains, "they are assigned writing tasks requiring them to shift points of view in a given story or in a story of their own." For example, students are asked to retell, in writing, a story they have read from the point of view of a different character than the one featured by the author of the text. They might also be asked to retell the story from the point of view of a type of character not represented in the text, such as a young child or elderly person. Oster asserts that requiring students to read and write from multiple points of view develops their flexibility as readers and writers and enables them to increase their use of "significant detail and appropriate figurative language" (85).

Like Spack's, Jacqueline Costello's (1990) pedagogy encourages the use of meaningful prereading writing tasks as a way into literary texts. In her approach, these are writing tasks in which the students speculate about a text before they have read much, if any, of it. According to Costello (23), the instructor might, for example, have students write about the title of a story before actually reading the text, or the instructor might read aloud a short passage from the text and have students speculate on the story based on that passage. Subsequent work with the text itself involves what Costello calls "focused freewriting," in which students concentrate on specific textual aspects identified by the teacher. Later, they generate questions about the text and use these for class discussion. There is then a second round of focused freewriting, which Costello says is "both to promote close reading and to help [students] realize that each reading of a given work is a new experience, a *different* reading, however subtle that difference might be" (26). Students thus gain insight into reading while writing about their new reading experiences. Eventually they write a formal paper in which they describe and analyze a relevant experience from their own lives while incorporating references to events or characters in the story they have read. Classroom peer review of their papers follows. Through this reading-writing sequence, says Costello, students "have learned that reading and writing are reciprocal activities, each commenting on and enriching the other" (29).

Myra Shulman (1995), too, places considerable stress on the use of writing in prereading and postreading tasks and emphasizes the value of students comparing written responses to assigned texts within a collaborative approach aimed at creating a community of readers and writers within the classroom. Where her pedagogy differs from others is in her use of all genres of literature—ranging from 14th-century Middle English poetry to contemporary and popular literature—and in the amount of attention she asks students to pay to the linguistic aspects of assigned texts. Linda Gajdusek and Deborah van Dommelen (1993a) have likewise developed a pedagogy that aims in part to teach the grammar of English via analysis of literary texts while at the same time linking reading and writing through a variety of exercises involving journal and essay writing as well as through peer review of student writing.

Gajdusek and van Dommelen (1993b) have also described a pedagogy in which literature is used to link reading, writing, and critical thinking. This approach involves a four-stage sequence with considerable initial emphasis on Spack's "write-before-you-read" strategy: (1) "pre-reading activities" (partly involving writing), which prepare students to enter the text (203–5); (2) "surface level comprehension activities," which help students acquire a baseline understanding of the text (205–7); (3) tasks aimed at "deeper levels of exploration and analysis," which entail writing activities focusing on analysis and interpretation of the text (208–13); and (4) "extending activities," where students use writing to explore reasons underlying the behavior of characters in a story and respond to themes and characters in the text (213–14). Here, as in stage 3, students develop their critical thinking abilities after establishing the facts and structure of the story in the first two stages. In this approach, writing is used to bring form and meaning to reading and in the process connects the two skills while nurturing students' ability to critically analyze texts.

Linda Blanton (1994) discusses a pedagogy that to some extent echoes Costello's emphasis on students' writing about their own experiences via connections made to literary texts. Writing in the context of developing students' academic literacy, Blanton stresses the importance of student empowerment in that context. She believes that "personal/life experience provides a critical element in students' development as academic readers and writers—in relating to texts as academic readers and writers do." Blanton maintains that students need to learn to "talk" meaningfully to the academic texts they read and that this comes about through practice in "speaking and writing about texts; through developing individual responses to texts" (12). She asserts that the personal engagement involved in reading and writing about literary texts increases the possibility of such student empowerment occurring. As she describes it, her pedagogy is one in which

> [t]asks call for interacting with texts—reading them, talking about them, extrapolating from them, linking them to each other, relating one's own experience to them, calling on them to shed new light on one's own experience and one's experience on them, synthesizing them, and writing one's own texts that do any or all of the above. (13)

I have elsewhere outlined an approach (Hirvela 1994, 1998) that applies Bleich's notion of a response heuristic to writing in EAP courses. In my EAP pedagogy, students engage in a three-stage task sequence that moves from "writing before reading," to "writing while reading," to "writing after reading." The writing in the first two stages is usually in the form of journal entries and draws on Spack's ideas about the importance of writing before reading, while "writing after reading" involves writing a response to the text or texts involved. Here students are encouraged to compose response essays that draw from what they have written both in the prereading phase and during reading. EAP practice here occurs in two forms: (1) utilizing academic citation techniques while quoting from the text(s) to summarize a story or support a response to it and, (2) in assignments where students read more than one text, synthesizing relevant material from the texts. While sharpening their synthesizing, summarizing, and citation skills, students continually interweave reading and writing as they search for and write with and about material from the stories.

Meanwhile, they are encouraged to see their response writing as a form of argumentation or persuasion in which they attempt to convince readers of the validity of their responses. This task, too, links reading and writing, as students use reading to locate persuasive material in the stories and use writing to express what they have found in their reading.

Conclusion

Salvatori (1996) says: "the question of reading in the teaching of composition is not merely the question of whether reading should or should not be used in the composition classroom. The issue is *what kind of reading* gets to be theorized and practiced" (443). The authors of the L1 and L2 pedagogies just described are united in the belief that literary reading should be factored into the reading-writing equation. By responding in reading and writing to the imaginative qualities of literary texts, students experience firsthand the acts of reading and writing as meaning-making activities as they engage in the text world production at the heart of interactions with literary texts. With the aid of the response statements and other pedagogical devices already described, students recognize, as Bartholomae and Petrosky (1987) explain, that "readers learn to put things together by writing " (4). They add that " writing gives you a way of going to work on the text you have read" (4). They also encounter, in meaningful ways, the recursive nature of reading and writing, as Bartholomae and Petrosky once again point out.

> To write about a story or essay, you go back to what you have read to find phrases or passages that define what for you are the key moments, that help you interpret sections that seem difficult or troublesome or mysterious. If you are writing an essay of your own work, the work that you are doing gives a purpose and a structure to that rereading. (Loc. cit.)

In addition, say Beach and Marshall (1991), "reading, discussing, and writing about literature helps students to better understand what texts mean and how texts mean" (17). Beach and Marshall also note the transferability of literature-based reading and writing skills to reading and writing about other kinds of texts.

While literary texts may prove difficult for many NNS students, they also provide uniquely powerful opportunities for learners to experience the ways in which reading and writing resemble and sustain each other. As I have already described, literary texts leave readers with gaps that can only be filled by active, meaning-making reading. Such reading is often guided most effectively by writing, which enables readers to sort out and make sense of the textual negotiations and interpretations they are engaged in, just as rereading adds clarity to the writing of these responses to the text. Sustaining this continual movement between reading and writing is the personal and deep interest that stories evoke in readers. Stories impact on us in ways other texts can seldom match, making them an especially useful tool in connecting reading and writing for students.

As William Grabe's chapter in this volume demonstrates, we now have a growing body of research that reveals important information about L2 reading and writing and the connections between them. While there is a need for more research in these areas, we also need to look further into ways of bringing reading and writing together in our classrooms, especially in academic literacy instruction where students' writing is based on source texts and acts of reading. In this chapter, we have seen that significant progress has been made in the L1 domain in establishing pedagogical connections between reading and writing through literature. Drawing on this work and on the L2 literature-based reading-writing pedagogies already developed, we have a promising foundation from which to continue exploring ways in which literature, a reemerging resource in L2 instruction, can enrich our classroom practice and enhance our students' joint reading and writing abilities.

References

Abbs, P., and J. Richardson. 1990. *The forms of narrative.* Cambridge: Cambridge University Press.

Bartholomae, D., and A. R. Petrosky. 1986. *Facts, artifacts, and counterfacts: Theory and method for a reading and writing course.* Upper Montclair, NJ: Boynton/Cook.

———. 1987. *Ways of reading.* New York: St. Martin's.

———. 1996. *Resources for teaching: Ways of reading.* 4th ed. Boston: St. Martin's, Bedford Books.

Beach, R. W., and J. D. Marshall. 1991. *Teaching literature in the secondary school.* San Diego: Harcourt Brace Jovanovich.

Belcher, D., and A. Hirvela. 2000. Literature and L2 composition: Revisiting the debate. *Journal of Second Language Writing* 9:21–39.

Blanton, L. L. 1994. Discourse, artifacts, and the Ozarks: Understanding academic literacy. *Journal of Second Language Writing* 3:1–16.

Bleich, D. 1978. *Subjective criticism.* Baltimore: Johns Hopkins University Press.

Britton, J. N. 1984. Viewpoints: The distinction between participant and spectator role in research and practice. *Research in the Teaching of English* 18:320–31.

Cai, Mingshui. 1997. Reader-response theory and the politics of multicultural literature. In *Reading across cultures: Teaching literature in a diverse society*, ed. T. Rogers and A. O. Soter, 199–212. New York: Teachers College Press.

Carson, J. G., and I. Leki. 1993. Introduction to *Reading in the composition classroom: Second language perspectives*, ed. J. G. Carson and I. Leki, 1–7. Boston: Heinle and Heinle.

Chambers, R. 1984. *Story and situation: Narrative seduction and the power of fiction* Minneapolis: University of Minnesota Press.

Costello, J. 1990. Promoting literacy through literature: Reading and writing in ESL composition. *Journal of Basic Writing* 9:20–30.

Flynn, E. 1982. Reconciling readers and texts. In *Language connections: Writing and reading across the curriculum*, ed. T. Fulwiler and A. Young, 139–52. Urbana, IL: National Council of Teachers of English.

———. 1983. Composing responses to literary texts: A process approach. *College Composition and Communication* 34:342–48.

Gajdusek, L. 1988. Toward wider use of literature in ESL: Why and how. *TESOL Quarterly* 22:227–57.

Gajdusek, L., and van Dommelen, D. 1993a. *Literary contexts for ESL writers: Connecting form and meaning.* Dubuque, IA: Kendall/Hunt.

———. 1993b. Literature and critical thinking in the composition classroom. In *Reading in the composition classroom: Second language perspectives*, ed. J. G. Carson and I. Leki, 197–215. Boston: Heinle and Heinle.

Haas, C., and L. Flower. 1988. Rhetorical reading strategies and the construction of meaning. *College Composition and Communication* 39:167–83.

Hirvela, A. 1993. A study of the integration of literature and communicative language teaching. Ph.D. diss., University of Stirling.

———. 1994. The role of reader-response theory in ESL instruction. Paper presented at the TESOL Summer Conference, Cedar Falls, IA, July 15.

———. 1996. Reader-response theory and ELT. *ELT Journal* 50:127–34.

———. 1998. EAP students responding to literary texts. Paper presented at the Thirty-second Annual TESOL Conference, New York, March 20.

Horowitz, D. 1990. Fiction and non-fiction in the ESL/EFL classroom: Does the difference make a difference? *English for Specific Purposes* 9:161–68.

Howatt, A. P. R. 1984. *A history of English language teaching.* Oxford: Oxford University Press.

Kelly, L. 1969. *Twenty-five centuries of language teaching.* Rowley, MA: Newbury House.

Krashen, S. D. 1984. *Writing: Research, theory, and applications.* Oxford: Pergamon Institute of English.

Kucer, S. L. 1985. The making of meaning: Reading and writing as parallel processes. *Written Communication* 2:317–36.

Lunsford, A. A. 1978. What we know—and don't know—about remedial writing. *College Composition and Communication* 29:47–52.

Marckwardt, A. H. 1978. *The place of literature in the teaching of English as a second language.* Honolulu: East-West Center.

McCormick, K. 1994. *The culture of reading and the teaching of English.* Manchester: Manchester University Press.

Oster, J. 1989a. *From reading to writing: A rhetoric and reader.* Boston: Little, Brown, and Company.

———. 1989b. Seeing with different eyes: Another view of literature in the ESL class. *TESOL Quarterly* 23:85–103.

Petersen, B. T. 1982a. In search of meaning: Readers and expressive language. In *Language connections: Writing and reading across the curriculum,* ed. T. Fulwiler and A. Young, 107–22. Urbana, IL: National Council of Teachers of English.

———. 1982b. Writing about responses: A unified model of reading, interpretation, and composition. *College English* 44:459–68.

Probst, R. E. 1988. *Response and analysis: Teaching literature in junior and senior high school.* Portsmouth, NH: Boynton/Cook.

Reagan, S. B. 1986. Teaching reading in the writing classroom. *Journal of Teaching Writing* 5:177–85.

Richards, I. A. 1929. *Practical criticism.* London: Routledge and Kegan Paul.

Rosenblatt, L. M. [1938] 1976. *Literature as exploration.* 4th ed. New York: Modern Language Association of America.

———. 1978. *The reader, the text, the poem.* Carbondale and Edwardsville: Southern Illinois University Press.

Rutter, T. 1985. *English language and literature: Activity review no. 4.* London: British Council.

Salvatori, M. 1996. Conversations with texts: Reading in the teaching of composition. *College English* 58:440–54.

Shulman, M. 1995. *Journeys through literature.* Ann Arbor: University of Michigan Press.

Spack, R. 1985. Literature, reading, writing, and ESL: Bridging the gap. *TESOL Quarterly* 19:703–25.

———. 1988. Initiating students into the academic discourse community: How far should we go? *TESOL Quarterly* 22:29–52.

———. 1994. *The International Story.* New York: St. Martin's.

Spivey, N. N. 1990. Transforming texts: Constructive processes in reading and writing. *Written Communication* 7:256–87.

Stotstky, S. 1995. The uses and limitations of personal or personalized writing in writing theory, research, and instruction. *Reading Research Quarterly* 30:758–76.

Strevens, P. 1977. *New orientations in the teaching of English.* Oxford: Oxford University Press.

Tierney, R. J., and P. D. Pearson. 1983. Toward a composing model of reading. *Language Arts* 60:568–80.

Troyka, L. Q. 1986. Closeness to text: A delineation of reading processes as they affect composing. In *Only connect,* ed. T. Newkirk, 187–97. Upper Montclair, NJ: Boynton/Cook.

Vincent, M. 1986. Simple text and reading text, part 1: Some general issues. In *Literature and language teaching,* ed. C. J. Brumfit and R. Carter, 208–15. Oxford: Oxford University Press.

Widdowson, H. G. 1979. *Explorations in applied linguistics.* Oxford: Oxford University Press.

———. 1984. *Explorations in applied linguistics.* Vol. 2. Oxford: Oxford University Press.

Chapter 5

The Foreign Language Literacy Classroom "Translating Event" as Reading and Composing: Eighth Graders Read Cross-Cultural Children's Literature

Mary Ellen Malloy, Central High School, Champaign, Illinois

Translation for Language Acquisition

> Translation has come of age. Studying it is not a simple specialty. Students of translation need knowledge of linguistics, literary history, literary theory, and cultural history. The study of translation does not compartmentalize: it unifies. It does not leave scholars and students happily tending little plots of their own: it forces them to survey, question, examine the lay of the land time and again. The text of a translation has often been called a culture's window on the world. (Lefevere 1992, 11)

I begin this chapter with these powerful words from Lefevere because, as Dingwaney and Maier (1992) have pointed out in contrast, "[t]ranslation has long been considered a rather questionable tool for language acquisition" (48). Consequently, translation has not had a role in classroom research concerned with second language acquisition (SLA), because that research has a "communicative competence" emphasis on listening and speaking. Given translation's traditional place with the reading and writing "skills" as a grammar-translation exercise reserved for adult students at the upper-division foreign language (FL) levels (see Cook 1998), truly very little knowledge of it as a well-theorized literacy[1] activity with adolescents has been generated. This pedagogical lack is unfortunate, for in mediating cross-cultural texts, "the translator learns something hitherto

---

1. See McKay 1996 for broader definitions and an expanded view of literacy.

unnoticed about the source language (and) the target language" (Miller 1992, 124); in effect, translation is a powerful learning activity.

As I incorporate authentic texts and complex literacy activities in my teaching, my students consistently demonstrate that translation "is not a simple specialty" but rather a process through which they learn FL. Moreover, because my middle schoolers are beginning learners of German, I have been able to watch how, in their translating, they become apprentices of literary and cultural history and theory, as well as linguistics. In the data to follow, they can be heard "surveying, questioning, and examining" the text at hand. Cook (1998) writes, "[S]o strong has been the influence of the grammar-translation method that many critics have been unable to envisage any other approach to translation in language learning" (119). This chapter offers a view of a pedagogical approach to translation as a literacy activity. The transcriptions of instructional conversations included herein are intended to provide readers with the classroom culture's "window on the world."

After two years of reading aloud and simultaneously translating authentic contemporary German picture books with my students, I would now feel very uncomfortable handing out to my eighth graders only little notional-functional reading dialogues of shopping at the KaDeWe in Berlin or ordering a bratwurst at the Oktoberfest. My students are literate in English, and they want something substantial to read in German as well. In the long term, they will want to interact with the highly literate Germans whose acquaintance they will actively seek out and in whose literate culture they will want to participate. In the short term, literacy-based curricula and instruction, especially the classroom genre (Pappas 1998) that I call here the "translating event," have legitimized our FL class by aligning it with the sophisticated reading and writing activities of my students' other middle school content area classes (Irvin 1998). I present here several actual translating events in the form of transcribed classroom talk to delineate, define, and describe them as grounded examples of how a teacher and her students use literacy skills to teach and learn FL.

The Significance of the Problem

All children, both Anglophones and speakers of other languages, should have regular literacy instruction in their own as well as another language. Hudelson (1996) insists, "Like native speakers . . . second language learners need to be read to on a daily basis" (146). Through my teacher research, I want to better support the Anglophone adolescents in my charge to accomplish three goals: (1) to become FL literate, both in a specific FL and in the argot of the FL content area;[2] (2) to join the ranks of the millions of regular, lifelong users of another language on this planet; and (3) to develop a finely grained sense of what it means to interact with nonnative users of English. We can build, extend, and deepen what U.S. Americans know about second language (SL) teaching and learning by promoting and researching their own participation in comprehensive, core curriculum FL classes. As indicated by the comparatively low FL learning activity in our country and by the public discourse and recent vote in California on Proposition 227, it is no exaggeration to say that such knowledge is desperately needed.

Picture Books, Reading Aloud, Translating Events

My own work on the intersection of literacy and FL with Anglophone middle schoolers (Malloy 1997) has led me to research the use of authentic children's picture books in the FL classroom (Malloy 1999). The two small K–8 Catholic neighborhood schools in Columbus, Ohio, have excellent teachers of both children's and young adult literature. My middle schoolers themselves act as reading buddies[3] for the early elementary grades. From my first skeptical and tentative attempts to read FL picture books as a part of formal instruction, the 11, 12, and 13 year olds in my classes have led the way, proactively co-constructing translating events.

What happens in our FL classes when I open up a German picture book to read aloud? After each page, the students spontaneously raise their hands so they can be called on to tell the group, in English, what they understand is being said and how they think the story is developing. They learned how to do this interactive literacy activity at their kindergarten teacher's knee, and they welcome each opportunity to do it now in their middle-grade FL class through the content area–appropriate mode of translating from one language into another and giving that protocol orally. Cathy Hirano (1999), translator of children's books from Japanese, describes translating such works as requiring "fairly strenuous cultural and mental gymnastics." She calls it "a balancing act, requiring sensitivity

---

2. Fifth graders can know what an infinitive is, what *conjugate* means, what a cognate is, that inanimate nouns can have gender, what a stem-changing verb is, and that they will address a stranger differently from a peer. Why not teach students this vocabulary and these concepts long before ninth grade?
3. Individual eighth graders are paired with individual kindergartners to sit down regularly together and read a book.

and intuition, a combination of humility, vigilance, and arrogance" (34–36), and she talks about struggling to "maintain a feeling for the way North American children speak" (38). I believe having Anglophone language learners do the translating themselves is an excellent way for them to access children's books from abroad (cf. Tomlinson 1998). Throughout the following transcriptions, my frequent "Yeah?" is an invitation to a bidding student to contribute what she or he wants to say about the text.

This combination of face-to-face, live reading and listening in German with immediate and socially constructed response and feedback among the participants makes for what Dingwaney and Maier (1992) call "a potentially disquieting but highly interactive situation," "by ensuring," they continue, "that the mediations in cross-cultural literary texts, including the mediation of reading itself, will be recognized and scrutinized" (48). Based on several recordings from the last week of middle school German class in May 1998, I offer here a sense of how my own students and I perform translating as "mediations of culture and literacy" and mediations of Benjamin's (1961) "translatability"[4] of the text itself. While our teaching and learning is not as politically charged as that of Dingwaney and Maier's college classes, my students and I nevertheless experience much trouble in our understanding and many successes as we use translating to make meaning with text.[5] What can be heard on the tapes is what Dasenbrock (1992) casts as a "model of reading, of interpretation, which redescribes the scene of reading not as a scene of possession, of the demonstration of knowledge already in place, or as a failure of possession, but as a scene of learning" (39). In the following transcriptions of such scenes of FL learning, one can actually hear the students becoming sharper readers, developing cross-cultural competencies, and acquiring German language through translating as the mediations of culture and literacy.

---

4. Benjamin's (1961) *Ubersetzbarkeit* is the expression of the most intimate relationship of the two languages to one another. What seems untranslatable in one language is precisely what offers possibilities for poetic expression in the other. The translation must have not only the sense of the original but also the code for understanding the meaning.

5. Little is known about how to help scaffold young Anglophones into the upper-division levels of L2 reading. Secondary and postsecondary transitions are exacerbated if students are exposed only to texts with tightly controlled vocabulary. Early, frequent negotiations of meaning with authentic, age-appropriate, cross-cultural texts lead 11, 12, and 13 year olds into later and more critical engagement with difference in literature and society and into lifelong FL learning.

Biliteracy Research Methodology: Protocols and Translating, Discourse Analysis

The practice of employing L2 reading protocols in the L1 (Bernhardt 1991) and the theory of translating as cross-cultural teaching (Dingwaney and Maier 1992) offer great promise to those of us biliteracy teachers who also need more good reasons for deconstructing the hegemony of the notion "target language only" in our FL instruction.[6] While reading protocols in the L1 have been used for gathering data about comprehension and for assessing students, similar practices in an FL classroom (not a research clinic) and for instruction (not just assessment) have not been widely implemented or are at least not widely documented. Just as most content area teachers across the curriculum rarely include reading lessons in their thematic units, FL teachers also do not frequently teach the reading of authentic texts (Vacca and Vacca 1997, 3; Alvermann and Phelps 1998, 16). When they do, they do not want to be documented as specifically encouraging students to say in English what they have understood, and they in fact often discourage direct translation.[7] However, live classroom reading and simultaneous translating in an L1 protocol mode offer student-driven and pedagogically sound ways to bring back vocabulary-rich and conceptually complex literacy activities in FL classrooms.

The biliteracy lessons in my classes are not monolingually German, and the books we read contain much more vocabulary, grammar, and syntax than we have yet covered, but the students, nevertheless, are busy at real literacy work in an FL. I regularly tape these lessons for discourse analysis, but neither in a quasi-experimental approach (see Brooks 1992), nor to analyze the data in the cumbersome methods of quantitative reading research (see Bernhardt 1991), nor to outline the kinds of lessons plans found in teaching publications. Rather, I am after a better understanding of what that biliteracy activity is all about and of how we do it. The nature of L2 reading development is that of learning to deal with text that is not mastery level. FL education methodology, therefore, should regularly include the orchestration of in-class events that may include the use of the

---

6. Phillipson (1992, 185) deconstructs the belief that a language should be taught monolingually.

7. The phenomenon of real-time classroom translation as a sort of schizophrenia would be fascinating to research. I have attended many FL classes where I was told not to use a dictionary and not to translate, although what we actually did to process texts looked a lot like translation.

L1 and that are based on translation as mediation of authentic texts. The kinds of standard FL curriculum and instruction for Anglophone middle schoolers could be greatly enhanced if we had better, larger libraries of FL children's picture books[8] and a better understanding of how adolescents read those books to learn FL. My data, analysis, and conclusions will support these views, though I hope they go beyond their goal of making useful points about translation and the more technical aspects of FL learning. Ideally, something of the joy of language learning will also emerge. My students are real Anglophone classroom FL learners, not objects of an anonymous short-term clinical study.[9] I hope readers find them and their practical action delightful, despite how the medium of transcription leaves much that is unrenderable for an academic essay.

The thematic unit of the entire literacy event, based on a picture book described later, included three phases: (1) introduction and discussion of vocabulary, (2) oral reading and simultaneous translating with the picture book in class, and (3) students reading aloud and retelling the story from a handout. The following 26 transcriptions from splices of the tape were recorded in two different eighth-grade class sessions of phase 2. They have been typed according to the guidelines in Hatch 1992, and the unit of analysis is the interactional sequence. My analysis consequently follows L2 discourse analysis methodology (McCarthy 1991), with the additions that I am both teacher and researcher using my own subjective experience to listen to and interpret the tapes in a narrative mode.

The Data and Analysis

On day 1, in phase 1 of our translating events, I write some 30 vocabulary items on the board in one eighth-grade room; these are present throughout the lesson as FL classroom environmental print and in the students' handwritten notes. On that particular day, we have a full 45 minutes, so we can go over vocabulary and read the book aloud handily in the period. In the other group, time that day is a bit short; I use a prepared transparency of the German words, and students write them and their definitions into their

---

8. The funding for printed matter in FL simply must be expanded to more closely match that for the other humanities subjects: social studies and English. Media centers should include FL sections, and class sets of quality FL books should be made available in the languages taught.

9. See Meara 1998 for an overview of translation and vocabulary learning research that is based on "lists of words" rather than connected discourse and "learning methods" (34–35) that are not typical of formal instruction. My contribution here is less concerned with assessment and more with instruction.

notebooks for reference the next class time. Throughout the translating event, after a short section has been read aloud, students are to figure out words and phrases across several turns. They thereby have "multiple opportunities to learn how words are conceptually related to one another" (Vacca and Vacca 1997, 133) in the FL text they are reading.

The vocabulary comes from Sabine Jörg and Danielle Winterhager's picture book, *Wiedersehen in Falun* (1996), a folk story based on an actual historical occurrence. To define each word, I flip around to different pictures in the book itself not only to teach vocabulary but also to give a text preview: as we learn words like *Bergmann* (miner) and later *Knall* (explosion), students are already surmising some turns of events. When we learn the names of the two protagonists, Maria and Julius, one boy quips, "Is this like a Romeo and Juliet story?" The cognitive work to puzzle out the German, the aesthetic pleasure through literate engagement with a sophisticated story presented with beautiful pictures, and the construction of knowledge about life in a 19th-century European mining village all make for worthy language/literacy/culture pedagogy, which my students and I carry out through means of translation.

Scene 1—Orientation to the book

1. T (teacher): Michael, can you read the title of the story? (showing book) Start here.
2. M: (8.0 seconds) *Wieder Sehen*
3. T: um-hmm
4. M: *in Falun.*
5. T: When a German says, *Auf Wiedersehen,* what's that mean, Michaela?
6. Ma: (shrugs)
7. T: We all say *Tschüß* to each other, but what's *Auf Wiedersehen* mean?
8. Ma: Good-bye.
9. T: OK, *Auf Wiedersehen* is more formally "good-bye."
10. T: *Falun ist eine Stadt in Schweden. Schweden* is what country? Sten?
11. St: Sweden.
12. T: (showing pages in book) *Und hier ist Maria und hier ist Julius. Und da ist Schweden.* Read the title, Bernd.
13. B: (3.0)
14. T: um, um-hmm, Hans.
15. H: *Wiedersehen in Falun.*
16. T: um-hmm, Lisa.

17. L: *Wie Wieder Wiedersehen in Falun.*
18. T: Um-hmm, *Wiedersehen in Falun.* The author is Sabine Jörg, (point-ing) OK; that's her name. Now this is an old, old folk story, so she just, she didn't invent the story, she just took the old material and wrote it anew for this picture book. (Opening book and flipping a page) I also look where books are printed. Here it says, *Stuttgart, Wien, und Bern. Stuttgart, Wien, und Bern.* Stuttgart is a city in what country?
19. S (student): Germany.
20. T: OK, what, how do you say "Germany" in German?
21. S: *Deutschland.*
22. T: Um hmm. Wien is a city in what country?
22. S: Austria.
23. T: *Sehr gut,* and how do you say "Austria" in German?
24. S: *Österreich.*
25. T: And Bern is a city in what country? Jessica.
26. J: *Deutschland.*
27. T: Not *Deutschland.* What do you think?
28. J: Switzerland?
29. T: Ok, *die Schweiz.* Bern *ist die Hauptstadt der Schweiz,* the capital city of Switzerland.

Moll and Dworin (1996) state, "The formation of 'habits of using texts' is of both theoretical and practical interest" (222). I include this introduc-tory section, which includes numerous interactional sequences, to show how teachers can use books to help novice readers of FL form those habits. Learners can read titles and recognize FL proper names as authors and illustrators; they can make meaning with these and other blurb and verso bits of information; they can aesthetically appreciate the sophisticated artifact of a picture book; they can become immediately engaged in a col-laborative story-reading event, and they can display their knowledge of the geography of the German-speaking countries in German. Holding classroom reads of an FL picture book is developmentally appropriate, content rich, and highly pleasurable.

Scene 2—*Llächeln*

T: *Lächelte sie, ihr liebstes Lächeln.* What was that? *Lächeln* was what, Anja? What do you have in your notes? *Lächeln* was one of the verbs we've had. Who can find it? *Lächeln* is
A: Smiled.

Scene 3—*Wartete*

T: OK, now, I'm gonna use the word *wartete*. What did *wartete* mean?
Check your notes. *Wartete* is what? *Wartete,* OK, whaddya have?
S: Waited?
T: She waited, it says: *Maria wartete schon.*

My directions in scenes 2 and 3—"What do you have in your notes?"
and "Check your notes"—direct the students again and again actively to
access literate resources for information that helps us understand the
story. While they are looking, I say the key words *(lächeln, wartete)* numerous times to reinforce them for the students and to buy search time. My
intimation that they need to look at verbs helps narrow the search. I had
nominated Anja for *lächeln,* but my "Who can find it?" opens the process
up for everyone and encourages collaboration and participation during
each others' turns. I anticipate for the group the use of the word *wartete,*
and once we are all sure of it, I incorporate it into the sentence "Maria
wartete schon." Reading L2 text takes tenacity and use of resources, both
written and social; I encourage the students to have such tenacity, and I
try to show them how to have it in our collective making of glossaries and
through my in-class instruction to use them.[10] Sometimes, this takes some
explicit admonishment about process.

Scene 4—"You can't . . . say you don't know; you need to start looking
for it."

1. T: Un kay, now here's this picture again. (4.0) *Dort traf Julius die
    anderen*
2. *Kumpels.* Whaddya make of that sentence? *Dort traf Julius die anderen*
3. *Kumpels. Kumpels* were what, Karsten? What were *Kumpels*?
4. K: (3.0) (shakes his head)
5. T: Oh!
6. K: (4.0)
7. T: (softly) I'll never ask you a word unless we have it on the board,
    so you

10. As Leinhardt (1983, cited in Alverman and Phelps 1998, 159) pointed out about
    homework in general and I have found in particular with reading homework in the
    FL, very little guiding and monitoring through text by the teacher takes place in
    advance of assigning. No time is taken for lessons in reading comprehension. Stu-
    dents are given a text and told to have it read for tomorrow's discussion. If they
    have little practice or tenacity with FL literacy tasks, however, their attempts at
    doing such homework often fail.

8.   can't shake your head and say you don't know; you need to start looking
9.   for it. *Kumpels* is what word?
10. K: (8.0)
11. T: Let's see, let's look up at the board, (2.0) (one, two, three, four) (2.0) It's
12. the fourth word down. *Die Kumpels* are yer what?
13. K: Friends.
14. T: OK, the guys that he works with, his buddies. *Dort traf Julius die anderen*
15. *Kumpels*—there he met the other buddies, his buddies—*mit denen er in den*
16. *Schacht hineinfuhr. Schacht* was what word? *Mit denen er in den Schacht*
17. K: The shaft.
18. T: OK, that he went down into the shaft with.

The German sentence in line 1 is long, but I want students to work with it. I repeat it several times and then key in on a single lexical item. The word *Kumpel* is fun; we'd talked about it a lot, and it is reflected in the picture (line 1). Karsten does not like to speak in class at all, though he is an otherwise cooperative boy, so I ask him to supply the word. He much too quickly wants to eject from the situation (line 4), and I feel a responsibility to not let him off without a try. I also publicly reinforce for the others what we are about here: all students are able to and are supposed to participate; I am asking fair questions, and it is their job to work with me (lines 7–9) and the materials we have. For a student to say he or she does not know is stating the obvious—we are in the process of learning. When Karsten balks again, I physically go to the board to demonstrate myself what they are all to do (lines 11–12), and he finally offers an audible answer. For him, every correct elicitation in German class is a quiet victory. Already with the next word, *Schacht* (line 17), he follows the required protocol and more easily supplies a correct answer as soon as he hears it, not waiting for me to finish the sentence.

Work with notes and the board is difficult and can be tricky, as can be seen in the next sequence: Jörg is an excellent student of German and is self-confident about speaking in class. I am, therefore, genuinely puzzled (scene 5, line 4) at the difficulty he has in supplying the needed word. We are talking about the chemistry of when the two young people meet: Julius's heart pounds and Maria smiles at him.

Scene 5—*Lächeln und Leiche*

1. T: *Wenn Maria Julius sah, lächelete sie ihr liebstes Lächeln.* Whad she do?
2. *Lächelte sie ihr liebtes, liebtes Lächeln.* Ahh, Jörg, whaddya think? *Lächeln* was wut?
3. J: (6.0)
4. T: Aw come on.
5. J: (1.0)
6. T: It's on the board.
7. J: (4.0)
8. T: *Lächeln,* what was *lächeln*?
9. J: Corpse?
10. T: (1.0) Umm, Oh no, OK,
11. Ss: (chuckle)
12. T: That would be sort of a sad (chuckle) sad return to his h-heart pounding.
13. Yeah?
14. S: Uh, she smiled a smile.
15. T: Exactly! Un-kay, *sein Herz pochte, sie lächelte.* (1.0)

Jörg himself is confused and does not know how to transmit this to me (lines 3 and 7). He has found *Leiche*'s corpse on the board and sees it as the closest equivalent to what he is hearing in *lächeln*. At this point in the story, however, it makes no sense to him, and he proves himself right, as can be seen in the classes' and my reactions in lines 10–11. I mitigate things by pointing out in line 12 the incongruity he saw. A fellow student bids. I call on her, and she supplies the correct answer. In line 15, I reinforce the semantic match of the two lines with my iambic intonation.

With longer sentences, I reduce the students' translation work by offering part of the text and inviting them to complete it with a logical and correct answer.

Scene 6—"Exhausted but happy"

1. T: (big sigh) *Erschöpft aber froh. Froh* means "happy," so he was *erschöpft aber*
2. *froh.*
3. S: He was exhausted but happy,
4. T: OK, exhausted but happy, *erschöpft aber froh setzte Julius sich an den*

5. *Tisch. Setzte Julius sich an den Tisch.* Now canye finish that? *Setzen* is
6. what I'm doin now.
7. S: (1.0)
8. T: OK *setzte.*
9. S: He
10. T: *sich*
11. S: sat down at the table?
12. T: He sat down at the table. OK, good working-guy here.

I had emphasized the word *erschöpft* earlier by contrasting it with the word *müde,* one we know well by saying *Ich bin müde* in response to *Wie geht's?* after a tiring German class. We had briefly seen the word *froh* at Christmastime. In this scene, I read the line, supply the new word, and repeat the line to be translated. The student in line 3 gives a quick rendering of it, and I proceed to the next part of the sentence. Seeing the picture, watching my movement, and knowing the word *Tisch* from other units enable the student to understand what is going on. However, he must work at getting the floor back away from me when I surmise from the pause in line 7 that I need to repeat. By line 11, he has completed the translation, and I then add a context note (line 12) about someone taking a seat after a hard day's work.

Once we've established that individual words—appearing as I read them aloud in our progression through the story and with the accompanying pictures—will help us comprehend the story and coproduce our translating event, I push the students to give more, different linguistically or metaphorically accurate renderings of what they are hearing. What follows are two versions of the same section.

Scene 7—"That's the gist, can you tell what the *sen*tence is saying?"

1. T: And when that happens, he says to her, *Laß uns heiraten.* What does he
2. suggest? Yeah?
3. S: Get married?
4. T: OK, can you translate the sentence when he says to her, *Laß uns heiraten?*
5. What is he saying? That's the gist, can you tell what the *sen*tence is saying?
6. S: (1.0)

7. T: Cuz he says—*uns* is one of our pronouns—he says, *Laß uns heiraten.*
   He's
8. saying, "let's," let-us, "get married." *Laß uns heiraten.*

In line 5 I validate that the student has found an important word and understands what is going on. In line 4, however, I want to hear something a little closer to the literal German sentence. Our text, for the first time, is using dialogue, and I am interested in hearing my students speak what Julius does. At the same time, at the gap in line 6, I realize how much is going on between the contraction in English (line 8), which cannot be done with the German, and the single word in German (line 8), which needs two words in English, so I shift to a more direct teaching mode.

In the next version, students come up with both figurative and literal productions of the German. Kristina gives us the key word, and Anna is able to supply what is certainly a "proposal" (19 8, line 1).

Scene 8—"What does he say in the sentence . . . ?"

1. T: Now he makes a proposal, *Laß uns bald heiraten.* Kristina, what
   would
2. that be?
3. K: (1.0)
4. T: Here's our word *heiraten,* so what does he say to her?
5. K: (1.0) To marry.
6. T: Well, what does he say in the sentence then? He says to her, *Laß uns*
7. *heiraten. Ja,* Anna.
8. A: Let's get married.
9: T: Let's get married, excellent. *Laß uns heiraten.*

When students give a speedy and accurate translation, as with Anna's in line 8, I sometimes simply latch with a teacher echo (line 9). But sometimes my feedback takes more of a communicative and informing twist, as the next four scenes make visible.

Scene 9—Michael

T: *Er schaufelte und hämmerte und schaufelte.* Whaddya make of that, Michael?
M: (2.0) He shoveled 'n hammered 'n shoveled.
T: (dramatically) It's the life of a miner.

Scene 10—Daniela

T: It says then, *Das war eine harte Arbeit.* What would that be? Yeah, Daniela, what do you think? *Das war,* I'm sorry, did you have your hand up? Yeah?
D: That was hard work.
T: It was *very* hard work. *Das war eine harte Arbeit.*

Scene 11—Lisa

T: . . . *daß Maria und Julius verlobt waren.* So what did the pastor say?
Ss: (2.0)
T: Lisa, what did he say?
L: That they were engaged?
T: Un kay, of course.

Scene 12—Exactly.

T: *Da fanden sie die Leiche, da fanden sie die Leiche eines jungen Mannes, eines jungen Mannes.*
S: They found the corpse of a young man.
T: Exactly.

In scene 9, the text feature of cognates set up in a pattern of three allows Michael to present an effortless, hearable, and poetic translation. Echoing his response would seem especially inappropriate because the item is so clearly his. Therefore, I add a comment that refers back to the picture of the group of young miners. Daniela not only knows the translation and bids for the line, but through facial expressions she lets me know she does not need a repeat. She gives a clear English translation, and in my feedback, I am not echoing but in effect saying a different sentence, emphasizing by adding "very" and repeating the German. Lisa, selected after no one bids on this item, dependably comes up with a perfectly inverted English dependent clause, to which I can only add a self-evident "of course." And when the student in scene 12 gives his full, elegant sentence to the grammatically complex inverted subject/verb and genitive of the German sentence, I congratulatorily add, "Exactly." Students listen to the German and make meaning with it via oral translations that are positively acknowledged. Not only do translating events allow students to deliver FL information, but they also create moments in which that work can be done, that information can exist, and a text world can accrue.

In the next two scenes, the students offer both viable interpretations of the story and linguistically accurate renditions of the German: they experience that both belong in translating events. In scene 13, S1 picks *sie sah* out of the text and uses it to give her answer (line 3). This is indeed a good rendering, but I want to hear that students can produce "disappeared" for *verschwand* as well and can use it to complete the fairly straightforward prepositional phrase that relates back to *er*, not *sie* (my "he" in line 4). The two students and I neatly perform this sequence. It is exemplary for the "translating event" genre of our class: the reading aloud, partial translating by the expert, generous interpretation by the literate novice, exact linguistic version by a fellow classmate, and pleased acknowledgment at the end.

Scene 13—"That's a good translation of that."

1.   T: *Sie sah ihrem Julius nach, bis er hinter dem letzten Haus verschwand.*
2.   She watched him until what? *er hinter dem letzten Haus verschwand.*
3.   S1: She couldn't see him anymore.
4.   T: OK, that's a good translation of that. She watched him until he what? *Er*
5.   *hinter dem letzten Haus verschwand.*
6.   S2: He disappeared um
7.   T: Yeah?
8.   S: (2.0)
9.   T: Behind the, *dem letzten Haus*
10. S2: The last house.
11. T: Very good.

Accordingly, in the next scene, Gustaf makes a contribution to the story based on the cavelike entrance to the mine in the picture, though the German word meaning "cave" is not used in the text. With a bit of focusing, however, he can also use the German text to drive our collective understanding of the story.

Scene 14—"I'll take that . . ."

T: *Julius war in den Schacht gefahren,* Where was he? *Julius war in den Schacht.* Gustaf, where was he?
G: In the cave.
T: Oh, uh, en, well OK in a cave, I'll take that, but *Schacht* is what? It's our miner word.

G: Shaft.

T: OK, he was down in the shaft.

Using the pictures to help make meaning with the accompanying text is certainly a strategy I want to support. At one point with another student, I read a line of German and say: "Whaddya make of that, Hannes? We'll take it bit by bit." Scene 15 is an example of how Toni and I negotiate—bit by bit and with the help of the picture—a lengthy piece of information that he can supply to lead me to a short teacher lecture on culture. I had talked at length with the students earlier about seeing skilled workers on the streets of Berlin dressed with 19th-century detail according to their profession, as well as villagers in Austria wearing dirndls and knitted vests indicating what part of the Alpine valley they were from. The idea that craftspeople may wear clothing that signals their professions was new to the students and central to understanding the story. Toni gives me "national costume" and "miner" (lines 12 and 14), which I blend (line 15).

Scene 15—"You see how that's in the picture . . ."

1. T: Toni, what would that be, *Sie stickte für Julius ein schwarzes Tuch,* and you see it in the picture. (moving out to him so he can see better)
2. To: She made a uniform for him.
3. T: Well, what was *Tuch?*
4. To: Scarf.
5. T: Unkay *schwarz* is what color?
6. To: Black.
7. T: OK, *sticken* is what verb?
8. To: (4.0) Embroider.
9. T: OK, I'm gonna say that sentence again. *Sie stickte für Julius ein schwarzes Tuch.*
10. To: She made Julius a scarf.
11. T: OK, and you see how that's in the picture. *Sie stickte für ihn ein schwarzes*
12. *Tuch* (1.0) *für seine Bergmannstracht, für,* Toni can you finish it, *für seine*
13. *Bergmannstracht.*
14. To: For his national costume
15. T: I-in fact, for hi-, an *Bergmann* is what?
16. To: Miner.
17. T: OK, so like, his miner national costume. Of-often people would

have an extra little scarf. People do that here, too, like racing car drivers will wear a scarf, and scarf is often associated with what you do in your work. People have them for luck.

Once Toni works through the words and puts the information together in line 10, I repeat the German with a pronoun (*ihn* in line 11 for his "Julius") and continue with the sentence, making a reminder nomination to Toni in line 12 to translate the next bit as well. Across 15 turns, Toni has supplied all the necessary information for understanding the sentence and getting the notion of professional uniform onto the table.

Scene 16—"It's so easy that you can't tell."

1. T: *Am Sonntag, in der Kirche.* Wha-wuz the time and place did I say?
2. Actually, ya see that in the picture. *Am Sonntag, in der Kirche.* Yeah,
3. Sten, whaddya think?
4. S: At noon, in the church.
5. T: OK, almost, but ra-, noon is *Mittag*. What day is *Sonntag*?
6. S: Afternoon?
7. T: No, what day of the week, *Wochentag*?
8. S: (2.0)
9. T: *Sonntag*. It's so easy that you can't tell.
10. S: Tuesday?
11. T: (smiling) NO! *Sonntag*!
12. Ss: Sunday, Sunday.
13. T: *Sun*day. *Am Sonntag in der Kirche.*

Stories have numerous settings (time and place in line 1), so I want to take advantage of that text feature to drive our talk. Sten might well be stuck in the word field of "times of day," not being able to switch to "days of the week." He is a good student, and as often happens automatically with them, I give clues and explanations in German (*Mittag* in line 5, *Wochentag* in line 7) and do not capitulate: I continue saying the German word *Sonntag* throughout. His "on" moment and initial error stymie him. My good-natured dismay (line 11) at his offer of "Tuesday" for what is obviously a cognate with a cultural condition (church on Sunday) makes an entry for other students to chorus the answer in line 12. Sten, a bit chagrined, is puzzled himself for not coming up with the answer.

Throughout the reading, I often use spot here-and-now examples to help comprehension, as in the next two scenes with *Paar* (*Schuh*e we'd had in our unit on articles of clothing) and the extrapolation from *Woche* and *Monat* to *Jahr,* all of which we'd had when we did a Morgenstern poem with Zwerger pictures. Jörg recognizes *Gottes* from the Agnus Dei *(Lamm Gottes)* prayer we had been saying to start class.

Scene 17—A couple and a pair

1. T: *Alle wünschten dem jungen Paar. Paar* would be what? If I say *ein Paar*
2. *Schuhe?* Yeah?
3. S1: Pair.
4. T: Ok, everybody wished the young pair *Gottessegnen. Segen* means
5. blessing, so *Gottessegen* would be what? Kristof, what would that be?
6. *Gottessegen?*
7. S1: (4.0)
8. T: Whaddya think?
9. S1: God's blessing.

Scene 18—"That's where our story jumps to."

1. T: *Viele, viele Jahre später.* If we have *die Woche* is the week, *und der Monat*
2. is the month, what's *das Jahr?*
3. Ss: The year!
4. T: OK, so it says, *viele, viele Jahre später.* What is that?
5. S: Many years later
6. T: That's where our story jumps to. This picture is the same, but it's many years later.

Though it is not evident in the pictures, I want the students to have a sense that much time has passed (line 6), again as evidenced by the text.

Scene 19—"Is it something about . . . ?"

1. T: *Das war der Tod.* Who was the person? *Das war der Tod.*
2. Who came to interrupt things in the wedding? *Das war der Tod.* (smile in
3. voice) We've had this word so many times. Whaddya think?
4. S1: Is it something about dead or dying?
5. T: OK, and if you think of it metaphorically, who is *der Tod?*

6. S1: God?
7. S2: A skeleton or something?
8. T: OK, like the Grim Reaper. OK, you wanna think of something that would embody death, OK? So Death was the person who stepped in and said this wedding isn't going to happen.

"Death" as a personification often causes both linguistic and cultural snags for Anglophone students (line 4).[11] Nevertheless, the student in line 4 knows *tot* from the last line we had in *Der Erlkönig* and can offer several candidates. Because of English's less pronounced use of the definite article (we will also encounter *das Leben* in this story) and perhaps the modern less spiritual concept of death in the United States (the student's line 6 "God" and my own oxymoronic "something that would embody death"), *der Tod* needed direct teaching in this sequence based on the students' hypotheses. Even in the picture, there is no depiction of *der Tod,* just a gloomy, omen-filled predawn scene. To decipher the text at hand and figure out the cultural code for understanding what was about to happen from the point of view of northern Europeans both now and at that time, student translators needed to conceptualize a character who was to "speak now or forever hold his peace."

The deciphering work of translation is talked into the real-time process here; the student's "Is it something about . . . ?" and the proffered candidates (God, a skeleton or something) show the kind of pinpointing of the possibilities and then the decision making that go into L2 text comprehension.

Scene 20—"Tell me in English . . ."

1. T: Tell me in English, how would you describe this picture. Look at the
2. difference between this one (takes a second to flip pages) and this one
3. here. What do you think? I'll take Jessica first.
4. J: It's like gloomy and dark.
5. S: It looks like it's going to rain.
6. T: Un kay, anything else, un how is it different from this one? Yeah?
7. S: Night 'n day.
8. T: OK, like night 'n day. How besides time of day?

---

11. German teachers spend much time explaining the difference between *der Tote* and *der Tod.*

9.   S: (says an inaudible sentence about the moon)
10.   T: Un huh, OK, right, oh yeah, so actually it *is* the difference between night 'n day; (chuckling) literally and figuratively it's the difference between night and day.

There is so much bidding when I openly offer to the cohort, "Tell me in English," that I have to number the talkers (line 3). Students want to talk about what they have understood of a cultural artifact like an FL picture book. The book itself drives our talk and my instructional role in this sequence as I encourage students to use their visual literacy to contrast the golden-hued scene of public congratulations on the previous page with the somber blue-gray unpeopled landscape of the page at hand. A very interesting thing happens here. The text says, *Am nächsten Morgen* [the next morning], but the student in line 7 notices the moon in the upper left-hand corner and mentions "night." Being more text-driven with *Morgen*, I haven't noticed the moon, but fortunately for me, I don't want to "correct" him. Instead, I take it metaphorically in line 8 and push things a bit with "How besides time of day?" When he clarifies the difference in line 9, I make my own translating point in line 10: there are both literal and figurative renderings of readings, and they work together, especially when they seem to be at odds.

My same point about encouraging students to share what they make of a story however they can and beyond what the text is transmitting can be heard in my elicitation in the next scene. The student gives a "scientific" explanation that leads me to offer a cross-cultural example (pharaoh's tomb) as well as to model cognitive work in a translating event ("I'm trying to think. I think the word is . . . ").

Scene 21—"Can you guys explain to me what must have happened?"

T: Can you guys explain to me what must have happened to the air in that shaft? It sort of was like a what?
S: He was preserved, with all the air out.
T: Un kay, un kay, so I'm trying to think. I think the word is like "hermetically sealed." The rocks fell in such a way that the air was so completely closed off that it was kind of like he was in a, like in a pharaoh's tomb or something, like he was mummified in there.

The tacit curricular point here is that an FL class will help expand vocabulary knowledge in English and cross-disciplinary content knowledge.

Scene 22—"We didn't go over these words, but what dya think?"

1. T: *Als mit einem gewaltigen KNALL! die Grube zusammensturtzte.*
2. Whaddya think happened? I'm gonna say this again. OK, Uschi, go ahead and try it.
3. U: He heard a loud noise,
4. T: OK.
5. U: and that killed him.
6. T: OK, we didn't go over these words, but what dya think? *Die Grube sturtzte*
7. *zusammen.*
8. U: It closed in on him.
9. T: OK, exactly. Anything else? That's the general gist.

Uschi does an excellent job here, bidding without waiting for a repeat, contributing full phrases rather than just single words, and forthrightly giving an understanding for material not yet covered. She hears my loud performing of the word *Knall,* and rather than offering the glossary meaning, "explosion," she says the equally acceptable and contextually appropriate "loud noise." "He" is in the picture, so she shapes her protocol as based on Julius's experience of the accident. She responds to my further prompting and offers a version even of words we "didn't go over." Uschi can move beyond them and, using contextual clues, including my hand gestures, offer a translation of German *zusammenstürzen,* which cannot be rendered word for word anyway. This is very sophisticated, high-level interaction with an FL text, Benjamin's (1961) "task of the translator": "Jene reine Sprache, die in fremde gebannt ist, in der eigenen zu erlösen, die im Werk gefangene in der Umdichtung zu befreien, ist die Aufgabe des übersetzers.[12] Uschi enjoyed being the one to explain this first little climax, freely translating, in the straightforward English of a middle schooler, story lines that are "locked up" in the German text. No one need add "anything else." My talk in line 9 and my proceeding to the next page demonstrate and emphasize the strategy "Once you have the gist, don't belabor things, but rather move on."

Scene 23—A transitional sentence

1. T: Now here's a little change after *Unglück, Unglück.*

---

12. "That pure language, which is bound up in the foreign—to release it in the [translator's] own, to set free the imprisoned meaning of the original work in the process of translating, is the task of the translator" (Benjamin 1961, 67).

2. S: (inaudible)
3. T: OK, you guys tell me what you think this transitional sentence is. It says,
4. *Aber das Leben ging weiter. Ging* was a verb we've had many times in the past.
5. *Ging*? Yeah?
6. S: Went.
7. T: Ok, so, *das Leben* is "life." *Das Leben ging weiter.* What happens?
8. S: Life goes on?
9. T: Life went on. *Das Leben ging weiter.*

I don't stop to ask for the English of *Unglück,* but it's hearable on the tape that a student supplied the word (line 2). The talk of these transcriptions is the translation work done by the students, but this sequence demonstrates that there is much active listening and thinking going on throughout translating events. Students will find significant FL text details that the teacher does not, and they will find auditory space to articulate that information. In this scene, I am clearly more intent on what I call here a "transitional sentence," on making use of student understanding of story grammar to begin mapping where the story might go now. The student correctly offers "went" (line 6) and correctly responds "goes" (line 8) to my present tense question (line 7). I make a repair that puts together the student's responses, and I repeat what is essentially an aphorism.

Scene 24—"Ok, not into the house, well, eventually into the house . . ."

1. T: *Die Bergmänner trugen den Toten durch das Dorf.* Yeah, whaddya
2. think, Anna?
3. A: They carried him into the house.
4. T: OK, not into the house, well, eventually into the house, but *durch das Dorf.*
5. S1: Through the door,
6. T: Oh, no, "door" is *Tür.*
7. S2: Through the town.
8. T: Through the town, through the village.

The accompanying picture here shows the group of miners carrying the corpse along a path in a field, not through the village or into the church as stated in the text. Anna perhaps acoustically hears something from *durch das Dorf* she can logically turn into "house." The miners will eventually set Julius up not in a house but in the church mentioned earlier, but I can still mitigate and accept her offering: the dead were given wakes in homes in earlier times, and *Haus* in German can mean any building. I work with interference from *Tür* for *Dorf;* students know both words, and line 5 is a logical translation, but when I caution, "Oh no," and say *Tür* (line 6) to distinguish it from *Dorf* (line 4), the student in line 7 takes the floor and supplies the word. My urgency about accuracy will prompt confident students to jump in neatly with correct answers.

Scene 25—More cognates and more mime

1. T: Whad she do?
2. B: She kissed him and whined.
3. T: Ok, *weinen* is this. (demonstrates)
4: B: Cried.
5. T: She wept 'n kissed him 'n everybody's going. What's going on here?

I mime frequently while reading aloud during translating events, for example, waving when I read, *Maria winkte* [Maria waved]. I also gesture as prompts to help elicit vocabulary. For example, I gesture appropriately as I say, "*Segen* is when the priest does this." Nothing is "wrong" in scene 24, and many possibilities occur in the flow of turns: *weinen*, whine, cry, weep. In fact, they work together to give a sense of the confusion I point out as part of the story grammar in line 5. We are the audience who knows what is going on when the character audience does not.

Scene 26—Rhetorical questions

T: What does she still have here? (showing book) *Maria legte das schwarze Tuch um seinen Hals.*
S: She laid it on his throat.
T: *Um seinen Hals.*

My question functions as accompaniment to pointing at the picture and reading aloud again *das schwarze Tuch.* A typical good picture book will introduce key items and vocabulary early and repeat them throughout. My question does not need an answer, because we can see the black scarf; what is important is what she is doing with it. To translate, the student skips a word-for-word rendering and jumps to syntax and meaning, substituting with pronouns: "she" for *Maria* and "it" for *Tuch*. "Laid on his throat" are what make it into the oral protocol. I repeat the new review item as it appears in the prepositional phrase (we had this in our unit on body parts) to legitimize the student's appropriately streamlined emphasis. For a translating event in a group of biliteracy learners, this scene's language and interaction as reading aloud and composing via translating in a recall protocol mode is exemplary.

Conclusion

> Denn *man muß* nicht die Buchstaben in der lateinischen Sprache *fragen, wie man deutsch reden soll*, wie diese Esel tun; sondern man muß die Mutter im Hause, *die Kinder auf der Gasse*, den einfachen Mann auf dem Markt *danach fragen, und denselben auf das Maul sehen, wie sie reden, und danach übersetzen, so verstehen sie es denn, und merken, daß man deutsch mit ihnen redet.* (Luther [1530] 1983, 85)

I roughly excerpt and muddily translate the italicized part of the preceding quote: "One must ask the children in the street how German is supposed to be spoken, and 'look them in the mouth' as to how they speak, and then translate accordingly. That's how they will understand and notice that German is being spoken with them." My FL pedagogical interest with middle school learners of FL and my taping and transcribing of our German classroom talk can be linked to many of the assumptions in Luther's 16th-century foundational text on translation. How do schoolchildren, in the context of the structures for and attitudes toward SLA in the United States, manage to talk their way through FL lessons? What is their logic about biliteracy teaching and learning, as evident in how they are actually doing it? Transcriptions help us to "look our FL learners in the mouth," to better understand that logic and to inform our interaction with them. A literature-based curriculum gives literate FL learners a chance to read and talk with each other about cross-cultural FL text via literacy-based instruction that includes translation. If I want my students ever-increasingly to "understand and notice that German is being spoken with them" as they grow into young adulthood and become lifelong SL users, I must get a better understanding of our interactions with text from their perspective. Our translating events help them become FL literate with all the attendant, defining competencies—linguistic, social, and cultural—such a fine state of being entails.

My emphasis here on translation as a biliteracy exercise has focused on reading as composing (Tierney and Pearson 1983) and social discourse

(McKay 1996, 428), not on pen-in-hand or fingertip-on-the-keyboard writing as such. Moll and Dworin (1996), however, support "a focus on children's actions with literacy within the social contexts that constitute classroom life," arguing, "what goes on in classrooms, and why and how it takes place, count" (221–22). The scenes here count: these transcriptions are intended to give not an idealized view of biliteracy teaching and learning but rather a phenomenological one. As stated earlier, my classes read *Wiedersehen in Falun* in the last week of class and did not have time to do a follow-up writing activity. The lack of time for FL teaching in schools in the United States (the classes discussed in this chapter meet twice a week for 40 minutes) is unfortunate for more comprehensive biliteracy instruction. Vacca and Vacca (1997) point out:

> When reading and writing are taught in tandem, the union influences content learning in ways not possible when students read without writing or write without reading. When teachers invite a class to write before or after reading, they help students to use writing to think about what they will read and to explore and think more deeply about the ideas they have read. (282–83)

With more time, any of the writing exercises mentioned in Huck, Hepler, and Hickman's (1993) section "Writing from Children's Books" (794–811) would have been appropriate as extensions to the reading-as-composing scenes presented in this chapter. Additionally, students could produce their own written translations of this or another authentic picture book (Malloy 1998) and then workshop them, so they could experience the variety of meaning-making possibilities with cultural texts. Luther, in translating a major world text, had a finely developed sense for processing, both top-down (conceptually complex and sociopolitical understanding) and bottom-up (scrupulous microlevel accuracy). All 26 classroom scenes presented in this chapter demonstrate translating at these and many other levels of meaning on that continuum. Luther's understanding of translation as a procedural, collaborative, and time-consuming enterprise with a direct connection to spoken language is reflected in the unique microcosm of our 20th-century FL classroom interactions around text. I delineate here some of the context-specific aspects of FL classroom translating events as evident in my data.

1. Students want and need high-interest, sophisticated FL texts, such as picture books, which are not mastery level, to read beyond their FL textbook chapters.
2. Literacy approaches including translating during in-class reads are

viable ways to acquire FL, and they are fully linked to the immediacy skills.

3. Translating ("not a simple specialty") is a process that requires guiding, time on task, and opportunities to practice in the classroom during formal instruction.

4. During classroom events, much about the skill and art of translation itself can be established for when students later continue to produce and consume target-language and translated texts through a lifetime of FL use.

5. Translators use many literate resources, for example, glossaries and pictures, including visual literacy, to read FL text. Students need to be taught about them and how to use them.

6. Students work collaboratively with each other (fellow novices) and the teacher (helping expert) across many turns to arrive at viable renderings of FL text via the social construction of knowledge in a classroom.

7. Misconceptions and "trouble" in translating can be frustrating (as in scenes 5 and 16 in this chapter), but they can also provide learning opportunities as well as fun language play and positive interaction with others.

8. Students like Daniela (scene 10) and Uschi (scene 22) exhibit mature self-efficacy with FL text when they bid, take the floor, and offer fluent, accurate translations and interpretations.

9. Complex grammar and syntax (e.g., "They found the corpse of a young man," in scene 12) can be introduced early and meaningfully through translating events; such moments provide advanced organizers for when these structures are later formally taught.

10. Intertextuality (see references to prayers, *Der Erlkönig*, and the Morgenstern poem at scenes 17–19) is invoked and expanded to accomplish the work of translation.

11. Cultural knowledge (e.g., death personified [scene 19] or national and professional costumes [scene 15]) is constructed, and cultural acts are performed through the human activity of translation.

12. FL students expand both their literary knowledge for language arts classes and their subject-matter knowledge for other content areas (as in the scenes built around the vocabulary and concepts of "transitional sentence" [scene 23], "hermetically sealed" [scene 21], and life in a 19th-century mining village [scene 9]).

Coda: Pleasures of the Text

Luther ([1530] 1983) wrote:

> Denn ich habe deutsch . . . reden wollen, da ich mir beim übersetzen deutsch zu reden vorgenommen habe. [For I wanted to speak German, because I had set myself the goal—by translating—of speaking German.] (84)

My front-of-the-room view of my seated students during translating events is an invariably gratifying one. I see them engaged in German class and in understanding German as at no other time in our lessons. The students were especially mesmerized by this particular book because of its beautiful artwork, unusual cultural scenes, and serious treatment of the story. Most analyses of FL reading comprehension are completely absent of attention to students' desires with literacy and of how bright, capable middle schoolers appropriate text via formal instruction during a thematic unit. Throughout the events described here, I saw and heard how my students "wanted" this story, how interest in language and text like that of *Wiedersehen in Falun* legitimized their being in German class, cultivating their goodwill not only to the school subject but also to the people and culture the word *German* represents. They wanted, by translating, to speak with their FL learning peers about the story. During phase 3, on the last day of German for the year, I handed out a typed-up version of the story text, and the students then took over all the work of reading aloud and translating in German. "I had set myself the goal" of encouraging my middle schoolers to develop and pursue desires and needs with FL text and of showing them how to do it via our translating events.

References

Alvermann, D. E., and S. F. Phelps. 1998. *Content reading and literacy: Succeeding in today's diverse classrooms.* Boston: Allyn and Bacon.

Benjamin, W. 1961. Die Aufgabe des Ubersetzers. In *Illuminationen: Ausgewählte Schriften,* ed. S. Unself, 56–69. Frankfurt am Main: Suhrkamp Verlag.

Bernhardt, E. B. 1991. *Reading development in a second language: Theoretical, empirical, and classroom perspectives.* Norwood, NJ: Ablex.

Brooks, F. B. 1992. Can we talk? *Foreign Language Annals* 25:59–71.

Cook, G. 1998. Language teaching. In *Routledge encyclopedia of translation studies,* ed. M. Baker, 117–20. London: Routledge.

Dasenbrock, R. W. 1992. Teaching multicultural literature. In *Understanding others: Cultural and cross-cultural studies and the teaching of literature,* ed. J. Trimmer and T. Warnock, 35–46. Urbana, IL: National Council of Teachers of English.

Dingwaney, A., and C. Maier. 1992. Translation as a method for cross-cultural teaching. In *Understanding others: Cultural and cross-cultural studies and the teaching of literature,* ed. J. Trimmer and T. Warnock, 47–63. Urbana, IL: National Council of Teachers of English.

Hatch, E. 1992. *Discourse and language education.* Cambridge: Cambridge University Press.

Hirano, C. 1999. Eight ways to say *you:* The challenges of translation. *Horn Book* 75 (January–February):34–40.

Huck, C., S. Hepler, and J. Hickman. 1993. *Children's literature in the elementary school.* Fort Worth: Harcourt Brace College Publishers.

Hudelson, S. 1996. Literacy development of second language children. In *Educating second language children: The whole child, the whole curriculum, the whole community,* ed. F. Genesee, 129–58. Cambridge: Cambridge University Press.

Irvin, J. W. 1998. *Reading and the middle school student.* Needham Heights, MA: Allyn and Bacon.

Jörg, S. 1996. *Wiedersehen in Falun.* Illustrated by D. Winterhager. Stuttgart: Thienemann.

Lefevere, A. 1992. *Translating literature: Practice and theory in a comparative literature context.* New York: Modern Language Association of America.

Leinhardt, G. 1983. Routines in expert math teachers' thoughts and actions. Paper presented at the annual meeting of the American Educational Research Association, Montreal, April.

Luther, M. [1530] 1983. Sendbrief vom Dolmetschen. In *Luther Deutsch: Die Werke Martin Luthers in neuer Auswahl für die Gegenwart,* ed. K. Aland, 5:79–92. Göttingen: Van den Hoeck and Ruprecht.

Malloy, M. E. 1997. *Emergent biliteracy: A way to think about middle school foreign language learning and teaching.* Educational Reports, no. 29. Columbus, OH: Martha L. King Language and Literacy Center.

———. 1998. *German children's literature.* Cultural Mosaics, vol. 3. Columbus, OH: Martha L. King Language and Literacy Center.

———. 1999. "*Ein Riesen-Spaß!*" ("Great fun!"): Using authentic picture books to teach foreign language. *New Advocate* 12 (spring): 169–84.

McCarthy, M. 1991. *Discourse analysis for language teachers.* Cambridge: Cambridge University Press.

McKay, S. L. 1996. Literacy and literacies. In *Sociolinguistics and language teaching,* ed. S. L. McKay and N. H. Hornberger, 421–45. Cambridge: Cambridge University Press.

Meara, P. 1998. The classical research in L2 vocabulary acquisition. In *Words, words, words: The translator and the language learner,* ed. G. Anderman and M. Rogers, 27–40. Philadelphia: Multilingual Matters.

Miller, J. H. 1992. Translation as the double production of texts. In *Text and context: Cross-disciplinary perspectives on language study,* ed. C. Kramsch and S. McConnell-Ginet, 124–34. Lexington, MA: D. C. Heath and Company.

Moll, L. C., and J. E. Dworin. 1996. Biliteracy development in classrooms: Social dynamics and cultural possibilities. In *Discourse, learning, and schooling,* ed. D. Hicks, 221–46. Cambridge: Cambridge University Press.

Pappas, C. C. 1998. The role of genre in the psycholinguistic guessing game of reading. *Language Arts* 75:36–44.

Phillipson, R. 1992. *Linguistic imperialism.* Oxford: Oxford University Press.

Tierney, R. J., and P. D. Pearson. 1983. Toward a composing model of reading. *Language Arts* 60:568–80.

Tomlinson, C. M. 1998. *Children's books from other countries.* Lantham, MD: Scarecrow.

Vacca, R. T., and J. A. L. Vacca. 1997. *Content area reading.* New York: Harper-Collins College Publishers.

Chapter 6

Learning to Assume the Role of Author: A Study of Reading-to-Write One's Own Ideas in an Undergraduate ESL Composition Course

George E. Newell, Ohio State University; Maria C. Garriga, Thomas More College; and Susan S. Peterson, Veritas Christian School

Typically, undergraduate English as a second language (ESL) students are required to take one or two composition courses to fulfill graduation requirements. Such courses usually have two general goals: to support students in learning to become more fluent writers of English and, at least, to introduce them to the demands and conventions of academic writing. At times, ESL educators have looked to composition theory to conceptualize what it means to write successfully in the academy. For example, Bartholomae (1985) argues that native English-speaking students need to be socialized into the academic discourse community, which does not, as Rose (1989) has argued, easily welcome novices. Consequently, the need to "invent" the academy seems most evident in the academic experiences of ESL students who must "learn to speak as we do, to try on the peculiar ways of knowing, selecting, evaluating, reporting, concluding, and arguing that define the discourse of our (academic) community" (Bartholomae 1985, 134). However, with some scrutiny, the assumption that the goal of enabling ESL students to use academic "practice" to transform their knowledge and experience raises significant theoretical and pedagogical issues.

On the one hand, we wonder how, if at all, explicit teaching of rhetorical structures and strategies should be used to ensure that students are learning new academic genres—a concern reflected in debates outside the ESL community (Freedman 1993) as well as within it (Blanton 1994; Ellis

1990; Krashen 1984). On the other hand, how might writing instruction enable ESL students in creating and supporting their own visions and interpretations, which are necessary if they are going to contribute to academic discussions? These two orientations seem to suggest that formal, academic writing requiring discipline-specific knowledge represented in the impersonal, detached stance of published scholars is always distinguished from and exclusive of more personal ways of writing that rely on general knowledge that can be applied to any writing context. Rather than two distinct constructs, however, we believe that these orientations are best understood from a developmental perspective that assumes a reciprocal relationship between general and specific knowledge about writing. Accordingly, we are interested in the ways instruction may support ESL students as they read and then shape their own interpretations, using formal academic structures as they advance their own ideas. Specifically, to understand how students mediate and make sense of complex writing tasks, this chapter focuses on three ESL students' rhetorical practices as they construct their own analytic essays out of source texts or reading passages.

The three ESL students at the center of this study of authorship were asked on three separate occasions by their instructor to write analytically about informational and literary texts. Specifically, they were asked to read and respond to reading passages in order to evaluate the quality of arguments in a series of brief texts, to explain what they found significant in two short stories, and finally to read and write about a lengthy literary text in order to consider how they constructed textual meaning over a period of time. This way of sequencing reading-to-write assignments parallels those Bartholomae and Petrosky (1985) propose to "provide a method to enable students to see what they have said—to see and characterize the acts of reading and writing represented by their discourse" (7).

Theoretical Orientation

But how might we conceive of ESL undergraduate students as authors who are learning to position and reposition themselves in relation to a range of ideas and values? We believe that ESL students, like other beginning writers, can develop a sense of authorship of ideas and experiences as opposed to just writing to present what they have learned for evaluation. By "authorship" we mean the critical thinking skills that students use in their efforts to contribute to a conversation about ideas, texts, and experiences (Greene 1995). This requires that ESL students learn to synthesize information from a range of sources to represent a community of writers (the instructor and peers) and their abiding interests, concerns, and issues. Accordingly, source texts (reading passages) provide a means of support and elaboration as ESL students learn what other writers have said and then find something new to say. In this context, writing an effective essay requires not only that ESL students restructure information gleaned from a reading passage but that they do so within the bounds of acceptable academic discourse. This restructuring may include developing new organizational patterns not found in the source text or readings, appropriating ideas as evidence to support their own arguments, and making connective interpretations between their own knowledge and experience and the contents of the reading passage. In this chapter, representations of how the ESL students restructured information, ideas, and experiences from source texts to make them their "own" are captured with various text analytic methods. Such analyses allow us to show how the students of different writing backgrounds (successful or less successful) tended to construct different representations of meaning, which we describe using the different structuring principles they performed.

Although educators (e.g., Bartholomae 1985; Spack 1988) value students' abilities to analyze, synthesize, and integrate others' ideas with their own visions, few studies have looked closely at how ESL students organize their essays to advance their own ideas. Put another way, our work as writing instructors is to establish mediating links between what students bring to our academic community and what the academic community will ultimately expect of them. The ESL writing course in which three ESL students learned to write analytically about reading sought to provide what Spellmeyer (1989) calls "common ground" between the individual author and the academy. In writing such essays, argues Spellmeyer, ESL students make a "first step in . . . progress toward work that is more complex intellectually [and] more self-conscious stylistically" (274). Accordingly, we chose to study authorship in an ESL composition course that presented students with the challenge of moving from more familiar to more formal reading-to-write contexts, in a three-assignment sequence.

Three primary questions motivated this study of how ESL students integrate the ideas of others in writing analytically about text: (1) How did these students organize their essays? (2) What strategies did they use to advance their own ideas? and (3) What, if any, evidence can be provided that they internalized these academic practices across a 10-week course? Of interest are the rhetorical strategies and discourse structures students relied on in fulfilling these tasks. Although students may adopt a particular stance, conveying what might be considered their "own" ideas in authoring a text, the ideas they articulate are expressions of shared beliefs that are rooted in different contexts, including their own experiences outside of class and shared experiences within the instructional context. Accordingly, an additional concern shaping this study is the instructional context of the course. We also wondered how the instructor typically represented the task of writing the three essays based on different sources and how the instructor represented the process of writing in the classroom.

Context of the Study and Research Methods

Research Site and Participants

The study was conducted in two sections of an undergraduate ESL composition course, Advanced English as a Second Language, taught at a large state research university. The course is the second in a series of three required writing courses for nonnative undergraduate students. Most of the university's international students must take the program's sequence of courses unless they demonstrate that they should be exempted after taking a placement test.

At the time of the study, the course's main goals were to develop students' academic writing and reading abilities through instruction in rhetorical modes as well as through their reading of informational and literary texts. The first five weeks of the course were devoted to the introduction of rhetorical conventions (topic sentence, conclusion, thesis, etc.) and four rhetorical modes (exemplification, comparison and contrast, cause and effect, and classification). The second five weeks allowed students to apply the conventions and modes as they wrote analytically about texts—students were encouraged to organize their essays using one primary rhetorical mode per essay. To support the ESL students as they worked on outlines and drafts of their essays, the instructor held four individualized tutorials for each of the 32 students.

Students were required to write three major out-of-class essays, and these essays were the primary focus of this study. Each was a response to an assigned text. Essay 1 required the students to respond to a newspaper essay by Wendell Berry (1990a) entitled "Against PCs: Why I'm Not Going to Buy a Computer," two letters (Inkeles 1990; Koosman 1990) written in response to Berry's essay, and Berry's (1990b) rejoinder. Essay 2 was a response to either "Reflections of a Seventeen-Year-Old" by Sylvia Plath

(1990) or "Child of the Dark: The Diary of Carolina Maria de Jesus" (de Jesus 1990, translated by David St. Clair). Here students were encouraged to do a comparison-and-contrast paper. Finally, essay 3 was based on the short story "To Room Nineteen" by Doris Lessing (1963). Given the length (35 pages) of the story, students were assigned the story in six segments and then given a series of choices as to how they might write about their responses.

The primary participants in the study included the writing instructor, who was a second-year doctoral student in foreign language education at the time of the study, and three students enrolled in the course. Based on instructor recommendations, writing ability, and willingness of the students to be interviewed, we selected three students from the two sections as illustrative case studies. Sung-Ho (a less successful writer) was a 24-year-old Korean student majoring in journalism, who began the study with only the vaguest notions of formal, academic writing. He reported (in an interview) that he had little experience with such writing prior to the start of his undergraduate work but wanted to improve quickly due to the demands of his major. Yucuanto (a successful writer), a 21-year-old Indonesian student majoring in electrical engineering, brought with him a great deal more knowledge and experience with formal writing than the other case study students. He had a clearer sense of the connection between the use of rhetorical conventions and the readability of his formal essays. Finally, Kamran (a less successful writer) was a 20-year-old Pakistani student majoring in marketing. His prior experience was limited to "personal writing about me," as he stated in an interview. He often attempted to integrate his own experiences into his essay writing, leading to a fluency unlike the other two case study students. On more than one occasion, however, Kamran's efforts to shift from his well-elaborated personal explorations of "what happened" to more analytic writing requiring explanations and reasons caused him to struggle with a more focused attention on the topic. Throughout the course, he sought ways to construct top-down (thesis and support) essays to present his ideas more coherently.

Design

Twice a week throughout the 10-week course, we observed at least two class meetings of the instructor's two sections of an undergraduate ESL composition course, taking field notes and tabulating the number of times various instructional activities occurred. These observations enabled us to draw a portrait of the instructional contexts, including the way assign-ments were made and how students' efforts were supported. The instruc-tor was interviewed on two occasions, once at the beginning of the study, to understand her instructional goals, and again at the end of the study, to debrief her on the students' progress. We also conducted retrospective interviews of three case study students to explore their interpretations of each of the three assignments and the instructional activities. As they completed each writing assignment, the case study students met with coinvestigators outside of class to answer questions for the interviews. They were asked questions about the task, about how they began writing, about what they did as they wrote the essay, about their reactions to their completed essays, and about their perceptions of the instructional support for each essay assignment. These sessions were audiotaped and tran-scribed for later analysis. In addition, we also collected data from all 32 students in the two sections: background and writing questionnaires and all drafts of each writing assignment for all 32 students. However, for pur-poses of this chapter, we will focus only on a brief description of the instructional context and various analyses of three analytic essays written by each of the three case study students.

Essay Analysis

For the analysis of the three case study students' writing, we used the three papers written by each student during the quarter. Although these papers are a small sample of the full class, the instructor felt them to be representative of the successful and less successful performances of all 32 students. Three separate analyses were conducted on the nine essays writ-ten by the three case study students to examine how they organized their ideas and the strategies they used to advance their own ideas. All of the essays were analyzed to reveal the underlying logic, or frame, shaping a given essay, with each essay subjected to (1) an analysis of the types of issues and claims (Herrington 1988) that represent lines of reasoning the case study students included in their essays; (2) an examination of level of abstractness (Durst 1987); and (3) a measure of the hierarchical organiza-tion of the content at two levels (Meyer 1985).

Lines of Reasoning

To analyze lines of reasoning the ESL students employed, we examined the issues and claims appearing in nine essays. For the initial analysis of types of issues, "issue" was defined broadly as the primary problem, question, or concern that the paper tries to address. We identified issues in all papers by a critical analysis of the essays' introductory sections (Herrington 1988).

"Claims" were defined using Toulmin, Rieke, and Janik's (1979) definition: "assertions put forth with the implication that there are underlying 'good reasons' that could show them to be 'well founded'" (29). For purposes of this chapter, we identified only the major claims, which were most often included in the "thesis statements" in the essays. In doing so we were able to examine the interpretive inferences about the source texts that the students were to read and respond to in the three writing assignments. After one analyst completed the analysis, a second analyst checked it. Disagreements about the analyses were resolved through discussion.

Level of Abstractness

Analyzing level of abstractness involved holistic coding of each essay for the degree to which the writer was able to move beyond a summary of the reading passage to develop a focus and a coherent analysis and interpretation. The analysis has three categories in ascending order of abstractness.

1. *Thesis and summary restatement*—an essay that begins with a thesis statement but reverts to a restating of the reading passage with little attempt to argue and present evidence for the thesis
2. *Unfocused analysis*—an essay that includes a thesis but the body of the essay contains a series of points or minor claims strung together without explicitly supporting, elaborating, or connecting them
3. *Focused analysis*—an essay that moves away from a restating of plot and/or ideas from the reading passages to form a thesis statement (e.g., claim or generalization) that is clearly supported with and argued for using textual evidence and/or personal experience

After one rater coded the essays for levels of abstraction, the entire set was coded again by a second rater. Differences between raters were resolved through discussion.

Hierarchical Organization of Content

Each of the essays was examined for hierarchical structuring of information using a procedure based on Meyer 1985 and modified by Langer 1986 and Durst 1987. This analysis represents essay content in a tree diagram of text organization. Interpropositional relationships are governed by rhetorical predicates that specify superordinate and subordinate relationships among the propositions. The text is first divided into T-units (Hunt 1977), then each T-unit is coded as representing a particular type of rhetorical predicate, the categories for which follow.

1. *Evaluation*—an opinion or commentary statement
2. *Sequence*—steps, episodes, and events ordered chronologically at equal levels in the passage hierarchy. Summaries of content from the reading passages were also included in this category.
3. *Causal*—both cause and effect specified at equal levels in the hierarchy
4. *Description*—various kinds of illustrations, such as manner, attribution, setting, and identification
5. *Explanation*—causal statements, lower in the hierarchy than the event being explained
6. *Evidence*—a statement supporting a previous point
7. *Alternative*—two or more equally weighted views or options compared and contrasted

The Meyer system differentiates between top-level, superordinate predicates, around which the entire text may be organized, and lower-level predicates (e.g., "explanation" and "evidence"), which elaborate on previous points. "Collection" was treated as an optional grouping of any category. Thus, a "cause" could have a collection of "effects," an effect a collection of causes. Because we were interested in only the overall structure of the essays, only the top two levels of the essays' content hierarchies were examined—a level consists of all predicates and embedded points from the essay occurring at the same point in the hierarchy.

These analyses were completed by one analyst, and the top-level and second-level structures were checked by a second analyst. Differences between analyses were resolved through discussion.

Results and Discussion

The Instructional Contexts for Analytic Writing

In this section, we examine the teaching of analytic writing in the two ESL classrooms, focusing on how the instructor supported the students in developing their own stances toward and responses to the reading. To teach students to write analytically requires the introduction of the ground rules (Sheeran and Barnes 1991) for arguing and reasoning, especially in the case of undergraduate ESL students, who are sometimes new to the demands of formal, analytic, academic writing. Accordingly, the instructor first introduced the rhetorical conventions (e.g., thesis statement, supporting evidence, etc.) early in the quarter and then presented a series of lessons on the four rhetorical modes (exemplification, comparison and contrast, cause and effect, and classification). Many of these lessons involved analysis and discussion of sample essays taken from instructional materials. The rhetorical conventions and the modes played a bigger role in instruction early in the quarter as compared to later in the quarter, when students were expected to have internalized some of the ground rules and strategies for analytic writing. At that point, the instructor focused more on the content and ideas in the students' writing, spending more class time on discussing the reading passages and on teaching analytic strategies through such activities as instructor-guided peer review of student writing and in-class writing and evaluation of "mini-essays" (Peterson 1996). This sequencing not only introduced the ESL students to strategies for presenting their ideas but also provided them with a set of choices as they became progressively more independent writers.

To enable the students to experiment with new forms and to practice a range of writing techniques (various ways of selecting topic sentences, making word choices, and developing style) without the fear of failure, the instructor assigned "mini-essays" (small paragraphs that follow the outline of a particular rhetorical mode). The inclusion of the mini-essays provided students with the opportunity to practice their writing in a more controlled environment, and students enjoyed writing them: one student reported in an interview, "I like the mini-essay because I can practice without taking a lot of time, and I can see results quickly." In addition, the mini-essays were also designed to make students feel comfortable about their writing. As Yucuanto commented, "[writing a mini-essay] gives me an opportunity to practice all in a small paragraph." That students were encouraged to develop their own ideas in writing without concerns for instructor grading fostered a sense of experimentation—the students were able to learn conventions for analytic writing before being assigned the more formal essays that were evaluated. In this way, the instructor was able to create a context in which students felt they could learn new strategies that they could then apply to the formal writing assignments.

How the ESL Students Articulated Their Own Responses to the Reading Passages

If we are to understand how ESL students internalize the ways of knowing that they encounter both from the social context of the classroom and from their own reading, we need to listen carefully to their ideas and to follow their ways of reasoning about and with those ideas.

Lines of Reasoning

The lines of reasoning used in the nine analytic essays by the three case study students reflect not only the issues addressed in their thesis statements but also the students' approaches to those issues. As we noted earlier, one of the instructor's goals was to enable the students to move beyond summaries of concrete information in the readings to the development of a framework to analyze and explain what the students construed as the meaning of the reading passages. Accordingly, she used the mini-essays, class discussions of the rhetorical conventions, and the readings to support students in developing their own approaches to issues articulated in the three essay assignments.

Although the students were encouraged to write about their responses to the reading passages, the issues actually addressed in the nine student essays we analyzed corresponded closely to those suggested in the essay assignments. All three essays from assignment 1 considered both Wendell Berry's intentions in his essay "Against PCs" and the validity of the criticisms of those intentions presented in the two letters written in response to the essay. For example, the thesis statement from one student's essay states, "But the purpose of Berry's essay is not to force a person not to use a computer but he and his wife only express their lifestyles. Therefore, both of them who wrote a letter misunderstood the idea of Wendell Berry's essay." For essay 2, the three case study students employ comparison and contrast—a strategy suggested by the assignment—either comparing their own lives with that of one of the authors or comparing the lives of the two authors. Finally, for essay 3, again following a strategy reflected in the essay assignment, the three students attempt to interpret the motives of Susan, the central character in "To Room Nineteen," as she sinks more deeply into mental depression and self-destruction.

Although each case study student's set of three essays includes issues referred to in the respective essay assignment, there was a great deal of variation in approaches to the issues. These variations reflect not only individual interests but also differences between Yucuanto, the more successful student writer, and Sung-Ho and Kamran, the less successful student writers. In general, Yucuanto's essays are more clearly focused on a specific issue: "Compared with Sylvia [Plath], my seventeen-year-old moment was better than that of Sylvia"; and his essays were more exploratory, taking him into more substantial analysis: "However, after Matthew told Susan that he cheated with other women, the great situation they had before no longer maintained. Since that moment, Susan, the main character in the story, changed drastically; and it caused my reactions toward her to change also." In fact, Yucuanto's essay 3 accomplishes three things that are largely absent from his other two essays: (1) it focuses not only on the relationship between two characters but on that between the reader and one of the characters; (2) it focuses on some dissonance that he sensed: "How could such an intelligent woman make such a tragic mistake"; and (3) it explores aspects of the literary work in some depth. This last point requires some explanation.

In most of the essays, the other two case study students were more inclined to focus on issues in a rather simplistic way. For example, one essay begins, "Regarding the lives of both ladies, Sylvia Plath as compared to Dona Carolina had a splendid and enjoyable life," lists elements of the two women's lives, and concludes, "Sylvia Plath had it easier than Donna Carolina." However, to some extent in essay 1 and more clearly in essay 3, Yucuanto tries to examine issues from more than one vantage point. In essay 1 he attempts to answer three questions about Wendell Berry's argument in "Against PCs," but in doing so he fails to find a central issue to pursue, which leads to an elaborated but largely incoherent essay. However, in essay 3, which he completed several weeks later, he includes two interrelated claims, each with a personal response tagged on: (1) " 'To Room Nineteen' is about a failure of intelligence but how could such an intelligent person [Susan] make such a mistake"; and (2) "As Susan changed so did my feelings for her." He concludes his essay not with a more typical generalization about the character's behavior but with a question: "Why did she not use her intelligence and think more to solve her problem instead of doing something stupid? I am confused by this kind of behavior."

In contrast to these more successful efforts, the essays of the less successful students did not always focus on issues that would lead them to integrate their interpretations. For the most part, they seemed bound to a

"What is x?" question that tied them to restating, describing, or summarizing the content of the reading passage. For example, one essay of a less successful student compares the life of Sylvia Plath with his own life; one paragraph focuses on a discussion of Plath's anxieties, and another paragraph focuses on the more positive experiences of the student writer. The essay concludes, "In fact, everyone has a different way of life because it is impossible for people to have the same experiences"—ignoring reasons why Plath's life was so unhappy and what the student had learned through his comparisons.

Rather than a criticism of the instructor or the students, our comments here suggest some of the complexities and nuances students must come to terms with when learning to authorize their own ideas. Of course, one of the most significant demands of such writing is the development of a coherent presentation of one's analysis. How the students dealt with this challenge is examined in the next two sections.

Level of Abstraction

Coding the essays for level of abstraction reflects the position each essay occupies on an abstractive scale ranging from the retelling or summarizing of events, steps, or ideas to interpretation of content. We expected all of the analytic essays to be categorized as either "focused" or "unfocused" interpretations; however, our analysis led us to the development of a new category, "thesis and summary restatement."

Table 1 reveals that Sung-Ho and Yucuanto began by writing essays that included a thesis statement but then reverted to a summary of the reading passage. Kamran's essay 1 was more analytic yet not consistently so—his analysis shifted abruptly from an evaluation of Berry's attitude toward his wife to the benefits of the personal computer. The effects of instruction become more evident in the second set of essays, especially for Yucuanto, the more successful writer, who moved beyond summarizing to a focused interpretation more quickly than did his less successful peers. By essay 3 and the end of the quarter, all three student writers were able to produce analytic essays, although only one of the three final essays was a "focused analysis" that provided an explanation for a thesis statement. That four of the total nine essays were more summary than analysis is consistent with findings from earlier studies of analytic writing (Applebee, Durst, and Newell 1984; Durst 1987) that found that less successful L1 student writers often fell back on summary or description of content. However, we believe that the type of instructional activities the case study students encountered enabled them to develop new analytic strategies for authorizing their own interpretations as they moved to the second and third writing assignments.

To examine the kind of effects the instruction had on the students' efforts to learn to analyze texts leading to authorization of their own ideas, we can consider Sung-Ho's first essay and the progress he made toward analysis in his third essay. Recall that "thesis and summary restatement" differs from "focused analysis" in that the latter contains an overarching generalization or a statement that moves beyond the events or ideas in the reading passage to develop support, evidence, and examples for the thesis. "Thesis and summary restatement" offers a thesis but little support, shifting instead to a summary of the reading passage or to a series of generalizations unconnected to the thesis.

In his first essay, Sung-Ho presents a thesis (both letter writers misunderstood Berry's intention), but rather than pursuing his interpretation, he summarizes the content of the two letters: "They wrote about writers who usually try to use a computer for editing and correcting words." He wanders from the focus of his essay (how and why the two letter writers misunderstood Berry's intention) to unpacking the content of the letters in a lengthy summary.

In contrast, in his essay at the end of the quarter, Sung-Ho is able to successfully explain why Susan, the central character in "To Room Nineteen," feels alone.

> This story made me rethink this choice. She [Susan] started to feel alone because she does not know what she wants or how to enjoy her life.
>
> Susan, the main character, started to feel alone because she did not know what she wanted anymore. When her kids started to go to school, she had a lot of time. However, she did not know what to do with free time. She kept herself busy, working for no reason.

TABLE 1.   Levels of Abstractness in Student Essays

Student	Essay 1	Essay 2	Essay 3
Sung-Ho (less successful)	Thesis and Summary Restatement	Thesis and Summary Restatement	Focused Analysis
Yucuanto (successful)	Thesis and Summary Restatement	Focused Analysis	Unfocused Analysis
Kamran (less successful)	Unfocused Analysis	Unfocused Analysis	Unfocused Analysis

In this essay, Sung-Ho establishes a general thesis ("This story made me rethink this choice [between career and family]") offering two explanations for the character's loneliness, a thesis that contains his own opinions about and responses to the story. He then cites specific examples from the story, but he also makes a clear connection between the example and his thesis: "Throughout this event she started to realize that she feels alone." Put another way, he has shifted comfortably between generalization and supporting details, a strategy he had only a superficial understanding of when he composed his first essay earlier in the quarter. As will be seen in our examination of the organizational features of the essays, across the quarter all three case study students broadened their notions of how to analyze and interpret the reading passages and thus began to make sense of the information in the passages rather than summarizing them.

Hierarchical Organization of Content

Seven types of organizing predicates were identified as comprising the top two levels of the students' essays—evaluation, sequence, causal, description, explanation, evidence, and alternative. The higher-level structures employed in this study represent the superordinate content structures that give shape to the essays as a whole. We anticipated that the essay assignment for the three essays and the nature of the writing instruction would lead to the inclusion of thesis statements to organize the top structure. Table 2 contains the results for the higher level of the content hierarchy for the students' nine analytic essays.

As we expected, the essays were organized primarily around three types of thesis statements: evaluation for essay 1, alternative (comparison and contrast) for essay 2, and causal (cause and effect) for essay 3. Kamran's essay on "To Room Nineteen" was one exception for assignment 3—his essay offered an opinion that described Susan's fall into despair as

TABLE 2.   Use of Top Level Predicates, by Student

	Essay 1			Essay 2			Essay 3		
	S-H	Y	K	S-H	Y	K	S-H	Y	K
Predicates									
Evaluation	X	X	X						X
Sequence									
Causal							X	X	
Description									
Alternative				X	X	X			

indicative of "abnormal thoughts." These patterns are depicted in the following example thesis statements taken from each of Yucuanto's essays.

Essay 1: Evaluation
"In his essay 'Against PCs,' Berry acts as if he takes advantage of his wife."

Essay 2: Alternative
"Compared with Sylvia [Plath], my seventeen-year-old moment was better than that of Sylvia."

Essay 3: Causal
"Since that moment, Susan, the main character in the story, changed drastically; and it caused my reactions toward her to change also."

Each statement requires a different kind of supporting evidence: the first requires evidence from the reading passage alone, the second from the reading passage and the student writer's own experiences, and the third from a more tightly integrated use of text-based and reader-based evidence. These patterns are indicative of what we found in all three students' essays: (a) across the quarter, the instruction supported the students' explorations of the reading passages in a variety of ways, allowing them to articulate their own responses to and positions about the essay and short stories; (b) the second-level structures contained a wide range of both text-based and reader-based supporting evidence; and (c) development in analysis for these students consisted of a coherent integration of various kinds of evidence.

The second-level predicates can represent, in a thesis/support essay, the main points supporting the thesis as included in the introductory paragraph and in other parts of the essay. Table 3 includes the number of second-level predicates (evaluation, sequence, description, explanation, evidence, alternative) for each case study student for each of the three essays. Across the three essays, there are two interesting changes in the type of supporting evidence the students employed as they attempted to argue for their thesis statements. First, in essay 1, the students used twice as many summary restatements of the reading passages (4 sequential and 8 description statements) than statements of analytic evidence (1 evaluation, 1 explanation, and 4 evidence statements) for their theses, with an accompanying shift in essay 3 toward less description (6 statements) and sequencing (1 statement) and toward more analysis (1 evaluation, 5 explanation, and 4 evidence statements). Second, across all three sets of essays, there was a gradual increase of analytic statements (evaluation, evidence, and explanation) and a gradual decrease of summary statements (description and sequence).

These patterns found in the essays written earlier in the quarter and near the end of the quarter are here described using excerpts from Sung-Ho's writing, accompanied by tree diagrams depicting the top two levels of the essays' hierarchies. The first example is from Sung-Ho's essay on Wendell Berry's "Against PCs," while the second is from his essay on "To Room Nineteen." Numbers in brackets signify the positions the T-units occupy in the content hierarchies as diagrammed in figure 1.

Sung-Ho's Essay 1: Top Two Levels of the Hierarchy

It is certain that using a computer does not always satisfy everyone. [1] But the purpose of Berry's essay is not to force a person not to use a computer but he and his wife only express their lifestyles. [2] Therefore, both of them who wrote a letter misunderstood the true idea of Wendell Berry's Essay. [3]

Both of them who wrote against Berry's essay were only talking about the advantages of using a computer. [4] They wrote about writers who usually try to use a computer for editing and correcting words. [5] So Inkeles wrote, that "Berry's wife is cheap" [6] and Koosman has also a similar opinion. [7] The two letters did not mention the disadvantages of the computer. [8] For example, Berry concentrated only on a computer. [9]

Sung-Ho's Essay 3: Top Two Levels of the Hierarchy

This story tells about typical middle aged and married women in most of our society. [1] Like this modern character, Susan, many young couples fall in love while they have their careers. [2] When they get married and have a child, women usually sacrifice their careers over family. [3] This story made me rethink this choice. [4] She [Susan] started to feel alone because she does not know what she wants or how to enjoy her life. [5]

Susan the main character started to feel alone because she did not know what she wanted anymore. [6] When her kids started to go to school, she had

TABLE 3.   Rhetorical Predicates in Second Level of Content Hierarchy, by Student

	Number of Predicates									
	Essay 1			Essay 2			Essay 3			All Essays
	S-H	Y	K	S-H	Y	K	S-H	Y	K	N = 9
Predicates										
Evaluation	0	0	1	0	0	0	1	0	0	2
Sequence	2	2	0	0	1	0	0	1	0	6
Description	1	2	5	5	2	1	1	2	3	22
Explanation	1	0	0	2	1	0	4	1	0	9
Evidence	2	2	0	0	2	0	0	2	2	10
Alternative	0	0	0	0	0	3	0	0	0	3

a lot of time. [7] However, she did not know what to do with free time. [8] She kept herself busy, working for no reason. [9]

Another reason Susan feels alone is that she did not know how to enjoy her life. [10] She believed that staying away from her family and having her own time was going to make her feel better. [11] So she decided to have her own space which was a Mother's room. [12] This made her more lonely. [13]

In figure 1, we see that in Sung-Ho's essay 1, he first describes the background of the reading passage, but rather than going on to offer evidence or explanatory remarks for his thesis, he then summarizes the content of the two letters that comment on Berry's essay. Later in his essay, Sung-Ho does cite some evidence for his thesis, but this seems added on rather than central to his analysis. In his essay 3 (fig. 2), Sung-Ho demonstrates a stronger understanding of analytic writing as authorizing his own ideas—he offers some background to the short story and for his essay, then contributes a personal evaluation of his thesis, moving then toward elaborated explanations of the two major features of his thesis. He develops these explanations by relying on textual evidence from the story, citing the main character's behavior, and then commenting on how it is connected to his main argument or thesis. Our analysis demonstrates that from essay 1 to essay 3, Sung-Ho was beginning to perform different transformations in his responses to the reading passages. In particular, he used different principles to restructure ideas from the reading passages, a pattern that was evident in the essays of all three case study students across the quarter.

	Evaluation [3]	
Description (Collection) [1] [2]	Sequence (Collection) [4] [5] [6] [7]	Evidence (Collection) [8] [9]

Fig. 1. Content organization for Sung Ho's essay 1

	Causal [5]		
Description (Collection) [1] [2] [3]	Evaluation [4]	Explanation (Collection) [6] [7] [8] [9]	Explanation (Collection) [10] [11] [12] [13]

Fig. 2. Content organization for Sung-Ho's essay 3

Conclusions

The central issue shaping this study was how ESL undergraduate students learned to authorize their critical responses to texts. We considered how they organized their essays, what strategies they used to advance their own ideas, and what evidence might be provided that they internalized academic practices across a 10-week course. First, the study of a small group of ESL students provided a way to look at their intellectual activities through the lenses of three different essay analyses. It was important to also study students' writing within the somewhat naturalistic contexts in which the students' essays were very much part of the goals of the course they took. Accordingly, we are able to get one more glimpse into the special nature of school settings and their influences on students' writing. A key point is that students' interpretations of the three writing assignments as represented in the essay analyses suggest the slow, deliberate, and constructive nature of writing development. Regardless of their earlier achievements as writers (successful vs. less successful), students relied on their previous understandings of analytic writing and on the cues of the immediate classroom setting to use different sources of information in creating their own texts.

Second, the course seemed to provide students with the means both to explore their own literary responses to the readings and to begin to employ more formal academic thinking and reasoning strategies. This is especially useful knowledge given the long-standing debates regarding the role of personal writing in the development of academic writing abilities. Specifically, the ESL students' writing became progressively more elaborated as they turned their attention to analysis of the readings, to their responses to those readings, and then to the representation of those responses within the formal organization of academic essays. Such development seems likely within a supportive instructional context that provides students with the means of enlarging their current understandings of what it means to write analytically in the academy.

Implications for Teaching and Research

Because this study focused on a small number of students in one ESL composition program, it is inappropriate to use it to suggest far-reaching recommendations for teaching. However, several issues raised by the study merit consideration by instructors and writing curriculum specialists. Our analyses of the essays suggest that Hillocks's (1995) argument about the value of direct instruction, at least in terms of specifying goals and criteria for success, is worth further consideration—the students should be taught what counts as effective writing within the context of the course. Therefore, ESL writing instruction probably should include rhetorical patterns and organizational schemes to teach students strategic use of structural knowledge, especially if we are to enlarge their repertoire of strategies to enable them to negotiate complex reading-writing tasks. Note, however, that we are not suggesting a return to traditional practices. If ESL students are to make contributions as authors, we must help them to weigh options when setting goals, to use strategies appropriately and flexibly, and to monitor the appropriateness of their choices and decisions.

As part of their response and analysis, the students in our study may have benefited from more opportunities to discuss and explore the literary texts with the instructor and with one another. Given the rather full agenda of the course, there was not much class time given to interpretation and analysis of the literary texts beyond occasional checks on students' understanding of the plot and characters in the narratives. Concerns over ESL students' "literal" text comprehension can result in less time for discussion of issues concerning deeper, more interpretive responses. Because students learn analysis through discussion as well as through writing, we recommend that instructors experiment with more time for discussions of literature, the results of which may be more engaging essays. Here, too, new strategies are necessary. For example, ESL students should know how to develop a scholarly project by placing their ideas amid what other authors have said and by justifying their decisions in determining what is important.

Much work remains if the ESL profession is to have a fuller understanding of what works in teaching analytic writing in ESL composition courses and of how, if at all, such writing skills are applied in other writing contexts. Future efforts should include a larger sample of ESL students of both genders and a consideration of the cultural backgrounds and the school writing experiences that they bring to various instructional contexts. Moreover, we would like to see more studies that connect process and product. For example, we think a significant line of research would include an examination of the effects of a wide variety of instructional contexts on the development of ESL students' writing and reasoning: How do certain instructional practices shape students' ways of composing, or, more specifically, what are the effects of instruction on students' utilization of structural knowledge for authorizing their own ideas? How do instructors' uses of terminology for analytic writing—terms reflecting a description of structure (e.g., topic sentence) versus terms reflecting an interpretation of the content (e.g., claims)—influence how students make procedural decisions during the act of composing? Relying on recent studies in contrastive rhetoric (e.g., Connor and Kaplan 1987), ESL composition research might study how an instructor's awareness of students' growing structural and conceptual knowledge for analytic writing shapes his or her instructional decisions as new and more demanding reading and writing tasks are introduced. During our study, for example, we recognized the potential benefit of knowing how ESL students from a wide array of cultural and national settings translate their own structural knowledge about academic writing into successful ways of writing in the American university.

Finally, an issue that we have discussed among ourselves many times since the outset of this study is the appropriate mix of instruction focused directly on prescribed forms of organization, such as thesis and support, and instruction that provides ESL students with the opportunity to construct their own interpretations of the topics that, in turn, become the focus of their writing assignments. The instructor we studied tried to develop a creative blend of the two, yet the major emphasis of the course was clearly on the structure of the analytic essay rather than on literary understanding and interpretation. Indeed, like freshman composition courses, the very point of most ESL composition courses is to teach student writers not how to write in a specific academic area, such as literary studies, but more general principles of analytic inquiry and argumentation that may be applied in a range of academic contexts.

In a collection of essays edited by Petraglia (1995), the contributors debate the adequacy of instruction in general writing skills. For example, Russell (1995) argues that because such courses have no specific content, they create an ambiguity of purpose: "There is no autonomous, generalizable skill or set of skills called 'writing' that can be learned and then applied to all genres or activities" (59). If this argument is correct, how, if at all, do ESL students apply general writing skills to writing in various disciplines? We do not necessarily believe, as Russell does, that instruction in general writing skills has no place in undergraduate ESL composition courses, but we need more studies like Leki 1995 and Spack 1997 that trace the development of ESL student writers from their experiences in general composition courses into their endeavors with the discipline-specific writing courses that are now becoming part of university requirements. The questions and issues addressed in this chapter suggest future endeavors as we explore ways of supporting ESL students in learning to read and write analytically in the American university.

References

Applebee, A. N., R. K. Durst, and G. E. Newell. 1984. The demands of school writing. In *Contexts for learning to write: Studies of secondary school instruction*, ed. A. N. Applebee, 55–77. Norwood, NJ: Ablex.

Bartholomae, D. 1985. Inventing the university. In *Writer's block: The cognitive dimension*, ed. M. Rose, 134–65. Carbondale: Southern Illinois University Press.

Bartholomae, D., and A. Petrosky. 1985. *Facts, artifacts, and counterfacts: Theory and method for a reading and writing course.* Portsmouth, NH: Boynton/Cook.

Berry, W. 1990a. Against PCs: Why I'm not going to buy a computer. In *Changes: Readings for ESL writers*, ed. J. Withrow, G. Brookes, and M. C. Cummings, 179–81. New York: St. Martin's.

———. 1990b. Wendell Berry replies. In *Changes: Readings for ESL writers*, ed. J. Withrow, G. Brookes, and M. C. Cummings, 188. New York: St. Martin's.

Blanton, L. 1994. Discourse, artifacts, and the Ozarks: Understanding academic literacy. *Journal of Second Language Writing* 3:1–16.

Connor, U., and R. R. Kaplan. 1987. *Writing across languages: Analysis of L2 texts.* Reading, MA: Addison-Wesley.

de Jesus, C. M. 1990. Child of the dark: The Diary of Carolina Maria de Jesus. Trans. D. St. Clair. In *Changes: Readings for ESL writers*, ed. J. Withrow, G. Brookes, and M. C. Cummings, 132–35. New York: St. Martin's.

Durst, R. 1987. Cognitive and linguistic demands of analytic writing. *Research in the Teaching of English* 21:347–76.

Ellis, R. 1990. *Instructed second language acquisition: Learning in the classroom.* Oxford: Blackwell.

Freedman, A. 1993. Show and tell? The role of explicit teaching in the learning of new genres. *Research in the Teaching of English* 27:222–51.

Greene, S. 1995. Making sense of my own ideas: The problems of authorship in a beginning writing course. *Written Communication* 12:186–218.

Herrington, A. 1988. Teaching, writing, and learning: A naturalistic study of writing in an undergraduate literature course. In *Advances in writing research*, vol. 2, *Writing in the academic disciplines*, ed. D. A. Jolliffe, 133–66. Norwood, NJ: Ablex.

Hillocks, G., Jr. 1995. *Teaching writing as reflective practice.* New York: Teachers College Press.

Hunt, K. W. 1977. Early blooming and late-blooming syntactic structures. In *Evaluating writing*, ed. C. R. Cooper and L. Odell, 91–104. Urbana, IL: National Council of Teachers of English.

Inkeles, G. 1990. Letters. In *Changes: Readings for ESL writers,* ed. J. Withrow, G. Brookes, and M. C. Cummings, 182. New York: St. Martin's.

Koosman, T. 1990. Letters. In *Changes: Readings for ESL writers,* ed. J. Withrow, G. Brookes, and M. C. Cummings, 182–83. New York: St. Martin's.

Krashen, S. D. 1984. *Writing: Research, theory, and applications.* Oxford: Pergamon.

Langer, J. A. 1986. *Children reading and writing: Structures and strategies.* Norwood, NJ: Ablex.

Leki, I. 1995. Coping strategies of ESL students in writing tasks across the curriculum. *TESOL Quarterly* 29:235–60.

Lessing, D. M. 1963. To room nineteen. In *A man and two women,* 253–88. London: MacGibbon and Lee.

Meyer, B. F. 1985. Prose analysis: Procedures, purposes, and problems. In *Understanding expository text,* ed. B. K. Britton and J. B. Black, 11–64. Hillsdale, NJ: Lawrence Erlbaum.

Peterson, S. 1996. Maximizing class time with the mini essay. *Ohio TESOL Newsletter* 20, no. 3:10–11, 21.

Petraglia, J., ed. 1995. *Reconceiving writing, rethinking writing instruction.* Mawhah, NJ: Lawrence Erlbaum.

Plath, S. 1990. Reflections of a seventeen-year-old. In *Changes: Readings for ESL writers,* ed. J. Withrow, G. Brookes, and M. C. Cummings, 123–25. New York: St. Martin's.

Rose, M. 1989. *Lives on the boundary.* New York: Penguin.

Russell, D. 1995. Activity theory and its implications for writing instruction. In *Reconceiving writing, rethinking writing instruction,* ed. J. Petraglia, 51–78. Mahwah, NJ: Lawrence Erlbaum.

Sheeran, Y., and D. Barnes. 1991. *School writing: Discovering the ground rules.* Philadelphia: Open University Press.

Spack, R. 1988. Initiating ESL students into the academic discourse community: How far should we go? *TESOL Quarterly* 22:29–51.

———. 1997. The acquisition of academic literacy in a second language: A longitudinal case study. *Written Communication* 14:3–62.

Spellmeyer, K. 1989. A common ground: The essay in the academy. *College English* 51:262–76.

Toulmin, S., R. Rieke, and A. Janik. 1979. *An introduction to reasoning.* New York: Macmillan.

Chapter 7

A Cognitive Modeling Approach to Teaching Critique Writing to Nonnative Speakers

Barbara Dobson and Christine Feak,
University of Michigan

Among the many different types of writing assignments that undergraduates must do, the critique is quite common. In this assignment, students must read and then respond critically to a written text, which may be either literary or nonliterary. Writing a critique of a nonliterary text, the focus of this chapter, is described by Mathison (1996, 315) as an "important literate activity across all disciplines" in which students are expected to read a disciplinary text evaluatively to develop and support their own position on it.

One reason this quintessential reading-to-write assignment is so widespread may be that a well-written critique provides instructors evidence that a student has engaged the critical thinking skills that are so highly valued[1] in the academy in North America (Shepelak, Curry-Jackson, and Moore 1992). According to current formulations of the construct, critical thinking is a two-stage process (ibid.). The first stage, *critical reasoning*, requires one to understand a text well enough to assess it. The second stage, *creative reasoning*, requires one to create a new, logically defensible text, whether oral or written, related to the original one. In short, critical thinking means more than simply comprehending a text well enough to summarize it or agree or disagree with it. It requires, to use Bereiter and Scardamalia's terms (1987), not merely "knowledge-telling" but "knowledge-transforming." And a well-written critique is a text that reveals such a transformation. Writing a critique involves analyzing mul-

---

1. For another view, see Atkinson 1997; that author urges caution in adopting pedagogies in critical thinking.

tiple, and sometimes competing, knowledge claims in a discipline to create one's own perspective.

Although the critique is not a fixed text type—just as other pedagogical genres, such as the undergraduate "research paper," do not have fixed forms (Johns 1997)—it is nevertheless possible to make some generalizations about typical critique assignments for undergraduates. Outside the literature classroom, students are generally asked to write critiques of a published article that has been assigned as a reading in addition to their usual textbook readings. Usually, the articles do not simply present accepted fact or the canon of a field. Instead, they tend to somehow challenge accepted views or approaches within the field or perhaps illustrate an application or extension of those ideas. The task of the students, then, is to weigh what they have read in the article against what they have learned as "fact" either through lecture or through other reading, such as that found in a textbook. Their goal is to demonstrate that they have integrated this disciplinary knowledge and that they can apply it to develop observations of their own.

This reading-to-write task presents numerous challenges for both native and nonnative speakers. First of all, as a "hybrid" act of literacy (Bracewell, Frederiksen, and Frederiksen 1982), critique writing is inherently complex—writers must first be readers. It places high demands on reading, writing, and thinking skills. For young undergraduates not yet affiliated with a discipline, the reading demands of the critique assignment can be significant. Most of the reading they do in their introductory survey courses is from textbooks, a pedagogical genre written with them in mind as audience.[2] An article they are asked to critique, however, is likely to be an instance of a "professional academic genre" (Johns 1997) and, as such, written for an audience (primarily disciplinary experts) of which they are not a principal part. Therefore, the article may be more challenging to them as readers than is the textbook.

Critique writing requires not only in-depth comprehension of a text but evaluation of it as well, often in light of multiple texts, such as course lectures, other readings, and personal experience. Students in introductory survey courses often have not been called on to do much evaluation of what they read. Their main disciplinary reading experience, the textbook, presents relatively uncontroversial information that students are

---

2. Swales (1995) argues that a second and important audience for textbooks is "evaluator-readers," the professors who select textbooks for their students. The professors, though, are being targeted in their role as instructors of undergraduates rather than as disciplinary peers of the textbook author.

expected to absorb rather than evaluate. Their lack of evaluative reading experience may lead them to view academic texts as mere storehouses of facts, not subjects for evaluation (Haas 1994; Johns 1997), and may contribute to their being relative novices at evaluating and synthesizing contradictory claims.

A second cause for the difficulty students have with critique writing is that few of them understand what a critique is. A survey we did this year of 23 first-semester undergraduate students taking an EAP academic writing class at our university showed that only four of the students had ever written a critique.[3] Of those four critiques, only one was of a nonliterary text (it was written as part of a writing portfolio that the student was required to submit when applying for admission to our university). Some who claimed to have written critiques apparently had not; when they described their critiques, they described papers that were argumentative essays on a controversial issue (e.g., capital punishment and drug legalization), not a critique of a nonliterary text. The majority of students said they did not know what a critique was, many using phrases like "I have no idea [what a critique is]." Many appeared to misunderstand what professors expect in a critique. Those of our students who ventured opinions about what professors look for in a critique typically missed the mark. Students tended to see the critique as an exercise in finding weaknesses in an article and/or as an assignment in which they should show the professor either their personal view of an article or that they understand the article.

This conceptualization of a critique is similar to that evident in critiques written by sociology students who were studied by Mathison (1996). In examining the critiques that they wrote of a sociology article, Mathison concluded that the majority of students in her study performed critique as a report and a personal response. Where they evaluated, they did so in terms of their personal beliefs rather than in terms of how the article related to the discipline of sociology. Professors evaluating these critiques valued disciplinary-based arguments for or against aspects of the article. They gave higher grades to critiques in which students went beyond personal reaction to make evaluations related to the content of what had been studied in their classroom. They valued commentary that showed the student was aware of discourse-community issues. The students, however, failed to recognize that their professors were looking for

---

3. We wish to acknowledge the help of Theresa Rohlck, ELI lecturer and regular instructor of undergraduate academic writing classes, in conducting this survey and in sharing with us her experience and perspectives on teaching critique writing.

the critique to be contextualized in a disciplinary framework. In this sense, Mathison found they were unable to meet professors' expectations.

Even if students are made aware of the need to evaluate and to support evaluations with disciplinary evidence, writing a critique poses difficulties because students are being asked to assume an unfamiliar writing persona, that is, one of an authority. Though they are the most junior members of the academy, they are being asked to position themselves in the role of someone with enough knowledge and experience to challenge the written word, often the written word of disciplinary experts. As Belcher (1995) points out, many students feel they do not know enough to be critical. Questioning the written word is difficult enough for native speaker (NS) undergraduates. It is likely even more challenging for many nonnative speakers (NNS), many of whom come from educational traditions in which absorbing and memorizing scholarly work—rather than evaluating it—is emphasized (Ballard 1984).

Teaching the Critique

Because we are convinced of both the importance and the difficulty of writing a critique, we believe it is important to incorporate this reading-writing task in our EAP writing courses. In this section of this chapter, we will discuss an approach to the teaching of critique writing that has been used successfully with NNS undergraduate students in a course at the University of Michigan called Integrated Academic Skills. What follows is to be viewed not as a lesson plan but rather as a description of ways to explore a topic and eventually a single text through a sequence of activities that move students through three different stages of critical inquiry—understanding and reacting, evaluation, and reasoning.

The undergraduate students in Integrated Academic Skills are advanced users of English, with TOEFL scores well above 550 (213 on the computer-based TOEFL). Students are placed into this class as a result of weak performance on the reading-writing part of the Undergraduate Writing Assessment (Feak and Dobson 1996). The class, which meets four hours a week for 10 weeks, is aimed primarily at improving the students' academic reading and writing using source texts.

Because students must understand an article and be able to accurately express that understanding in writing before they can successfully write a critique, the course covers summary writing before working on critique writing. In working on summary writing, students learn to identify the main issue of an article, the author's perspective, support for a claim, and other relevant aspects of a text, such as its rhetorical structure, all of which are useful for the writing of a critique. The final summary assignment requires students to take the role of a very junior member of the academic community, summarize an article on current research in a field (e.g., research on animal language), and make a recommendation to a committee as to whether a particular project in that field should receive funding. While the focus of this writing task is summarizing, the recommendation gives students the opportunity to offer an opinion. For some students, this opinion is limited to a one-sentence acceptance or rejection of the proposal in light of the research presented in the article, while for others the opinion expands to also include commentary on the general area of research. Thus, the recommendation serves as a useful link to the critique.

Student success in writing a critique is largely dependent on two main factors: having adequate background knowledge of the topic being dealt with (Mathison 1996) and having a useful set of evaluative criteria that can be applied to a text (Shepelak, Curry-Jackson, and Moore 1992). As our classroom includes students from a wide range of disciplines, from music to engineering, we do not assume that the students have shared academic knowledge. Stage 1 of our approach is thus devoted to providing sufficient background knowledge by centering the critique unit around one research topic that is accessible and, ideally, interesting to most students in the class. Topics chosen are those that the instructors have some familiarity with (allowing for some content teaching) and have ranged from language acquisition to education to intelligence.[4] The main goal of stage 2 is to introduce students to evaluative criteria that, though not discipline-specific, are nevertheless appropriate in many disciplines and that move students away from simple reaction to a text. Finally, stage 3 focuses students on developing a new text from one they have read—transformation of the source text through the creative application of their own ideas.

Stage 1: Understanding and Discussion

In stage 1 of our approach to teaching critique writing, students read four or five short articles that present different views on a single topic, including competing and previously rejected ideas. The goal of this preliminary reading is for students to understand content, each author's purpose in writing, and the rhetorical aspects of the texts. In addition to providing

---

4. Some very interesting readings on intelligence can be found in Rose and Kinery 1998.

students with information on a topic, the articles are also a source of support for their own points in the critique they finally write. Initially, students discuss the articles in small groups and then write either short summaries of these articles or respond (in writing) to comprehension questions that probe their understanding. Students are not asked to rigorously evaluate the articles but are encouraged to form opinions about them. Here we expect nothing more than low-level evaluations, such as "I liked the article," "The article was interesting," "The article was hard to read." Any type of reaction is encouraged, since one goal at this point is for students to see that different readers can react to readings in different ways and that there is no right or wrong answer when they are asked to give an opinion. Students are also asked to try to give reasons for their opinions, which is generally challenging for students who may be "intimidated by the authority of established knowledge" (Belcher 1995, 137), who may have been taught to "revere" the written text (Matalene 1985), or who may never have been exposed to multiple texts on a single topic because such texts simply were not available (Grabe 1991).

Reading several articles on one topic yields several benefits. First, students become aware that experts do not always agree, that there is debate, and that perspectives change over time. Second, they begin to realize that given differences in expert claims, they cannot simply passively absorb what they read; they need to be able to assess it. If they are unable to assess, there is little to prevent them from accepting whatever claim they have read last. Third, the students also gain an awareness that academic texts are parts of larger disciplinary discussions and that students in the disciplines need to be able to find ways to meaningfully participate in those discussions as "professionals in training."

Armed with various kinds of information on a topic, the students are now ready to begin working on critically evaluating an article on that topic. The challenges at this stage are many. For one, students tend to act like sponges (Browne and Keeley 1998), absorbing everything they read and failing to discriminate between what is worth discussing and what is not. For another, students have little experience using evaluative standards that move them beyond their personal experience. If all they do is agree or disagree, their evaluation may take the form of an argument for their point of view, rather than an evaluation that may approximate the type that would be expected of them in their other courses. They need to be able to sift through information to determine what information might be valued and how that information is positioned in relation to other information, a process that Browne and Keeley (1998) describe as "panning for gold." In "panning for gold," students interact with the knowledge they have absorbed and are absorbing as they read a new text.

The following approach to dismantling an academic, nonliterary text is likely to be too general to be applied in a specific discipline, but it provides a good first step to evaluation using standards that are appropriate for an academic setting. Although there are approaches to critique that rest on a particular school of thought, the approach offered here is intended to emphasize making nonpersonal evaluative commentary and providing nonpersonal support for that commentary. Later, in their content classes, students need to become aware of the disciplinary standards against which published work is measured.

Stage 2: Evaluation

As Belcher (1995) has noted, simply having read a lot on a topic does not necessarily translate into a student's ability to critique. Providing model critiques written by other students can help students see the different ways background knowledge can be used in a critique and the aspects of a text that can be critiqued. However, models cannot reveal the thinking processes that underlie them (Cumming 1995; Gajdusek and van Dommelen 1993). Thus, we model in stage 2 the type of thinking that experienced readers and writers use as they prepare a written critique, so that students can "become aware of, and can practice, the complex mental activities that characterize expert composing" (Cumming 1995, 383) and, we should add, reading. Without such modeling, students may fail to fully grasp the ways in which expert readers dismantle a text and select aspects from which to create a new text.

One approach to highlighting the cognitive processes that go into writing a critique is to provide a set of questions that guide the students' reading of a text they need to evaluate. As Shepelak, Curry-Jackson, and Moore (1992) state, to understand and critically assess a text, students need a fundamental set of analytical questions. Such questions not only emphasize the importance of asking and answering questions while reading but also provide the foundation for critical inquiry.[5] These questions

---

5. The set of questions that we provide our students, which continues to evolve, has been adapted from Browne and Keeley 1998. For a thorough treatment of what lies behind these questions, we encourage the reader to see this reference, which is an excellent guide to developing good skills for text analysis.

are intended not as an outline of a critique but rather as a guide to help move the students beyond comprehension and low-level reaction to the consideration of different components of a text vis-à-vis their knowledge.

1. Who is the audience?
2. What is the author's purpose?
3. What is the issue? (What question is being addressed?)
4. What conclusions does the author draw?
5. What kind of evidence or reasons does the author offer to support those conclusions?
6. How good is the evidence?
   a. How sound is the logic?
   b. What, if any, evidence was omitted?
   c. What is the quality of the references?
7. How good is the study, if one is presented?
   a. Was the sample size used in the study adequate?
   b. Was the study properly carried out?
   c. What is the significance of the study?
   d. How do the results relate to other similar research?
   e. What areas of future research does the study suggest?
   f. How reliable do the statistics seem, if any are provided?
8. Are any key terms ambiguous?
   a. Do some key terms have multiple meanings?
   b. Is the author's position or conclusion reasonable in light of other possible meanings of the key terms?
9. Is the author's position valid based on the evidence?
10. What assumptions does the author make?
    a. Are these assumptions valid?
    b. Why are the assumptions valid or invalid?
11. How does what the author states relate to other perspectives on the topic?

Because space constraints do not allow us to discuss each of these questions, we will address only questions 1, 2, 6, and 8. The first two questions may appear to be rather simple, but in fact they are essential to getting the critique off to the right start. In question 1, the issue is best described as the focus of the article. We encourage students to frame the issue as a yes-no question so that they do not simply say what the article is about—the topic. If students simply say that an article is about intelligence, they will likely miss both the point of the article and the author's perspective. Rather than saying that an article is about intelligence, we want students to focus on such questions as "Are there different kinds of intelligence?" or "Can traditional IQ tests measure intelligence?" By framing the issue as a question, students can then focus on the author's conclusion, which is one response to question 2. Identifying the author's conclusion may seem to be an easy task; however, often authors do not explicitly state their conclusions. Readers can be left to infer the conclusion based on what they find in the text. If students cannot identify the issue and the conclusion of a text, the critique will "get off on the wrong foot" and likely fail.

Framing the issue as a question and then identifying the author's answer to the question also encourages students to look for the reasons or evidence that support the answer and to identify the way in which the author arrived at his or her conclusion. Evidence, of course, must be evaluated. But first students need to be aware of what kind of evidence is typically offered in various kinds of academic articles and what kind of evidence (anecdotes, research results, analogies, generalizations, etc.) is valued. This discussion is important later when the students begin to write their own critiques and need to evaluate their own claims. In question 6, students are asked to judge the quality of the evidence based not only on principles of logic but also on content. Students are also encouraged to consider what type of evidence was omitted or could have been offered to support the argument—information that would cause a reader to perhaps evaluate the article differently if it had been provided. This question is quite difficult, even for students who may be familiar with ways of critiquing an article. But sometimes what has been omitted is even more important in the evaluation of an article than what has been included.

Since our students are generally concerned about their level and understanding of vocabulary, we also encourage them to look for key terms that have multiple meanings. Thus, the purpose of question 8 is to make students aware that if a key term potentially has more than one meaning, one's understanding of the text will vary according to these different meanings. If we take the term *discriminate,* for example, the sentence "It is important for intelligence tests to discriminate" can have different meanings depending on whether the author intended *discriminate* to mean "to make a distinction" or "to treat differently because of prejudice or bias."

The set of questions we provide as a guide to our students allows us to model the thinking processes that expert readers might engage in during and after reading as well as while writing, that is, to cognitively model

(Cumming 1995) the reading-writing process for critiques. Minimally, by providing criteria, these questions allow the students to see the kinds of things they can evaluate. Ideally they help students to see that there is more to reading a text than simply understanding content and more to writing a critique than simply reacting.

Stage 3: Constructing the Critique

After carefully thinking through various aspects of the article they are critiquing as well as any supporting or competing knowledge claims that they are aware of, the students need to construct their own perspective (Mathison 1996, 315), which they reveal in a new text of their own. The critique assignment attempts to establish a reasonable rhetorical context. It first provides students with some background of the article they will analyze and reveals that the article has generated considerable debate. It then explains why the students have been asked to critique the article (usually the university is considering a policy change that will affect current or future students) and gives the purpose and intended audience for the critique (generally a mixed group of peers and professors on a committee discussing the change in policy). Recently, for instance, we worked with an article that dealt with multiple intelligences, a theory that supposedly was giving rise to changes in our university's admissions policy. In providing the purpose and audience, it is hoped that the students can see themselves as members of the academic community who have something to say. In preparing their critiques, students are to view their audience as largely unfamiliar with the article they are working with, although they likely have some familiarity with the topic. Thus, the critique must stand on its own and not rely on a reader having read the source text. Providing a context for writing also allows students to select from the article some content over other content and consider ways to reorganize material and establish connections for the particular purpose.

The students are required to demonstrate an understanding of the source article, place their discussion into a larger context, provide evaluation based not on personal experience but rather on the evaluative criteria suggested by the question prompts, and use other readings to provide "disciplinary" support for their evaluation. We do not prescribe the number of pages or the number of words; however, most students have noticed that the critiques written by previous students have often been longer than the original article that they are critiquing, which can range from 900 to 1,200 words. Although we do not impose any particular organization on the texts that students write, generally they begin with a discussion of a context to establish the relevance of the issue raised in the article and continue with a topic-comment text configuration, where the topic is some aspect of the article they are working with while the comment is their critique. For example, they may begin with a brief summary of the source article and continue with their own commentary. Alternatively, they may repeat the topic-comment pattern, a text configuration Belcher (1995) describes as a "cycling summary/critique review" (140). In this type of critique, the writer refers to something from the article and critiques it, refers to something else from the article and comments on it, and so on. During the early development of this unit, insufficient emphasis was placed on the topic-comment approach, which often resulted in students simply providing comments with a very loose connection to the source text; their papers were more similar to argumentative essays than to critiques. We provide students with sample student critiques to demonstrate various topic-comment configurations and the importance of sequencing ideas for the greatest effect.

Considerations

Earlier we said that student success in critique writing depends on background knowledge and an appropriate set of evaluative criteria. Though these factors are clearly necessary, they are not sufficient. Success also depends on other factors that need to be considered by the instructor. In our experience, NNS students are not ready to attempt this critique assignment sequence when they first begin the class. In addition to needing time to read articles and participate in class discussions to build disciplinary knowledge related to the topic of the critique, students need to develop and practice certain component skills of critique writing.

For example, before trying to write a critique, students should have practiced summarizing and paraphrasing. Learning to objectively and accurately report what an author has said is a prerequisite for critique writing. Other writing skills to introduce early in the term and then recycle for the critique include incorporating borrowed material from one or more sources into one's own text, properly attributing borrowed material, and interweaving borrowed material with one's own views clearly and smoothly.

Course work to practice certain critical reading skills should also be helpful before and during the critique assignment. Among the reading skills to strengthen are distinguishing fact from opinion, recognizing the strength of claims, attributing ideas appropriately when reading a text that includes the views of several sources, identifying the author's intended audience and purpose, evaluating the author's arguments, mapping the rhetorical "moves" of an article, comparing the ideas in one reading to the ideas in another, recognizing the author's ideology, and deciding what aspects of a text one agrees with and what aspects one disagrees with.

As students write the critique, many opportunities arise for contextualized grammar and vocabulary instruction. Focused "language work" can help students acquire the sophisticated vocabulary and syntax they need to convey their critical reactions. Thus, on an ongoing basis, we deal with such language issues as semantic ambiguity, hedging, and evaluative vocabulary (e.g., such adjectives as *simple, complex, limited, flawed, elegant*). We teach students to construct sentences of concessive contrast (e.g., "Although the author cites many sources, the quality of those sources is questionable"). We also have them work on counterfactuals (e.g., "The author would have been more convincing if he had related his findings to previous research on the subject").

To improve our students' chances for success, we provide focused practice on critical reading and evaluative writing before the critique assignment is given. We start small. For example, we might ask students to paraphrase and then evaluate a sentence, such as "Nine out of ten doctors surveyed who recommended any pain reliever at all for their patients recommended Tylenol." Before the final critique assignment, we might ask students to apply to a short text only a single critical reading question from our set. For example, students might be asked to answer question 6 from the set: How good is the evidence? These short critique exercises help us recognize, in a controlled context, problems and misunderstandings students might have. The students begin to appreciate the difficulty of the task and also to judge their ability to handle it. We learned the hard way that starting students out with a full-length critique risks receiving a critique that went wrong at such an early stage of the reading-writing process that it is virtually unsalvageable, a demoralizing experience for teacher and student alike.

We have learned that it is essential to choose one topic to explore, to provide articles for reading and writing about, and to select a single article for the class to critique. If the instructor does not provide sufficient background, time, and instruction, choosing instead to present articles on unrelated topics that are selected primarily because they are "thought-provoking," students may leave the classroom thinking that critiquing means simply presenting their personal reactions. They may fail to recognize the importance of content knowledge in critique writing.

Teachers, rather than students, should choose the final article to be critiqued. Even if students have learned about a topic in class, they may choose a relevant article that either does not lend itself to critique or is too difficult for them to critique at their educational level. In the case where students have not worked with only one topic in the classroom, they may select a topic about which they have insufficient background knowledge—one they are ill prepared to evaluate effectively with disciplinary evidence. Alternatively, they might pick an article on a controversial issue that they are very emotionally involved with. In this case, they may not be able to stand back from the text and evaluate it without their own personal filter. They may end up evaluating the article in merely personal terms that are unconvincing or irrelevant to others. Some may even write about their views on the issue rather than present views of what the author said in the article. Some topics that we have found to lead to this problem include abortion, creationism, and euthanasia. The highly emotional nature of these topics, their connection with religious beliefs, and the semantic ambiguities rampant in articles on these topics make them poor choices for the purpose of critique.

Conclusion

Our three-stage approach to teaching critique writing allows us to reveal to students much of what underlies the writing of the pedagogical critique. Students begin to realize the importance of understanding disciplinary knowledge and being able to apply that knowledge. In addition, they become aware of the kind of evaluative criteria that might be used by members of the academy. As a result of cognitive modeling and working through the evaluative criteria, students gain practice in the kind of thinking that enables them to do more than just react to a text. Of course, the set of questions we presented in this chapter cannot be applied to all disciplines. It is not a template for thinking and evaluation across the disciplines. Rather, the approach represented by the questions opens the door to an unfamiliar, yet important, literate activity involving meaningful interaction between reading and writing and provides students with some useful strategies for how to handle it.

References

Atkinson, D. 1997. A critical approach to critical thinking in TESOL. *TESOL Quarterly* 31:71–94.

Ballard, B. 1984. Improving student writing: An integrated approach to cultural adjustment. In *Common ground: Shared interests in ESP and communication studies,* ed. R. Williams, J. Swales, and J. Kirkman, 43–53. Oxford: British Council/Pergamon.

Belcher, D. 1995. Writing critically across the curriculum. In *Academic writing in a second language: Essays on research and pedagogy,* ed. D. Belcher and G. Braine, 135–54. Norwood, NJ: Ablex.

Bereiter, C., and M. Scardamalia. 1987. *The psychology of written composition.* Hillsdale, NJ: Lawrence Erlbaum.

Bracewell, R., C. Frederiksen, and J. Frederiksen. 1982. Cognitive processes in composing and comprehending discourse. *Educational Psychologist* 17:146–64.

Browne, M. N., and S. Keeley. 1998. *Asking the right questions: A guide to critical thinking.* 5th ed. Upper Saddle River, NJ: Prentice-Hall.

Cumming, A. 1995. Fostering writing expertise in ESL composition instruction: Modeling and evaluation. In *Academic writing in a second language: Essays on research and pedagogy,* ed. D. Belcher and G. Braine, 375–97. Norwood, NJ: Ablex.

Feak, C., and B. Dobson. 1996. Building on the impromptu: A source-based academic writing assessment. *College ESL* 6, no. 1:73–84.

Gajdusek, L., and D. van Dommelen. 1993. Literature and critical thinking in the composition classroom. In *Reading in the composition classroom,* ed. J. G. Carson and I. Leki, 197–217. Boston: Heinle and Heinle.

Grabe, W. 1991. Current developments in second language reading research. *TESOL Quarterly* 25:375–406.

Haas, C. 1994. Learning to read biology: One student's rhetorical development in college. *Written Communication* 11:43–84.

Johns, A. M. 1997. *Text, role, and context: Developing academic literacies.* Cambridge: Cambridge University Press.

Matalene, C. 1985. Contrastive rhetoric: An American writing teacher in China. *College English* 47:789–808.

Mathison, M. A. 1996. Writing the critique, a text about a text. *Written Communication* 13:314–54.

Rose, M., and M. Kinery. 1998. *Critical strategies for academic thinking and writing.* 3d ed. Boston: Bedford Books.

Shepelak, N. J., A. Curry-Jackson, and V. L. Moore. 1992. Critical thinking in introductory sociology classes: A program of implementation and evaluation. *Teaching Sociology* 20:18–27.

Swales, J. M. 1995. The role of the textbook in EAP writing research. *TESOL Quarterly* 14:3–18.

Interlude: Developing Meaningful Literacy Courses

Ilona Leki, University of Tennessee

In this interlude, I would like to explore just a few of the points made in this volume that strike me as especially intriguing, provocative, or ironic.

In their introduction, Diane Belcher and Alan Hirvela raise, among other issues, the astonishing question "Do our students actually become better L2 readers and writers as a result of our integrated reading and writing instruction?" Presumably the authors and the readers of the chapters of this book believe that they do. As Bill Grabe notes, literacy research in both L1 and L2 contexts seems to show that reading improves writing and, at least to some degree, that writing improves reading. But that says nothing about the role our classes play in this interaction or might play if the classes were different.

Furthermore, although research appears to support the assumption that literate activities increase literate skills, as Grabe again notes, we have insufficient empirical evidence that "reading and writing as a collaborative activity" improves learning, despite the appeal of such an idea. Yet in academic settings (except perhaps in literacy classes themselves), reading and writing are done nearly exclusively for the purpose of learning some disciplinary content or to display that learning.

The relative importance of the two literacy skills varies, however, with the academic status of the student, as we learn from Joan Carson's investigation. In the U.S. tertiary system, nearly all undergraduates are required to take a freshman writing course. Yet Carson shows us that the greatest literacy need of undergraduates in U.S. tertiary institutions involves not writing but reading. Furthermore, this reading is presumably the kind of extensive reading Grabe refers to, involving large amounts of text to be read for gist (and some detail), often from textbooks whose goals are to introduce students to a disciplinary area and that therefore necessarily range widely in an attempt to define the field.

This type of reading is exactly what is not taught much in literacy classes, perhaps, as Grabe notes, because results are slow to show themselves and because teachers feel a stronger sense of accomplishment when they focus on what Grabe characterizes as a "less important skill," working intensively with a reading. Or perhaps, while we have well developed methodologies for teaching writing to L2 students with intermediate and more advanced language proficiency, our reading methodologies (beyond quick tips, such as advising students to read the subheads of a chapter first) are not very well developed for helping with extensive reading. Our literacy courses for undergraduates, then, may focus on the wrong literacy skill (writing) and may treat the right literacy skill (reading) in the wrong way. The result for L2 undergraduates may be that (1) they are left on their own to deal with the huge amount of reading they are required to do in general education courses and (2) they get intensive instruction in writing but do not need writing skills until a couple of years after the writing course is over, by which time surely some of what might once have been learned has slipped away.

Carson's findings indicate that graduate students are required to do more writing and more intensive, close reading than undergraduates. Yet graduate students may not have writing courses as available to them as is the ubiquitous freshman course to undergraduates, and when graduate students do turn up in literacy courses, we L2 writing teachers may not be familiar enough with disciplinary knowledge to help them through intensive reading requirements or familiar enough with the specifics of disciplinary genres to offer much more help in writing than the rather general kind of help that first-year writing courses offer.

For all these reasons, our L2 literacy classes may be less useful to both undergraduate and graduate students than we might hope or expect. Moreover, in addition to these possible limitations on the effectiveness of our L2 literacy classes, and returning to Diane Belcher and Alan Hirvela's question, it is possible that the positive impact of our literacy courses is reduced by yet another peril. It is the privilege and the potential disadvantage of language/literacy classes to have wide latitude—in fact, nearly complete freedom—in determining the content of the course, in terms both of the literacy skills to be addressed and the unavoidable subject matter to read and write about. The advantages seem obvious. The disadvantages, however, may not be.

It is probably the case that most classroom teachers and program directors feel it is important to try, as Bill Grabe recommends, to select literacy course content and language tasks based on the literacy demands students will presumably encounter. Yet I suspect that the frank and arresting remarks of the Chinese students Joel Bloch cites in reference to plagiarism may find echoes in the opinions of many of our literacy students: the writing assignments (and perhaps the reading assignments) that students are given in language/literacy classes are viewed as "meaningless school-based . . . assignments." It is far from easy to avoid assigning such meaningless work. Our choices of literacy skills to develop may not reflect literacy needs the students are facing across the curriculum, and the subject matter, since it is essentially arbitrary and often externally imposed by the teacher or the textbook, may also seem irrelevant. In addition, many of our literacy courses enroll students with diverse intellectual interests and educational backgrounds, thus multiplying the difficulty in selecting course content that will inspire intellectual engagement and commitment in all or nearly all of the students.

Several of the chapters of this book present attempts in one way or another to solve this problem of the content of literacy courses. While all approaches to a literacy syllabus almost invariably include attention both to literacy skills development and to subject matter to practice the literacy skills on, different approaches usually highlight one or the other of these two facets of the course, concentrating more intensely either on literacy skills themselves or on the subject matter of the reading-writing assignments. Presumably no teacher or program wants to be seen as requiring meaningless assignments. So, what informs decisions about literacy course content, and how successful are these sources of information in helping practitioners to create meaningful assignments?

One traditional solution to the question of the content of literacy courses has been to use personal history and self-exploration as a jumping-off point in the development of academic literacy. While this option has the advantage of being intrinsically compelling to some students, it may be perceived by others as meaningless because it is not directly related to academic work—how time is spent is an area of vital concern to many L2 students. The argument that, regardless of its lack of strictly academic value, such writing is empowering may be specious (see Benesch 1999), and in any case, since this option is not examined in the chapters of this book, I will pursue it no further.

One source of information for our decisions about course content is the kind of research findings and theoretical considerations described in Grabe's chapter, exploring what promotes L2 literacy development and how L2 literacy development promotes learning academic content and fills other literacy needs. Yet the complexity of the picture painted by these findings makes it difficult to know how to take these findings into account.

Another approach is to teach what we know as literacy teachers, for example, rhetorical devices, techniques, and stances. The courses that follow this line of reasoning focus on features of rhetoric, for example, on teaching students how to write thesis statements or generalizable genres, such as critiques, as described by Barbara Dobson and Christine Feak. The relevance and, therefore, potential meaningfulness of this focus are often asserted by appealing to a conviction (not always an accurate reflection of fact) that students will have to manipulate these types of rhetorical techniques in other courses eventually and so should learn how to do so in a literacy class. Other justifications include Tony Silva's (1997) contention that if we advertise our class as one that teaches writing, we should, in effect, use writing as the content of the course and not spend time teaching other things, like literature or culture (including cultural critiques) or even the currently much beloved "critical thinking." Presumably, whether or not the assignments in courses following these rationales are meaningful would depend in great part on what literacy needs the students are experiencing. It should also be noted that courses like these, ironically, may run the same risk that courses focusing on personal exploration face: privileging English department genres like argumentation and persuasion. Again, the contention that these genres should be taught because they are prevalent in undergraduate education appears not to be borne out by Carson's study.

Others agree that we should teach what we know and perhaps enjoy ourselves while focusing not directly on developing literacy skills but rather on developing knowledge of subject matter. The interest in teaching literature as a link between reading and writing falls into this category. Although I have no proof of this, I suspect that the many L2 literacy researchers and practitioners, such as Alan Hirvela, who advocate the teaching of literature know and enjoy literature so much that they urgently want others to experience the same enjoyment and, presumably, benefit; that is, the argument for teaching literature these days is post hoc. Advocates begin not with the perception that using literature as the content of literacy courses solves literacy problems but rather with the need to justify their sense of the value of teaching literature by detailing how it might or could help to develop literacy. Those who use literature in literacy classes, being knowledgeable themselves about literature, heed Spack's (1988) often cited argument that we should not attempt to teach literacy in disciplinary domains where we know less than our student writers.

Yet Currie (1999) argues not only that it is possible to help students develop literacy in disciplinary domains unfamiliar to literacy teachers but that it may be a positive advantage to put students, not the teacher, into the role of knowledge holders by having students use the literacy course as a place to analyze concepts from other disciplinary courses. Debbie Barks and Patricia Watts suggest a similar possibility in their description of the disciplinary ethnography assignment in their literacy course. This kind of approach turns the literacy demands themselves into the content of the literacy course.

Finally, an approach not explicitly addressed in this volume but implicit in the idea of using students' current academic lives as the content of literacy courses is the recommendation of advocates of critical pedagogy like Benesch (1999). Critical pedagogy invites students to use the literacy skills they develop in our courses to explore, analyze, and address unsatisfactory conditions of their academic, work, or personal lives. These types of approaches that focus on students' real lives tap into the energy of students' personal experiences without locking them into nonacademic genres and cognitive exercises, as personal and expressive writing might do.

Each one of these approaches is open to criticism, namely, that creating literacy classes following any one of these approaches still cannot guarantee that the work we ask students to do in literacy classes is meaningful. Or put another way, each of these approaches could produce meaningful literacy work but will not do so inevitably or invariably. Joel Bloch and Janina Brutt-Griffler's admirable chapter on technology suggests a means of bolstering the probability of creating meaningful assignments. I confess that I nearly did not read that chapter, having become jaded about technology and the exaggerated claims made for its wonders. Research reports in our discipline seem likely to gloss over curricular failures; while we often read testimonials from students about how our literacy courses changed their lives, we rarely see quotations from students who did not appreciate curricular changes that we support strongly or that we believe will be in the best interests of our students. But Bloch and Brutt-Griffler implement systematic, continuous, and probing course evaluations combined with a matter-of-fact willingness to alter the course in light of students' negative experiences.

When developing literacy courses, we need to go beyond the findings of research, the arguments of theoretical considerations, our own preferences, and insights gained from professional experiences in teaching L2 literacy. We need to gather, repeatedly, information and reactions from students, as Bloch and Brutt-Griffler did, and to listen carefully to those students' voices when they tell us they are not interested in our assignments, when they tell us they do not have enough information on a topic to write or read about it with understanding, or, most especially, when they—or an evident lack of commitment to what we do in these literacy courses—tell us that they find our assignments meaningless.

References

Benesch, S. 1999. Rights analysis: Studying power relations in an academic setting. *English for Specific Purposes* 18:313–27.

Currie, P. 1999. Transferable skills: Promoting student research. *English for Specific Purposes* 18:329–45.

Silva, T. 1997. On the ethical treatment of ESL writers. *TESOL Quarterly* 31:359–63.

Spack, R. 1988. Initiating students into the academic discourse community: How far should we go? *TESOL Quarterly* 22:29–52.

Part 3

(E)Merging Literacies and the Challenge of Textual Ownership

Chapter 8

Plagiarism and the ESL Student: From Printed to Electronic Texts

Joel Bloch, The Ohio State University

The integration of previously published written texts into a new text is governed by a set of rules, the violation of which is called plagiarism. These rules concerning writing based on source texts have not always been as clear-cut as many teachers and students have assumed, particularly with regard to teaching about plagiarism. Moreover, as will be discussed in this chapter, the development of the Internet as a source for texts may create additional complications. For all composition teachers, the proliferation of electronic texts has meant both that there are more opportunities for students to conduct research and that there are more opportunities for them to copy texts and pass them off as their own. The World Wide Web allows for the easy copying of electronic source texts, whose numbers are growing as the supply of electronic magazines and journals expands. This trend has already caused a number of lawsuits concerning what constitutes plagiarism on the Web. The *New York Times,* for example, filed suit against a Web site for reprinting its articles. The owner of the Web site countered by arguing that such reproduction was protected by copyright law under the doctrine of fair use. The outcome of such lawsuits has sometimes been ambiguous or less than straightforward, and as a result, the issue remains highly contentious. A more insidious problem can be found on such Web sites as *Schoolsucks* (http://www.schoolsucks.com/) or *Term Papers Etc.* (http://pages.prodigy.net/bertrand1/webpage.html), which allow for ready access to term papers for sale. Moreover, students can easily "cut" pieces of texts directly from the Internet and "paste" them into their papers. Consequently, many ESL teachers have expressed concern about accessibility to texts on the Internet accentuating the practice of plagiarism.

Although it has been argued that in the future the Internet may reduce expenditures for technology in lesser-developed countries (Negroponte 1996), currently many countries do not have the foreign currency to pay for large quantities of such technology. Nevertheless, the rapid development of on-line journals and other materials on the Internet will mean that people in these countries will have access to information they could not previously afford to purchase. This prospect raises questions about students in or from those countries who do not know the appropriate rules for paraphrasing and citing texts and who thus may plagiarize in the process of working with these new sources of information. It also raises questions about how to approach teaching related to plagiarism in light of these new conditions and evolving notions of intellectual property and authorship. This line of questioning likewise touches on reading-writing relationships and how academic reading and writing should be taught with respect to proper source text use and avoidance of what is generally considered plagiarism. Plagiarism, whether of print or electronic texts, is not only an act of writing. It begins with how students read and process source texts as they prepare to incorporate relevant material from them into their own papers. It then carries over into their writing as they select from their reading what they consider to be appropriate source text content and then situate that content within their own writing. The expanding world of electronic texts, then, creates new challenges for teachers in terms of addressing issues concerning plagiarism as well as the reading-writing connections central to effective appropriation of source text material.

Regardless of the degree to which the Internet allows global access to new forms of information, it has been argued that its development will challenge concepts of intellectual property in lesser-developed countries, just as it already has in the West. This challenge to intellectual property has, in turn, created questions throughout the world about various existing definitions of plagiarism and whether these definitions can be extended to the use of electronic texts as source texts. Some people, such as Bolter (1990), argue that electronic texts are antithetical to printed texts and that they thus generate copyright issues far different from those regarding print texts. Barlow (1994), moreover, questions how the same copyright laws that protect print works can protect electronic works, which can be reproduced infinitely and in any country in the world. This position is not, however, universally held. There are people who believe that since cyberspace is simply an expansion of the print culture, there has as yet been no real change in our concept of intellectual property, allowing current copyright laws to facilitate the dissemination of information in cyberspace (Lichtenberg 1995).

Underlying the intellectual property/copyright debate is the question of what is meant by authorship and the ownership of a text. Traditionally, the copyright rests on a distinction between what is public and what is private (Rose 1993). Frequently, teachers hear students say that they do not need to cite an idea because it is "common knowledge" and therefore is in the public domain. The problem with the Internet is that the distinction between public and private is blurred (Elkin-Koren 1998). As Kolko (1998) has argued, writing comes in many forms, ranging from journal articles to E-mail messages or transcripts of MOO (multi-user domain, object-oriented) sessions. She asks whether all of these forms should be considered the same in terms of whether they should be cited.

In discussing plagiarism among Chinese students, Scollon (1995) argues that differences in the concept of authorship explain in part why Chinese students often follow rules about plagiarism that are not operative or readily accepted in the West. In a similar vein, there is the question of whether authorship is similar across the various forms of texts. Being cited is part of the capital authors receive for having their scholarly work published. Rather than being paid money, authors receive citations as part of their reward for their work (Mulkay 1972). Here the question of whether publishing on the Internet is the same as publishing in print becomes especially important, since authors of Internet publications may lose the currency of being cited. Citing the work of Esther Dyson, Lunsford and West (1996) argue that this electronic form of writing will result in a more "depersonalized" form of authorship where traditional forms of citation will not be as highly valued. In this case, the laws or norms applying to electronic texts may not be the same as for printed texts.

It has often been argued that ESL students have different conceptions of plagiarism. Matalene (1986), for example, maintains that Chinese students plagiarize because of their Confucian traditions, which emphasize the memorization of a canon of texts. Fox (1994) has gone so far as to argue that while for American students plagiarism is a violation of accepted cultural norms, for ESL students, plagiarism may be a product of their own cultural norms. In other words, there may be fundamentally different notions of authorship in operation, and these contrasting views may go to the heart of the problem of plagiarism among ESL students. Scollon (1995) has also asserted that cultural differences in the concept of authorship often lead students from other cultures to violate Western rules for plagiarism. Not everyone, however, agrees that culture is the crucial factor. Others have argued that ESL students simply may never have been taught any norms (something that could also be said of many American students). For instance, Deckert (1993) argues that Chinese students overuse source materials because of "an innocent and ingrained habit of giving back information exactly as they find it" (133).

No matter how this controversy is viewed, it has been generally assumed that ESL writers, particularly those from Asia, lack a basic understanding of how teachers and scholars in the West view plagiarism. How, then, will the development of new forms of electronic texts affect this problem? Will it further confuse ESL students as to what is meant by plagiarism, or, because the network is global, not local, will it allow room for new concepts of authorship that may be more compatible with those often found in other cultures? These new views of intellectual property may offer ESL students a greater opportunity to exploit their cultural traditions in their use of the Internet. As teachers and researchers in the West are confronting changes in the traditional views of what is meant by intellectual property and plagiarism, it may be useful to understand alternative views of these concepts. Rather than becoming simply a new place from which to steal texts, then, the Internet may emerge as an extension of the traditional ways in which these writers have viewed themselves in relationship to texts.

In this chapter, I want to explore how the changes discussed earlier may affect how researchers and teachers think about plagiarism and how they approach teaching about plagiarism to ESL students. The particular focus of this discussion will be on Chinese students. While these issues touch on ESL students from many cultures, much of the focus of research has to date been on Chinese students (e.g., Deckert 1993; Matalene 1986; Scollon 1995), who not only are the largest segment of the ESL population in the United States but also bring with them a long history of ideas about authorship and intellectual property and an approach to literacy that greatly values the written text. To increase understanding of the potential problems as well as the opportunities that computer-mediated discourse may create for these students, I will examine what traditions and attitudes toward plagiarism Chinese students may carry into the writing process; how Anglophone teaching of plagiarism has attempted, sometimes unsuccessfully, to respond to these attitudes; and finally, how the increasing use of on-line texts may be addressed in reading and writing instruction.

Influences on Views of Intellectual Property in Chinese Rhetoric

The assumption that there are differences between China and the West in how plagiarism is defined presupposes differences in cultural traditions and historical developments. Any such cross-cultural comparison runs the danger of dichotomizing the two cultures into polar opposites, presenting one culture as the opposite of the other. Actually, differences between China and the West should be seen as ranging along a continuum of perspectives, rather than as in opposition to each other (Bloch and Chi 1995; Scollon 1995). It is important, therefore, that we examine the issue of plagiarism in China in the context of a complex and continually changing culture, as has been done in explorations of plagiarism in Western culture.

Social Influences

It has been argued that the Western concept of plagiarism developed in response to changes in how intellectual property was viewed due to the rise of capitalism and the merchant classes in England during the late 17th and early 18th centuries (Gross 1990). The concept of the individual ownership of intellectual property had its roots in the particularities of the philosophical and artistic developments of the time. Rose (1993) argues, for example, that this was a period when the ownership of a work shifted from the publisher to the author. This claim seems to support the argument that there is no comparable concept of intellectual property in China, since capitalism has never existed in China for any substantial period of time. Rather, social conditions in China have traditionally been family- or clan-oriented (Creel 1970). Except for during brief periods of capitalist activity in regions like Shanghai during the 1920s and 1930s, the social conditions that underlie the Western concept of intellectual property did not emerge in China. Therefore, the type of individualism often associated with capitalism never developed in China; instead, the traditional collectivist nature of Chinese society has dominated. However, this does not mean that China did not develop concepts of authorship and intellectual property. Certainly in the 20th century, we have seen the strong development of Chinese essayists and novelists that would belie any argument that Western concepts of intellectual property do not exist in China. It seems more appropriate to say that whatever concepts of ownership exist in China did not necessarily develop in the same ways as did the concepts in the West.

Numerous factors in the intellectual life in China are thought to have played an important role in establishing the Chinese view of intellectual property. One possible factor is the importance given to the translation of foreign texts. Qian (1985) called China a "translation society," a place where translations are valued as much as original research. In fact, translations of academic articles are a major occupation in Chinese academic circles. Since many Chinese academics do not know other languages, and since, compared to the West, there are significantly fewer researchers in China to create original research and far fewer places in China to publish research, the translation of foreign articles has become an important academic activity. Financial rewards for translations of articles are similar to those for original articles. There are also Chinese literary traditions in which translation has been considered an art form. For example, Link (1981) points out that translations of Western romances into classical Chinese were popular at the turn of the 20th century. There was no intent to steal in these translations, since the authors of the original texts were widely known. What is significant about these practices is that the Chinese literary tradition assigns greater importance to the author of the translation than is given in the West, where the translator rarely achieves any prominence. In this sense, the voice of the translator and the voice of the individual author merge, which, as Scollon (1995) argues, submerges the individual voice into a more collaborative voice.

An older literary influence on the development of authorship in China can be found in the Chinese examination system for civil servants, which elevated the recitation of the Confucian classics to the level of being the basis for obtaining a government position. By the T'ang dynasty (618–906), the examination system was used to identify an intellectual elite that commanded much prestige in the society. The examination system became an important route for social advancement; a means for supporting state policies; and, to varying degrees, a way of encouraging social mobility (Elman 1991; Lee 1989). Needham (1969) argues that the examinations had the effect of "democratizing" the feudal system—a development not seen in the feudal system in the West, and a point we need to consider in understanding the historical development of intellectual property in the Chinese and Western contexts. The examination system also elevated the status of writing; beyond that, it influenced literacy practices throughout the educational system. Literacy education for children evolved into rote memorization of the classics as well as copying model texts to improve writing skills (Rawski 1985). From an early age, students concentrated on "the Four Books and the Five Classics," which are the core texts of Confucian thought (Chaffee 1985). It has been argued that this approach to education has had important implications for past and present notions of intellectual property.

The Concept of Intellectual Property

Chinese educational and literary traditions have often been cited as reasons why Chinese students feel they do not need to actually cite texts in

English, particularly well-known works by prominent scholars. Not citing such texts is often considered plagiarism in the West. Rules governing citation practices in Anglophone discourses make a distinction between ideas, which can be freely used if they are not identified with a particular scholar, and the expression of those ideas, which must always include appropriate acknowledgment. Such a distinction was not as clearly drawn in traditional Chinese rhetoric. In the civil-service examinations, as in the practice of translation, there was a blurring in the distinction between an idea and its expression.

Both Chinese and Western traditions share the importance given to the social context of the production of texts. Although citation norms may differ, both cultures have acknowledged the importance of integrating the ideas of other authors into a text. Chi and I have argued elsewhere (Bloch and Chi 1995) that this strategy of integrating the author's voice with other textual voices can be found throughout Chinese rhetoric. As in the West, the purpose is to show how ideas found in classic texts substantiate one's own claims. We have asserted that this process gives the text a hypertextual feeling, in that the authors seamlessly link their voices to those from the canon of significant texts, whether they be from Confucious or from Mao Tse-tung. While the lack of formal acknowledgment in these texts might be considered plagiarism in the West, the term *plagiarism* in fact has little or no meaning in this context. Instead, this practice of integrating voices demonstrates a shared sense of audience but not necessarily a different view of intellectual property.

Changes in the Definition of Plagiarism

Recently, Chinese academicians have been trying to demonstrate that plagiarism is as repugnant in China as it is in the West. In three highly publicized cases, Chinese researchers caught plagiarizing from both Chinese and Western sources were given severe punishments (Li and Xiong 1996). In one case, a researcher was attempting to publish papers that had been previously published. In another case, two researchers were punished for copying parts of another paper into their own. Li and Xiong (1996) cited a recent survey showing that plagiarism "arouses general indignation in scientists," and they quoted a government official as saying that "whenever such a phenomenon occurs, investigations must be conducted and due punishments imposed" (338). This attitude toward plagiarism may indicate how Chinese researchers who have studied in the West—which includes many of them—have been influenced by that experience. The Westernization of China, however, cannot totally explain this attitude. In recent times, material changes in Chinese economic life could have produced an evolution in the Chinese view of plagiarism in the same way that changes in Western economic life have led to revisions in the Western view of plagiarism. More and more, Chinese scholars have come under the same pressures as Western scholars to have their research published and acknowledged.

However, there are still some interesting differences between how plagiarism is viewed in China and the view in the West. For example, in the West it is common for both academic and nonacademic writers caught plagiarizing to blame their acts on forgetfulness; that is, they claim they did not remember the source of their ideas. It is also typical in the West to claim that the plagiarism was accidental, as in the case where Mike Barnacle, a well-known newspaper columnist, claimed he "forgot" he read a book he was accused of plagiarizing. In contrast, Li and Xiong (1996) quote the aforementioned Chinese researchers caught plagiarizing as admitting they plagiarized parts of the paper because of their weak English, while arguing that the important part of the paper was their own. The Dutch editor of the journal in which the plagiarized article was published responded in the traditional Western way: "It is not acceptable practice to copy texts—not even small passages—from published materials without reference" (Li and Xiong 1996, 337). These differences exemplify the conflict between traditional Chinese discourse, in which the individual voice becomes interwoven with previously published texts, and modern Western discourse, in which the individual voice must be distinct from the general community.

Chinese Students' Perceptions of Plagiarism

We have seen that many Chinese academics and officials have strong opinions about plagiarism, but are these opinions shared by Chinese students? In this section of this chapter, I want to explore the attitudes of Chinese students themselves toward these issues. As part of a larger project on comparative rhetoric, I interviewed 16 Chinese graduate students (half in the physical sciences and half in the social sciences) about their attitudes toward plagiarism. Each interview lasted about one hour. Since few of these students had had much experience with electronic texts, the focus of my discussion with them was on traditional academic writing. Nevertheless, their opinions may reveal much about the attitudes Chinese students hold toward plagiarism.

The Nature of Plagiarism

My interviews with Chinese graduate students confirm that plagiarism both exists and is recognizable in Chinese academic life. Many of the participants in the study told anecdotes about well-known scholars found plagiarizing academic papers. For example, one participant told a story about a professor who published a paper that had previously been published in the West without mentioning that he had translated it directly from English.

Another student, who herself admitted to plagiarism in school, distinguished between plagiarism in popular science magazines or in newspapers, which might be considered acceptable, and plagiarism in serious research journals, which would not be acceptable.

> It depends what kind of paper. If it is a magazine for popular science, it is not a serious problem. If you write an academic paper, it is a serious problem. Such a problem. This is also a difference between scientific and social science area. For example, my boss in China made a research on technology but some person from another government agency . . . published [his paper]. My boss was very annoyed, but he could do nothing about it.

The distinction this student makes is important in understanding how Chinese students define plagiarism. We can see in her comments contradictory attitudes toward what is considered plagiarism. On the one hand, the student's attitude toward the plagiarism of popular writing seems to epitomize how Westerners have traditionally viewed Chinese attitudes. On the other hand, she recognizes that certain forms of writing are the property of the author and cannot be appropriated by someone else.

The Causes of Plagiarism

From my earlier discussion, one would expect that there have been changes in Chinese views on plagiarism due to larger changes in the country's political and social life. We saw earlier how individuals, thinking that their actions are acceptable, may be entrapped by changes in the society. Likewise, some of the participants in my study felt that it might have been acceptable to plagiarize in the past but not necessarily today. For instance, a student in educational psychology, who had been a college administrator in China, said that in the past it was common practice to hand in essays that had been copied. She felt that this practice might have

resulted from teachers trying to push their students to read more. Consequently, the students only had time to copy what they had read—a practice another participant called the "cut-and-paste" strategy—but did not
have the time to think about what they had read. However, the former
administrator went on to qualify her claim by noting that conditions are
changing and that she personally would be upset if somebody plagiarized
her papers.

The students also provided evidence of how plagiarism could result
from a lack of knowledge. In the following comment, an engineering student connected the problem of plagiarism to Chinese students' lack of
writing training in college.

> The kind of training I received in university does not emphasize how we
> should write or how we should cite. So I think that . . . the academic standards
> are not really so formalized. Some Chinese students did not learn this tradi-
> tion very fast and they were basically going their own way. I don't think that
> it is intentional.

This student seems to say here that since the Chinese college students
never learned this new "tradition" of using source texts, it was acceptable
for them to "go their own way."

Among the participants in my study, there was also an acknowledgment that there are differences in attitudes toward plagiarism relative to
the kind of text being written. These differences sometimes reflect different attitudes toward the texts. Note, for example, how a graduate student
in physics describes her own experiences of plagiarizing in college.

> Generally, people think if you are not going to publish this, [plagiarism] is not
> a serious problem, for course paper not a big deal. But if you want to publish,
> it's a serious problem if you publish some paper and figure out it's copied and
> not yours.

While this student's attitude may account for some instances of plagiarism, it is not completely dissimilar from the attitudes often displayed by
American college students toward their classroom assignments, particularly when these assignments are considered meaningless. Their attitudes
toward such assignments are reflected in the proliferation of Web sites
offering to sell term papers. This Chinese student similarly makes an
important distinction between what she sees as meaningless school-based
writing assignments and more meaningful ones, such as publishing, that
are important in her life.

This attitude may reflect a general cynicism that has developed in

Chinese life. This cynicism is often the result of students' being forced in the past to write about political matters in which they had no interest. In that context, plagiarism became a writing strategy that not only simplified a boring task but also protected the writer from the consequences of political deviations. One participant described how in high school she would copy from the newspapers when she had to write political criticism. Her strategy was "use glue and scissors to make your paper." In situations where students do not feel that it is important to say anything original, they may resort to this "cut-and-paste" strategy. In the past, cutting and pasting from a politically acceptable text was one way students could ensure they would be considered politically correct. Deviations from the party line could be detrimental or even dangerous to students' careers. They therefore had no incentive to say anything original.

The same participant went on to recall how she had plagiarized while in college because she felt that her Chinese writing assignments were often meaningless and boring while also requiring adherence to established patterns of political thought and expression.

> First, you have to have some argument. First, there looks like some kind of framework, but that framework must be based on Marxism. Once you put the argument, you have to convince the person that the argument is right by quoting more Marxism and so on. I don't like writing in Chinese because I feel so dull because you have to use statements to confirm statements. Then generally, in that period of time, I read a lot of journals and copy it together and make a paper.

Here, this student describes plagiarism as a potential writing strategy to be used only when the writing context is judged not to be important or when the writer does not know of other approaches to the situation. This explanation reflects her belief that a writing assignment had to be considered important or meaningful to generate the effort to be original and not plagiarize. The view that "academic" (excluding personal or expressive) writing falls within the category of meaningless writing was common among the participants in my study.

In general, the participants in my study shared a sense of the general parameters of what is considered plagiarism, although there was not unanimity on the specifics of plagiarism. As in the plagiarism case described by Li and Xiong (1996), the students' intent was clearly not to "steal" but rather to borrow. Therefore, although my study indicated, among Chinese students, some acceptance of plagiarism as a valid writing strategy in both English and Chinese, this acceptance may not have resulted from laziness on the students' part or from traditional Chinese rhetoric. It may have been a result of linguistic insecurity and a fear of making mistakes, or it may have been an act of what Pennycook (1996) has called resistance against writing that has no significance.

The Problem of Teaching about Plagiarism

I have tried to show that plagiarism may result not only from deep-seated cultural differences but also from writing strategies that could change as the learner's language skills develop or as the rhetorical context changes. Nevertheless, students entering Anglophone universities must confront new writing contexts without necessarily understanding the cultural norms that govern these contexts. Therefore, most ESL teachers believe it is necessary to explicitly teach the norms of plagiarism as an integral part of their composition courses.

Unfortunately, some of the cultural stereotypes associated with ESL students have led to oversimplification in teaching about plagiarism. For example, the assumption that Chinese students have a radically different concept of plagiarism has sometimes led teachers to over dramatize that difference by comparing the plagiarizing of a paper to the theft of a personal item. ESL teachers operating in this manner commonly illustrate plagiarism by "stealing" a student's bag or jacket. However, this metaphor is problematic on several levels. First, it assumes that the Chinese have no sense of intellectual property, an assumption that, as I have already shown, is not accurate. Where Chinese societies have had an economic interest in protecting intellectual property, they have developed copyright laws. Cox and Chow (1996) point out that such Chinese locales as Hong Kong and Taiwan, which have developed commercially important intellectual property industries, have also developed strong intellectual property laws. There is reason to believe that as China develops its own sources of intellectual property, the Chinese will develop their own pertinent laws (Miller 1996).

The second problem with using the metaphor of theft to illustrate plagiarism is that it assumes a clear and consistent definition of plagiarism. In the West, both the number of court cases concerning intellectual property and the controversies over what constitutes plagiarism seem to belie the existence of a clear-cut definition (Wallace and Mangan 1996). Recent incidents concerning accusations of plagiarism in academic writing illustrate the difficulty in defining the phenomenon. A recent charge of plagiarism concerning an article about high school football published in the journal

Sociology of Sport has raised several questions (Mooney 1992). For example, is intent, which is a factor in intellectual property law, a factor in plagiarism? Is accidentally copying another author's work without crediting it plagiarism? The author accused of plagiarism maintained that in his *Sociology of Sport* article he was only using the structure of the allegedly plagiarized article and that it was not his intent to plagiarize, even though his article contained numerous uncited passages similar to those found in the other article. Other people, however, felt that intent was not the issue; if the article had passages similar to those in another one already published, then its author was guilty of plagiarism. This example and numerous other court cases concerning various forms of intellectual property over the last few years suggest that confusion as to what constitutes plagiarism is as prevalent in the West as in China.

Further complicating the problem of teaching about plagiarism is the ambiguity of the "crime" of plagiarism. The "theft" of intellectual property is not necessarily the same as the theft of physical property. Copying intellectual property does not necessarily result in loss of property for the author (Mulkay 1972); in fact, the copying of software may even result in additional revenue for the software companies. Moreover, the "stealing" metaphor does not account for the rhetorical dimension of citations. The need for the attribution of sources is not only a question of acknowledging ownership. There is also a rhetorical purpose for citing sources. Academic writing in particular relies on a kind of social cohesiveness, what Myers (1985) refers to as the need for writers to demonstrate how their ideas are connected with what has already been published. Thus, there is rhetorical value in demonstrating how one's own claims either are consistent with or extend beyond what has previously been claimed. Achieving this social cohesiveness can be problematic for ESL students. Lacking formal knowledge of the rules governing the use of intellectual property, these students may produce texts that generate charges of plagiarism when there in fact was no actual intent to steal or cheat.

Electronic Texts and Teaching about Plagiarism

ESL students who lack knowledge of rules regulating the use of intellectual property face not only the danger of being accused of plagiarism but also the problem of writing ineffective texts. The increase in on-line information, usenet groups, news lists, and electronic journals adds a new dimension to this discussion of plagiarism. These new electronic resources provide a vast new supply of texts that can be added to the network of texts available for student use; at the same time, however, their rhetorical value is unclear, since their status in the academic world has yet to be determined. An important question now being addressed by scholars and teachers is, Does the citing of a text from the Internet carry the same weight as the citing of a text from a print journal? This question raises a number of related questions regarding teaching about plagiarism and regarding how reading and writing are taught in the context of source text use. For example, does an E-mail message or a Usenet posting need to be cited or attributed in the same way as passages from printed texts? Should E-mail messages be cited without permission? We see here that the distinction between what is private and what is public, the basis for determining whether something has been plagiarized (Rose 1993), is even less clear in the electronic medium than in the medium of print. Given that ESL students may already be confused about plagiarism, how will the growing use of these new forms of texts affect their attitudes?

Electronic Texts as Intellectual Property

The question posed in the preceding paragraph becomes more complex if electronic texts are considered different from printed texts. As Barlow (1994), Bolter (1990), and others have argued, electronic texts and printed texts are not the same, partly because the electronic medium is not the same as the printed page. This point of view can have a profound affect on whether a text is considered plagiarized, since where information is published is traditionally an important consideration in determining plagiarism. Fields (1996) notes that an idea is copyrighted when it is fixed in a "tangible medium," that there is thus no difference between an idea placed on paper and an idea placed on a server, and therefore that plagiarism can be defined the same way in both contexts. This position has never been clearly established, however, either legally or theoretically. Numerous court cases, many of them still wending their way to the Supreme Court, have questioned whether the Internet is, in fact, simply an extension of traditional media and therefore governed by existing law. Is the Internet, for example, an oral medium like a phone company, where ideas are not fixed in a tangible medium, or is it a written medium like a magazine, where they are? Since the nature of intellectual property varies across different media, so would the laws and norms concerning its appropriation. If scholars' and teachers' views of the nature and use of electronic texts are unclear, working with those texts may be an even greater problem for ESL students, who may have far less exposure to and understanding of the Internet than do other students.

Authorship and Electronic Texts

While electronic texts may present difficulties for ESL students with respect to issues of authorship and intellectual property, there is an alternative possibility: that the Internet may prove less problematic for some ESL students than for Anglophone students. In some instances, how electronic texts are viewed as intellectual property may not be that different from the way intellectual property has traditionally been conceptualized in China or in other countries from which students come to American colleges. Still, the globalization of the Internet has complicated perspectives on plagiarism by challenging conventional views of authorship and of what constitutes the ownership of intellectual property. Barlow (1994) has argued that since the posting of information on the Internet can be read anywhere in the world, it poses a unique question regarding a fundamental concept of intellectual property. For instance, although the Internet remains distinctly "American," can or should Americans impose their views of intellectual property on all writers, regardless of their geographical location? An affirmative answer to this question would challenge the conventional distinction between public and private property, the assumption underlying what any culture considers plagiarism. Furthermore, LeBlanc (1995) argues that even policies of fair use do not make sense in electronic environments, since it is easy for one copy of a text to be more widely distributed there than in the traditional classroom. Similarly, Lunsford and West (1996) argue that in electronic texts, the traditional view of the individual author dissolves. The ease with which individuals can access and revise texts electronically, sometimes without the consent of the author, may have a profound affect on how traditional authorship is viewed. Woodmansee and Jaszi (1995) likewise argue for a radical view of authorship on the Internet, where vast amounts of information are exchanged with little concern for claims of authorship. Can the traditional concept of authorship be maintained in a medium where one text can be easily linked to an infinite number of other texts? If different contexts allow for different forms of authorship, it is possible that at least some of them may resemble concepts of authorship found outside of the West. As a result, what is proposed as a radical view of authorship in the West may not be so radical for writers from other cultures, since they do not necessarily share the traditions that produced Western concepts of authorship. What Woodmansee and Jaszi call the "romantic model of sole, original authorship" (783) may not be as prevalent in China as it is in the West. If there is a more collaborative voice in Chinese rhetoric, what may be problematic for Chinese students about plagiarism in regard to printed texts may be less problematic in regard to electronic texts.

Implications for Teaching about Plagiarism

As Pecorari argues elsewhere in this volume (chap. 9), "plagiarism is anything but a cut-and-dried concept" among institutions, despite their assumptions that definitions of plagiarism are universal. Regardless of how our views of electronic texts evolve, the existence of these new textual forms challenges the conventional ways in which plagiarism has been addressed in ESL composition classes. Some people have proposed technology solutions to what are considered to be technological problems. Such Web sites as *Glatt Plagiarism Services, Inc.* (http://www.plagiarism.com) purport to be able to detect plagiarism from the Internet. Other people, however, are calling for a redefinition of what we consider to be plagiarism. We are beginning to see new definitions of plagiarism and copyright that may be more useful in understanding differences between Western and non-Western views of intellectual property and plagiarism. What we cannot assume, however, is that the same strategies for teaching that were used with print texts can be used with electronic texts. I have tried to show that Chinese students in particular bring to the West a complex set of ideas regarding what is intellectual property and what is plagiarism. With the Internet developing as a new source of information, plagiarism has become an even more complex problem, particularly for students coming from or living in cultures where these issues have not received much attention. It is already common knowledge that students are often confused about plagiarism. It is important that we understand the sources of this confusion in all their complexity before we attempt to help students engage the issues involved. Otherwise, our solutions may be simplistic and detrimental to their development.

In part, the confusion results from both cultural and material factors, neither of which can be considered alone. This chapter's discussion of plagiarism presents contradictory evidence about the influence of culture that makes any definitive statement about ESL students' attitudes toward plagiarism rather difficult to defend. The introduction of electronic texts into the academic curriculum as well as into the professional lives of Chinese academics has added a new dimension to the problem. As China's economic situation has changed and as China has attempted to integrate itself into the world economy, Chinese attitudes toward intellectual property have likewise changed. How will these changes affect Chinese writers as they adapt to the new technologies? How will similar changes affect writers in other cultures? The answers, in part, depend on what is thought to be the nature of the Internet. Is it simply an extension of the world of printed texts, or is it a new domain where texts will be viewed differently? The more conservative view, that the Internet will simply provide more texts for researchers to have access to, means that, as mentioned earlier, the existing rules for attribution, as well as existing rules of copyright, can be applied in cyberspace. As a result, Chinese students and researchers may have to learn even more about intellectual property and plagiarism if they want their work to be recognized in the West.

The radical view provides a different challenge. This view holds that computer-mediated discourse will look dramatically different from its print-based predecessor and that, as a result, cyberspace will have different rules regarding what is public and what is private. As I have attempted to show, Chinese writers already bring to the composition classroom a long tradition and healthy respect for the kinds of intertextuality and hypertextuality found on the Internet. Thus, the ability of the Internet to integrate an infinite number of texts may be viewed very positively by Chinese students.

The pedagogical implications for discussing the plagiarism of electronic texts are equally complex. The core question teachers face is less about whether cyberspace will provide an easier method for plagiarizing texts and more about how this new world of electronic texts fits into the overall purposes of the second language composition classroom. Approaches to teaching about plagiarism as well as related reading and writing strategies may depend on how the role of the classroom is viewed. ESL composition pedagogy has long been divided into at least two camps (whose views are not necessarily mutually exclusive): (1) those who believe that the ESL composition classroom should be a place where students primarily explore the nature of language and (2) those who believe the ESL composition classroom should be a place that prepares ESL students for the kinds of academic writing they will encounter in their course work. In the former type of classroom, there is great opportunity to explore how these new kinds of text challenge the traditional forms of authorship in ways that may be consistent with traditional forms of Chinese rhetoric. In the latter type of classroom, teachers can focus on acclimating students to ways of utilizing the vast number of texts and resources available in cyberspace.

In both types of classroom, the cultural traditions of ESL students can be an asset in their creation and use of electronic texts. Their traditions can also be a stimulus by which to challenge conventional thinking about classroom writing, in ways that meaningfully embrace issues surrounding use of the Internet and computer-mediated discourse. The various problems concerning plagiarism have long motivated ESL teachers to find reading and writing strategies and create assignments that can combat whatever tendencies students may have for plagiarizing. It is crucial, for example, to engage the students in meaningful writing so that they do not feel that they are engaged in empty or unproductive tasks (as the Chinese students felt they had been in writing political criticism) and to create an atmosphere where they do not need to bind themselves to the act of copying texts out of a fear of making mistakes in their own writing. Cyberspace, then, adds new challenges to ESL teaching, but these challenges may bring greater rewards. I do not want to minimize the problems surrounding plagiarism, such as the easy ability to "cut and paste" from the Internet, for as long as students feel insecure about their writing, they will try to mimic standard forms of English. However, the Internet can also become a place where Chinese (and other) students, with their long and varied traditions of authorship and intertextuality, may feel more at home than in traditional classrooms. This impact may be felt beyond the writing classroom. Many have believed, or hoped, that the Internet will change political and social life in China, but few have considered the impact that the Chinese may have on the Internet. As the most populous nation in the world gains more and more access to cyberspace, its impact on what is considered to be the authorship of electronic texts may be considerable. Far from having to be taught about this new world of intellectual property and plagiarism, the Chinese may have something to teach the West.

References

Barlow, J. P. 1994. The economy of ideas: A framework for rethinking patents and copyrights in a digital age. *Wired* 2 (March): 85–90, 126–29.

Bloch, J. G., and L. Chi. 1995. A comparison of the use of citations in Chinese and English academic discourse. In *Academic writing in a second language: Essays on research and pedagogy*, ed. D. Belcher and G. Braine, 231–47. Norwood, NJ: Ablex.

Bolter, J. D. 1990. *Writing space: The computer, hypertext, and the history of writing.* Hillsdale, NJ: Lawrence Erlbaum.

Chaffee, J. W. 1985. *The thorny gates of learning in Sung China: A social history of examinations.* New York: Cambridge University Press.

Cox, R. E., and D. D. Chow. 1996. Checkered Chinese policy. *Intellectual Property.* <http://www.ipmag.com/summ962.html>.

Creel, H. G. 1970. *The origins of statecraft in China.* Chicago: University of Chicago Press.

Deckert, G. D. 1993. Perspectives on plagiarism from ESL students in Hong Kong. *Journal of Second Language Writing* 2:131–48.

Elkin-Koren, N. 1998. Public/private and copyright reform in cyberspace. <http://www/ascusc.org/jcmc/vol2/issue2/elkin.html>.

Elman, B. A. 1991. Political, social, and cultural reproduction via civil service examinations in late imperial China. *Journal of Asian Studies* 50:7–28.

Fields, T. G. 1996. Copyright on the Internet. <http://fplc.edu/fields/cOpyNet.htm>.

Fox, H. 1994. *Listening to the world: Cultural issues in academic writing.* Urbana, IL: National Council of Teachers of English.

Gross, A. 1990. *The rhetoric of science.* Cambridge: Harvard University Press.

Kolko, B. E. 1998. Intellectual property in synchronic and collaborative virtual space. *Computers and Composition* 15:163–83.

LeBlanc, P. 1995. Pulling out the rug: Technology, scholarship, and the humanities. In *The politics and processes of scholarship,* ed. J. M. Moxley and L. T. Lenker, 115–25. Westport, CT: Greenwood.

Lee, T. H. C. 1989. Sung education before Chu Hsi. In *Neo-Confucian education: The formative stage,* ed. W. T. de Bary and J. W. Chaffee, 106–36. Berkeley: University of California Press.

Li, X., and L. Xiong. 1996. Chinese researchers debate rash of plagiarism cases. *Science* 274:337–38.

Lichtenberg, J. 1995. Academic property and new technologies: Protecting intellectual property is the key. In *The politics and processes of scholarship,* ed. J. M. Moxley and L. T. Lenker, 89–95. Westport, CT: Greenwood.

Link, E. P. 1981. *Mandarin ducks and butterflies: Popular fiction in early twentieth-century China.* Berkeley: University of California Press.

Lunsford, A. A., and S. West. 1996. Intellectual property and composition studies. *College Composition and Communication* 47:383–411.

Matalene, C. 1986. Response to a comment on contrastive rhetoric: An American writing teacher in China. *College English* 48:846–48.

Miller, H. L. 1996. *Science and dissent in Post-Mao China: The politics of knowledge.* Seattle: University of Washington Press.

Mooney, C. J. 1992. Plagiarism charges against a scholar can divide experts, perplex scholarly societies, and raise intractable questions. *Chronicle of Higher Education,* February 12, A1, A14, A16.

Mulkay, M. J. 1972. *The social process of innovation.* New York: Macmillan.

Myers, G. 1985. The social construction of two biologists' proposals. *Written Communication* 2:219–45.

Needham, J. 1969. *The grand titration.* London: Allen and Unwin.

Negroponte, N. 1996. The next billion users. *Wired* 4 (June):220.

Pennycook, A. 1996. Borrowing others' words: Text, ownership, memory, and plagiarism. *TESOL Quarterly* 30:201–30.

Qian, W. L. 1985. *The great inertia.* London: Crown Helm.

Rawski, E. S. 1985. *Popular culture in late imperial China.* Berkeley: University of California Press.

Rose, M. 1993. *Authors and owners: The invention of copyright.* Cambridge: Harvard University Press.

Scollon, R. 1995. Plagiarism and ideology: Identity in intercultural discourse. *Language and Society* 24:1–28.

Wallace, J., and M. Mangan. 1996. *Sex, laws, and cyberspace.* New York: M&T Books.

Woodmansee, M., and P. Jaszi. 1995. The law of texts: Copyright in the academy. *College English* 57:769–87.

Chapter 9

Plagiarism and International Students: How the English-Speaking University Responds

Diane Pecorari, University of Birmingham

When students gather facts and opinions from written sources and report them in their writing assignments, a connection is forged between reading and writing skills. When this connection emerges in the expected way, it is called citation and is valued as one attribute of successful academic writing. When the conventions are not adhered to, it is called plagiarism and treated as a serious violation of academic standards.

Meeting expectations about the use of citations can be especially difficult for international students in English-speaking universities. Various explanations have been offered for this, including limited language proficiency (Cammish 1997), which might cause students to mistrust their language skills and follow a source text too closely; past experience in an educational system that encourages close modeling of other texts (Bloch and Chi 1995); and cultural attitudes toward authorship and originality (e.g., Matalene 1985; Pennycook 1996; Scollon 1995). Scollon (1995) observed that "the concept of plagiarism is fully embedded within a social, political, and cultural matrix that cannot be meaningfully separated from its interpretation" (23). International students in an English-speaking university must attempt to interpret the concept without the benefit of a lifetime spent in the culture that produced it. At the same time, the standards and rules of their universities are applied to them.

Howard (1995) points out that such rules are often inappropriate for addressing the problems novice academic writers may face. She argues that "a textual strategy" she terms "patchwriting," involving too-close paraphrasing, "has traditionally been classified as plagiarism" (788) but does not represent a conscious violation of the rules; it is a developmental stage for writers who "are working in unfamiliar discourse, when they must work monologically with the words and ideas of a source text" (796).

She observes that teachers whose students engage in patchwriting may find themselves in an unenviable position if their institutions require an inflexible, punitive response to plagiarism.

These two issues—the difficulty of source use for inexpert academic writers and the possibility of harsh consequences if they fail in meeting the target—provide the background to the research reported here. It had two goals: (1) to determine whether the English-speaking academic discourse community can be said to have a common view of plagiarism and (2) to explore the policies and practices universities have in place for dealing with plagiarism and assess how appropriate they are for international students.

Background to the Problem

Evidence that international students often encounter difficulties with plagiarism is plentiful. Although many of the accounts found in the literature are anecdotal, they are nonetheless valuable in indicating the sources of the problems. Based on the literature on plagiarism and international students, we can identify six features believed to be desirable in university policies and mechanisms for dealing with plagiarism: (1) a definition of plagiarism; (2) a broader discussion of the acts that fall under that heading; (3) an explanation of the reasons plagiarism is objected to; (4) a constructive approach focusing on educating about the use of sources, rather than threats of punishment; (5) appropriate procedures for cases of suspected plagiarism and suitable sanctions for it; and (6) recognition of the complex nature of plagiarism and the lack of universal standards for the use of sources.

A Definition of the Term

Plagiarism is such a common concept in the English-speaking academic community that it may seem unnecessary to explain what plagiarism is or that it is considered to be a bad thing. Yet there is evidence that some students do indeed need such an explanation.

One example comes from Pennycook (1996), who assigned his students in China to write about a famous person. Pennycook writes that one response to this assignment "had the ring of a text from elsewhere, of language borrowed and repeated." He continues:

> I sought out the. . . student and asked him about his text. He explained that although he felt that he had not really done the task I had set, because I had

asked them to do some research prior to writing, he had felt rather fortunate that I had asked them to write something which he already knew. Sitting in his head was a brief biography of Abraham Lincoln, and he was quite happy to produce it on demand. (201–2)

The student did not attempt to conceal that he was not the original author of the Lincoln biography. The implication is that he did not consider reproducing a text without citation to be something that needed to be concealed. To understand rules about plagiarism, students like this would first need to have the word defined and explained and to be taught that copying all or part of a piece of academic writing from another source is considered to be wrong.

Illustrations and Examples

A definition alone may not be enough. It was not sufficient for a group of Malaysian students who had been accused of plagiarism but told another teacher that they had not plagiarized: "They knew what plagiarism was, they said, and they had not copied word for word. They had memorized the textbook and repeated that back on the exam" (Leki 1992, 72). Incidents like this demonstrate that providing students with a definition of plagiarism and a warning not to commit it is often not enough. Examples and illustrations of the many and varied acts that come under the heading of plagiarism are needed to show students how their writing practices may violate the rules.

Reasons for Not Plagiarizing

Students who are learning to incorporate sources into their writing often ask such questions as how many words in a source text must be changed to make a paraphrase. Students asking such questions show a lack of understanding about the reasons why plagiarism is held to be wrong. They do not understand that teachers want their students to go through the process of reformulating an idea in their own words—that a paraphrase is acceptable if the writer has expressed an idea in his or her own words (in which case there may be superficial similarities between the original source and the paraphrase) but not if the writer has simply substituted synonyms for key words.

Deckert's 1993 research showed that first-year students in Hong Kong had a limited understanding of the reasons why plagiarism was wrong, and he concluded that "their past educational experience simply had not exposed them to a Western conception of the broader consequences of misusing source materials" (142). Students may find it easier to follow a rule if they understand the reasons for it. Thus, university policies and practices on plagiarism may be more useful if they set forth explicitly the values and attitudes that underlie the prohibition against plagiarizing.

A Constructive Approach

It has been suggested that universities couch warnings about plagiarism in a harsh, legalistic tone, treating students "as potential or actual criminals" (Pennycook 1996, 220). According to Macrae (1997, 141), "plagiarism and fabrication of results are virtually a crime" in British universities.

If it is recognized that students may copy without any intention of violating the rules, such an approach to plagiarism has several potentially damaging consequences. First, students who view copying or closely modeling as good writing strategies may not connect the dire warnings of an illegal activity with their own work and may simply disregard the warnings. Second, as Howard (1995) notes, teachers who view overdependence on sources as a developmental stage "might find themselves professionally compromised if their institutions' regulations provided only for juridical responses," and they "may therefore be forced into counter-pedagogical responses" (797).

Finally, teachers who have limited contact with international students may not recognize or fully understand unintentional misuse of sources. By following harsh, legalistic procedures, they may initiate disciplinary proceedings ending in punishing students who do not really understand their crime.

Appropriate Procedures and Penalties

Especially where the prescribed disciplinary procedures seem harsh, staff may be reluctant to follow them to the letter. The university-wide policy of an Australian institution that responded to the survey discussed later in this chapter dictates: "Staff are required to report all cases of suspected cheating to the Unit Coordinator. If the Coordinator believes cheating has taken place, this must be reported to the Dean before any penalty is imposed." But in a personal communication (and with regard to all students, not only international students), one of the institution's unit coordinators wrote: "While the penalties seem very harsh, and they have been invoked, the way in which they are run depends very much on the level of the student in the system. . . . I would leave most of the issues . . . to be dealt with by my tutors and not involve the university at all." This example suggests that if teachers suspect, for any or all of the reasons already mentioned, that their students have plagiarized without a full awareness of what they were doing, they may be reluctant to set in motion cumbersome procedures that could result in the student suffering serious consequences. A further desirable feature of university disciplinary procedures, then, is that they permit action that is appropriate to the situation, so that teachers can implement them in good conscience.

Addressing the Gray Areas

Plagiarism is far from a clearly defined construct. Pennycook (1996) argues persuasively that "plagiarism cannot be cast as a simple black-and-white issue" and that "it needs to be understood in terms of complex relationships between text, memory, and learning" (201).

The illusive nature of plagiarism is seen at many levels. Postmodern thought calls into question the idea of an autonomous author. Writer Kathy Acker, for example, has received favorable critical attention for using plagiarism as a form of expression: "Acker's (auto)plagiaristic technique foregrounds issues that are crucial to critical theory" (Sciolino 1990, 442).

Not every discipline views plagiarism in the same way, and scientists do not adopt the view of plagiarism as a creative act. "Incidents of plagiarism in science corrupt the soul of the perpetrator [and] erode the integrity of the discipline," according to the editor of the *Canadian Journal of Physics*, who promised, after publishing a plagiarized article, "to avoid such a deplorable occurrence in the future" (Betts 1992, 289).

Often there is disagreement about whether allegations of plagiarism have merit. The scholarly journals of every field report disputes between academics who cannot agree whether plagiarism has occurred. For example, Mark Twain's *A Connecticut Yankee in King Arthur's Court* was published in 1890, but the debate about whether Twain plagiarized continues (Kruse 1990). In a case involving medical researchers at the University of Hong Kong, three court decisions and a university committee's ruling were required to reach a decision on whether a questionnaire had been plagiarized, with expert witnesses from the field testifying on both sides (Brahams 1995; Dyer 1995).

Howard (1995) points out that institutional policies castigate plagiarism as a moral crime, making intent paramount, but look to textual similarities as proof that it happened. Is plagiarism, then, a defect in the product or in the process?

The rapid expansion of the Internet complicates the matter further. In chapter 8 in this volume, Bloch discusses additional complexities involving citation that have risen with the advent of new electronic media and points out that there is not as yet scholarly consensus as to whether electronic sources should or should not be treated as distinct from more traditional media for the purposes of debate about intellectual property.

These are just some of the complexities that surround the concept, and there is no reason to think that students are unaware of them. Indeed, precisely because international students approach the question from a different background, they may perceive subtleties that are not readily apparent to their teachers. An insistence that plagiarism is always clear and always wrong may simply be rejected. Instead, it may be more productive to discuss the area where good and bad practice approach each other. In chapter 10 in this volume, Barks and Watts call for precisely this approach in the classroom; university policies that aim at combating plagiarism would do well to set the example and provide a more complex treatment of the issues surrounding source use and plagiarism.

Methods

An international survey on plagiarism was carried out with two goals: (1) to investigate which of the six features described earlier were present in the policies and practices of English-speaking universities and (2) to explore whether those universities share a common definition of plagiarism. One hundred and forty universities—72 in the United States, 42 in the United Kingdom, and 26 in Australia—were asked for four types of information: (1) a formal definition of plagiarism, (2) regulations about plagiarism, (3) a set of procedures that teaching staff should follow if they find or suspect plagiarism in a student's writing, and (4) guidance for students on appropriate ways to use source material.

Fifty-four universities responded with information in a variety of forms, including university statutes and regulations, student handbooks, and brochures (written for students) explaining research and citation skills. A total of 74 documents were provided. Table 1 details the responses and the types of material received.

The materials were examined for a formal definition of plagiarism and to see which of the aforementioned six features they incorporated.

TABLE 1

	United States	Great Britain	Australia	Total
Institutions Responding	21	20	14	54
Documents Sent	31	23	20	74
Types of Documents				
Student Handbooks	10	7	7	24
University Regulations	2	10	3	15
Procedure Manuals	4	1	4	9
Guides to Citation, Plagiarism, and Academic Misconduct	15	5	6	26
No University-Wide Definition	7	3	4	14
Documents That Speak of Plagiarism but Do Not Define It	7	3	4	14

Findings

A Common Definition of Plagiarism?

Fifty-three definitions were present in the documents. The definitions mentioned some or all of six elements: plagiarism is (1) material that has been (2) taken from (3) some source by (4) someone, (5) without acknowledgment and (6) with/without intention to deceive. Typical was the definition from a British university:[1] "Plagiarism is defined as the use of other people's work and the submission of it as though it were one's own work."

The definitions were very consistent and differed primarily in the level of detail they provided. For example, one British university supplied the definition

> Plagiarism is the substantial use, without acknowledgement and with intent to deceive the examiners or knowing that the examiners might be deceived, of the intellectual work of other people by representing, whether by copying or paraphrase, the ideas or discoveries of another or of others as one's own in work submitted for assessment; . . .

Meanwhile, an Australian university contented itself with the definition "Plagiarism is the passing off of the thoughts or works of another as one's own."

The single area where an important disagreement emerged among the definitions was with regard to whether plagiarism may occur unin-

---

1. To avoid the appearance of singling out universities for criticism, institutions are not identified here by name.

tentionally. On the one hand, 7 of the documents defined plagiarism as an intentional act. For example, a university in the United States described plagiarism as "the deliberate copying, writing or presenting as one's own . . . " In addition, 36 documents used such phrases as "taking credit falsely," "stealing," "representing as one's own," "passing off as one's own," and so on, which would seem to suggest an intention to deceive. On the other hand, 11 documents accepted that plagiarism can be unintentional, although not without reservations. For example, an Australian university said it "can sometimes occur unintentionally, but is more frequently a deliberate attempt to deceive." Inadvertent plagiarism was attributed by three universities to sloppy writing practices and by three to lack of familiarity with citation conventions.

Since plagiarism by international students is believed often to be unintentional, whether institutions accept unintentional plagiarism is an important question. Those that accept the existence of inadvertent plagiarism may be better equipped to help students in whose writing it appears. Apart from this point, the definitions were quite consistent, supporting the idea that the English-speaking academic discourse community has a common view of plagiarism.

The Presence of a Definition

Fifteen of the institutions responding to the survey, or 27.7 percent, had no university-wide definition of plagiarism. While it is recognized that individual units, departments, programs, and so on may provide students with a great deal of useful information about plagiarism, the absence of a definition and policy at the university level is significant. Where there is no university-wide definition, students in different departments have different standards to live up to. An Australian university addressed this issue by stating that students should take responsibility for understanding the rules of each area of the university in which they take classes. An American university took a similar view: "students should request a delineation of [honor code] policy from each professor if none is given at the beginning of each semester." This approach seems, however, to put a heavy and perhaps unrealistic burden on students, especially undergraduates, who take classes in several departments.

An administrator at an American university described a similar situation and called it "the weakest link in the chain, in that, for many of the cases I have seen involving plagiarism, the accused student did not understand the proper use of citation and did not fully understand the concept of plagiarism." The administrator continued, "Occasionally, you will find a faculty member who provides additional information and guidance in a specific class, but this is the exception rather than the norm."

Fifteen of the 74 documents, or 20 percent, did not define plagiarism although they referred to it. An additional document provided no definition of plagiarism but also contained no direct reference to plagiarism; and two contained definitions of plagiarism but did not use that term, simply including the definition under types of academic misconduct.

The definitions from the remaining institutions were found in a variety of contexts. The sources ranged from brochures with eye-catching illustrations, aimed at educating students about plagiarism, to student handbooks and university statutes. The documents fall into four categories: brochures, guides, and so on about plagiarism, citation, and academic misconduct in general (26 documents); student handbooks and catalogs (24 documents); university regulations (15 documents); and manuals of university procedures (9 documents).

Two of the handbooks suggested the level of engagement they expected from their target audience. One from a British university began, "You are not expected to read, learn and inwardly digest the whole of [this handbook] but you are strongly advised to keep it safely for easy reference." An American university's handbook had this entry on its first page: "Please read the section titled . . ." Presumably university statutes are even less likely to be read by students. It is perhaps fair to wonder whether definitions found in documents students are unlikely to read closely are intended primarily to inform students or to serve as a basis for taking action against those who have violated the rules.

A Detailed Discussion of Plagiarism

A detailed discussion of plagiarism with examples of the practices the term encompasses was one of the positive features that the survey sought in the plagiarism materials. The universities surveyed were thorough in listing practices that could be termed plagiarism: copying or paraphrasing without attribution, insufficient paraphrasing, purchasing a paper, and translating a work from another language and presenting it as original. One U.S. university listed "the verbatim repetition, without acknowledgement, of the writings of another author"; "borrowing without acknowledging the source"; and "paraphrasing the thoughts of another writer without acknowledgement." The substantial overlap between those categories—it is hard to imagine what kind of "borrowing" would not be either "paraphrasing" or "verbatim repetition"—is presumably intended to leave no possible gaps.

There were examples of correct and incorrect ways to incorporate material from a source into a writing assignment, and there were lists of the kinds of material that must be cited if used, including unpublished materials, information in electronic form, graphs, charts, maps, and illustrations. Students were told that not only words and ideas but also the organization of a piece of writing could be said to be plagiarized if followed too closely.

The lists were comprehensive enough to include activities that may not be widely accepted as plagiarism. For example, one university mentioned citing something from a secondary source in such a way as to make it appear that the writer had gone to the primary source. While many teachers would object to students' "padding the reference list" in this way, not all would agree that it constitutes plagiarism.

In general, the universities surveyed were very informative on the subject of what writing practices might be termed plagiarism.

Why Is Plagiarism Wrong?

The documents sent in response to the survey gave much less guidance about why plagiarism is prohibited. Only 13 of the 74 documents included one or more reasons why plagiarism is considered to be wrong. A further 14 documents presented plagiarism as being detrimental to standards of integrity and honesty, but without any clarification of what is dishonest about plagiarism; the simple assertion that plagiarism is harmful seems to fall short of being an explanation.

Five reasons for prohibiting plagiarism were offered: that students who do not plagiarize are placed at a disadvantage when their work is compared to a plagiarized piece of writing (in five documents), that plagiarism undermines the university's reputation since credit is granted for work not actually done by the student (in five documents), that plagiarism circumvents the learning process and works to the disadvantage of the plagiarist (in three documents), that good citation practices make the work stronger (in two documents), and that not acknowledging sources is unfair to their writers (in one document). The absence of more explanation is especially unfortunate given the wide variety of activities that were labeled as plagiarism. To join under one heading the seemingly disparate acts of insufficient paraphrasing, reporting a secondary source as if the primary source had been seen, and buying a piece of writing with the full consent of its author suggests that these acts all violate a common set of principles. With the exceptions already mentioned, these documents did not explain what those principles are.

Treating Plagiarism as a Crime

As I previously discussed, treating plagiarism as a crime may be a counterproductive approach to inadvertent plagiarism. The tone of the definitions collected through the survey was found to be surprisingly neutral in categorizing plagiarism. However, the documents discussed plagiarism in extremely harsh terms in other places. An Australian university's characterization of plagiarism as "an extremely serious academic offence" was typical. According to a British university, plagiarism is "an act of academic fraudulence." One American university used the words "academic fraud"; another called plagiarism "nothing less than an act of theft."

Policies for handling cases of suspected plagiarism evoked the language of the law court: the terms *allegation, hearing, trial, jury, prosecutor, defendant, witness, evidence, verdict,* and *acquittal* all appeared. Documents from two universities said proceedings should begin when it is determined that the accused has a "prima facie case to answer." Another two documents spoke of charges being proved "beyond reasonable doubt." While it is true that this kind of language could be expected in statutes and bylaws, that universities chose to deal with plagiarism through their internal judicial system is in itself significant. Plagiarism was lumped together with all sorts of misbehavior, banned along with "violent, indecent, disorderly, threatening or offensive behaviour or language"; "dropping or throwing objects from a high-rise building"; and the "sale, possession, manufacture, distribution, or consumption of alcoholic beverages on the University campus" (quotes drawn from two British university documents and an American one, respectively).

Two problems may arise as a consequence of plagiarism being presented as a criminal offense. First, students who have no intention of breaking the rules may not understand that the crime they are warned about is something they are likely to do. Second, students and teachers may feel uncomfortable about discussing the embarrassing possibility that the student is an academic criminal. When this happens, students who use source material in inappropriate ways may not get the help they need.

Dealing with Plagiarism

Forty-three of the 54 institutions responding to the survey provided information about the procedures that should be followed when plagiarism is suspected. The procedures fall into three categories: (1) those where the teacher is permitted to resolve the matter; (2) those that require the matter to be referred to an authority or body at the level of a department, school, college, or other internal division; (3) those in which a university-wide authority deals with the case. Thirty-nine of the 43 institutions reported having a university-wide procedure in place; 18 reported that individual administrative units dealt with the problem; and only 9 allowed the teacher to handle the matter autonomously (the total for the three categories is higher than 43 because some institutions have several levels of procedures in place for more or less serious occurrences).

Although more universities reported high-level procedures than any other procedures, it cannot necessarily be concluded that the high-level procedures are the most frequently used. The more complex and serious the official process is, the more likely it would seem that teachers will try to resolve cases of plagiarism on their own.

The rationale for university-wide procedures is easy to imagine: they are an attempt to guarantee that similar offenses receive similar treatment, regardless of the department they occur in, and to ensure that the teacher is not simultaneously accuser and judge. But the penalties reported show that once a question of plagiarism passes from the hands of the teacher to the academic judicial system, the outcome is more likely to be judgment and punishment than additional help with citation skills.

Thirty-nine institutions provided information about penalties. The most frequent set of punishments, used by 33 institutions, involved reducing or withholding academic awards. Grades for the plagiarized work or for the entire course could be reduced, possibly to zero value. Seven of those 33 institutions listed denying or revoking a degree as the highest penalty. The next most frequent type of punishment was suspension or expulsion (listed by 27 institutions). At 18 universities, an official reprimand or warning or a note in the student's record could be used to sanction plagiarism. Finally, a group of penalties in place at only six universities—two in the United States, one in Britain, and three in Australia—aimed at educating a student who is believed to have plagiarized through an imperfect understanding of what was expected, by requiring the student to attend a seminar on writing, frequent the writing center, and so on.

Given such a range of penalties, it may seem that there is ample scope for making the punishment fit the crime. But when plagiarism is unintentional, a productive response is to educate about, rather than punish, the offense, and only six institutions offer a constructive, rather than a punitive, option.

Examining the Gray Areas

As I previously discussed, plagiarism is anything but a clear-cut matter. However, in general, the documents collected through the survey ignored the potential difficulties for students in this area, making it appear that not plagiarizing was a simple matter of being careful to provide citations. A British university, for example, prefaced its discussion by saying that examples were drawn from two disciplines but that "the issues are the same in all disciplines." Another assured students: "a simple rule dictates when it is necessary to acknowledge sources. If a student obtains information or ideas from an outside source, that source must be acknowledged." An American university assured students, "The instructor can provide clear guidance on how the student can avoid committing this act of academic misconduct."

Only three documents hinted at the complexity surrounding the question of plagiarism. An American university acknowledged that attribution may be a difficult question in some disciplines, particularly in the fine and performing arts. One Australian university recognized that university-level students may discover more stringent standards for originality than those that are applied at lower school levels, and another offered its faculty members the advice to "be aware of and responsive to different cultural backgrounds of students, especially in relation to the use of the work of others and to writing skills."

Apart from the exceptions just mentioned, the institutions that responded to the survey failed to recognize the difficult issues involved in plagiarism and the use of sources. A few, however, provided an unwitting illustration of the point. Figure 1 gives some examples.

Examples 1a and 1b, from two British universities, are identical except that 1a includes the words "or inventions" while 1b does not. However, given that both are similar to many other definitions, that they are relatively short, and that the options for expressing the same idea are limited, it could plausibly be argued that they were created independently and that the resemblance is coincidental. Examples 2a and 2b are not identical, but they have many points of similarity, across many lines of text, and

Example 1

a. . . . to take and use another person's thoughts, writings or inventions as one's own. *(from a new British university)*

b. To plagiarise is to take and use another's thought or writings as one's own. *(from an older university in the north of Britain)*

Example 2

a. Plagiarism: Presenting the work of another as one's own (i.e., without proper acknowledgment of the source). The sole exception to the requirement of acknowledging sources is when the ideas, information regarding, etc. are common knowledge. (Note: for more information regarding plagiarism, see below.)

   Typical Examples: Submitting as one's own the work of a "ghost writer" or commercial writing service; directly quoting from a source without citation; paraphrasing or summarizing another's work without acknowledging the source; using facts, figures, graphs, charts or information without acknowledgment of the source. *(from a small university in the eastern United States)*

b. Plagiarism. Plagiarism is knowingly representing the work of another as one's own without proper acknowledgment of the source. The only exceptions to the requirement that sources be acknowledged occur when the information, ideas, etc., are common knowledge. Plagiarism includes, but is not limited to, submitting as one's own work the work of a "ghost writer" or work obtained from a commercial writing service; quoting directly or paraphrasing closely from a source without giving proper credit; using figures, graphs, charts, or other such material without identifying the sources. *(from a state university in the U.S. Pacific Northwest)*

Fig. 1. What is plagiarism?

include rather unusual expressions, such as "ghost writer," which was not found in any of the other definitions. Because of these many similarities, the explanation that leaps to mind is that one was copied from the other, with only minor alterations.

   These examples are not offered as a criticism of institutions that produced them. In fact (assuming that they are in fact instances of copying), it would be hard to find grounds for a serious criticism. Since no author is identified on any of these documents, no one is taking credit for another's work. Since promotion or other honors are unlikely to have been the result of the definitions, there is no question of anyone receiving unearned benefits. At a practical level, greater uniformity in institutional views of plagiarism can only be beneficial to students, and it seems unnecessary for every university to "reinvent the wheel," producing policies and definitions in isolation when useful ones already exist.

The examples are offered to illustrate the point that, despite the ease with which it is discussed, plagiarism is anything but a cut-and-dried concept. The writers of these documents decided that the usual rules about attribution—the rules they were in fact setting forth—did not apply to their particular case. So some understanding is called for when international students, who have even less experience within the English-speaking academic community, cannot see that the rules apply to their writing either.

Conclusions

With few exceptions, the policies examined through the survey discussed in this chapter appeared to assume a universal view of plagiarism as an academic crime. Inadvertent plagiarism was rarely acknowledged, and even then it was attributed as much to carelessness as to lack of citation skills. Universities that respond to plagiarism with an attempt to educate students are few; punishment is the norm.

However, if it is true that students may copy without any intention of violating the rules, such an approach to plagiarism has several potentially damaging consequences. First, students who view copying or closely modeling as good writing strategies may not connect the dire warnings of an illegal activity with their own work and may simply disregard the warnings. Second, teachers who view overdependence on sources in the more positive light of a development stage writers must pass through "might find themselves professionally compromised if their institutions' regulations provided only for judicial responses," and "[t]eachers may therefore be forced into counter-pedagogical responses" (Howard 1995, 797). Angelil-Carter (in press) points out another harmful effect: "the inappropriate monitoring of plagiarism actually encourages what it purports to condemn: the parroting of sources, though acknowledged, and discourages what it purports to protect: 'originality' of ideas" (122).

By ignoring or denying the possibility of inadvertent plagiarism, universities do international students a disservice in several ways. First, they make an assumption that the reasons why plagiarism is wrong are widely understood. In this way, they lose the opportunity to teach the values and attitudes behind the rules against plagiarism. Second, by focusing on plagiarism as a violation of the rules, universities leave teachers with the options of ignoring it or punishing it but not with the option of referring students for help with using sources. Finally, when the disciplinary mechanism is set into motion, students may be punished for the "crime" of not understanding.

Because the conventions for citation are not universal, both students and their teachers need policies that permit new practices to be absorbed gradually, like all other new skills, and that allow students a margin of error as they try to hit a new target. Unfortunately, the majority of institutional responses to plagiarism surveyed here deny students that support.

References

Angelil-Carter, S. In press. *Stolen language? Plagiarism in writing.* London: Longman.

Betts, D. D. 1992. Retraction of an article published in the *Canadian Journal of Physics. Canadian Journal of Physics* 70:289.

Bloch, J., and L. Chi. 1995. A comparison of the use of citations in Chinese and English academic discourse. In *Academic writing in a second language: Essays on research and pedagogy,* ed. D. Belcher and G. Braine, 231–47. Norwood, NJ: Ablex.

Brahams, D. 1995. Hong Kong plagiarism case concludes. *Lancet* 346:1420.

Cammish, N. K. 1997. Through a glass darkly: Problems of studying at advanced level through the medium of English. In *Overseas students in higher education: Issues in teaching and learning,* ed. D. McNamara and R. Harris, 143–55. London: Routledge.

Deckert, G. D. 1993. Perspectives on plagiarism from ESL students in Hong Kong. *Journal of Second Language Writing* 2:131–48.

Dyer, C. 1995. Hong Kong doctor cleared of plagiarism. *British Medical Journal* 310:618.

Howard, R. M. 1995. Plagiarisms, authorships, and the academic death penalty. *College English* 57:788–806.

Kruse, H. H. 1990. Mark Twain's *A Connecticut Yankee:* Reconsiderations and revisions. *American Literature* 62:464–83.

Leki, I. 1992. *Understanding ESL writers: A guide for teachers.* Portsmouth, NH: Heinemann.

Macrae, M. 1997. The induction of international students to academic life in the United Kingdom. In *Overseas students in higher education: Issues in teaching and learning,* ed. D. McNamara and R. Harris, 127–42. London: Routledge.

Matalene, C. 1985. Contrastive rhetoric: An American writing teacher in China. *College English* 47:789–807.

Pennycook, A. 1996. Borrowing others' words: Text, ownership, memory, and plagiarism. *TESOL Quarterly* 30:201–30.

Sciolino, M. 1990. Kathy Acker and the postmodern subject of feminism. *College English* 52:437–45.

Scollon, R. 1995. Plagiarism and ideology: Identity in intercultural discourse. *Language in Society* 24:1–28.

Chapter 10

Textual Borrowing Strategies for Graduate-Level ESL Writers

Debbie Barks, University of Michigan, and Patricia Watts, University of Illinois at Urbana-Champaign

A crucial aspect of the reading-writing connection at Anglophone colleges and universities is the appropriate integration and documentation of other texts, or textual borrowing, in light of the innately intertextual nature of academic practices in such settings. Many of the genres commonly found in graduate-level writing require sophisticated weaving of prior texts into a larger piece of written discourse. Accordingly, graduate-level writers require facility with the linguistic and sociolinguistic aspects of textual borrowing to write successfully within their respective academic communities. Yet, as the experience of many EAP instructors and researchers has shown, the development of appropriate borrowing practices presents a daunting challenge for many ESL writers. Several recent studies have suggested that current instructional practices for teaching textual borrowing to international students in the EAP classroom may be inadequate. While the pedagogical suggestions in the professional literature are helpful, little attention has been given to examining how such suggestions can be implemented effectively. In this chapter, we review several issues related to textual borrowing and examine current ESL writing texts and practices pertaining to this area of academic writing. We then present a set of practical strategies and activities aimed at improving instruction in textual borrowing for ESL students at the graduate level. While doing so, we demonstrate how the reading-writing connection is strengthened when students are able to write successfully using source texts and appropriate textual borrowing techniques.

Issues Surrounding Textual Borrowing

A fuller understanding of the complexities involved in textual borrowing is essential in developing effective EAP pedagogy in this area. Our purpose here is to examine in particular the role of problematic and dynamic concepts of authorship, different cultural and educational practices, and the complex nature of language learning itself.

Problematic and Dynamic Concepts of Authorship and Originality

Authorship and originality may appear to be fixed concepts with clear definitions. Recently, however, as these concepts have been examined more critically, a less clear-cut picture of them has emerged. Pennycook (1996), drawing on the work of Richard Kearney, traced the history of authorship in Western culture. Pennycook noted that it was not until the modern period in Europe that authorship began to be associated with originality, a change that led to the development, in the West, of the concept of plagiarism and the notion of intellectual property rights. As a result of this change, authors came to be viewed not only as creators but also as owners of language and ideas. While the view of author as owner-possessor prevails in Western culture, it has not been universally adopted (Deckert 1993; Pennycook 1994, 1996). For example, many Asian cultures are said not to subscribe to this view at all or to subscribe to it only to some degree. As is often the case when different perspectives about a concept exist, there is an inclination to see one's own view as the norm and other views as nonstandard. In contrast to this sentiment, Pennycook (1994) has argued for recognition of the view that all notions of authorial ownership are culturally derived and thus should carry equal merit. He maintains that forcing the Western view of authorship and originality on other cultures is a form of cultural imposition. Deckert (1994), however, contends that most of the writers on whom this view is being "imposed" belong to the international community of science and technology, a community that communicates in English and for which the Western view of plagiarism dominates.

Further complicating the picture is the lack of consistency within Western culture about what is considered plagiarism. Pennycook (1996) has noted the extensive amount of literary plagiarism that has occurred in the West and the eagerness of academicians to defend these writers, a defense he finds ironic considering the lack of such a defense for ESL writers, who are certainly less skilled and experienced writers than the literary figures accused of the act. He has also pointed out inconsistencies within academia, such as graduate students authoring papers for which advisors receive credit, regardless of whether the advisor contributed to the creation of the product.

The issue of constancy is also relevant. Whether Western views about plagiarism will remain static in the future is uncertain. Postmodern views of authorship and originality differ widely from many recent assumptions. Pennycook (1996, 209–11) notes that the notion of an author creating individually derived meaning is challenged in the postmodern view. Following that line of reasoning, he says, a written product cannot be seen as completely original, for all language is based on the words and ideas the author has previously encountered; writers, thus, are "authored by texts" rather than authoring them, and they recirculate words and ideas rather than creating them anew. Another topic of much interest recently is how hypertext and electronic media will change current conceptualizations of both author and text.

Different Cultural and Educational Practices

Several cultural and educational practices bear a relationship to the broad issue of using prior texts and, more specifically, to the issue of plagiarism. The body of research exploring these practices has focused primarily on Chinese culture in both mainland and Hong Kong contexts. Many authors have discussed the role memorization plays in education and in Chinese culture (Bloch and Chi 1995; Deckert 1993; Pennycook 1996). It is a widely held belief that this custom contributes to unacceptable borrowing practices found in the writing of Chinese ESL students, such as plagiarism and the recycling of ideas without transformation. The apparent connection between an emphasis on memorization and plagiarism has contributed to the view that memorization is an inferior educational practice. However, Pennycook (1994, 1996) has called for the reexamination of this view. Through interviews with students accused of plagiarism, he found that the presence of plagiarized passages did not necessarily indicate a lack of knowledge about the topic. Further, as Marton, Dall'Alba, and Kun (1996) pointed out in their study of educational practices in China, memorization can serve as a tool to further understanding and thus should not be dismissed as merely parroting source texts.

Another cultural practice examined in the literature is social harmony. Taylor and Chen (1991) examined the connection between the cultural concept of social harmony in Chinese culture and Chinese writers' willingness to criticize the texts of others. They found that Chinese writers did not criticize other authors in the introductory sections of their articles. Deckert (1993) speculated that adherence to social harmony conventions prevents Chinese writers from developing an original stance and instead results in simple recycling of information from texts. Bloch and Chi (1995), in an examination of citation practices in research articles, found that Chinese writers did criticize the work of previous researchers, though most of these criticisms were constructed indirectly for social appropriateness in the Chinese context.

Another cultural practice that has received some attention in the literature is the tendency for Chinese writers to rely on classic texts as sources. In their comparison of source use between Chinese and American writers, Bloch and Chi (1995) found that Chinese writers used fewer recent citations (0–5 years) and more older citations (15 years or more) than did American writers. They also found an interesting difference within their sample of Chinese writers. Writers in the physical sciences used more recent citations than did writers in the social sciences, an area for which more accountability to Marxism would be expected. Bloch and Chi speculated that their findings could be attributed in part to the effects of modernization. As China has modernized, achievements in the natural or physical sciences have been accorded higher status than those in the social sciences, resulting in reduced access to recent material published in the social sciences, while the physical scientists have increased access to the latest publications originating outside China.

The Complex Nature of Language Learning

Achieving the level of language proficiency necessary not just to survive but to thrive in the English-speaking academic context is clearly a complex task for a nonnative speaker (NNS). The cognitive and social demands of graduate-level academic writing, especially in source-based writing, are likewise considerable. For example, accurate and effective paraphrasing alone requires sophisticated knowledge of English syntax, an extensive vocabulary, and a high level of reading comprehension ability.

Research in this area has focused in part on students' attempts to cope with the complexity required to work with source texts. Britton et al. (1975) discussed the developmental nature of writing from sources and listed several stages necessary to achieve full command of the use of source texts, beginning with mechanical copying and culminating in synthesis. Regarding students' coping strategies, they argued that it may be natural for writers to progress through various degrees of copying before being able to succeed at more sophisticated tasks, such as synthesis. While their research focused on the development of native language writers, it seems equally, if not more, applicable for ESL writers. Indeed, Pennycook

(1994) maintains that an inherent part of the process of language learning is assimilating words and phrases in the target language into one's own use of that language.

Campbell (1990) investigated degrees of copying on a timed writing test for college freshmen and found that both native and nonnative writers plagiarized frequently. Her findings regarding the relative popularity of plagiarism as a coping device provide further evidence of the complexity of achieving desired levels of intertextuality. Yet ESL writers in the Anglophone academic context, many of whom have little experience writing in English upon arriving at Anglophone universities, face immediate pressure to produce texts that incorporate the research of others in appropriate ways. These texts, like those of their native-speaking counterparts, must conform to general academic conventions. ESL writers are doubly challenged by these conventions, both by their lack of familiarity with the expectations for academic writing and also by limitations in their linguistic proficiency. Thus, the emergence of copying as a survival or compensatory strategy (as noted in Bloch and Chi 1995, Currie 1998, and Spack 1997) is not surprising given students' need to write with clarity and accuracy in a tone appropriate for a discourse community to which they have just been introduced.

While plagiarism has been traditionally viewed as a writing problem, a body of research indicates that difficulties with reading may help explain plagiarism and other problems in source use. Kirkland and Saunders (1991) note that reading-into-writing tasks call for interactive and recursive composing processes. Students travel back and forth between source texts and their own text as they revise. Recursion requires a high degree of cognitive development and can be impaired by problems in reading comprehension. In particular, Kirkland and Saunders contend that students who read by processing texts in a bottom-up fashion often do not grasp the overall purpose and message of the text, a problem that may eventually result in plagiarism when students cannot rely on their own understanding of the text while attempting to borrow from it. In a similar vein, Howard (1995) says students' reliance on a coping strategy she calls "patchwriting," that is, copying passages while making only minor changes in vocabulary and grammatical structures, is due in part to their difficulty in comprehending texts. Such problems are common not just at the undergraduate level; inexperienced writers at the graduate level may also approach reading-to- write tasks with limited or misguided strategies and inadequate task interpretation. (Their problems may also stem from badly constructed and poorly explained tasks.) Kantz (1990) suggests another cause of textual borrowing problems: many new writers use a nonrhetorical approach to reading, in which they read texts as stories and as collections of facts instead of recognizing that in many cases they are reading texts constructed as arguments. She goes on to claim that if students are taught how to read rhetorically—that is, to consider such factors as intended audience for the text and the author's purpose in writing the text—they will be able to write like scholars and will use their source material more effectively.

While most writing in an academic context involves considerable reading, the two skills are often dealt with as separate entities in EAP programs, often in separate courses. This artificial separation persists despite research that demonstrates close parallels in the cognitive processes involved in reading and writing, and it has resulted in what Carson and Leki (1993) have called "impoverished EAP." In this model, reading instruction has tended to focus on the cognitive strategies involved in text comprehension, while writing instruction has concentrated on text production; that is, reading has been taught as a passive skill and writing as an active skill. EAP students are regularly required to perform reading-into-writing tasks in their academic careers (Johns 1993), but they remain unprepared or underprepared to complete such tasks if they treat reading passively and writing actively.

Though cognitive issues certainly play a role in the complexity of textual borrowing for ESL students, lack of attention to the interrelated social aspects of reading and writing within discourse communities may also lead to problems in textual borrowing practices. As students enter a discourse community, they may engage in extensive borrowing of phrases and other uses of language they find appealing in the process of developing their authorial voice. Howard (1995) emphasizes that this is a natural stage in the process of learning to write, although ultimately unacceptable in a final draft. Another problem, particularly for new graduate students, results from a lack of necessary background knowledge in their field of study. Students lacking necessary background knowledge in a subject may compensate by providing an inappropriate level of background information about sources that they cite, that is, too much or too little detail about the sources (Sternglass 1986). Insufficient background knowledge in a subject may also lead to an overreliance on quotation or to Howard's (1995) aforementioned practice of patchwriting.

Patchwriting is likely to be especially prevalent among new graduate students, who are not yet familiar with the discourse community they are joining, but it can also be found among any students who must grapple with unfamiliar readings. Even though it is often assumed that international graduate students bring considerable subject area knowledge with them to their graduate program, there may still be culturally bound references and text types that are not familiar to them. For example, architecture students might have to read texts from a wide range of disciplines, including postmodern literary criticism, anthropology, and philosophy, in addition to the literature associated with their discipline. Given the complexities involved in processing such texts with sometimes limited language proficiency, it is not surprising that they rely on copying or patchwriting as they attempt to assimilate such texts into new pieces of writing.

Current EAP Instructional Practices

Despite the complexity of textual borrowing in the ESL writing classroom, many of its related issues and problems tend to be overlooked or insufficiently addressed in ESL writing textbooks. Many of these textbooks contain limited emphasis on source-based writing at best and often relegate it to a chapter on the research paper. In general, we have found that these textbooks address plagiarism and the broader issue of writing from sources in the following limited fashion: first, they provide a black-and-white definition of plagiarism, often presenting the borrowing of a "string of three words or more" as the magical boundary over which one crosses into plagiarism; second, they warn students of the seriousness of plagiarism in the U.S. academic context and often include a list of possible penalties for plagiarism; third, they introduce the three means for incorporating a source into writing—paraphrase, summary, and quotation. Isolated practice of these skills is sometimes included, but these exercises do not go as far as, say, providing students with more integrated practice, such as asking them to incorporate a paraphrase into a piece of writing or to think about how information from a reading could be used in the accompanying writing assignment.

While some texts have expanded treatment of source-based writing beyond the limited triadic model already mentioned, more often than not they are the exception to the rule. As Deckert (1993) and Currie (1998), among others, have noted, a sequence like the triadic one just described fails to take students' backgrounds and beliefs into consideration and does little or nothing to support linguistic development. Such practices are not only pedagogically unsound; Pennycook (1996) has argued that merely teaching ESL students to follow certain accepted norms is "intellectually arrogant" (227). Further, it ignores the need for students to acquire a sufficiently deep understanding of how texts are used in various academic and professional genres, thereby failing to prepare students to carry out source-based writing assignments effectively.

Instructional Strategies for Textual Borrowing

Beyond developing increased understanding of the complexity of textual borrowing, EAP instructors need to critically examine current practices and be willing to change or amend what has not proven to be effective. Certainly, many EAP instructors are well aware of the limitations of the aforementioned triadic model, yet there are few appropriate models available for improving instruction in this area.

In the remainder of this chapter, we present an application of three pedagogical strategies taken from various sources to investigate how to better inform and instruct graduate ESL students in the practice of textual borrowing. The strategies are (1) discussing with students the complexity of authorship and plagiarism, (2) helping students develop a range of effective borrowing practices, and (3) using ethnographic approaches to enhance both teacher and student understanding of students' educational practices and backgrounds as well as the literacy demands of their chosen disciplinary communities. Adoption of these strategies will enrich students' awareness of connections between academic reading and writing and thus strengthen their core academic literacy skills. We will draw from our own materials as well as from texts that are commercially available for teaching writing to graduate students.

Discussing the Complexity of Authorship and Plagiarism

Pennycook (1994, 1996), in particular, has argued that it is unfair to present plagiarism to our students as an easily understood black-and-white issue. His solution to this problem, one also advocated by Currie (1998), is to raise students' awareness of textual borrowing practices in their own culture and then have them compare those with the practices commonly adopted in Anglophone discourse. He also encourages delving in some depth into the complexities of the notions of originality and authorship. This practice seems especially appropriate for graduate students, who are immersed in a complicated and ongoing socialization process as they become increasingly specialized in their academic discipline. A discussion of the use of textual borrowing and citation practices within the context of this process is quite natural.

Yet, however natural this kind of discussion may appear, it also can move both student and instructor beyond their personal comfort zone and thus away from, rather than closer to, the instructional goals being pursued. It is much easier to present these issues in unambiguous, black-and-white terms than to engage in the give-and-take of class discussion, where a certain amount of ambiguity and uncertainty is likely to occur as these issues are addressed. Furthermore, students often are more receptive to such apparently easy solutions. As with many consciousness-raising activities, in the discussion mode there is always the possibility of complicating issues rather than simplifying them, but there is also great potential for the kinds of lively exchange and intellectual engagement that ultimately lead to greater understanding.

Our first example of this kind of discussion-oriented activity, one employed in our own writing course for graduate students, is a true-false exercise used at the beginning of a unit on textual borrowing and designed to draw students' attention to some of the complexities involved in using material from other authors while writing an academic text. For many students, this may be the first time they have really thought about such issues, which signifies that they may not be fully aware of the differences in source text use across cultures. The value of this activity, then, is that it encourages students to seriously consider these issues and to make comparisons beyond the EAP writing classroom as they complete their academic writing tasks in the writing class and in their own disciplinary contexts. As is shown in table 1, students are asked to make direct comparisons between textual borrowing practices in their native country and, in this case, the United States.

A second example drawn from the same academic writing course has a broader focus on the concepts of authorship and originality across disciplines and cultures. Students who have been in the Anglophone academic context longer often have much to contribute to what can be a very lively discussion on the topic. As is shown in figure 1, the questions are deliberately open-ended to encourage wide-ranging discussion; by design, then, they do not lend themselves to easy answers. In question 2, the term *original* is intentionally vague, again with the purpose of stimulating further discussion of and investigation into the questions of what constitutes an original idea and whether originality in writing truly exists.

TABLE 1

True or False?	In Your Country	In the United States
1. Much academic writing involves reading background information, studies, and other sources related to your topic.		
2. It is acceptable to copy passages from a source text and use them in your paper without attribution.		
3. When non-native speakers of English are writing academic papers in English, it is better for them to use the original words from other authors than to paraphrase or summarize, because a native speaker of the language can always express ideas better than a non-native speaker.		
4. When you use material from another writer in your own paper, it is often necessary to summarize or rephrase it so that it is expressed in your own words.		
5. If you rephrase something from another author and use it in your paper, you do not need to acknowledge it within your text with a footnote or parenthetical documentation.		
6. Taking good notes while you read your source material is a good way to avoid plagiarism.		

1. On average, what percentage of the academic papers that you write now is material from another source? Does it vary according to the type of paper you are writing? Explain.
2. What percentage of your academic papers consists of original ideas?
3. What does the term *intellectual property* mean to you?
4. How do you define the term *author*? Do you consider yourself an author?
5. Have you noticed any differences in the ways you use texts by other authors in your academic writing here in the United States with your writing in your own country?

Fig. 1. Textual borrowing in academic writing

Such consciousness-raising activities are not common in commercially available writing texts. There is, however, a good example of this approach in *Academic Writing for Graduate Students* by Swales and Feak (1994, 179–81). In this activity, students are asked to consider various theories that have been proposed to explain why citations are used in academic writing in the Anglophone academic context. The activity shows students that even among the experts, a considerable amount of variation exists in opinion. Here are a few statements included in the activity (the statements are cited in Swales and Feak's text).

> Citations are used to recognize and acknowledge the intellectual property rights of authors. They are a matter of ethics and a defense against plagiarism.

> Citations are tools of persuasion; writers use citations to give their statements greater authority. (Gilbert 1977)

> Citations are used to create a research space for the citing author. By describing what has been done, citations point the way to what has not been done and so prepare a space for new research. (Swales 1990)

Again, the discussion is open-ended, leaving room for students to formulate their own answers and to compare perspectives. Rather than having citation practices dictated to them, students acquire awareness of them in a more engaging and interactive, hands-on manner that may add impact or depth to the knowledge they gain.

Helping Students Develop a Range of Effective Borrowing Practices

Establishing membership in an academic discourse community involves adopting new language and knowledge, which is in part accomplished through reading-to-write activities. Thus, learning appropriate ways of borrowing the words of others is an integral and important part of the learning process and a necessary step toward students' successful participation in their academic communities (Howard 1995; Pennycook 1996). The challenge for NNS writers is learning how to integrate the words of others in ways that are acceptable within their academic community, knowledge that can be obtained by capitalizing on the learning opportunities inherent in the reading-to-write process. As Pennycook (1996) has argued, "all language learning is to some extent a process of borrowing others' words" (227). EAP instructors can play an important role in this process by helping students to learn to incorporate language from sources into their writing without crossing the line into plagiarism. The goal of this strategy is therefore to help students understand and differentiate among various types of borrowing, ranging from intentional copying to sophisticated intertextual practices, and then to develop practices that will help them borrow in ways that foster language learning and lead to successful participation in their respective academic discourse communities.

Students do need to know what the institution's definition of and policy on plagiarism is, but, as we have already seen, plagiarism as it is traditionally viewed is not a particularly useful pedagogical construct, for various reasons. Particularly relevant here is Howard's (1995) distinction between the traditionally negative understanding of plagiarism as a result either of intentional copying or lack of attribution caused by ignorance of the conventions of citing source material, on the one hand, and her more positive view in which plagiarism occurs as a result of the learning process, on the other. Seeing "positive plagiarism" or patchwriting as a pedagogical opportunity is an important step for instructors in designing materials that move beyond the usual treatment of plagiarism in many academic writing classes.

Once this view is adopted, patchwriting can be seen as an intermediary step toward more effective integration of material from other sources. It can also be seen as a valuable step in helping students not only understand the texts they are reading but also learn to use some of the language of their discipline. It may be helpful to think of borrowing in this sense as a continuum, as Swales and Feak do in the following exercise from their textbook (1994, 126).

> Here are some approaches to writing, beginning with a plagiarizing approach and ending with an acceptable quoting technique. Where does plagiarism stop? Draw a line between the last approach that would produce plagiarism and the first approach that would produce acceptable original work.

1. Copying a paragraph as it is from the source without any acknowledgment.
2. Copying a paragraph, making only small changes such as replacing a few verbs or adjectives with synonyms.
3. Cutting and pasting a paragraph by using the sentences of the original but leaving one or two out, or by putting one or two sentences in a different order.
4. Composing a paragraph by taking short standard phrases from a number of sources and putting them together with some words of your own.

5. Paraphrasing a paragraph by rewriting with substantial changes in language and organization, amount of detail, and examples.
6. Quoting a paragraph by placing it in block format with source cited.

Even though students may understand, at an intellectual level, the types of borrowing considered acceptable in the university context, they may need additional practice and training before they can use sources in ways that are acceptable. In the Swales and Feak exercise just cited, all but number 6 and possibly number 5 are considered to be plagiarism, yet many students commonly use the first four strategies, which fall under Howard's definition of patchwriting. It is here that our pedagogical opportunity lies. Currie's (1998) case study shows that students may actually be aware of this learning possibility but unsure of how to proceed without crossing the line into negative borrowing practices, that is, plagiarism.

One type of appropriate borrowing is the use of technical terms and specialized vocabulary. Swales and Feak (1994, 113–14) address this type of borrowing in their section on paraphrasing strategies. Their list of strategies includes "Always try to use your own words, except for technical terms" and "Do not try to paraphrase specialized vocabulary or technical terms." These strategies provide a good starting point, because graduate students tend to be quite familiar with the specialized vocabulary in their discipline, and if they are not, this exercise should motivate them to try to understand the distinction between terms that should and should not be paraphrased. This exercise could be extended by having students summarize a text from their field, a task that would require them to consciously decide which terms they can borrow before they write.

In a related exercise in Arnaudet and Barrett's textbook (1984, 137–38), students compare an original text and a summary of it. The original text, which defines what a neuron is, runs 267 words in length, with extended and very detailed, technical definitions of four key terms: *neuron, dendrite, axon,* and *nerve.* The 87-word summary, which is printed parallel to the original passage, draws students' attention to how technical terminology can be converted into simpler language. The following excerpt from the first part of the activity illustrates how the explanation for the term *neuron* has been paraphrased in an appropriate manner.

Original Passage

The Neuron
    The number of cells, or neurons, that make up the nervous system has

been estimated at 100 to 200 billion. Although neurons come in many different shapes and sizes, they are specialized to receive and transmit information.

Summary
In *Psychology,* Charles G. Morris explains that the nervous system consists of cells called neurons, whose purpose is to convey information.

Another useful activity along the borrowing continuum is one designed to focus students' attention on possible expressions used for a particular pragmatic function within the context of an academic text, followed by "borrowing" of those expressions in a revision exercise. Students first scan a section of a journal article for terms that are useful for certain functions (comparing results, giving an explanation for results, etc.). This is done individually, and the information is then shared in groups or as a class so that students acquire a number of key stock phrases that can be used to express a certain function. Students next draw on their stockpile of terms to write a section of their own or to revise a text using the terminology they have learned. An example of this activity is seen in figure 2.

Using Ethnographic Approaches

EAP instructors often teach students from a wide range of academic disciplines. At the graduate level, this becomes a considerable challenge, as instructors must teach from the elusive perspective of "generic" academic writing while trying to meet the disciplinary needs of individual students from a variety of discourse communities. In this setting, ethnographic approaches are particularly useful, for both student and instructor, because they encourage students to make a connection between the EAP writing course and the "real world" of their own academic discipline. By referring to the use of ethnographic approaches, we mean implementing tasks that involve asking students to function as participant observers in the academic culture by gathering and analyzing articles, texts, and assignments from their academic field. EAP classrooms become, in effect, "laboratories for the study of texts roles and contexts, for research into evolving student literacies and developing awarenesses and critique of communities and their textual contracts" (Johns 1997, 19). This "examine and report back" approach (Hirvela 1997) is particularly useful for advanced-level EAP students and especially for graduate students as they are becoming socialized in their academic fields (Johns 1993; Swales 1987). In the case of textual borrowing, the use of structured ethnographic activ-

Part A

In your group, examine the results and discussion sections of your journal articles. Make a list of phrases and sentences used to convey the following information:

generalizations from the results
    Ex: "The data show that . . ."
explanations of the results
    Ex: "One explanation for this may be . . ."
comparisons of the results to findings from other research
    Ex: "The results agree with . . ."
expressions that limit the findings
    Ex: "It should be noted that . . ."

Look over your list to detect any patterns in verb tense, voice, and vocabulary. Be prepared to discuss your findings with the whole class.

Part B

Read the following passage from a results and discussion section of a paper from the field of communication entitled "Leadership and Listening: A Study of Member Perceptions." Revise the passage by using relevant constructions and vocabulary you identified in part A to replaced underlined information. You may need to change the entire sentence to use the phrase correctly.

   To determine the relationship between perceived leadership skills and perceived listening skills, the Spearman correlation statistic (Wiersma 1986) was used to analyze the data. For the 23 groups, the mean correlation coefficient for subject rankings of leadership and listening was .497 ($p =$ .01). A significant positive correlation between member rankings of leadership and member rankings of listening skills <u>exists</u>. Thus, the data <u>leads one to believe</u> that there is a positive relationship between perceived leadership behavior and perceptions of listening performance. Those subjects ranked as most like a leader were also typically ranked as good listeners. The anecdotal evidence and prescriptive models offered by many textbook authors encouraging the development of effective listening skills to enhance perceptions of leadership performance <u>is supported</u> by this finding. Individuals perceived to be leading the groups were most commonly believed to be listening to the groups.

Fig. 2. Effective textual borrowing

Find an article from a professional journal in your field and write responses to the questions below.
Title of article:
Author(s):
Title of journal, date:
Page numbers:

1. What kind of article is it (e.g., research report, review of the literature, analysis, argumentation, etc.)?
2. Does the article have an abstract at the beginning? If yes, approximately how many words? What headings and subheadings are used in the article?
3. How are citations documented within the text (e.g., by author, date, and page, as in "Smith 1989, 20")?
4. Give an example of a citation from within the text.
5. Is there a list of sources at the end of the paper? What is this section of the paper called?
6. Give an example of the form used in the bibliography of the paper.

Fig. 3. Academic writing: formats and citations

ities helps the students (and their EAP instructors) learn about the specific conventions and practices in their departments and fields. The instructor's role is to train and guide students in developing an analytical approach to texts in their own fields. The following examples illustrate a range of ethnographic activities we have used with our graduate-level ESL writers.

The first example (fig. 3), adapted from Frodesen 1995, calls attention to the formats and citation conventions across disciplines by asking students to analyze a journal article from their field. Students do this assignment individually and then share their results in small groups or with the class.

Our next example (fig. 4) is a similar, but more involved, activity. In this task, students examine some surface features of source use and also explore the roles sources play in a text.

In the following excerpt from one student's analysis, the student identified at least three different reasons (highlighted in bold) for using citations in an article from the field of statistics.

In the article, the outside source functions as **providing some background information** (e.g., "Likelihood and procedure for autoregressive models have

Length: 1½–2 pages, typed double-spaced
Purpose: To raise awareness about how sources are used in academic writing in the United States

Instructions: Choose a sample academic article from your field. Use the following questions to guide your analysis about source use in your sample. The answers [to the questions] should become the basis of a report you will write about the use of sources in the genre you selected (library-based research report, literature review, experimental research report, etc.).

Questions:

1. How many references are made to outside sources in each section of the paper? Does frequency of source use vary with the section? If so, where are sources used most frequently? Where are they used least frequently?
2. What is the proportion of original ideas to ideas from sources?
3. When an outside source is used, how is it incorporated into the paper? As a quotation or as a paraphrase or summary?
4. If quotations are used, can you think of any reasons why the author chose to quote the material rather than to paraphrase or summarize it? To present the material exactly as it was stated in order to comment on it? To draw on the words of an authority? To distance himself/herself from the quotation? To maintain language that is powerful or technical/legal in nature?
5. How does the source material function in the paper? For instance, does it provide an example? Give a definition? Support an idea being advanced? Provide background information? Help situate the research in a context of other research? Provide motivation for carrying out the present study? Allow comparison of research results? Refer the reader to standard methodology? Justify a methodological choice? Serve other functions?
6. (a) When a source is used, how is it documented within the text? Is a number system or an author-date system used? What punctuation is used? Are page numbers ever included? If attributive phrases are used, write down a couple of samples (e.g., "Jones argues," "According to Jones").

   (b) How is the source documented at the end of the text? What style manual is followed for citations?

Fig. 4. Analysis of source use

been well studied (Box and Jenkins, 1970)" and "Regression models for censored independent Gaussian data have also been investigated," **providing motivation for carrying out the present study** (e.g., "This expression for the beta score equation is in the sprit of the iterative procedure suggested by Stampford and Taylor (1959) and further developed by Wolynetz (1974, 1979) for censored independent Gaussian data.") and **giving a definition** (e.g., "Note that the term pseudolikelihood is used in the sense of Besag [1975] rather than that of Gong and Samaniego [1981]").

Another student from the field of social work observed in her analysis:

> The reason why the author used quotations is probably to introduce the ideas precisely to make them support the author's idea. In addition, it is likely that [the author] wants to avoid using her own words and quote the words of other researchers to distance herself from the quotation because she does not have any convincing proof to provide or not agree to the idea. She seems to use quotations at places where she wants to emphasize her ideas.

Whether or not she is right, she has formulated an interesting hypothesis with which to approach further reading in her field. Doing such an exercise helps students to focus on some of the rhetorical features of texts they are reading and provides them with a richer, more critically astute model of reading, along the lines suggested by Kantz (1990). The input they gain as readers in such tasks then informs their writing practices as they apply what they acquired through such close reading. Hence, connections between students' reading and writing are strengthened as they complete such exercises.

Swales (1987) recommends an even more ambitious sequence of activities that begins with students considering and comparing their own citation practices in class by interviewing each other. They next compare a written academic text that has citations with an audiotaped interview of the author talking about how or why he or she used certain citations. Finally, the students choose a paper written by one of their professors, identify the citations in the paper, and then interview the professor about the citations.

Two further examples of ethnographic activities are variations on this theme. In one activity, the instructor uses a text she wrote as a graduate student and has students work through a sequence of exercises involving analysis of the citations used in the excerpt, comparing the excerpt to the original texts from which she took the citations. Depending on an instructor's ability to remember back to his or her days in graduate school, this variation solves the problem of finding cooperative professors/authors.

Students can also be asked to examine, in similar fashion, a portion of a text they have written and to write a brief report on their use of citations in that text.

In another variation of this theme, students analyze the citations in a paper written by one of their peers in the class. (This exercise assumes that the students are using the same source material and are writing on the same subject matter.) In this way, they have ready access to the author(s) of the text and can discuss the ramifications of citation choices as well as the efficacy of textual borrowing in the paper. They could also bring in several related articles from their field and compare citations with the original sources to analyze how one author has cited another.

As a means of helping NNS graduate students assemble an individualized "portrait" of their academic discourse communities, Hirvela (1997) recommends using "disciplinary portfolios" in which students collect the results of their ethnographic research. A primary advantage of using portfolios is that they extend the "examine and report methodology" of ethnographic approaches to foster a more unified reflection on the specific conventions of texts within each student's academic field.

Conclusion

Effective textual borrowing hinges on various players, including the graduate student writer, EAP instructor, and content area instructor. Student writers cannot use sources effectively in their academic writing without a clear understanding of their writing tasks or without effective reading-to-write strategies. Content area instructors obviously play an important role here by negotiating tasks clearly with their students as well as modeling reading strategies for the discipline (Kantz 1990; Spack 1997). They also serve as expert informants about the specific conventions and practices of the disciplinary community the graduate student is entering. Ethnographic approaches that involve interviewing discipline area professors are one means of developing the mentoring relationship between student and professor as well as creating a link back to the EAP instructor.

Further research in the cognitive processes involved in "reading into writing" practices of students may also help EAP practitioners design more helpful learning tasks, as Johns (1993) suggests. Thus, in an integrated reading and writing approach, students could be taught strategies and sequences that, through appropriate reading, would lead to more effective use of sources in their writing. This should be particularly helpful when teaching the second instructional strategy we described in this chapter: helping students use intermediary borrowing practices to their benefit.

Certainly there is a need for ongoing research in the textual borrowing practices of international graduate students within the larger process of academic literacy acquisition. Much of the existing research has focused on a limited cultural range; thus, one potential focus would be to examine other cultural groups. Indeed, the influence of culture on textual borrowing practices is not entirely clear. When presented with the true-false consciousness-raising activity provided in table 1 in this chapter, our students tend to answer that textual borrowing practices are the same in their culture as in the Anglophone culture. Is this a matter of ignorance or lack of experience, or is it possible that culture is not as influential as other, more immediate factors, as noted by Spack (1997) and Currie (1998)? Longitudinal research with graduate-level writers would also provide insights into the process of academic literacy acquisition experienced by this diverse group of learners.

Finally, the artificial separation of reading and writing in EAP courses for graduate students needs rethinking. While theme-based integration of reading and writing tasks may not be as practical for graduate-level students as it is for undergraduates, other means of addressing reading-to-write issues for graduate student writers should be explored. We feel the ethnographic approach holds great promise in helping students explore the rhetorical aspects of the texts they are reading in relationship to writing tasks. It is our hope that the strategies and materials presented in this chapter will provide a stepping-stone to further developments in the instruction of textual borrowing for international graduate students.

References

Arnaudet, M., and M. Barrett. 1984. *Approaches to academic reading and writing.* Englewood Cliffs, NJ: Prentice-Hall.

Bloch, J., and L. Chi. 1995. A comparison of the use of citations in Chinese and English academic discourse. In *Academic writing in a second language: Essays on research and pedagogy,* ed. D. Belcher and G. Braine, 231–74. Norwood, NJ: Ablex.

Britton, J., T. Burgess, N. Martin, A. McLeod, and H. Rosen. 1975. *The development of writing abilities.* Houndmills, Hampshire, UK: Macmillan.

Campbell, C. 1990. Writing with others' words: Using background reading text in academic compositions. In *Second language writing: Research insights for the classroom,* ed. B. Kroll, 211–30. Cambridge: Cambridge University Press.

Carson, J. G., and I. Leki. 1993. Introduction to *Reading in the composition classroom: Second language perspectives,* ed. J. G. Carson and I. Leki, 1–7. Boston: Heinle and Heinle.

Currie, P. 1998. Staying out of trouble: Apparent plagiarism and academic survival. *Journal of Second Language Writing* 7:1–18.

Deckert, G. 1993. Perspectives on plagiarism from ESL students in Hong Kong. *Journal of Second Language Writing* 2:131–48.

———. 1994. Author's response to Pennycook's objections. *Journal of Second Language Writing* 2:131–48.

Frodesen, J. 1995. Negotiating the syllabus: A learning-centered, interactive approach to ESL graduate writing course design. In *Academic writing in a second language: Essays on research and pedagogy,* ed. D. Belcher and G. Braine, 331–50. Norwood, NJ: Ablex.

Gilbert, G. N. 1977. Referencing and persuasion. *Social Studies and Science.* 7:113–22.

Hirvela, A. 1997. "Disciplinary portfolios" and EAP writing instruction. *English for Specific Purposes* 16:83–100.

Howard, R. M. 1995. Plagiarisms, authorships, and the academic death penalty. *College English* 57:788–805.

Johns, A. M. 1993. Reading and writing tasks in English for academic purposes classes: Products, processes, and resources. In *Reading in the Composition classroom: Second language perspectives,* ed. J. G. Carson and I. Leki, 274–89. Boston: Heinle and Heinle.

———. 1997. *Text, role, and context: Developing academic literacies.* Cambridge: Cambridge University Press.

Kantz, M. 1990. Helping students use textual sources persuasively. *College English* 52:74–91.

Kirkland, M., and M. A. Saunders. 1991. Maximizing student performance in summary writing: Managing cognitive load. *TESOL Quarterly* 25:105–21.

Marton, F., G. Dall'Alba, and T. Kun. 1996. Memorizing and understanding: The keys to the paradox. In *The Chinese learner: Cultural, psychological, and contextual influences,* ed. D. Watkins and J. Biggs, 69–83. Hong Kong: Comparative Education Research Centre.

Pennycook, A. 1994. The complex contexts of plagiarism: A reply to Deckert. *Journal of Second Language Writing* 3:277–84.

———. 1996. Borrowing others' words: Text, ownership, memory, and plagiarism. *TESOL Quarterly* 30:201–30.

Spack, R. 1997. The acquisition of academic literacy in a second language: A longitudinal case study. *Written Communication* 14:3–62.

Sternglass, M. 1986. Writing based on reading. In *Convergences: Transactions in reading and writing,* ed. B. T. Peterson, 151–62. Urbana, IL: National Council of Teachers of English.

Swales, J. 1987. Utilizing the literatures in teaching the research paper. *TESOL Quarterly* 21:41-68.

———. 1990. *Genre Analysis.* Cambridge: Cambridge University.

Swales, J., and C. Feak. 1994. *Academic writing for graduate students: A course for nonnative speakers of English.* Ann Arbor: University of Michigan Press.

Taylor, G., and T. G. Chen. 1991. Linguistic, cultural, and subcultural issues in contrastive discourse analysis: Anglo-American and Chinese scientific texts. *Applied Linguistics* 12:319–36.

Part 4

Technology-Assisted Reading and Writing

Chapter 11

With the Dictionary and Beyond

Terence Odlin, Ohio State University

Introduction

As research on English as a second language (ESL) progresses, the scope
of the problems that investigators address becomes ever clearer and ever
vaster. Even though encounters between speakers of English and speakers
of other languages have been occurring for centuries, the development of
highly specialized approaches has taken place only in about the last hundred years. In the United States, moreover, the establishment of a major
professional organization, Teachers of English to Speakers of Other Languages (TESOL), did not occur until the 1960s. Not surprisingly, then, it
has taken quite a while for subfields to develop. In the case of ESL writing,
the interest has been there for a long time—writing has obviously been a
concern of teachers for centuries—but even so, some of the most cited articles and books (e.g., McKay 1984) showed a very heavy reliance on the
principles and practices of writing instruction for native speakers. However, more recent work (e.g., Belcher and Braine 1995; Connor 1996) indicates very rapid changes in the field of ESL writing, with questions that do
not necessarily involve concerns important in native speaker contexts
now often being asked. Indeed, few specialists would now claim that writing for speakers of other languages should look exclusively—or even primarily—at L1 writing research for further progress.

While the principles and practices of L1 writing instruction will no
doubt continue to be a valuable source of new ideas, the fact remains that
ESL writing by definition entails distinct concerns, since the speaking and
writing as well as the listening and reading abilities of nonnative speakers
differ in countless ways from those of native speakers. Research on second
language acquisition has made considerable progress in characterizing
how competence in a second language evolves, and SLA research is therefore a natural starting point for thinking about some of the principles and

practices of second language writing instruction. This chapter, then, will use some insights from work in SLA to address the following questions:

1. What is the relation between reading and writing in a second language?
2. What role should dictionaries play in ESL literacy instruction?
3. What implications do digital technologies have for such instruction?

The issues raised by each of these questions are clearly too vast to explore in a single essay. Nevertheless, research on language transfer, that is, crosslinguistic influence, can help to inform theory and practice in second language literacy.

The plan of this chapter is thus to look first at some implications of transfer research, one of the most important being that it is unrealistic to expect most acquisition to take place within any ESL classroom. The discussion will then turn to how dictionaries and some forms of digital technology can help foster learning independent of classroom instruction.

Transfer and Implications for Second Language Learning

Other areas of second language research can no doubt provide insights for work in second language literacy, but research on the native language factor (often termed *transfer*) has a special place because of its relation to the history of writing. Foreign language pedagogy has relied on written crosslinguistic comparisons, also known as contrastive analysis, ever since the earliest literate cultures of the Middle East (Kelly 1969). The fact that from antiquity onwards people have tried to compare languages systematically suggests a long-standing assumption: that conscious study of the points of similarity and differences between languages can help in overcoming the difficulties of the target language.

It would not surprise me at all if archaeologists eventually find a clay tablet that reads, in translation:

> We assume that the student who comes in contact with a foreign language will find some features of it quite easy and others extremely difficult. Those elements that are similar to his native languages will be simple for him, and those elements that are different will be difficult.

This archaeological find that I am predicting bears a curious—indeed, a verbatim—resemblance to Robert Lado's often quoted claim (1957, 2) about second language acquisition. In such discussions as those of Rod Ellis (1985) on the so-called Contrastive Analysis Hypothesis, the views of Lado are usually Exhibit A. For many people, including Ellis, the Contrastive Analysis Hypothesis is discredited. However, the very expression "Contrastive Analysis Hypothesis" has had some negative effects, leading some (though not Ellis) to conclude that transfer plays only a minimal role in second language acquisition if the hypothesis is discredited. Much of the research in the 1960s and 1970s did in fact show that it is a mistake to regard language transfer as the sole explanation for all ease or difficulty in acquisition: in this sense, we can indeed say that an idea called the CAH is discredited. However, the most inflexible difficulty for adults learning a second language is crosslinguistic distance. Virtually everybody would agree that learning to speak or read Chinese will take an English speaker much more time than will learning French. The crosslinguistic distance between Chinese and English is obviously vast, and this distance accounts for the planning made by the Foreign Service Institute (FSI) and other language teaching units of the United States government. The FSI routinely plans for many more hours of instruction not only in Chinese but also in Japanese, Korean, Arabic, and several other languages (Odlin 1989; Ringbom 1987).

That all the languages just cited are Asian might suggest that second language learning difficulties mainly arise from cultural differences between Eastern societies and English-speaking societies. No doubt, cultural factors explain some of the difficulty, but they do not account for all of it. In fact, some languages spoken in European countries are notoriously difficult for English speakers, and the reasons for the difficulty have relatively little to do with culture. Finnish, Estonian, and Hungarian all belong to the Uralic language family, which differs considerably from English and all other Indo-European languages, and other languages (e.g., Basque) could be cited as similarly difficult. One Foreign Service Institute catalog indicates that 44 weeks of instruction are needed for Finnish whereas only 24 weeks are required for Swedish, a Germanic language having many points in common with English (Odlin 1989). While it is possible to argue that the culture of Finnish speakers diverges from that of Swedish speakers, Ringbom (1987) goes so far as to claim that Swedish and Finnish-speaking Finns live in a monocultural country.

One way to appreciate the importance of crosslinguistic distance is to examine texts that are the common cultural property of various speech communities. The first few sentences of the Lord's Prayer follow in five languages.

1. Our Father, who art in heaven, hallowed be thy name. Thy kingdom come, thy will be done on earth as it is in heaven.
2. Faeder ure, Þu Þe eart on heofonum, si Þin nama gehalgod. To becume Þin rice. GewurÞe ðin willa on eorðan swa swa on heofonum.
3. Fader vår, som är I himmelen! Helgat varde ditt namn; Tillkomme ditt rike; ske din vilja såsom I himmelen så ock på jorden.
4. Isä meidän, joka olet taivaissa! Pyhitetty olkoon sinun nimesi; tulkoon sinun valtakuntasi; tapahtukoon sinun tahtosi myös maan päällä niinkuin taivaassa.
5. Meie Isa, kes oled taevas! Pühitsetud olgu sinu nimi; sinu riik tulgu; sinu; tahtmine sündigu nagu taevas, nõnda ka maa peal.

The second language, Old English, shares a great deal with the third, Swedish, including some points where Old and Modern English diverge. While the fourth and fifth languages, Finnish and Estonian, differ strikingly from the three Germanic ones, parallels in vocabulary and grammar indicate that the last two languages are closely related historically.

What implications do these crosslinguistic differences and similarities have for research and teaching in English as a foreign language (EFL) or ESL? If native speakers of English find it decidedly harder to learn Finnish than to learn Swedish, the converse conclusion seems plausible as well: speakers of Finnish will have greater difficulty acquiring English than will Swedish speakers. This conclusion is in fact not just a speculation. Considerable research in Finland, especially Ringbom's 1987 book cited earlier, has made it abundantly clear that Finnish-speaking Finns have a great deal more difficulty learning English than do their Swedish-speaking counterparts. Later in this chapter, I will discuss some examples of this difficulty, but for now it is sufficient to note that Robert Lado was not quite so mistaken in his beliefs on the effects of similarities and differences in foreign language learning (cf. Selinker 1992).

If it is true that the most inflexible difficulty for adults learning a second language is crosslinguistic distance, it naturally follows that the most inflexible problem for teachers is the lack of time to work with students. It will help here to discuss some figures I provide in the introduction to a collection of articles on pedagogical grammar (Odlin 1994). Four years of instruction in a high school will result in about 800 contact hours if classes meet one hour per day, five days a week. This is comparable to the 720 hours that students in the Foreign Service Institute would spend on Swedish. While the comparison might suggest that four years of high school instruction will suffice to learn a closely related language, two caveats are necessary. First, the 720 hours spent on Swedish occur in rapid succession in an intensive language program with a norm of 30 contact hours per week as opposed to 5 in the high school setting. Second, class sizes in the FSI are much smaller than in many high school settings. Many other factors can make secondary school instruction less effective, but even in exceptionally good high school programs, the 800 contact hours still do not come near the 1,320 hours of instruction for such languages as Finnish (which the FSI has designated as a language warranting 44 weeks of intensive instruction). Moreover, the number of contact hours in ESL courses, such as those in the Ohio State ESL writing programs, amount to only 130 extra hours.

The numbers thus offer some insight as to why speakers of such languages as Chinese and Korean so often find reading and writing in English difficult: the structural distances between their languages and English are vast, and the related problem of cultural differences can also occasion great difficulty (cf. Connor 1996). If it is true that few (if any) teaching programs offer students enough time to learn in the classroom everything that they need to know, the efforts of learners outside the classroom must be a key concern. Students obviously differ considerably in how successful they are, and while not all of the success (or lack thereof) results from efforts outside of class, we all know that some students do more work and that some manage to use their time extremely well, solving problems that take other learners many more hours. To use a well-worn but accurate phrase, successful students have learned to learn.

Dictionaries and Learner Autonomy

When structural contrasts are great and where classroom hours are few (and these conditions obtain in most cases of instructed second language acquisition), a key goal of any teaching program must be learner autonomy. Many techniques and materials can contribute to that goal, but dictionaries remain among the most important. To consider just how dictionaries can best contribute to autonomy, it will be necessary to compare their use in reading and in writing—and to consider some of the claims and counterclaims about dictionary use.

A brief historical look at English lexicography will help explain how design factors in dictionary making can affect reading and writing. The dictionary is in many ways an invention of the modern world. Chaucer was long dead, and Shakespeare had already written most of his plays, by the time Robert Cawdrey wrote the first dictionary for the English language in

1604, and its name, *A Table Alphabeticall* [sic] *of Hard Usual English Words,*
suggests how limited his scope was (Baugh and Cable 1993; Cawdrey [1604]
1966). Dictionaries of hard words remained the norm for quite a while, but
in 1755 the first serious dictionary of English, the famous creation of Samuel
Johnson, appeared, and by 1828 Noah Webster had published an American
English rival. As historical linguistics became a dominant concern in the
same century, an even more ambitious project got underway: the *Oxford
English Dictionary.* Since then, countless other dictionaries have appeared to
help users in a wide range of fields, including dialectology, computer science, and language teaching (cf. Murray 1977; Sledd and Ebbitt 1962;
Spencer 1992; Wilson, Hendrickson, and Taylor 1963).

It is no secret that many publishers have noticed the worldwide boom
in English language study, and with this boom have come ever more dictionaries tailored for the needs of second language learners. Oxford University Press was one of the first to appreciate the need—and the market—
for lexicographical work aimed primarily at English teaching involving
nonnative speakers. Following on the success of A.S. Hornby's *Oxford
Advanced Learner's Dictionary of Current English* (1974), which first
appeared over fifty years ago, other publishers, including Longman and
Collins, have introduced rivals that have added features not seen in
Hornby's contribution. Even Cambridge University Press, which for years
shied away from most lexicographical projects involving English, has
recently launched its own *Cambridge International Dictionary of English*
(Procter 1995). The competition between the dictionary makers has been
healthy, and a couple of examples will suggest some of the improvements
that have appeared. The Hornby dictionary now has versions for speakers
of a number of different languages, including Chinese and Indonesian. In
the Chinese version, for example, students can read a Chinese translation
of an English word but still get most of the information available in the
monolingual English version (Hornby 1988). The new Cambridge dictionary gives line numbers for every entry, which is part of a new technique
to help users look up idioms. A survey by MacFarquhar and Richards
(1983) indicates that ESL students prefer some conventions over others in
the content of dictionaries, and such preferences will no doubt continue to
be a concern for publishers.

The translations in the newer Hornby dictionaries show that second
language lexicography increasingly considers specific user-groups, and it
is noteworthy that Oxford University Press has seen fit to blur the traditional line between monolingual and bilingual dictionaries. Among teachers and researchers, debate continues over how advisable it is for students

to use bilingual or monolingual dictionaries: for example, there have been recent exchanges on TESL-L, a computer list widely read by teachers, on the pros and cons of various dictionary strategies. Whatever the definitive answers are, they doubtlessly hinge on the purposes that individual learners have. Before those purposes are considered, however, it will help to consider research on the advisability of using any dictionary at all. Not surprisingly, many of the debates over dictionary use are related to larger questions in literacy studies, most notably the following two:

- How much vocabulary can learners pick up in context?
- What differences are there between L1 and L2 vocabulary acquisition?

The issue of context clearly has implications for using—or not using—a dictionary. If students could learn all new vocabulary simply from reading or listening, there would be no need for dictionaries. There are indeed researchers and teachers who have considerable faith in the power of contextual learning (e.g., Nagy, Herman, and Anderson 1985), and apart from actual research, intuition suggests that children acquiring their native language can pick up a great deal from context. Moreover, there are distinct hazards in using dictionaries. If learners interrupt their reading or writing frequently to consult a dictionary, the overall communicative purposes of engaging with a text are put at risk.

While there are indeed reasons to be skeptical about dictionaries, the most plausible answers to the two questions just posed do not give strong support to the skeptics. In fact, a number of researchers have argued that context is unreliable. Schatz and Baldwin (1986), for example, criticize earlier studies of contextual learning with native speaker readers. They note that the texts used in these studies were often artificial and tended to provide considerable redundancy, which could aid learners in their guesses. It is just as easy, though, to construct sentences with minimal redundancy: for example, in the sentence "Mike is a scurrilous person and I have never liked him," there is not enough context to allow readers unfamiliar with the word *scurrilous* to infer the exact meaning. Instead of also using artificial texts in their study, however, Schatz and Baldwin used prose passages taken from modern fiction and also from history and science texts, and they found that low-frequency words often proved too difficult for students to understand in context. Schatz and Baldwin emphasize, moreover, that the effects of contextual learning in the study by Nagy, Herman, and Anderson (1985) cited earlier were relatively weak—though the results did indicate that at least 10 percent of unfamiliar word meanings might be inferred simply from context.

Whether or not 10 percent is an accurate figure (and whether or not it is realistic to expect that a single statistic could summarize the advantages), the implications of such work on context would be less straightforward if research had been done only with native speakers. In fact, however, there is considerable work on the effects of context in second language reading, and the results argue strongly against claims that context alone is sufficient help. For example, Haynes (1984) found that while ESL college students could identify some words in a highly redundant "local" context, they had considerable difficulty guessing the meanings of words when there was little textual redundancy.

While the Haynes study might suggest that native and nonnative speakers perform the same way with regard to learning in context, there are strong reasons for arguing that L2 vocabulary acquisition can be a very different process from what goes on in first-language settings. Most crucially, language transfer can provide considerable advantages to some learners. In the versions of the Lord's Prayer given earlier, anyone who knows Modern English can make an easy guess as to what *Faeder* means in Old English and what *Fader* means in Swedish. In such cases, then, there will be some context for inferring that *ure* and *vår* are equivalent to *Our*. In general, crosslinguistic similarities can make a considerable amount of vocabulary learning unnecessary. Conversely, large differences in vocabulary mean that much more learning will be needed. The Finnish phrase *Isä meidan* could be equivalent to either *Our Father* or *Father our*, and there is insufficient context to help English-speaking readers decide (the latter translation happens to be the correct one). These informal examples are supported by the systematic comparisons of Ringbom (1987), the main difference being that the target language in his research was English. Not surprisingly, L1 Swedish speakers had a strong advantage in vocabulary over speakers of L1 Finnish (cf. Ard and Homburg 1992).

While inferring from context and transfer from the L1 are separate cognitive processes, they may interact, as seen in a recent study by Nagy, McClure, and Montserrat (1997). In that study, Spanish-English bilinguals seemed to have used syntactic information from Spanish to make inferences about the meanings of some nonsense forms put into English sentences. While Nagy, McClure, and Montserrat focused on negative transfer, their results suggest that the native language can facilitate good guessing in the target language. In fact, Holmes and Ramos (1993) found considerable evidence of mainly positive transfer in the reading strategies used by Portuguese readers of English. By the same token, though, when the crosslinguistic similarities are few, much more vocabulary remains to be learned. Several researchers have pointed out that one of the biggest obstacles to using contextual clues is that second language learners often know too few words for there to be a clear context in the first place (e.g., Hunt 1996a). A study by Laufer (1992) did not look directly at the question of context, but it did compare the reading comprehension scores of students with varying degrees of knowledge of English vocabulary. The threshold for good comprehension proved to be 3,000 words: that is, learners whose lexical knowledge exceeded the threshold had dramatically higher scores in contrast to those who knew somewhat fewer than 3,000 words.

If the threshold seen in Laufer's study applies to other situations as well, it suggests that advising learners with small vocabularies to rely heavily on context would be a mistaken teaching strategy. In fact, Sanaoui (1995) found that students who relied only on informal lexical strategies (including contextual learning) had less success in remembering new vocabulary in comparison with individuals who employed a range of formal strategies, including making lists and consulting dictionaries. Similarly, Laufer and Kimmel (1997) argue that such dictionaries as the versions of Hornby's adapted for specific L1's allow for greater success in mastering new vocabulary. Another recent investigation (Hulstijn, Hollander, and Greidanus 1996) focused on the effects of using and not using a dictionary. In comparison with a control group, Dutch students who consulted a dictionary showed much better retention of L2 French words, but, most significantly, this success was only evident in the cases where learners actually looked up the words. When they did so, they outperformed a third group, who had been given glosses in the text they would read, but when the students in the dictionary group neglected to look up words, they performed much worse than the group given the glosses.

The studies of Nagy (1995; Nagy, Herman, and Anderson 1985; Nagy, McClure, and Montserrat 1997), Laufer, Sanaoui, and others suggest that the benefits of learning vocabulary in context are real but also limited (cf. Coady 1993). Moreover, work on transfer by Ringbom and others makes clear what the implications are when large amounts of English vocabulary are unfamiliar to learners whose native languages are vastly different. In such cases, learning from context is hardly a viable option in the earlier stages of acquisition—including the intermediate stages of proficiency shown by many learners in university ESL programs. Furthermore, the studies by Hulstijn, Hollander, and Greidanus (1996) and Laufer and

Kimmel (1997) indicate that dictionary work can indeed help readers to learn—and retain—new vocabulary. The question is thus not whether dictionaries help but rather how they can best help.

Most of the research reviewed so far has focused on reading comprehension, and this is the area where learners can have the greatest autonomy. Yet, since reading is not the only skill needed for academic literacy, it is natural to wonder just what role dictionaries may play in the connections between reading and writing. For those kinds of writing that are closely related to reading tasks, there can be little doubt that students able to use a dictionary well have a major advantage. Writing summaries and abstracts will be one of the most common tasks awaiting new university students, and a study by Hatzitheodorou (1994) suggests that the single biggest factor in failures to write good summaries is unsatisfactory reading of the original text. The reading research cited earlier indicates that inaccurate identifications of words in context are commonplace, and while not all reading failures arise from inaccurate lexical inferences, there is clearly a need to encourage some readers to rely more on dictionaries.

The uses of dictionaries in writing are not confined to specific genres, such as abstracts. Proficiency in grammar is obviously necessary for constructing the sentences of any text and for editing the text later. Just as they can become independent analysts in deciphering the vocabulary of the texts they read, foreign language learners can—and should—become aware of many of the most common grammatical patterns of the target language. This awareness may never be thorough: indeed, no native speakers can really say that they thoroughly understand just how the morphology and syntax of their mother tongues work. Even so, some second language research (e.g., Hulstijn and Hulstijn 1984) indicates that awareness need not be total in order for benefits to come from focusing on form. Special learning materials, such as dictionaries, can contribute to such focusing.

It must be conceded that for some grammatical structures, such as word order, dictionaries offer only minimal help (unless they include a section specifically on grammatical points). However, learners can certainly profit by using a dictionary with regard to such problematic areas as articles. Master (1987) found that systematic instruction in the uses of articles led to significant gains that were not seen in a control group not given any instruction. It is especially noteworthy that the distinction between count and noncount nouns constituted one major part of the instruction that students received. The countability of nouns in English affects meaning in English, as can be seen in the difference between the sentences "I was looking for mint" and "I was looking for a mint." In the former example, the noun *mint* is noncount and denotes some unspecified quantity, whereas in the latter, the presence of the indefinite article indicates a countable noun, here a single referent very different in form (and usually in color) from herbal mint.

Because the count/noncount distinction matters so much for deciding whether or not to use an article and for deciding what article to use, second language learners must be certain about the countability classification of every noun in their writing. This is indeed a formidable problem, but it is also one where dictionaries can be tremendously helpful. The Hornby dictionary was among the first to distinguish count nouns, such as *tree,* and noncount nouns, such as *information,* and also to distinguish countability according to the diverse senses, as in the case of countable *mint* and uncountable *mint.* Since Hornby, most other learners' dictionaries have adopted similar classification systems, and even if there were no other reason to recommend these dictionaries over those intended for native speakers of English, the information on countability would be sufficient justification. Once again, transfer research is also relevant, as it has clearly shown that speakers of languages with no articles have an especially difficult time with English articles (e.g., Master 1987; Odlin 1989). For speakers of such languages, then, dictionaries remain one of the most powerful tools for dealing with an extremely difficult problem.

Most of the discussion of dictionaries up to this point has focused on monolingual dictionaries, but bilingual dictionaries are obviously a related concern. I have mentioned that some versions of the Hornby dictionary provide translations in students' native languages. Even with such a desirable feature, however, the structure of the dictionary is based clearly on the English lexicon, as are all L2-to-L1 dictionaries. For students only interested in receptive skills, the L2-to-L1 structure will help a great deal with reading and listening comprehension. For productive skills, however, every learner should have access to an L1-to-L2 dictionary, where, for example, Turkish students can find an English word by looking up Turkish words that are close translation equivalents. It is conceivable, of course, that a learner in a writing course might compose everything in English without even thinking of what the native language equivalents are. However, the L1-to-L2 format will no doubt help students to hit upon words they had never encountered before or words that they have forgotten.

Even though bilingual dictionaries have an important role to play in second language instruction, they can present pitfalls if learners do not use them carefully. As Hunt (1996b) notes, learners can come to rely too heavily on bilingual dictionaries, which can perpetuate the erroneous belief that the meanings of every native language word correspond exactly to the meanings of one and only one target language word. Moreover, even carefully constructed bilingual dictionaries may have some unreliable advice, as Hunt (1996b, 16) illustrates with the following sentences taken from a Japanese/English dictionary: "He won't see being used" (i.e., "He won't allow himself to be used") and "We went around to drop into the drugstore on our way home" (i.e., "We went out of our way to drop by the drugstore on our way home"). Even when the accuracy of the dictionary is not in question, there remain other problems. One is that learners may not necessarily select the most accurate information from either a monolingual or a bilingual dictionary (Parry 1993). There is also the problem of making learners aware of the limits of any dictionary and especially of bilingual dictionaries. Teachers should accordingly encourage a two-dictionary strategy, at least with intermediate learners who do not know enough words to recognize many new ones in context and who do not yet have a good sense of all the possible word choices available in the target language—but who do have enough sophistication in lexis and grammar to begin using a monolingual dictionary, such as Hornby's.

These comments on dictionaries may seem obvious to many who have taught EFL or who have learned a second language (including, of course, English). Nevertheless, if it is true, as suggested by Nation (1990), that learners underuse the resources in dictionaries, instructors will need to check just what their students are or are not doing. Nation's assertion is in fact supported by studies from France (Béjoint 1981) and Japan (Baxter 1980) showing that while university students do use dictionaries, relatively few consult them for problems related to grammar. Moreover, even though many students in the French study recognized the value of dictionaries for reading, far fewer seemed aware of all the help dictionaries could provide for writing. I myself have encountered many language learners who are unaware of the value of a two-dictionary strategy for learning to write in English. Furthermore, many have seemed unaware of the advantages of specialized EFL dictionaries, such as Hornby's, in such areas as noun countability. In such cases, students have a long way to go in developing their capacities as independent analysts. Accordingly, an important role of a language teacher is to be an advisor on how to make the best possible use of low-tech tools, such as dictionaries, as well as the wonders of the digital age.

Dictionaries and the New Technologies

While print dictionaries will continue to play an important role for the foreseeable future, there is good reason to wonder what their relation is—and will be—to emerging technologies, such as handheld electronic devices. At present, there are some clear advantages to small but detailed print dictionaries. For the time being, they are cheaper than the best electronic ones, and the cheaper electronic lexicons that I have seen provide only a fraction of the information supplied by a good print dictionary. Handheld electronic lexicons will probably continue to improve, but it remains to be seen how well they will cope with long-standing technical problems, such as a small screen, a vulnerable power source, and an even more vulnerable memory.

Although some believe that print technology will go extinct, a more likely scenario is that information users, students and teachers among them, will continue to do what they are already doing: relying on print technology for some purposes and on digital technology for others. While television certainly changed the future of radio in drastic ways, radio has had its own niche for decades now. Likewise, there will probably remain an important niche for printed matter, including dictionaries. Even if the printed book is low-tech by today's standards, it is the outcome of centuries of experimentation with the technology of writing. Its flexibility and durability will probably assure its survival for a long time to come.

A continuing coexistence of print and digital technology will force us to think more and more about the comparative advantages of each. Since I have discussed some advantages of print dictionaries, it is now appropriate to consider a new technology that is beginning to make an impact on lexicography and on teaching: concordance programs. In comparison with concordances, print dictionaries are quite rigid. Any word a user wants to look up has a fixed place in what is usually an alphabetical sequence. On-line dictionaries, such as the electronic version of the *Oxford English Dictionary,* allow for much more flexibility, but they still do not provide users with access to the databases from which they were originally compiled. For example, the electronic *OED* cites Shakespeare's *Hamlet* (act 1, scene 1) to exemplify the use of the word *philosophy:* "There is more known under heaven than is dreamt in your philosophy, Horatio." However, very few uses of this word by Shakespeare are there cited. A printed Shakespeare concordance lists every occurrence in context for this word and every other word in Shakespeare. Concordances have long been available for Shakespeare, the Bible, and other highly revered works. However, computer programs, such as TACT, now allow for concordances to be developed very easily for any text by any author. TACT, which stands for Textual Analysis Computing Tools, is available on the Internet (http://www.chass.utoronto.ca:8080/cch/tact.html) and is now being widely used.

Several researchers have discussed the value of concordances for dictionary making and for classroom teaching (e.g., Hunt 1996b; Johns 1994; Sinclair 1991), but relatively few have considered the benefits of concordances for research on language transfer or for solutions to learners' problems that are rooted in crosslinguistic influence. Accordingly, this section of this chapter will focus on the benefits of such an application. The examples to be considered come from a database compiled by Jarvis (1997), consisting of 316 narratives written by schoolchildren in the fifth, seventh, and ninth grades in Finland and the United States. The young writers were all shown part of the Charlie Chaplin film *Modern Times* in class and asked to write down an account of the events. The largest number of narratives came from 140 students whose native language is Finnish; another 110 came from L1 Swedish speakers, and 66 were written by the L1 English schoolchildren in Indiana. There were actually more participants in the study, but Jarvis randomly selected a smaller sample from each of the three groups for controlled comparisons.

The Finnish speakers had studied English for varying periods, between two and six years. Not surprisingly, many problems involving vocabulary and grammar emerge in the corpus, some of which are discussed in a recent article (Jarvis and Odlin in press). In that research, we focused on locative expressions with certain verbs. In this regard, the verb *put* is interesting because it invariably requires some kind of adverbial complement, whether an adverb phrase or a prepositional phrase. Figure 1 shows some typical problems that arise in the L1 Finnish students' attempts to use *put*. The first two examples do not involve errors: in the first, *put* is followed by the preposition *in*; in the second, *put* is followed by *into*. All of the next three examples, however, show some of the problems that arise from differences between Finnish and English. While Finnish does have some prepositions, it makes much greater use of postpositions and of case endings (Finnish nouns can be inflected for 15 different cases). One outcome of this difference is sometimes the omission of a preposition in English, as in the third example. This problem is comparatively rare in the corpus, but it occurs not only with *put* but also with other locative verbs, such as *take* and *sit*. Still another outcome—and a more frequent one—is an inaccurate choice of preposition, as in the fourth and fifth examples, where *to* follows *put*. The choice of *to* is no doubt due largely to the influence of Finnish. The student who wrote these examples was probably making an interlingual identification between English *to* and the illative case in Finnish. In a control group of Finnish schoolchildren who wrote a narrative of the film in their native language, several chose the form *poliisiautoon* (police auto), a noun phrase marked by the illative case. It is significant, moreover, that the L1 Swedish group writing in English never chose *to* to follow *put,* nor did they omit prepositions as occurs in example 3.

From these observations, one conclusion of interest to SLA researchers is that crosslinguistic differences do not invariably lead to the same outcomes. Some Finns omitted prepositions whereas others chose ones that were consonant with the semantic structures in their native language. To reach this conclusion, a corpus is necessary even though a concordance program is not. However, the concordance program allows for much easier investigations of certain kinds of problems, such as the occurrences of various types of adverbial constructions with locative verbs.

Concordances can likewise help teachers to construct exercises that save a great deal of time. The sixth and seventh examples in figure 1 are instances of *put* as used by the American schoolchildren in Indiana. One possible activity would be for students to compare what native speakers actually do in repeated instances: many more Americans also used *put*, and, interestingly, none chose *into* even though this would be an accurate choice—one that some Finnish students actually made. For teachers in Finland who might not be sure about what the most likely choices of native speakers in such a context would be, the corpus could provide much more information than could a dictionary. Some of the writing problems evident in both the native and nonnative speakers' writing should no doubt be edited out in some exercises to allow learners to focus on a specific problem. Another option, of course, would be to choose a model text written in standard English. Even so, I think there is a lot to be said for the idea of students in one country seeing authentic language from students in another country.

In comparison with a print dictionary, then, a computer corpus can provide learners and teachers with much more information about lexical occurrences, including how frequent some constructions are and what native speakers seem to prefer in certain contexts. With a little training, then, the corpus can be a valuable supplement to, though not a replace-

(1) Police is very angry and say: Now we going to the police-station and they live.
Police put Chaplin in the car.
He sit down and girl come in.
Chaplin asks: Do you remember me, and the bread?

(2) something to the kids who were standing right beside him.
Then the police saw what he was doing and he took Charlie away.
Soon there came police car and the police put Charlie into that car.
After a few minutes the car stoped again and there came the same girl who had steel that bread.

(3) He eat like that horse.
Then he is ready he says a waitress I haven't got money.
Policeman caught he and put he a police car.
That woman who stole bread Charlie give he place in woman.
Policecar almost drove crashed.

(4) then a policeman whit a girl.
Charlie went ot the restaurant and he ate a very big meal there, but he couldn't paid and a policeman put him to the policecar, there were some another robbers too.
Then a car stoped and a girl who stole that bread came in.

(5) prisoners (at some point C. plays with a cigar(?)).
The girl is put to the buss, too.
She and Chaplin meet again.
The girl decides to run away, so she and Chaplin jump to the street.

(6) And they were chasing her agian.
So he went in the cafataria and ate lots of food and didn't pay for it.
So they arrested him and put him in the back of a police van and drove away.
And not to long later they caught the lady and put her in the back to.
Not to long in the drive they jumped out of the van and were knocked out

(7) He got a segre and took it and smoked it and gave some kids some.
And after the police man got off the phone the man would not pay.
So the put him in a van, and took him off.
The the lady who stoled the bread got on their and had to stand up so the man let her sit down.

Fig. 1. Selected examples from a corpus generated by TACT

ment for, the dictionary. Both tools together can do much to help learners become independent analysts.

Summary

Research on language transfer (i.e., crosslinguistic influence) suggests that it is unrealistic to expect most acquisition to take place within any ESL classroom. Both dictionaries and digital technologies can help foster learning independent of classroom instruction.

Dictionaries have grown more sophisticated and specialized over the centuries, but there continues to be skepticism about their value in second language learning, with some teachers and researchers pointing to the importance of learning vocabulary in context. However, considerable research indicates that the benefits of learning vocabulary in context are real but also limited. Moreover, work on language transfer makes clear the implications when large amounts of English vocabulary are unfamiliar to learners speaking languages vastly different from the target. In such cases, learning from context is hardly a viable option in the earlier stages of acquisition.

Research indicates that dictionaries constitute a very useful backup when contextual strategies do not result in accurate inferences. Reading and writing interact in vocabulary acquisition as in other areas: writing good summaries (among other genres) depends on good reading, which in turn depends on good understanding of the individual words that collectively shape a text. Dictionaries can contribute not only to solving vocabulary problems but also to making correct decisions about morphology and syntactic structure in writing, as seen in the information that Hornby's dictionary and other dictionaries provide about noun countability, information that is essential for using definite and indefinite articles accurately.

Since students are not always aware of all the kinds of help that a good dictionary can offer, teachers should make sure to raise the level of awareness. Digital technology has already made an impact on language learning, but it seems unlikely that it will supersede the printed dictionary any time soon. Print and digital technologies will probably coexist for many years to come, and teachers should try to use the complementary advantages of print dictionaries and computer corpora. Both have an important role to play in helping learners achieve greater autonomy.

References

Ard, J., and T. Homburg. 1992. Verification of language transfer. In *Language transfer in language learning,* ed. S. Gass and L. Selinker, 44–70. Amsterdam: Benjamins.

Baugh, A., and T. Cable. 1993. *A history of the English language.* New York: Prentice-Hall.

Baxter, J. 1980. The dictionary and vocabulary behavior: A single word or a handful? *TESOL Quarterly* 14:325–36.

Béjoint, H. 1981. The foreign student's use of monolingual English dictionaries. *Applied Linguistics* 2:207–22.

Belcher, D., and G. Braine, eds. 1995. *Academic writing in a second language: Essays on research and pedagogy.* Norwood, NJ: Ablex.

Cawdrey, R. [1604] 1966. *A table alphabeticall of hard usual English words.* Gainesville, FL: Scholars' Facsimiles and Reprints.

Coady, J. 1993. Research on ESL/EFL vocabulary acquisition: Putting it in context. In *Second language reading and vocabulary learning,* ed. T. Huckin, M. Haynes, and J. Coady, 3–23. Norwood, NJ: Ablex.

Connor, U. 1996. *Contrastive rhetoric: Cross-cultural aspects of second-language writing.* Cambridge: Cambridge University Press.

Ellis, R. 1985. *Understanding second language acquisition.* Oxford: Oxford University Press.

Hatzitheodorou, A.-M. 1994. An analysis of summary writing by students of English as a second language. Master's thesis, Ohio State University.

Haynes, M. 1984. Patterns and perils of guessing in second language reading. In *On TESOL '83— the question of control: Selected papers from the Annual Convention of Teachers of English to Speakers of Other Languages,* ed. J. Handscombe, 44–64. Washington, DC: Teachers of English to Speakers of Other Languages. ERIC ED 275149.

Holmes, J., and G. R. Ramos. 1993. False friends and reckless guessers: Observing cognate recognition strategies. In *Second language reading and vocabulary learning,* ed. T. Huckin, M. Haynes, and J. Coady, 86–108. Norwood, NJ: Ablex.

Hornby, A. S. 1974. *Oxford advanced learner's dictionary of current English.* London: Oxford University Press.

———. 1988. *Oxford advanced learner's English-Chinese dictionary = Niu chin hsien tai kao chi Yin Han shuang chieh tz'u tien.* Hong Kong: Oxford University Press.

Hulstijn, J., M. Hollander, and T. Greidanus. 1996. Incidental vocabulary learning by advanced foreign language students: The influence of marginal glosses, dictionary use, and reoccurrence of unknown words. *Modern Language Journal* 80:327–39.

Hulstijn, J., and W. Hulstijn. 1984. Grammatical errors as a function of processing constraints and explicit knowledge. *Language Learning* 4:23–43.

Hunt, A. 1996a. Constraints on inferring word meaning from context. *Kansai Gadai University Journal of Inquiry and Research* 63:239–49. ERIC ED 405738.

———. 1996b. Evaluating bilingual and monolingual dictionaries for L2 learners. *Kansai Gadai University Journal of Inquiry and Research* 65:15–27. ERIC ED 405739.

Jarvis, S. 1997. The role of L1-based concepts in L2 lexical reference: Second language acquisition, first language influence. Ph.D. diss., Indiana University.

Jarvis, S., and T. Odlin. In press. Morphological type, spatial reference, and language transfer. *Studies in Second Language Acquisition.*

Johns, T. 1994. From printout to handout: Grammar and vocabulary teaching in the context of data-driven learning. In *Perspectives on pedagogical grammar,* ed T. Odlin, 293–313. Cambridge: Cambridge University Press.

Kelly, L. G. 1969. *Twenty-five centuries of language teaching; An inquiry into the science, art, and development of language teaching methodology, 500 B.C.–1969.* Rowley, MA: Newbury House.

Lado, R. 1957. *Linguistics across cultures; Applied linguistics for language teachers.* Ann Arbor: University of Michigan Press.

Laufer, B. 1992. Reading in a foreign language: How does L2 lexical knowledge interact with the reader's general academic ability? *Journal of Research in Reading* 15:95–103.

Laufer, B., and M. Kimmel. 1997. Bilingualised dictionaries: How learners really use them. *System* 25:361–69.

MacFarquhar, P., and J. Richards. 1983. On dictionaries and definitions. *RELC Journal* 14:111–24.

Master, P. 1987. A cross-linguistic interlanguage analysis of the acquisition of the English article system. Ph.D. diss., University of California, Los Angeles.

McKay, S. 1984. *Composing in a second language.* Rowley, MA: Newbury House.

Murray, E. K. M. 1977. *Caught in the web of words: James A. H. Murray and the Oxford English dictionary.* New Haven: Yale University Press.

Nagy, W. E. 1995. *On the role of context in first- and second-language vocabulary learning.* Technical Report 627. Urbana: Center for the Study of Reading, University of Illinois. ERIC ED 391152.

Nagy, W. E., P. Herman, and R. Anderson. 1985. Learning words from context. *Reading Research Quarterly* 20:233–53.

Nagy, W. E., E. McClure, and M. Montserrat. 1997. Linguistic transfer and the use of context by Spanish-English bilinguals. *Applied Psycholinguistics* 18:431–52.

Nation, I. S. P. 1990. *Teaching and learning vocabulary.* New York: Newbury House.

Odlin, T. 1989. *Language transfer.* Cambridge: Cambridge University Press.

————, ed. 1994. *Perspectives on pedagogical grammar.* Cambridge: Cambridge University Press.

Parry, K. 1993. Too many words: Learning the vocabulary of an academic subject. In *Second language reading and vocabulary learning,* ed. T. Huckin, M. Haynes, and J. Coady, 109–27. Norwood, NJ: Ablex.

Procter, P., ed. 1995. *Cambridge international dictionary of English.* Cambridge: Cambridge University Press.

Ringbom, H. 1987. *The role of the first language in foreign language learning.* Clevedon, UK: Multilingual Matters.

Sanaoui, R. 1995. Adult learners' approaches to learning vocabulary in second languages. *Modern Language Journal* 79:15–28.

Selinker, L. 1992. *Rediscovering interlanguage.* London: Longman.

Schatz, E., and R. S. Baldwin. 1986. Context clues are unreliable predictors of word meanings. *Reading Research Quarterly* 21:439–53.

Sinclair, J. 1991. *Corpus, concordance, collocation.* Oxford: Oxford University Press.

Sledd, J., and W. Ebbitt. 1962. *Dictionaries and THAT dictionary.* Chicago: Scott, Foresman, and Company.

Spencer, D. 1992. *Webster's new world dictionary of computer terms.* New York: Prentice-Hall.

Wilson, K., R. H. Hendrickson, and P. Taylor. 1963. *Harbrace guide to dictionaries.* New York: Harcourt, Brace, and World.

Chapter 12

Lexis and Grammar in Second Language Reading and Writing

Georgette Jabbour, New York Institute of Technology

This chapter argues for using a lexical approach rooted in corpus linguistics when teaching second language academic reading and writing. The argument I advance builds on two assumptions. The first is that reading-writing instruction is based in part on text analysis and the conceptualization of text models (Swales 1981, 1990). The second is that since both reading and writing are text oriented, words and word combinations used in texts are of paramount interest, and the results of recent lexical studies concerned with word combinations and language chunks can contribute to reading-writing pedagogy (Johns 1991; Lewis 1993, 1997; Sinclair 1987, 1991; Willis 1990).

The outcomes of lexical studies have emphasized the value of the independent lexical item (be it a single-word or a multiword item), its immediate environment, and the meaning it projects, rather than the grammatical structure in which it occurs. These recent studies make use of computer software to analyze chunks of authentic language found in a wide variety of text types: newspaper and magazine articles, advertisements, letters, memos, and so on. If we consider the language classroom as a place to analyze texts and formulate text models, we should be able to use such linguistic corpora and current software packages (e.g., concordancers) to study the language we impart to second language learners. Tracing the use of words and word combinations in texts would enhance the quality and quantity of text models we formulate (Biber, Conrad, and Reppen 1996).

In a lexical, or corpus-based, approach, reading and writing depend on words and word associations that relate to the discourse community of the texts forming the corpus. This means that the traditional pedagogical separation of grammar from vocabulary is inappropriate and that every one word or group of words has its own behavior, value, and significance in the place where it occurs. In this chapter, therefore, the emphasis will be on why and how words have their own grammars and on how a lexically oriented reading-writing program—a natural by-product of the combination of computer technology and second language acquisition findings—benefits second language learners. In other words, the chapter deals with the rationale for implementing a lexical approach based on corpus linguistics research when teaching academic reading and writing.

The terms *lexical approach* (Lewis 1993, 1997), *lexical syllabus* (Sinclair and Renouf 1988; Willis 1990), and *corpus-based approach* (Biber, Conrad, and Reppen 1996) refer to the same notion of a teaching program that emphasizes language chunks elicited by corpus research, instead of emphasizing traditional grammar and structures. The term *lexical syllabus*, however, implies a more structured, selected, and thorough use of lexis, whereas *lexical approach* implies a methodology. More often than not, a syllabus dictates a methodology. Thus, the two terms are used interchangeably because both *lexical syllabus* and *lexical approach* denote a lexically oriented teaching program.

In this chapter, I first set the scene for the connection between reading and writing and look into how, in some theories of syllabus/curriculum design, the lexical approach operates much like the interactive reading approach promulgated by Carrell, Devine, and Eskey (1988). The connection between reading, writing, and lexical patterns is then dealt with. The principles on which a lexical approach functions are also presented. These include collocation, corpus linguistics, and word frequency. The last section provides sample materials, generated by corpus research, for use in teaching academic reading and writing.

The Reading-Writing Connection

Writing is an activity that is informed by reading, and influences reading, as learners become more proficient in their language use. In academia, the strong connection between these two activities is undeniable. Some writing textbooks for both native and nonnative speakers of English include large amounts of reading selections that serve as prompts and models for writing. For instance, Bazerman's textbook, *The Informed Writer: Using Sources in the Disciplines* (1985), includes three sections that guide the writing process from writing about readings, to writing using readings, then to writing in specific disciplines. The book assumes that writing develops from reading and in turn diverges from it in the sense that authors eventually attempt to provide their chosen disciplinary communities with new knowledge through their writing. The implication is that the discipline shapes the thinking of the writer. Swales (1981, 1990) makes a similar assumption about writing contributing new knowledge in his famous CARS (Create A Research Space) model.

Similarly, regarding studies on the acquisition of reading, Grabe (1986) suggests that a threshold language level in reading is achieved with the possession of a "critical mass of knowledge," a point at which "a learner stops learning to read and only reads to learn" (36). In this chapter, I further assume that past a threshold, reading and writing diverge in two directions. While, as Grabe states, reading turns into a tool to increase learning, writing turns into a tool to share contributions, leading into writing in the discipline, as Bazerman (1985) indicates. The reading-writing connection is framed as follows: relating textual information to discourse structures is achieved through reading, and writing, informed in part by reading, becomes a tool for creating knowledge and for representing new discourse structures. Similar approaches to learning are seen in Wilkins's (1976) concept of the notional syllabus; in a methodology for text analysis, for example, Sinclair and Coulthard's (1975, 1992) discourse analysis framework; and in Swales's (1990) genre and move analysis.

From a reading-writing classroom perspective, text is studied as discourse. This entails examining words, combinations of words, language patterns, and ultimately models that influence attitudes (Van Dijk 1993). The more we know about how attitudes are forged through word combinations, the more help we can offer to students as writers, and the more sensitive the students become, as readers and writers, to wording. Writing is involved with expressing ideas by means of acceptable sets of patterns and models, and acquiring information about those patterns and models occurs through reading, specifically reading centered on grammar and vocabulary.

Reading and Writing in Syllabus Design

Reading and writing are literacy skills, acquired gradually and based on the transfer of skills from one mode to another. In reading, the mode starts by recognizing the signs on paper and ends with an interpretation in the mind (Rayner and Pollatsek 1989). Conversely, the mode in writing starts by encoding meanings and ends in polishing the writing on paper for discourse structure, text organization, and language mechanics. No definite and reliable line can exactly be drawn between acquisition stages, since in both cases there is a part related to cognition that somewhat resists observation and measurement. However, as in all learning situations, assumptions can be made about the intellectual activities involved.

One particularly strong assumption views language learning as a product of habit formation. This view has resulted in teaching programs built on language structures, patterns, and oral drills, where rote practice and memorization instantiate the target in the learner (e.g., Lado 1964). Habit formation is a key concept motivating the structural approach to language teaching. This view has been especially influential in teaching beginning-level learners. A second assumption involves the communicative approach to language teaching (e.g., Wilkins 1976). In this approach, learners are geared toward higher order levels and intentions, with an emphasis on teaching and learning specific language functions and notions, albeit it in a more inductive manner de-emphasizing direct grammatical instruction. The success of the communicative approach is largely seen at the intermediate and advanced levels of second language instruction. Currently, a new approach that is gaining ground builds on each of the preceding approaches by bringing together an emphasis on both language structures and functions; this is generally called the interactive approach (e.g., Carrell, Devine, and Eskey 1988).

These three approaches are impacting simultaneously on reading theory and on writing. However, while in the first two approaches, the structural and the communicative, the focus has been on either language forms or functions, no specific language focus is associated with the interactive approach. This chapter argues for teaching reading and writing through an interactive approach rooted in a lexical approach embodied in corpus linguistics research, with lexis as the focus of the instruction, in the manner promulgated by Johns's (1994) tutoring program using class concordancing (see Odlin 1994).

In the lexical approach, entry-level learners, as well as more advanced learners, are acquainted with language forms, words, word combinations, and patterns, first in the context of their basic functions, then in the larger context of their use within the discourse in which they occur. A lexical approach befits teaching second language reading and writing, since both activities are text oriented and make use of words and word combinations, or lexical patterns, within the confines of discourse. This approach has been gaining momentum recently because there are now better technological means for identifying recurrent lexical patterns that speakers and writers use in their speech and writing.

Grammar, Vocabulary, and Lexical Patterns

Lexical patterns are commonly known as *lexical phrases, multi-word units, fixed phrases, formulaic phrases, chunks,* and *preassembled chunks.* Sinclair (1991) refers to such items as constituting "one choice," operating "as a whole, more or less like a single word," and enabling the learner "to produce with confidence much more idiomatic English with less effort." These "one choice" items are, however, related to the discourse and are appropriate to the intent of the message. For this reason, the study and elicitation of lexical patterns fit naturally with the study of discourse. In an interactive framework, the lexis used to formulate the message is highlighted; thus, it allows language forms to connect to discourse structures.

In this chapter, I am reporting on the use of a corpus of electronic texts[1] to illustrate how a lexical approach to teaching works in a framework of interaction. Unlike the traditional approach to teaching reading and writing where grammar and vocabulary are treated independently, the rationale underlying the lexical approach is that grammar and vocabulary, or lexis, are interrelated, interdependent, and somewhat inseparable (Lewis 1997). Halliday (1994) uses the term *lexico-grammar* to refer to grammar and vocabulary, or lexis, combined, which he considers to form the level of "wording" in language. While grammar and vocabulary have traditionally been assigned to the two poles of fixed items versus free-occurring ones, Lewis (1997) states that there is generally more interest in those items occurring in the middle of the spectrum. If learners become accustomed to looking at words in the context of other words, as word units and groups, their reading capacity and writing ability may increase. The position in this chapter is that the grammar of words is the grammar that second language learners need in their apprenticeship. This grammar of words is best studied and compiled by referring to the lexicon in a structured manner, as in collocation and concordance sets.

Lexical studies of large amounts of text using the computer reveal that the complexities of a language, like English, lay in the idiosyncratic behavior of particular words and their formulaic, routinized associations. If left unexamined, these complexities will remain an obstacle for learners of English. Hunston (1995) and Hunston and Francis (1998) studied the verb

---

1. This chapter makes reference to a corpus of medical research articles compiled by the author and used for Ph.D. research in ESP syllabus design (see the reference list).

patterns of the bank of English and elicited new categories for the description of the grammar of the language, in particular, the complement and prepositional phrases. For teaching purposes, if lexical studies are supplemented by text analysis, the relation between discourse structures and word combinations becomes obvious, and similarities between the acts of reading and writing are easier to observe. Reading represents models for writing practices (Jabbour 1992), and writing practices provide additional models for analysis and imitation. Long-term objectives of second language reading and writing instruction include the development of learners' capacity to connect reading to writing, to cite reading in writing, and to reach a reasonable stage of comfort with the procedures involved in textual borrowings. Achievement of these objectives lies in the ability to recognize text patterns and to develop flexibility in handling these patterns to express specific and new meanings.

The recent interest in "pedagogical grammars" (Odlin 1994) implies dissatisfaction with traditional grammars, which are mostly prescriptive in nature and far more abstract than can be handled in teaching situations. This further justifies the search for a grammar that accounts for variations in meaning within different contexts of the use of words, leading to a stronger relationship between lexis, grammar, and discourse and enhancing integrated reading-writing instruction. The pedagogical grammar advocated in this chapter, therefore, is the grammar of words that may be imparted to learners through significant language patterns, in accordance with the advances made by Lewis (1993, 1997), Nattinger (1980), Nattinger and DeCarrico (1992), Willis (1990), and Willis and Willis (1988). The kind of lexical approach to EAP reading-writing instruction advanced in this chapter has proved successful in general EFL/ESL language instruction.

Principles of Lexical Studies

Lexical studies have so far been intended for lexicography and dictionary compilation. However, it is only recently, beginning in the early eighties, that the flexible use of the computer, including its availability and the availability of software packages to describe the language, has made it possible to gear lexical studies toward language teaching purposes. Two principles underlie recent lexical studies. The first is collocation or word adjacency, and the second is word frequency. A teaching program benefits from these two principles. When words collocate, we must be able to point this out to the students for language awareness purposes, or what

Lewis (1997) calls "lexical awareness." When words collocate frequently, we are sure that such combinations are essential for students' language development in their search for language regularities (Willis and Willis 1996). A reading-writing program built on lexis brings to the fore frequent word combinations and demonstrates that there is more grammatical flexibility in the target language than learners may realize. Subordinate clauses (including complement clauses with *that* and *to*) and prepositional phrases, for example, may be seen as more accessible and subject to variation in a lexical approach than in traditional approaches to grammar instruction.

Lexical studies are conducted through a variety of methods. Applied linguists, such as Carter (1987), have devised tests to identify stretches of nouns and adjectives that collocate. Classroom-oriented researchers, such as Lewis (1993, 1997), have devised categories of word collocations. Corpus linguists, such as Sinclair (1987, 1991), have looked at computerized sets of word combinations using concordancers and frequencies. In all such cases, a corpus of texts is essential. Corpus linguistics is essentially analyzing computerized text using computer software. The terms *lexical studies, computerized language,* and *corpus linguistics* are closely interrelated, and they all serve language teaching purposes. By contrast, the term *computational linguistics* encompasses language and lexical studies that are not meant to relate to an immediate teaching purpose (Chapelle 1996, 139). What follows is a brief review of collocation, corpus linguistics and syllabus design, and word frequency.

Collocation

In general, vocabulary studies are involved with the semantic connotation of words, their sets, and their context of use. For example, Carter (1987) identifies a core word, generally a noun, in reference to a number of tests. A word is denoted "core" if it can substitute for other less common words. For instance, the word *eat* may substitute for *dine,* and the word *give* can substitute for *donate.* The range of collocability of the word is another test Carter uses to identify a core word. He explains, "Collocability describes the company a word keeps; that is, single words operate in a lexical environment of other words" (36). Words with a higher collocability range are more "core" than are words with a restricted range of collocability. The words *friendly* and *amicable* are synonyms, but the latter is less common and has a restricted usage, such as in the sentence, "The divorce was an amicable one" (Carter 1987, 52). The notion of core words and collocability in Carter's studies has been significant from the applied linguistics perspective. The objective of this kind of approach is to restructure the categories in the language and to provide grounds to improve the teaching of vocabulary in terms of giving emphasis to core words, which are generally considered less culture bound and therefore less threatening in second language environments. Lewis (1993, 1997) focuses on the lexical approach, a classroom pedagogy incorporating the notion of word collocability. The approach challenges the fundamental view of dividing language into grammar, or structures, and vocabulary, or words.

Lewis (1997) argues that the lexical approach views language as "chunks." He identifies four different chunk types: single words, collocations, fixed expressions, and semifixed expressions. Other than the single words, all the other types are multiword items. The rationale of the lexical approach is that the most common words and their combinations should form the basis of instruction. In this case, the most common words are those that can be traced through their recurrence in the spoken form of the language and in text.

From another perspective, one involving the range of different meanings a frequently used word may take, Sinclair (1991) uses the term *delexicalisation,* as opposed to the fixed referential meaning of words, to refer to English words that are not assigned set meanings, such as *give, have, make,* and *do.* Their meanings vary depending on their occurrences and on the words with which they collocate. Words with relatively fixed meanings belong to the terminology of a specific topic. Therefore, words can be considered as forming a continuum. At one end are the less frequently used words with fixed meanings; at the other end are the more frequently occurring words that form part of the idiomatic expressions of the language. A frequency list of a computer-held corpus indicates which of these words need to be examined for teaching purposes.

Linguistic studies of a corpus of cancer research articles (Gledhill 1995) and a corpus of medical research articles (Jabbour 1998) have provided additional interesting clues about collocation. Collocation reflects text type. Collocations found in article introductions, for example, are rhetorical in function and clustered around verb tenses. By contrast, collocations used in methods sections and results sections are geared toward research activities and use prepositional phrases. There is also an element of intertextuality in collocation, in that certain collocations may occur in a number of genre texts. Thus, the study of one collocation in a corpus is by itself the study of this combination in a number of texts.

Corpus Linguistics

Corpus linguistics entails the preparation of computer databases of texts and the use of text analysis software to elicit collocations. The dualistic nature of corpora—as (1) data samples in which the behavior of words can be checked through concordancing and (2) a source of meaning construction (since there is access to the text as a whole)—enables corpus work to be used in making the connection between language forms and language functions. This, in turn, further enhances the reading-writing connection, as is illustrated in the final section of this chapter.

The core belief underlying corpus linguistics, as a branch of linguistic inquiry, is that the concrete description of the patterns of the language will make possible the formulation of new linguistic categories that render traditional grammars inadequate. Teaching programs based on corpora give precedence to collocations rather than to sentences (see the section "Potential Class Implementation" later in this chapter). The teaching methodology that realizes these programs is therefore affected (Lewis 1997). Moreover, Biber, Conrad, and Reppen (1996) state that the impact of corpus linguistics on the discipline of linguistics is related not only to "language structure" but essentially to "language in use." Reinforcing the status of the outcomes of corpus research, Biber, Conrad, and Reppen further summarize three characteristics of a corpus-based approach to the study of language. They say that corpus work is empirical, uses the computer for analysis, and is both quantitative and qualitative.

Sinclair (1991) describes corpus linguistics as the study of language associated with the use of the computer because the computer helps in analyzing the discourse of a large amount of naturally occurring language, analysis that is essential for the reconstruction of the grammar of the language and thereof for a pedagogical grammar. From the applied linguistics perspective, teaching based on corpora is inductive, leading to the formulation of hypotheses about language, as well as deductive, drawing generalizations about the language, thus raising the learner's linguistic awareness. In the context of data-driven learning based on corpora, Johns (1991) states that the task of the learner is to "discover" the foreign language, while for the teacher the task is "to provide a context in which the learner can develop strategies for discovery" (2).

For designing a lexical syllabus, Sinclair and Renouf (1988) propose criteria based on "the commonest word forms, their central patterns of usage, and the combinations which they typically form." Similarly, Willis (1990) states: "The lexical syllabus does not identify simply the commonest words of the language. Inevitably, it focuses on the commonest patterns too. Most important of all, it focuses on these patterns in their most natural environment" (vi). A lexical syllabus, encompassing the lexical approach, therefore uses texts, word frequencies, and collocations to orient the activities in a teaching program (Willis 1996).

Traditional grammars do not give due attention to the fact that each preposition, for example, has its own pattern and its own semantic denotation. In traditional grammars, the tendency is to classify all prepositions under one grammar topic and then use the same pattern to teach all prepositions. For instance, in one textbook exercise (Immel and Sacks 1999, 121), learners are asked to identify prepositions and their objects. In the example sentence "Paula enjoys a bowl of soup," the word *of* has simply been denoted as the preposition followed by its object, *soup*, thus making essential the combination "of soup," not the combination "bowl of." In corpus research, the concordancer gives a clearer picture of how the preposition *of*, or any other word, behaves. Corpus research makes it clear that the preposition *of*, unlike many of its category, relates to the word that precedes it, despite the fact that what follows *of* is also a nominal (Sinclair 1991, 81).

Word Frequency

Raw frequency lists of the corpus are both frequency ordered and alphabetically ordered. A frequency ordered list shows how words are distributed in texts. It starts with the most common grammar words, such as *the, of,* and *and.* The last words in the list are those that occur once in the corpus and belong to the specific terminology of the topic covered by the texts. A frequency ordered list can further be scrutinized to delimit or identify the words most likely to form the core of a language course.

An alphabetical list shows how words and word forms, or lemmas, are distributed in relation to each other in texts. While a frequency ordered list is generally used to identify the most frequent words and patterns in a corpus, an alphabetically ordered list may form the background of the investigation in terms of finding out what word forms are more frequent in a particular corpus. Thorough use of frequency lists is related to the use of a concordancer. Each concordance line shows how specific words collocate within a short space of each other in the text (see the following section in this chapter for examples of concordance sets).

The study of words in lists, using concordancing and detecting collocations, provides a wealth of information about the texts that may eventually be used directly for class instruction by teachers and students alike. For example, Johns (1991, 1997) presents learners with concordance lines of the target language to work with in order to create their own picture of the language. Discourse analysis assists in identifying discourse patterns, while corpus linguistics provides the means to look at language patterns and the lexis that forms the patterns. Discourse models connect with text, with sentence, and with collocation. For example, in an argumentative text, an attribution, or report, entails the presence of an averral, or assertion, on the part of the writer. Therefore, the averral-attribution unit is identifiable in texts through the relation of one sentence to another. Interaction in discourse analysis relies on the predictive value each sentence or each word combination offers to the text. Corpus linguistics and discourse analysis are related (Sinclair 1994). However, instead of the more traditional notion of sentence, there is more reliance on the word and its collocations. Word frequencies and concordances are inherent in corpus work and for this reason in the analysis of the discourse.

Potential Class Implementation

I can now briefly show some ways in which reading and writing instruction can be linked with, and enhanced by, the components of the lexical approach just described. I will achieve this by describing classroom activities based on genuine lexical data acquired through corpus research. Data for the tasks that follow were retrieved from a corpus of medical research articles by means of concordancers[2] (Jabbour 1998). These preliminary tasks are geared for academic reading, but because of the relationship between reading and writing explained in this chapter and in other chapters in this book, they can be applied toward practice in writing as well, thus reinforcing reading-writing connections. Although the tasks are in principle related to only one primary medical research article, the data used in the tasks were retrieved from the whole corpus, consisting of about 200,000 words. The rationale for this approach to task design is that every article of the corpus shares a level of wording with other articles in the corpus (see the subsection on collocation earlier in this chapter), thus making the students' exposure to the language richer and more intensive.

The sample tasks relate to the study of the methods sections and results sections of one primary medical research article, entitled "Low-Rate Smokers" (Owen et al. 1995), and a secondary medical research arti-

---

2. The concordancers used were MicroConcord and WordSmith.

cle, entitled "Evaluation of a Dutch Community-Based Smoking Cessation Intervention" (Mudde, de Vries, and Dolders 1995). The methods sections and results sections, considered "past-texts" because they report what has already occurred (Jabbour 1998), form more than half of the length of the articles, thus making them a worthwhile focus of discussion here. Three tasks refer to the methods sections. The first, a matching exercise, concentrates on word associations that help provide background information about the research conducted, specifically the association that exists between data and the present and past passives of verbs. The second is discourse-related and forms a preliminary activity to effective reading. The beginning of the third task is based on word associations, followed by activities that move beyond the confines of the present study to the projection of a study of the same type conducted in a different environment. This approach provides students with an opportunity to use in writing the word combinations they have come across in their reading. There are also two tasks referring to the results sections. The first is a concordance set for the word *significant* that will enable the students to have a set of associations to draw from when they write their own review or response to the article. The second task is essentially related to reading and scanning.

I. Methods

1. The article "Low-Rate Smokers" describes a data-based study. Complete the following tasks:

a) Match the elements below to form complete sentences about the data.

(i) Data were	to a categorical form.
(ii) Data were weighted	by sex, five-year age-groups, and geographical area.
(iii) Data were collected	from a representative population survey.
(iv) Data for each of the other	predictor variables were converted solely by personal interviews.
(v) Data were analyzed	using the SPSS-PC statistical package.

b) Data are *collected* and *reported*. What else happens to data? Make a list of "methods" phrases using the concordance set below.

as the latter. Statistical analysis. All data are reported as means +/- SD. Statistical if
tial intent to breastfeed for longer. All data are expressed as mean (SD). The effects of d
rom the whole population. Statistics All data were analysed using the Cox regression model
eraged to estimate cost when IMS America data reported the use of generic drugs. For combi
ran overnight fast. Statistical analysis. Data are expressed as means +/- SD. Sensitivity a
es incurred during the screening. Revenue data were extracted periodically during the 3 ye
losely follow the interview was selected. Data were collected solely by personal interviews
rettes smoked per day, were self-reported data obtained by interviews or self-administered
tection. Statistical Methods Serological data were logarithmically transformed for analysi
ss than 0.05 were considered significant. Data were analysed with the SPSS statistical pack
land Inspection Institute for review. The data were analysed using the SPSS program in the
yatomic absorption spectrophotometry. The data were checked, coded and keyed into computers
oliovirus isolated from their stools. The data were analysed using Lotus-123 and EPI INFO s
age and postgraduate qualifications. The data were compiled, sorted and coded. Analysis wa
11 scores were not determined because the data were collected during rather than at the beg
the 488 nm line. STATISTICAL METHODS The data from the groups were compared using the Mann

2. There are six paragraphs in the methods section. Here are the opening words from each paragraph. Read each of these opening statements and then complete tasks a and b:

   (i) Readiness to quit smoking was measured using a 10-point scale . . .

   (ii) Data were collected solely by personal interviews conducted in . . .

   (iii) Data were analysed using the SPSS-PC statistical package.

   (iv) In order to increase the likelihood that we were examining . . .

   (v) Data were from a representative population survey, conducted . . .

   (vi) Data from each of the other predictor variables were converted to . . .

   a) How do you think the section is organized? Arrange the six statements in the correct order.

   b) Read the methods section to check your answer.

3. In a methods section, descriptions of procedures make use of the verb *was/were* followed by a participle. Complete the following tasks:

   a) Underline the verb groups in each statement.

      (i) A sample . . . was selected.

(ii)   A weighted daily average was calculated.

(iii)   These categories were then collapsed into three stages of readiness to quit smoking.

(iv)   An item from the Fagerstrom Tolerance Questionnaire . . . was used . . .

(v)   An index of perceived health risk of smoking was constructed . . .

(vi)   Responses were converted to categorical form.

(vii)   Sociodemographic variables were categorized.

(viii)   A logistic regression model . . . was then built.

b)   The following set is taken from another methods section of an article on smoking. Make a list of the verb groups in this set that are similar to the verb groups you underlined in task a.

(i)   The quit-line was staffed with trained counselors who advised . . .

(ii)   . . . while the panel in the treatment city was potentially exposed to the intervention messages . . .

(iii)   The group program was carried out by trained employees of the MHS, . . .

(iv)   . . . of the intervention at a population level was investigated through a population study, . . .

(v)   The panel in the control city was potentially exposed to all national smoking . . .

(vi)   . . . in which the self-help manual was used as a guideline.

c)   Go to the methods section of the article entitled "Evaluation of a Dutch Community-based Smoking Cessation Intervention" and identify the same kinds of verb groups.

d)   If you were to carry out a study on smoking in Syria, what procedures would you follow for collecting data and defining the sample? Using the kinds of verb groups found in the previous exercises, write a sentence describing each of your procedures.

II. Results

1. In a results section, there are numbers, graphs, and other presentations of statistics. The authors present the outcome of their research
   in this way for ease of reference. Complete the following tasks:

Look at the citations below. The first three refer to significant "differences." Identify what the other citations refer to.

> other smokers. There were statistically significant differences over the three smoking-ra
> ix or more a day). X 2 analyses revealed significant differences for perceived difficulty
> gnificance. There were few statistically significant differences between low-rate and oth
> sta oil whereas Robusta oil contained a significant amount of 16–0-methyl-cafestol, a sub
> 237 non-snorers. Table 2 represents all significant associations between IHD and signific
> ects (P<.I). Plasma epinephrine showed no significant change in either group during the old
> 'happiness' did not make a statistically significant contribution to the final model shown
> mental test score are shown in Table 1. A significant correlation was obtained for both te
> racellular volume, as suggested, showed a significant decrease in the hyperkalemic group by
> r men, there were no other statistically significant determinants of having sex while symp
> s acute hyperkalemia was accompanied by a significant increase in the Na PS of -40% (p <0.
> uring the reaction time test, there was a significant increase in Cl only in the borderline
> icity, and educational level demonstrated significant independent associations with each of
> l, the status of owning a car was still a significant indicator of long-term outcome. In ot
> contact before the infarct did not have a significant influence over the entire length of t
> type as factors indicated a statistically significant interaction for factor VIII in white
> patients than the controls; there were no significant intergroup differences. The blastogeni

2. In the statements in task 1, what are the predictors of membership of
   the low-rate smoker category? Identify each phrase that describes
   these predictors.

Conclusion

In this chapter, I have stressed two points. First, I have related outcomes
of lexical studies to the interactive approach to reading and writing,
because words, word combinations, and language patterns relate to
schema and shape knowledge. Lexis provides the basis of the bottom-up
linguistic elements that form the descriptive core of a piece of academic
writing, and these elements then connect to the conceptual framework of
the text and allow top-down reading and writing to occur. A key element
in teaching academic literacy, then, is raising students' awareness of the
lexical features of academic prose. That awareness can be built through
lexically based reading activities and can be reinforced through lexically
based writing tasks.

The second point this chapter has dealt with is the interdependency and inseparability of vocabulary and grammar. Traditionally, reading and writing have been connected to the study of vocabulary and grammar as two independent fields. Lexical studies show that words generate patterns, while traditional grammar textbooks leave students to discover in an ad hoc manner many of the problematic areas of language use. For example, words like *report* and *show* have two different behaviors in text. One provides an exact report, while the other is more flexible in accommodating the writer's position (Skelton 1997). Similarly, complement clauses with *that* and *to* may not be considered different in traditional textbooks, whereas research shows that these complement clauses have not only different structures but distinct discourse impact (Biber 1996).

As pointed out earlier, I have used the terms *lexical approach* and *lexical syllabus* interchangeably because these terms refer to interrelated stages of the process of lexicalization of teaching. The basis of the process rests in corpus linguistics, or corpus research, and in applications of the findings of such research to the reading-writing classroom. Current approaches to academic reading-writing instruction are not making effective use of these findings. I have also made clear that use of developing computer technology, particularly concordancing programs, is essential to a lexical approach to reading-writing instruction.

Concordancing yields the best results when related to text analysis and frequency lists. In a medical research article, for example, if we concordance an item in the verb group, we investigate relationships in the discourse, such as in report statements or assertions made by the writer, especially in introduction and discussion sections. If we concordance an item in a noun group, we investigate semantic categories, such as prepositional phrases; these are most frequently found in methods sections and results sections. Semantic groups form strings and chains of words needed to express meaning expansion and/or reduction, connecting to nominalization and grammatical metaphor. Johns (1991), for example, describes an approach to learning through a concordancing process involving three learner-based activities: "identify-classify-generalise."

To conclude, if instruction based on concordancing is successful, students should be able to connect lexis to meanings and to discourse structures through reading. They should also be able to apply these meanings and structures in writing. Hence, reading informs their writing, and a lexically based pedagogy extends students' academic literacy skills.

References

Bazerman, C. 1985. *The informed writer: Using sources in the disciplines.* Boston: Houghton Mifflin.

Biber, D. 1996. Investigating language use through corpus-based analyses of association patterns. *International Journal of Corpus Linguistics* 1:171–97.

Biber, D., S. Conrad, and R. Reppen. 1996. Corpus based investigations of language use. *Annual Review of Applied Linguistics* 16:136–55.

Carrell, P., J. Devine, and D. E. Eskey, eds. 1988. *Interactive approaches to second language reading.* Cambridge: Cambridge University Press

Carter, R. 1987. *Vocabulary: Applied linguistics perspectives.* London: Allen and Unwin.

Chapelle, C. A. 1996. CALL-English as a second language. *Annual Review of Applied Linguistics* 16:139–57.

Gledhill, C. 1995. Scientific innovation in the phraseology of rhetoric: Posture, reformulation, and collocation in cancer research articles. Ph.D. diss., University of Aston, Birmingham, UK

Grabe, W. 1986. The transition from theory to practice. In *Teaching second language for academic purposes,* ed. F. Dubin, D. Eskey, and W. Grabe, 25–48. Boston: Addison-Wesley.

———. 1994. *An introduction to functional grammar.* 2d ed. London: Edward Arnold.

Hunston, S. 1995. Grammar in teacher education: The role of a corpus. *Language Awareness* 4:15–31.

Hunston, S., and G. Francis. 1998. Verbs observed: A corpus-driven pedagogic grammar. *Applied Linguistics* 19:45–72.

Immel, C., and F. Sacks. 1999. *Sentence dynamics: An English skills workbook.* 4th ed. New York: Longman.

Jabbour, G. 1992. Improving the writing skills of ESPC medical students: An experimental approach. *Damascus University Journal* 8, nos. 29–30:33–47.

———. 1998. Corpus linguistics, contextual collocation, and ESP syllabus creation: A text analysis approach to the study of the medical research article. Ph.D. diss., University of Birmingham, UK

Johns, T. 1991. Should you be persuaded—two samples of data-driven learning materials. In *Classroom concordancing,* ed. T. Johns and P. King, 1–13. Birmingham, UK: Centre for English Language Studies, University of Birmingham.

———. 1994. From printout to handout: Grammar and vocabulary in the context of data-driven learning. In *Perspectives on pedagogical grammar,* ed. T. Odlin, 293–313. Cambridge: Cambridge University Press.

———. 1997. Contexts: The background, development, and trialling of a concordance-based CALL program. In *Teaching and language corpora,* ed. A. Wichmann, A. Fligelstone, T. McEnery, and G. Knowles, 100–115. London: Longman.

Lado, R. 1964. *Language teaching: A scientific approach.* New York: McGraw-Hill.

Lewis, M. 1993. *The lexical approach: The state of ELT and a way forward.* Hove, UK: Language Teaching Publications.

———. 1997. *Implementation of the lexical approach.* Hove, UK: Language Teaching Publications.

Mudde, A. N., H. de Vries, and M. G. T. Dolders. 1995. Evaluation of a Dutch community-based smoking cessation intervention. *Preventive Medicine* 24:61–70.

Nattinger, J. R. 1980. A lexical phrase grammar for ESL. *TESOL Quarterly* 14:337–44.

Nattinger, J. R., and J. S. De Carrico. 1992. *Lexical phrases and language teaching.* Oxford: Oxford University Press

Odlin, T., ed. 1994. *Perspective on pedagogical grammar.* Cambridge: Cambridge University Press.

Owen, N., P. Kent, M. Wakefield, and L. Roberts. 1995. Low-rate smokers. *Preventive Medicine* 24:80–84.

Rayner, K., and A. Pollatsek. 1989. *The psychology of reading.* New York: Prentice-Hall International.

Sinclair, J. 1991. *Corpus, concordance, and collocation.* Oxford: Oxford University Press.

———. 1994. Trust the text. In *Advances in written text analysis,* ed. M. Coulthard, 12–25. London: Routledge.

———, ed. 1987. *Looking up: An account of the COBUILD project in lexical computing.* London: HarperCollins.

Sinclair, J., and M. Coulthard. 1975. *Towards an analysis of discourse: The English used by teachers and pupils.* Oxford: Oxford University Press

———. 1992. Towards an analysis of discourse. In *Advances in spoken discourse,* ed. M. Coulthard, 1–34. London: Routledge.

Sinclair, J., and A. Renouf. 1988. A lexical syllabus for language learning. In *Vocabulary and language teaching,* ed. R. Carter and M. McCarthy, 140–60. London: Longman.

Skelton, J. 1997. The representation of truth in academic medical writing. *Applied Linguistics* 18:121–40.

Svartvik, J., ed. 1992. *Directions in corpus linguistics.* Berlin: Mouton de Gruyter.

Swales, J. M. 1981. *Aspects of article introductions.* Aston ESP Research Reports, no. 1. Birmingham, UK: University of Aston.

———. 1990. *Genre analysis: English in academic and research settings.* Cambridge: Cambridge University Press.

Van Dijk, T. A. 1993. Principles of discourse analysis. *Discourse and Society* 4:249–83.

Wilkins, D. A. 1976. *The notional syllabus.* Oxford: Oxford University Press.

Willis, D. 1990. *The lexical syllabus.* London: HarperCollins.

———. 1996. Language description in language teaching. Class notes. School of English, University of Birmingham.

Willis, D., and J. Willis. 1988. *The Collins COBUILD English course.* London: HarperCollins.

Willis, J., and D. Willis. 1996. *Challenge and change in language teaching.* Portsmouth, NH: Heinemann.

Chapter 13

Implementing CommonSpace in the ESL Composition Classroom

Joel Bloch, The Ohio State University, and Janina Brutt-Griffler, University of Alabama

A number of years ago, at a meeting of a CALL (computer-assisted language learning) special-interest group, a composition teacher asked whether any research showed that ESL students wrote better essays using computers. On hearing not only that was there little evidence supporting this claim but also that students wrote even weaker essays in some cases, she bemoaned that she could not ask her dean to purchase computers if there is no evidence that they help. Since that time, we have learned two important facts. First, despite occasional reservations, the use of computers has permeated the composition process. Students either use or are expected to use computers throughout the writing process. Second, research in reading and writing in one computer context may not be applicable to other contexts where there are different settings or configurations of machines. As Haas (1996) has argued, a myriad of factors, such as screen size and the use of printouts, can affect both reading and writing on a computer. Thus, we cannot discuss the use of the computer independently from all the factors that affect the interaction between humans and computers.

As Dix et al. (1993) argue, to understand the potential of any piece of software, there is no substitute for studying the process by which the software is implemented and used. Since, in the last few years, software has been developed specifically to facilitate reading and writing in composition classes, we were interested in how such software could be integrated into a computer-based course. Working on the assumption that the effectiveness of computer software depends as much (or more) on its particular implementation and usability as on something intrinsic to the nature of computing itself, we undertook a study that focused on how teachers implemented software for composition classroom purposes and how their students responded to the implementation.

In this chapter, we explore the different aspects of the implementation of a collaborative program called CommonSpace, designed for use in composition classes. Our focus in this HCI (human-computer interaction) study is on the way software like this program can be integrated into the composition classroom. In particular, we address whether the implementation affected the ways in which reading and writing were both taught and learned. We discuss the social and cognitive dimensions of reading and writing on-line and whether the students influenced the process of technology implementation in the composition classroom. We suggest that reading and writing on the computer is not an abstract concept but a product of a variety of factors that can change the dynamics of how the computer is used. Our study suggests that the implementation of a computer program can impact the process of second language reading and writing. Yet the process is not one-sided: the students can also be key players. Finally, we argue for the need to create space for CALL methodology within overall TESOL methodology in teacher education programs, so that the principles of second language (L2) education are not lost sight of in our eagerness to implement new technology.

Technological Determinism and the Empowerment of the L2 Writer

The installation of new technologies in any given institution presents a number of challenges. Sproull and Kiesler (1991) have argued that the installation of a software program can have profound effects on the goals of the organization where the software is installed. In short, technology may drive teaching practices. At the same time, any implementation faces constraints that come from the goals and structure of the program, as well as constraints that arise from the nature of the students. Howard (1997) adds an important dimension to our understanding of the installation of technology in an institution when he argues that new technologies must be seen from a dual perspective: how they accommodate the goals of one group of people and how they may be resisted by another group.

While institutional concerns are critical, it is also important to examine how technologies can affect reading and writing processes at the level of text construction and text processing on the computer screen. Here we may find it useful to take into account Haas's (1996) discussion of how computer use falls between two competing metaphors—the computer as deterministic and the computer as transparent. In the former metaphor, the computer has profound effects on the process being performed; in the latter one, the computer has no effect. As a result, it can be assumed that reading and writing on-line may not be exactly the same nor completely different from reading and writing print. More importantly, the degree to which the processes are similar or different may depend on a range of factors that affect the way computers intervene in the reading-writing process. The impact of computers on classroom literacy practices may depend greatly on the role of the teacher in the computer composition classroom (Palmquist et al. 1998) and on the perceptions of L2 writers—what they believe that the new technology can do for them versus what it actually does.

Understanding reading and writing on the computer screen requires examining how readers and writers interact with the computer. This interaction includes what Card (1993) refers to as

> the joint performance of tasks by humans and machines; the structure of human-machine communication; the social and organizational interactions with machine-design; human capabilities to use machines (including their learnability) . . . ; the process of specification, design, and implementation of interfaces; and design trade-offs. (xi)

The study of this joint performance constituted a guiding principle in our yearlong implementation of CommonSpace in the L2 writing environment for undergraduate and graduate writers in an ESL composition program at a large, midwestern university. In our study, we examined the nature of the processes of reading and writing on the screen and student perceptions of technology. Our ongoing evaluation and research in the process of implementing CommonSpace was guided by our determination not to isolate CALL methodology from the pedagogical principles that underlie L2 composition methodology. In other words, we attempted not to make this implementation a technology-driven enterprise but to search for a "fit" between computers, software capabilities, and the linguistic and cultural characteristics of L2 writing and writers.

We viewed the computer not as a tutor but as a tool. In the model of the computer as a tutor, the computer essentially replaces the instructor; in the conception of the computer as a tool, it is just one more material/resource that instructors bring to the classroom (cf. Levy 1997). In the model of the computer as a tutor, CALL exists in a realm of its own, often insulated from other developments in language pedagogy, including the learner-centered and interactive approaches. The conception of computers as tutors arguably encourages the naive belief that CALL would of itself promote the aims of language learning.

The conception of computers as tools, however, both preserves and alters the role of the teacher. Hence the question that we began with—whether the computer can make L2 writing better—was made more complex in our case, as meeting the goals of our study required our active involvement in using the computer. In this model, the role of the teacher dramatically changes from that of a recipient of technology to that of reflective, active teacher-researcher responsible for creating the space for effective usage of technology that matches the underlying philosophy of teaching writing.

Beginning the Implementation Process

Our initial goal was relatively simple. We thought that by installing software that allowed students to send their papers on-line, we could break down some of the artificial constraints of the classroom, specifically those of time and space. Dix et al. (1993) divided space into two categories: participants could be located in the same space (co-located) or in different spaces (remote). Time is likewise divided into two categories: synchronic, with people communicating directly with each other in real time, as when they are located in the same physical space, on a phone, or in a chat room; and asynchronic, which involves communication separated in time, including such forms as E-mail or comments written on the margins of papers. Writing classes are very much constrained by both factors. Students must often submit a paper at a certain time in a certain place, and students missing that deadline need to wait for the next opportunity for submission or find another place for it, such as the instructor's office. Instructors, as well as others responsible for commenting on papers, also face certain constraints. Papers can only be returned to the author in a specific place and at a specific time, regardless of when the process is completed. If one party cannot meet the deadline, the process is delayed until the next occurrence of the appropriate time and place. The constraints of time and space in a composition class are particularly problematic in process-oriented classrooms, where students may be assigned only a few papers but are required to revise them a number of times.

Our attempt to transcend some of the limitations of these constraints was facilitated by two factors: instructors in our ESL program had ready and inexpensive access to tools for sending and receiving E-mail and texts, and, similarly, the students all had at least some access to computers. At the same time, other constraints exist, such as the attitudes of the users and the goals of the instructional program, which can affect software implementation. For instance, Palmquist et al. (1998) point out that teachers are often resistant to using technologies they themselves are unfamiliar with, even though these technologies may help the students. Although there was great interest among our fellow teachers in using computers in more familiar asynchronic time—using E-mail to send and receive papers—none of the teachers was familiar with using the computer in synchronic time, and few were interested.

It was in this context that our ESL program was looking for software for its composition courses. We had already developed extensive Web pages for a number of the courses. There was a consensus that we needed to involve our students in the new technologies as well as to purchase software to help us with specific aspects of our teaching, such as making readable comments on papers or helping students work better collaboratively. We wanted software that allowed writers to send their papers for comment at the time they finished them and likewise allowed commentators to return the papers at any time.

We put forward the following specific criteria for selecting software, criteria largely based on the existing goals of the courses in which we were going to use the software:

1. Software that was relatively easy to use
2. Software that could be used across platforms and with other word-processing programs
3. Software that allowed instructors to type comments onto the papers
4. Software that was inexpensive for us—and, if need be, for the students—to buy

After evaluating a number of software packages, we decided on CommonSpace, a program that Sixth Floor Media had specifically designed for composition courses.

Before we discuss specific goals of the research, we want to note that we systematically collected longitudinal and cross-sectional data from students to help in our ongoing implementation. Our students were both graduate and undergraduate students in intermediate and advanced ESL academic composition classes. The study began in the spring term of 1997 and continued until the winter term of 1998. The number of classes in the study ranged from one to four per term. Graduate students were required to complete the classes during their first year of graduate school. The classes had approximately 15 students per section and met three times a week, with usually one meeting a week in a computer lab. The software program, CommonSpace, was installed in a number of labs across campus; moreover, the students could request that the program be installed in a more convenient public (university) lab, if there was one. We also ordered student versions of the software that could be purchased and used at home or in the graduate students' offices.

As a preliminary attempt to determine the computer background and attitudes of our incoming students, we surveyed all of the international students newly admitted by the university over a two-year period. Then, at the end of the second year of this period, we began surveying the students' perceptions on how they used CommonSpace in their writing process (see app. A). Our survey was administered each term and was continually revised as new issues and questions arose. In addition, after three terms, we felt that we needed to look in greater depth at how the implementation was proceeding; therefore, we conducted six one-hour semistructured interviews and two three-person focus groups with a total of 11 students who had volunteered to be interviewed after the term had ended (see app. B). We also kept informal journals of what we were doing as instructors in the classroom and had frequent meetings to discuss how the implementation was taking shape.

Four Goals for the Implementation of CommonSpace

Once we had purchased the software and had begun to use it with our students, we decided on four specific implementation goals that we wanted to investigate more systematically.

GOAL 1: To provide a new means for students to give and receive readable comments from their teachers and classmates, at the same time extending the traditional boundaries of the classroom during the process of text construction

Our first goal was mainly methodological in nature. To meet the first part of this goal, that is, to provide a platform for readable comments from peers and teachers, we relied on the fact that CommonSpace allows for columns to be created and for the reviewer to type in comments that are linked to a specific part of the text (see fig. 1). This was particularly helpful if the instructor's handwriting was not very clear. The advantages of

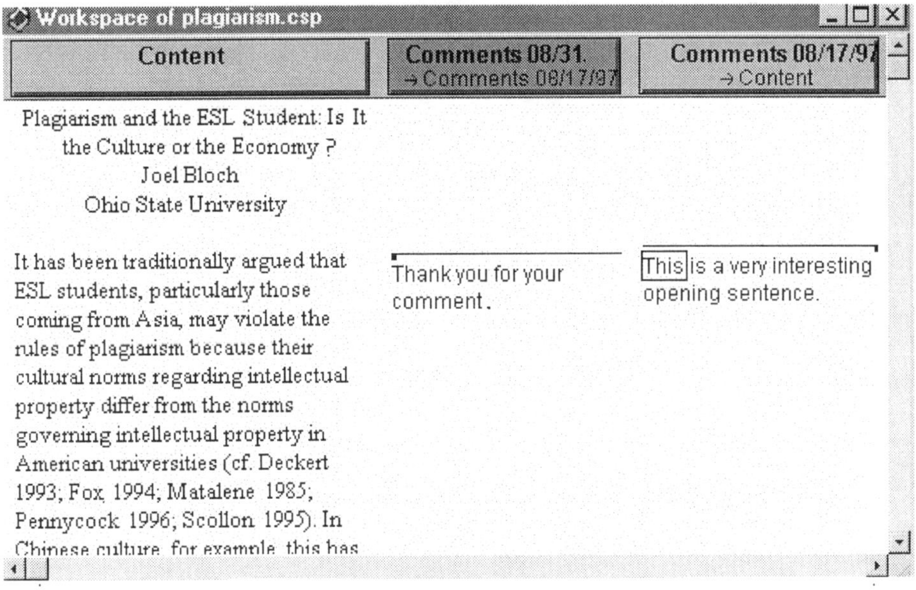

Fig. 1. An example of using columns in CommonSpace

this type of format were captured in the following comment from an instructor's journal:

> I enjoyed being able to respond to students with CommonSpace on drafts via email. It is far easier to write comments when a special vertical space is provided and you have the ability to highlight certain words or passages.

An important feature of CommonSpace was that multiple columns could be created where comments could be linked to specific portions of the writer's text. When the instructor or student clicked on a comment, the relevant portion of the text would be highlighted. In postcourse interviews, students confirmed that the on-line process of exchanging comments on papers was often very expeditious. One student reported:

> Very fast, usually one or at maximum two days. What I wonder is if that is good for you teachers because I think you can become a slave of the computer.

Another student wrote:

> Yeah, I had enough time to revise my paper. [I sent my papers] at least seven times; each paper had to have 2–3 drafts. I sent it to him and then he returned it with comments and I sent it back to him.

We were able to allow students to send in their papers as often as they wanted to or were able to. This meant that teachers could more easily focus on particular aspects of rhetoric and grammar on each draft. They were also freed from artificial deadlines. If they had not finished reviewing the papers by class time, they could return them later in the day without worrying about depriving the students of the time to revise. Of course, as one of the students already quoted pointed out, the instructors were often tied to their computers, a fact that bothered several teachers who were used to marking papers in a variety of places, on and off campus. And some students felt that, despite our efforts to make CommonSpace accessible, they still had limited access to the program.

The second aspect of our first goal was to expand the traditional boundaries of the classroom. This was attempted in at least two major ways. First, by increasing the number and quality of instructional materials available on our class Web sites, we had many elements of an on-line course in place. Second, since CommonSpace allowed us to send and receive papers on-line, teachers and students could return papers whenever they were finished writing or commenting, instead of being constrained by the class's actual meeting time When asked about this in the survey described earlier, 74 percent of the students reported that they preferred sending papers on-line to handing them directly to the teacher, just 13 percent indicated that they did not like the on-line method, and 13 percent expressed no preference between the two methods of submission. Meanwhile, 51 percent indicated that CommonSpace helped their writing, 30 percent stated that it made no difference in their writing, and 19 percent felt that it had not helped their writing. ($N = 63$ for all the items reported.)

Nearly every term, however, there were one or two students who, for whatever reason, had difficulty sending and receiving files. One such student said:

> Sometimes I attach files and mail [them to] him, but I don't know why he didn't get it. It's a problem. I had this problem. I had sent it 3 times but he didn't get it. The fourth time I just copied my paper [and] I gave it to him.

The problem was compounded by the lack of physicality of the on-line process. In the traditional classroom, students could physically hand in a paper and receive a paper back; in the on-line classroom, they do not nec-essarily know whether their paper has been received, unless they specifi-cally require a notice of receipt; nor do they know if the paper has been returned, unless they happen to be on-line. Thus, while the lack of need for the physical exchange of papers had a potentially liberating effect, the on-line process presented an additional challenge for some students.

Our research showed that a number of variables affect the process of implementation. Institutional goals or constraints play a major role, but the students are also key players in the process. In the classes in the fall term, particularly, we found that many of our students were unfamiliar with using the E-mail program Eudora (the most convenient E-mail pro-gram at our institution at the time), especially the attachment feature. To help the students get started, we devised two interactive tutorials for using CommonSpace and Eudora (Bloch 1998). Helping them use Eudora or whatever mail program they chose became an important subgoal of the course. One of the advantages of having the course in a lab, as opposed to in a regular classroom or even on-line, was that we could easily identify students who were having problems with the various technologies involved in the class.

Other systemic problems were beyond our control. For example, some teachers agreed with the student comment about being "a slave of the computer." Using CommonSpace meant more drafts had to be read. It also meant that teachers were tied to their computers and their Internet service providers. In training sessions for using CommonSpace, given both inside and outside our program, we found that being tied to com-puters was a negative factor. Teachers in our program who had larger numbers of composition students, for example, felt particularly troubled by having to read each paper on a computer screen. As one teacher at a neighboring institution interested in implementing CommonSpace put it, she read papers at stoplights and at her son's soccer match, so having to use a computer was not convenient.

In general, the extent to which we were able to meet our goal of extending traditional boundaries was strongly affected by balancing the advantages of the technology with disadvantages often rooted in institu-tional decisions: the size of classes, the availability of computers, and the accessibility of the Internet. In the same way, while we had to situate our goals within institutional considerations, we also had to consider the cur-ricular goals. In our case, it was a question of allocating time to the various goals of the courses. We neither could nor necessarily wanted to change the goals or even assignments. However, at the same time, it was clear that we would have to allocate class time to teaching the students not only how to use CommonSpace but also how to use auxiliary programs, such as mail programs, that were necessary to send papers on-line.

We also considered whether computers can actually substitute for the teacher. Since students received extensive feedback both from the instructor and from peers, did they still perceive a need for face-to-face, one-on-one conferencing (Ferris and Hedgcock 1998)? Our cross-sectional study shows that while students greatly valued on-line feedback, face-to-face conferencing was still felt to be indispensable. For example, just over 4 percent of the 63 students surveyed stated that they did not need a tutorial, that is, conference. Most (87 percent) agreed or strongly agreed with the statement that they "need to talk to an instructor," while the same percentage of respondents agreed or strongly agreed with a statement about preferring to receive on-line feedback prior to one-on-one conferencing. As for the idea of having both a face-to-face tutorial and on-line feedback, 74 percent expressed agreement. Just 39.2 percent of the students agreed or strongly agreed with the statement that they "prefer to have tutorial rather than on-line feedback."

While the students did not want to replace the teacher with technology, their use of CommonSpace led to notably increased interaction among them, including help that they gave each other with various problems. This was consistent with the findings of Palmquist et al. (1998), who compared computer classrooms with traditional composition classrooms. One instructor in our own study found,

> Initially, [CommonSpace] was rough for students to learn, but they were eventually helped by their peers.

In addition to students interacting more, we found that teachers had to work together more. In the initial stage of the implementation, all the instructors involved felt the need for biweekly meetings to discuss how things were working and to gain more in-depth knowledge of the software program.

GOAL 2: To provide a means for collaborative writing

While our first goal could be examined primarily from the standpoint of methodology, our second goal added a social dimension to our analysis of technology implementation. The second goal was to provide an improved means of student collaboration. Collaborative writing and peer review, which had already been an integral part of our curriculum, necessarily rely on students engaging in a social construction of text. We hypothesized that using CommonSpace could encourage and enhance student interaction in collaborative writing assignments. Collaborative essay writing was usually carried out in the second half of the term, at which time the students in computer-assisted classes would be familiar with the technology. In collaborative writing assignments, for which there was limited teacher intervention, the instructors placed a greater responsibility on the students for constructing their own text.

From students' journal writing and surveys, we found that many students, on their own initiative, extended the range of their use of the technology during the collaborative assignment. They reported that one of the most effective uses of CommonSpace was to provide feedback to each other.

In one of our focus interviews, one group of students discussed their experience in constructing an on-line collaborative essay. In their discussion, the students indicated that the technology helped them tell each other what they thought about a particular topic as well as share their writing. They also stated that CommonSpace was more convenient in giving comments and revising than was other word-processing software, because it integrated original content and comments in one work space so that they could be viewed at the same time. Moreover, its ability to highlight a specific section corresponding to a comment can make the comments clearer than if they had been written in the margins. Another reason this group found using the computer for collaborative essay writing beneficial was the opportunity to build a text together with one another's support. One student summarized the sentiment of the group:

> If peers of a student could find the mistakes or just tell him other strategies in writing from different angles s/he might benefit from such advice. Even the compliments could give him/her much confidence and enthusiasm in writing a paper.

This student captures to a great extent the potential of technology for creating meaningful interaction and, in particular, for facilitating the social as well as affective side of second language learning and writing.

GOAL 3: To explore the cognitive nature of the reading-writing processes in the context of the on-line writing environment

Since CommonSpace allows for various drafts of papers and comments to be saved in one file, it might be argued that it develops a particular reading-writing environment. Columns of comments from both the instructor and other students, along with the writer's own comments, can be saved in one file. Multiple drafts can also be saved together so that the student as well as the instructor can more easily trace the writer's development over the drafting process. The creation of this kind of environment is consistent with our process-oriented teaching philosophy, which assumes that revising is an integral part of learning to write. We hoped that CommonSpace would help improve student writing by creating a complete writing environment where students could track their development. Students could also retain a complete collection of comments, which could be used for reflection on the kinds of comments, either rhetorical or grammatical, they had received—of particular advantage in a class that employs portfolio assessment.

Therefore, while creating an on-line reading-writing environment, we sought to uncover reading-writing connections and how technology potentially plays a role in developing those connections. One very interesting finding that emerged from our cross-sectional study is that out of the 23 students involved in one of the courses, just over one-third (35 percent) stated that they liked reading papers on the computer screen, yet a sizable majority (70 percent) of all the students participating in the study ($N = 63$) liked commenting on classmates' papers on-line. These apparently conflicting findings imply that the computer is preferred when students are writers, not readers. Haas (1996) attributes readers' and writers' trouble with reading on-line to the limitations of the current state of the technology: ability to read on-line with (or without) ease can be directly related to the size and resolution of the computer screen. That reading was difficult on-line was confirmed by at least some of our participants. One student commented:

> Reading on the computer is more difficult; it is difficult to see the connection between the first paragraph and the later paragraphs in the paper . . . it is difficult to see the connections between paragraphs and parts of the paper.

Thus, there is the potential for differences between text processing strategies when students read from a hard copy as opposed to when they read from the screen. However, these differences may be intrinsic not to the computer itself but to the current limitations of the technology, in this case screen size. As the price of larger screens decreases, it may be possible to provide students with a larger area on which to read, which, as Haas argues, could change the reading-writing process.

In our peer review study, we sought to uncover whether there are differences in text processing and, if so, how they affect the extent to which students provide comments on peers' papers. We employed two methods of written peer feedback: what we called the "traditional" method (the pen-and-paper method using hard copy) and the on-line method using CommonSpace. In our postclass discussions, we found that both methods have advantages and disadvantages. The most frequently reported observations regarding the pen-and-paper method were that it is sometimes difficult to decipher handwriting, that comments are not detailed, that it takes longer to use comments, and that people make more general comments. As for CommonSpace, the primary observations made were that it is easier to identify what comments refer to; that users like highlighting and commenting; that comments are detailed; and that what comments refer to can be found quickly, which saves time. Some of these comments regarding CommonSpace were expected: for example, that it made it easier for the author to read comments and that it was easier to identify what the comments referred to were direct consequences of the technology, which allowed the respondent to type in the comment and highlight exactly the section of the text that the comment referred to. Two perhaps less predictable results were that the pen-and-paper comments tended to be general in nature and that the CommonSpace comments were usually much more detailed than those made in the pen-and-paper format.

Through a discourse analysis of students' peer reviews (those that students accomplished using the "traditional" method and those that they did on-line), questionnaire responses, and end-of-term interviews, a major tendency emerged that differentiated text processing and responding when using the different methods. When students did a peer review on the computer screen using the features of CommonSpace, they tended not to read through the full draft before commenting; however, when using a hard copy of the text, they were inclined to read the entire essay before making any comments. The greater emphasis on bottom-up processing when reading on the screen was reflected in some students' self-reporting of difficulty in keeping the whole text in focus during their peer commenting when using CommonSpace. This finding is consistent with the concern of the student quoted earlier on the difficulty of discerning the whole amid the parts of the paper.

These differences raise the further question of how written peer feedback may be affected by a program like CommonSpace. We addressed this question in our cross-sectional study of peer review using, as mentioned already, the pen-and-paper method for peer review in the classroom and CommonSpace for peer review in the computer lab. No special instruction was given on how to use either method (beyond the mechanics of on-line responding). Each student reviewed two different papers, one using each method. Twelve students were the subjects of this phase of the study.

The results indicated a consistent difference in the kind of feedback students provided to each other using the two different methods. The major finding is that students tended to focus more on grammar than rhetoric using CommonSpace, that is, to have more sentence-level concerns. In interviews, students expressed their concern that the type of feedback they received using CommonSpace was not as useful. Students reported concentrating on such things as "general impressions," "content," and giving "global comments" while using the traditional method, and they listed "grammar," "word correction," and "sentence correction" as their primary concerns while using the computer. When asked to further describe the process of providing feedback, the students who reported using both top-down and bottom-up strategies also reported that they moved from the discourse level to the sentence level while employing the traditional method, whereas they reversed the process when using CommonSpace. For example, one student noted that when using the traditional approach while responding to a classmate's paper, she "first thought about the general impression of the paper" and afterward moved on to a consideration of "particular mistakes," but when using CommonSpace, she first considered the particular mistakes. She goes on to say: "It was really hard for me to think about the paper as a whole. My feedback in this case was more concentrated on particular mistakes."

Interestingly, when asked about the usefulness of on-line comments, nearly three-fourths of the twelve students (73.9 percent) said that on-line feedback helped improve their writing, and a large majority of the students (65.2 percent) agreed that the on-line comments were important. However, with regard to specific kinds of feedback, rhetorical and grammatical, there was not a strong preference for either type: 43.4 percent indicated that they mainly made use of the rhetorical comments they received, and 43.5 percent indicated that they mainly utilized the grammatical comments. When asked to react to the statement that it was "easy to use on-line feedback," 73.9 percent of the students responded positively (agreed/strongly agreed).

This interaction between technology and the student in the new reading-writing context came to be a critical element in our implementation process. A later stage of this study and of the implementation itself consisted of developing CALL methodology to counteract this shift of emphasis to local-level feedback in peer review, to make better use of the inherent potentialities of the software.

Over the course of the implementation, we attempted to use different types of peer review exercises to exploit some of the advantages of the software while minimizing some of its limitations. For example, in an assignment requiring revising a formal academic paper for a more general audience, we asked students to comment on any part of a peer's text that they could not understand. In this way, we were asking students to focus on more global aspects of the rhetoric of the text (i.e., its ability to meet the needs and expectations of the audience) while they concentrated on only isolated pieces of text that could be easily processed on the computer screen. We also encouraged students to create separate columns for sentence-level/grammar correction, on the one hand, and rhetoric/content comments, on the other. We surveyed students on the ways in which they used CommonSpace for peer review by asking them to indicate their level of agreement (from "strongly agree" to "strongly disagree") on whether they focused mainly on rhetoric or mainly on grammar in their comments. Nearly two-thirds (65.2 percent) of the 23 student respondents selected "strongly agree" and "agree" to the statement that they offered mainly rhetorical advice in their reviews. A much lower portion (39.1 percent) indicated strong agreement or agreement with the statement that they provided primarily grammatical advice.

In conjunction with these exercises, students were encouraged to at least skim through the paper to form a general understanding of it before proceeding to make comments. This seemed to impress on them that they needed to address concerns about rhetoric and content and should not unduly focus on grammar. Also, we encouraged students to carry on a dialogue with the reviewer through CommonSpace, to make the learning experience interactive. The technology of the software was of great help in accomplishing this subgoal, since CommonSpace allows writers to create their own column in which they can attach responses to the reviewer's comments.

This dialogue had positive results in a couple ways. First, it helped the reviewers concentrate more on global rhetorical concerns (particularly when students were responding to the first or second draft of their papers), thereby encouraging negotiation of meaning. Second, the dialogue seemed to make the student authors more comfortable with receiving feedback, having given them a sense of voice and the ability to question the judgment of the reviewers. In many cases, the writer and the reviewer worked cooperatively through problems with the paper before the instructor joined in. This approach increased student responsibility and autonomy in the peer review process, and these benefits potentially could carry over later to students' independent writing.

This process of encouraging student autonomy in writing reached its peak in the collaborative writing assignment, focusing on a response essay for the undergraduate students and a data analysis paper for the graduate students. Peer review provided an important means for the collaborative construction of a group text and helped initiate negotiation of meaning in the writing process. The students reported that they used CommonSpace most effectively and extensively when the responsibility for implementing peer review fell entirely on them.

Goal 4: To provide an alternative computer program that had all the features of a word processor, including an on-line handbook geared toward ESL students

The most popular aspect of CommonSpace was its accommodation of columns. Another novel feature of CommonSpace (which also provides all the regular features of a word processor) was an on-line handbook with a section specifically designed for ESL students. Although we expected this feature to be attractive to our students, very few of them used it. CommonSpace also allows links to on-line resources to be placed in the files, and students and even instructors took advantage of these resources. Still other features allow for setting up on-line discussion. For example, CommonSpace also enables instructors to actually place links in the columns to guide the students to the handbook. However, in the first version of this software, the links to the on-line handbook were very unstable, and there was no ability to link to Web resources. Not until we received version 2.0 were we able to begin to use some of these features, and despite the improvements in version 2.0, we still found these features of the software difficult to use to full advantage.

Most of the students' resistance to the software could be attributed to the limitations of the technology. While very few students objected to working on-line, many were frustrated by the technical limitations of the software. Unfavorable comparisons with other word-processing programs have been among the most difficult problems we have encountered. Most of our students used MS Word 7.0 and had mixed feelings— often bordering on resistance—about using another word-processing program. Many of them preferred the features in MS Word 7.0; as a result, in some cases, they did not want to use, and especially did not want to buy, another software program. Therefore, many students insisted on using their own word-processing programs. Overall, among the 63 respondents to the survey, CommonSpace received weak ratings (using a 1–3 scale; 1 = superior, 3 = inferior) on word processing (2.24, sd = .68), sending and receiving files (2.35, sd = .82), and spell-checking (2.085, sd = .562).The latter finding was somewhat surprising but could be explained by the overall difficulty some students experienced when using CommonSpace. CommonSpace was, however, rated very highly on receiving comments (1.3, sd = .70) and had a somewhat positive rating on revising papers (1.92, sd = .967).

One of the consequences of student perceptions of their own word-processing programs as superior was that students frequently transferred files between CommonSpace and their word-processing programs. In fact, among the 49 students who responded to this area of the survey, 73 percent combined CommonSpace with another word-processing program although they were encouraged to use only CommonSpace, just 22 percent reported using CommonSpace alone, and 5 percent used only another word-processing program. In one case, a student cut his file out of CommonSpace and pasted it into an E-mail message.

> Actually, I used Microsoft Word for the first draft and then I transferred it to CommonSpace. I only used CommonSpace for the on-line feedback. Because I'm more familiar with Microsoft Word than with CommonSpace. There are some features that CommonSpace doesn't have. Right now if I am typing in Microsoft Word and I am typing some word wrong, the program will underline it.

The use of two different word-processing programs was somewhat cumbersome for the teacher, particularly since CommonSpace sometimes had difficulty reading other file formats. The spell-checker, which may be of even greater use to L2 students than to L1 students, also presented a problem, at least while using version 2.0 of the software. As one student observed:

> I used CommonSpace; I didn't have so many spelling problems. CommonSpace had a spelling checker but not so convenient. I still like Microsoft Word because it is much more convenient. I had been using Word for many years but CommonSpace for only 3 months. I felt more comfortable with Word.

While students who really objected to using computers may have dropped out of the classes using CommonSpace, it is still interesting to note that many of the objections were to the quality of the software. We found few if any objections to having to use computers; instead, most of the objections came from using what was perceived to be an inferior technology. One student commented:

> I like using Word because I think there are many functions in Word that you can use to edit my paper. I am more comfortable using Word because before I came here, I never used CommonSpace and I am quite used to Word.

But not everyone found CommonSpace to be inferior. As we had hoped, some of the students believed that the features allowing for comments made CommonSpace better than Word. One student wrote:

> When you are planning to correct the mistakes of the paper on line, I think that CommonSpace is better than Word because you can use the columns and associate your comments with the text, but to be honest, having it in hard copy easier because you can take a hard copy to highlight a region. It could be maybe spend much less time using hard copy than using CommonSpace but if the idea is to use online feedback, I think that CommonSpace is much better.

While not every student had such high expectations, it seems that any implementation of computer technology requires consideration of the quality of the technology. The challenge, then, of introducing technology into the composition classroom is to meet the expectations of the students regarding the benefits of the technology. Their perception of the technology goes beyond the frustrations of problems caused by computer bugs or lack of understanding about how the technology works.

Conclusion

The conclusion that we can reach from the preceding study is that CommonSpace as a tool for on-line student negotiation and construction of meaning can be successfully incorporated into L2 composition methodology without sacrificing the principles on which a class is currently based. We felt that we were able to meet most of our goals, although more empirical measures need to be developed to test more specifically the degree to which the computer program affected student writing. These findings do have more general implications for any form of computer use. This study suggests that CALL does not necessarily by itself promote goals, such as student autonomy, that play a central role in the student-centered classroom. However, when innovative approaches are developed, CALL methods can play an important part in striving toward such goals. Doing so requires the guidance of the instructor in shaping the students' use of the technology. As we move from conceptions of computer as tutor to computer as tool, the instructor's role necessarily expands.

What general conclusions can we reach about this technology implementation process? In considering its positive effects, it is important to note, first, that in comparison to similar classes that did not have this component, necessarily much more of the class time was devoted to learning to use computers, the Internet, and E-mail. We felt that this was a valuable consequence, since many of our students came from countries where these technologies were not pervasive, but they would now be expected to use them in their other courses. Second, the software provided a means by which teachers could write clear and concise comments that could be read and understood by students. Third, the software facilitated peer review by enabling students to send files to each other regardless of what platform they were using; or, students could respond to each other simply by exchanging seats in a computer lab. Fourth, the software provided an environment for students in which they could easily access on-line features, such as a writing handbook. Finally, the software allowed for the on-line exchange of papers, which broke down some of the constraints of time and space for both teachers and students.

We also faced a number of challenges in the process of technology implementation. The introduction of the software was constrained by such factors as the structure of the classes, which limited the time available for using the computer lab; the frustrations of teachers, some of whom felt that the software was too difficult to use since it required them to be tied to their computers; and the limited ability of teachers and students to log on to the Internet to send and receive files. The result was some resistance from teachers who did not want to invest the time required to overcome these problems and from students who already had access to software and did not want to pay for or use another program. Thus, during the process of implementation, we need to think about not only hardware and software but also "humanware."

Any software package should be flexible enough to allow for different needs of instructional programs, teachers, and students. Collaboration among teachers using the program is essential. This means, ideally, departmental support for release time so that teachers can work together. It also means that we need flexibility in the way the software is used. Students, as well as teachers, will adapt software use to their own needs and preferences. Thus, teachers should be flexible in their requirements for software use. Other problems may be beyond the control of the instructor. Problems that cannot be addressed, such as university infrastructure and software cost, will negatively impact the implementation of any software program. Moreover, software publishers need to be aware that "bugs" in their program will discourage all but the most dedicated users from working with their software.

Finally, we would like to reiterate that reading and writing on the computer are not autonomous phenomena but rather are affected by a variety of factors. We have focused specifically on software and how it is introduced; however, obviously other factors need to be explored. Perhaps our most important finding is that the process of implementation is a continually evolving task, one that is never fully completed. New problems (as well as possibilities) arise, for which new responses are necessary. As the technology changes, we need to change our pedagogical approaches as well. Because of these continual changes, we must talk about reading and writing on-line as a process in flux, just as in the age of the Internet, we no longer talk about writing on a computer in terms of how words are processed, as was often the case in the 1980s. In the context of second language acquisition, it is important to examine the cognitive, sociocultural, and affective factors that contribute to L2 writing via classroom empirical studies.

Such research as ours is relevant to teacher education in the computer age. We have tried to show that the implementation of a software package can be a long and complex process that can impact and in turn be impacted by the pedagogical considerations of a particular course. As long as we do not give specific attention to CALL's place in TESOL methodology and teacher training, we run the risk that the increasing implementation of CALL in the ESL curriculum might conflict with the pedagogical principles to which we strive to adhere, even while we assume that CALL promotes our methodological aims. Therefore, CALL pedagogy should not be determined by the computer's capabilities. Instead, we need to understand the demands that technology places on the L2 learner and how the implementation of computer-based approaches alters and possibly facilitates the different dimensions of language acquisition as well as the role of the instructor. We suggest that research, such as ours, in the field of human-computer interaction (HCI), in conjunction with second language acquisition research, serves as the basis for integrating CALL within TESOL methodology and teacher education programs. In pursuing these goals, approaching CALL research from an HCI standpoint holds important promise, particularly with respect to the teaching of reading and writing.

Appendix A. CommonSpace Questionnaire

We are evaluating our use of the program CommonSpace so that we can improve on the way we use the program. We hope you will help us with this evaluation by answering this short questionnaire. You do not need to put your name on this, and your instructor will not see it until after the grades are turned in.

1. I enjoyed using CommonSpace to send and receive papers from my instructor.

   Yes ___   No___   No Difference ___

2. I enjoyed working with my classmates using CommonSpace.

   Yes ___   No ___   No Difference ___

3. I felt I understood the comments my instructor and classmates sent me on CommonSpace.

   Yes ___   No ___   No Difference ___

4. I think using CommonSpace helped my writing.

   Yes ___   No ___   No Difference ___

5. I would take another class using CommonSpace.

   Yes ___   No ___   No Difference ___

6. It was troublesome for me to send files by E-mail.

   Yes ___   No ___   No Difference ___

7. I purchased a copy of CommonSpace.

   Yes ___   No ___

8. The comments I received on CommonSpace were clearer than the ones I receive by hand.

   Yes ___   No ___   No Difference ___

9. By the end of the quarter, I felt I understood how to use CommonSpace.

   Yes ___   No ___   No Difference ___

10. I enjoyed sending papers on-line rather than handing them in.

    Yes ___   No ___   No Difference ___

11. Outside of class, where did you use CommonSpace most often? (Check one.)

___ Office
___ Home
___ Computer Lab

12. Is there another lab where you would like us to install CommonSpace?

13. Which features of CommonSpace did you find most useful? (Check all that apply.)

___ Columns
___ Spell-check
___ Handbook
___ On-line capabilities

14. How do you normally write your papers for this class? (Check only one.)

___ Use CommonSpace for all drafts
___ Use a word-processing program (e.g., Microsoft Word) for the first draft and CommonSpace for the remaining drafts
___ Use a word-processing program for all drafts
___ Use other programs (e.g., E-mail)

15. Compared to the word processor you most frequently use, is CommonSpace better or worse on the following features?

Word processing	___ Better	___ Worse	___ No difference
Spell-checking	___ Better	___ Worse	___ No difference
Sending and receiving files	___ Better	___ Worse	___ No difference
Revising papers	___ Better	___ Worse	___ No difference
Receiving comments	___ Better	___ Worse	___ No difference

Appendix B. CommonSpace Interview Form

1. In using CommonSpace, did you have a copy of the software? Where did you install it?
2. Did you do all your writing on CommonSpace, or did you use another word processor?
3. Did you notice any particular changes in the way you wrote because you were using CommonSpace?
4. In your country, did you use a computer, or did you write by hand?
5. Were you used to writing on a computer in your native language?
6. When you were using CommonSpace, did you write first by hand or on computer?
7. How would you compare using a word processor and using CommonSpace? Did you feel as comfortable using CommonSpace as with your word-processing program?
8. When you were writing a collaborative essay with your partner, how did you use CommonSpace?
9. Did you use the column feature?
10. Were there any differences in using CommonSpace when you were working with a peer compared to when working by yourself?
11. Did you E-mail the papers to each other? Was that convenient? More convenient than exchanging hard copies?
12. Did you ever use E-mail to ask questions about the comments?
13. Did you have any trouble using CommonSpace? What about using Eudora? Were you able to attach files?
14. Did you use "attach files" to send the paper to your instructor? Did you like the fact that you could send it in whenever you wanted?
15. Do you remember what the turnaround time was? When you sent in the paper, how long did it take for you to get it back?
16. Did you feel you had enough revision time when sending the paper back and forth? Do you remember how many times you were able to send the paper in? Were you able to send the paper to your peers and get it back quickly?
17. Did you like working in a group situation?
18. Can you list some specific things that you learned from the comments of your peers?
19. Did you always understand the comments you received from your instructor? Were they always clear to you?
20. If comments were not clear, in what way were they not clear?

21. Did you save the comments from revision to revision, or did you delete the comments?
22. Was it convenient to have different files, or would you prefer to have one file?
23. Did you write in your native language or in English? Did you notice any differences when you used CommonSpace?
24. Did you use the CommonSpace spell-checker? Was it as useful as the one in the word processor?
25. Did you spend more time on your paper when you used Common-Space? If so, why?
26. Besides your English class, do you see any other use for Common-Space?
27. Normally, do you use CommonSpace or a word-processing program?
28. Did you know how to save the CommonSpace file as another format?
29. Did you exchange files in CommonSpace or by a word-processing program?
30. Do you think the cost of $30 is too much for purchasing Common-Space?
31. How often did your class go to the lab? What did you mostly do in the lab?
32. Did you actually create the paper together in the lab, or did you mostly do revision?
33. Did you meet with your peer, or did you do everything by computer?
34. Do your prefer the tutorials face-to-face, or would you rather be able to talk on-line?
35. Did you ever want to be able to communicate with your instructor outside of class?
36. Did you ever use E-mail to ask your instructor questions?

References

Bloch, J. 1998. Installing collaborative software in ESL composition courses. <http://www.esl.ohio-state.edu/comp/staff/bloch/uts/utscover.htm>.

Card, S. K. 1993. Foreword to *Human-computer interaction*, ed. A. Dix, J. Finlay, G. Abowd, and R. Beale, xi–xii. New York: Prentice-Hall.

Dix, A., J. Finlay, G. Abowd, and R. Beale. 1993. *Human-computer interaction*. New York: Prentice-Hall.

Ferris, D., and J. S. Hedgcock. 1998. *Teaching ESL composition: Purpose, process, and practice.* Mahwah, NJ: Lawrence Erlbaum.

Haas, C. 1996. *Writing technology: Studies on the materiality of literacy.* Mahwah, NJ: Lawrence Erlbaum.

Howard, T. W. 1997. *A rhetoric of electronic communities.* Greenwich, CT: Ablex.

Levy, M. 1997. *Computer-assisted language learning: Context and conceptualization.* New York: Oxford University Press.

Palmquist, M., K. Kiefer, J. Hartvigsen, and B. Goodlew. 1998. *Transitions: Teaching writing in computer-supported and traditional classrooms.* Greenwich, CT: Ablex.

Sproull, L., and S. Kiesler. 1991. *Connections: New ways of working in networked organizations.* Cambridge: MIT Press.

Afterword: Lessons on Linking Literacies for L1 Teachers

Andrea Abernethy Lunsford, Stanford University

Given the opportunity to respond to this exciting new collection of essays on the interactive relationship between reading and writing, I found myself enacting many of this text's major claims. Before reading the essays carefully, for example, I composed a brief list of questions and expectations I brought to the text (I was writing to read), and I skimmed the introduction and table of contents, looking for the kinds of connections I could discern among and across titles (I was reading to write). These acts further revealed some of the strategies I put to use every day and highlight their cultural context: I am relentlessly task-oriented (better not miss that deadline!) and intrigued by hierarchies (why are there four sections in the book, in this particular order?) and by the politics of academic publishing (what is the ratio of men to women contributors and what might this ratio suggest about the field of ESL studies today?). Then, of course, I read the book, careful to proceed in the order of the table of contents and to take notes that amounted to a reading journal in which I carried out a kind of collaboration with the editors, the authors, and their work. Finally, I began to write, out of a complex web of reading-writing connections characteristic of even apparently "simple" academic tasks.

All of the reading and writing I have done, however, has been as a native speaker of English reading work written in English. In his foreword to this volume, John Swales introduces himself with "I also happen to be an ESL writing instructor." I happen to be primarily a teacher of students for whom English is the first (and often only) language. Given this institutional and cultural position, I have found this set of essays provocative in extraordinary ways. While the primary audience for *Linking Literacies* is clearly L2 teachers and researchers, these essays should hail a strong secondary audience of L1 instructors. Certainly, those who come to this book can take away a number of valuable lessons.

The first and in some ways most subtle of these lessons for me echoes very much a statement articulated by Swales, who notes in the foreword, "I have taken reading skills too much for granted." In the same way, L1 teachers, especially of introductory composition courses, have also taken the reading part of writing too much for granted. Even those whose writing courses regularly incorporate formal readings (including literature—a practice that Alan Hirvela and Mary Malloy eloquently advocate in essays in this volume) often provide very little actual instruction in reading and rarely attend to and document the largely invisible reading practices of their students. I can identify several reasons for this situation: a persistent albeit very unfortunate backlash against cognitivist research in composition studies; the challenge to improve writing abilities in a very short span of time; the nagging suspicion that attending to reading, especially the reading of literary texts, is just one way faculty have had of not teaching writing. But the essays in *Linking Literacies* call for all teachers of writing to challenge old assumptions and to undertake the kind of research necessary to map the intricate relationships between reading and writing. From William Grabe's comprehensive review of research on these connections, to Joan Carson's meticulous analysis of the reading and writing tasks invoked in three different fields, to Barbara Dobson and Christine Feak's informative demonstrations of how students interrelate reading and writing to produce effective academic critiques, this collection lays the groundwork for an ambitious ongoing research agenda that should be followed carefully and, indeed, contributed to by L1 teachers of reading and writing.

A closely related issue, the relationship of speech to reading and writing, arises in Paul Kei Matsuda's exploration of why literacy was, in the early years of L2 research, marginalized by the primacy of speech. Matsuda's careful historicizing offers another lesson for L1 compositionists, one we began to learn when Janet Emig famously corrected the sharp binary between speech and writing in her influential essay "Writing as a Mode of Learning" (1977). More recently, L1 researchers and teachers are beginning to realize the degree to which oral and written forms of discourse are currently merging and combining in important, provocative, and still largely untheorized ways, especially on-line. Here, too, essays in *Linking Literacies* raise questions about our (at best) partial understanding of how digital literacy and technology are affecting reading and writing, though they do not go so far as to reveal the ways in which the terms themselves—*reading* and *writing*—are today inadequate for the freight they bear. Joel Bloch and Janina Brutt-Griffler, for example, analyze a specific software program, CommonSpace, and assess its usefulness in ESL composition classes, while Bloch provocatively suggests, in another essay in the book, that ESL students may use electronic texts in surprisingly challenging ways.

These essays are, in turn, closely related to others in the volume that touch on two issues of great current interest to L1 teachers and researchers: intellectual property and collaboration. In my mind, these two issues are themselves linked, since collaboration automatically raises questions about textual ownership and about just where acceptable modes of collaboration end and unethical practices (such as plagiarism) begin. Because I have spent so much of my career worrying about these questions, I found particularly compelling the part of the book titled "(E)Merging Literacies and the Challenge of Textual Ownership." While Bloch there traces the way ESL student use of the Web helps to challenge traditional Western concepts of intellectual property and plagiarism, Diane Pecorari's essay illuminates the large—and often harmful—gap between English-speaking academic expectations regarding the use of sources and ESL writers' efforts to meet those expectations. In these essays and especially in Debbie Barks and Patricia Watts's analysis of textual borrowing strategies for ESL writers and how best to teach them, L1 teachers will find much to learn from, for L1 writers at every level struggle to learn how the "experts" use and cite sources, practices that are changing in cyberspace in ways that increasingly challenge even the "experts." Research in L1 composition, then, stands to reap rich rewards for the same kind of research on textual borrowing that Barks and Watts have conducted.

Textual borrowing is, to my mind, one form of collaboration—a form demonstrated in this volume in the essays by Dobson and Feak and Barks and Watts. Several other essays in *Linking Literacies* gesture in intriguing ways toward the need to differentiate more carefully and clearly among such collaborative modes. Bloch and Brutt-Griffler, for example, touch on collaboration among peers and one form of software; Mary Malloy describes a collaboration among peers, teacher, and text; George Newell, Maria Garriga, and Susan Peterson discuss collaboration between students and teacher; and both Georgette Jabbour and Terence Odlin argue for the ongoing usefulness of collaborations between student writers and such technologies as dictionaries and word frequency programs. What marks these practices as collaborative, and what characteristics distinguish them from each other? Which may be especially amenable to the needs of ESL writers, which to L1 writers, and which, if any, to both? While these essays do not take the exploration of these questions as their goal, each does help to point up the social and collaborative nature of reading and writing. In fact, the linked literacies of this volume's title are everywhere here shown to be in constant rich collaboration with one another across a range of tasks, aims, and settings.

This book contains other lessons of importance to L1 researchers and teachers as well, reminding us that "new" is not always "better," that there is a need for more and better training in language study in general and discourse analysis in particular, and that balancing reading and writing activities in any language classroom is an ongoing difficulty. In retrospect, I am struck even more by the many insights I have gained by reading this book and by the many similarities, as well as the differences, between L1 and L2 teacher/researcher concerns. Throughout, I have been especially mindful of just how much L1 compositionists stand to learn from their L2 counterparts. There is all the more reason, then, to bemoan the growing separation of these two groups, as L1 scholars gather at the Conference on College Composition and Communication while L2 scholars cluster at the TESOL meetings. And there is all the more reason to call for more and better collaboration aimed at linking the different but closely related literacies of L1 and L2 readers and writers.

Reference

Emig, J. 1977. Writing as a mode of learning. *College Composition and Communication* 28:122–28.

Contributors

Debbie Barks is a lecturer in the English Language Institute at the University of Michigan, where she teaches courses in academic writing for graduate students. She is actively involved in EAP course development for the graduate students in architecture, and she coordinates the ELI's English for Business Studies Program.

Diane Belcher is director of the ESL Composition Program at Ohio State University; coeditor, with George Braine, of *Academic Writing in a Second Language: Essays on Research and Pedagogy* (1995); and former chair of the TOEFL Test of Written English Committee. She currently serves on the TOEFL Committee of Examiners and coedits the journal *English for Specific Purposes.*

Joel Bloch obtained his doctorate in rhetoric from Carnegie Mellon University and currently teaches in the ESL Composition Program at Ohio State University. Edited volumes he has contributed to include *Academic Writing in a Second Language,* ed. D. Belcher and G. Braine (1995); *Realms of Rhetoric,* ed. V. J. Vitanza and M. Ballif (1990); and *Second Language Reading and Vocabulary Learning,* ed. T. Huckin, M. Haynes, and J. Coady (1993).

Janina Brutt-Griffler is an assistant professor of English at the University of Alabama. Her work has appeared in *TESOL Quarterly* and *World Englishes* and in edited volumes. Currently, she is completing two books on EIL to be published by Multilingual Matters.

Joan G. Carson is associate professor and chair of the Department of Applied Linguistics and English as a Second Language at Georgia State University. Her recent publications include "Reading-Writing Relationships in First and Second Language," *TESOL Quarterly* (1990); *Reading in the Composition Classroom: Second Language Perspectives,* coedited with Ilona Leki (1993); and "Completely Different Worlds: EAP and the Writing Experiences of ESL Students in University Courses," *TESOL Quarterly* (1997). She has served on the editorial board of *TESOL Quarterly* and currently sits on the editorial board of the *Journal of Second Language Writing.* She has served as chair of the Test of Written English Committee and member of the TOEFL Committee of Examiners.

Barbara Dobson, a research assistant and adjunct lecturer in the English Language Institute at the University of Michigan, is coauthor of two ESL reading books, *Reader's Choice* (1994) and *Choice Readings* (1996). She has served as a consultant on language testing in Tunisia and Malaysia and given numerous presentations at TESOL, Language Testing Research Colloquium (LTRC), and National Association of Foreign Student Advisors (now the Association of International Educators).

Christine Feak has been a lecturer at the University of Michigan's English Language Institute since 1988. There she is the lead lecturer for writing courses for undergraduates. In addition to coauthoring, with John Swales, *Academic Writing for Graduate Students* (1994), she has coauthored articles on summary writing, data commentary, and academic legal writing.

Maria C. Garriga is assistant professor of Spanish and chair of the Department of Foreign Languages at Thomas More College. She obtained her doctorate in foreign and second language education from Ohio State University.

William Grabe is professor of English and chair of the English Department at Northern Arizona University. His recent publications include *Theory and Practice of Writing,* coauthored with Robert B. Kaplan (1996); *Communicative Language Proficiency: Definition and Implications for TOEFL 2000,* coauthored with Carol Chapelle and Margie Berns (1997); and "Discourse Analysis and Reading Instruction," in *Functional Approaches to Written Text,* ed. T. Miller (1997). He is a consultant with ETS on the TOEFL 2000 project and editor of the *Annual Review of Applied Linguistics.*

Alan Hirvela teaches in the ESL Composition Program at Ohio State University. He has published articles and reviews in *English for Specific Purposes, ELT Journal, System, Modern Language Journal, TESOL Journal, JALT Journal, Language Issues,* and other professional journals. He is currently an assistant editor for *English for Specific Purposes.*

Georgette Jabbour is assistant professor of English and coordinator of the ESL Program at the New York Institute of Technology, Old Westbury Campus. She holds a bachelor's degree in English from Damascus University, Syria; a master's degree in TESOL from the University of Illinois at Urbana-Champaign; and a doctorate in applied linguistics from the University of Birmingham, England. Her article "Where Is the Writer in a Frequency List? Using a Corpus of Medical Research Articles in Teaching" appeared in the proceedings of the International Conference on Practical Applications of Language Corpora (1997).

Ilona Leki is professor of English and director of ESL at the University of Tennessee. She coedits the *Journal of Second Language Writing,* is the author of *Understanding ESL Writers: A Guide for Teachers* (1992) and *Academic Writing: Exploring*

Processes and Strategies (1995), and is coeditor, with Joan Carson, of *Reading in the Composition Classroom: Second Language Perspectives* (1993). She has published widely on the development of academic literacy and is the winner of the 1996 TESOL/Newbury House Distinguished Research Award.

Andrea Abernethy Lunsford is professor of English at Stanford University. She has published numerous articles and reviews on composition and rhetoric and is the coauthor of *Singular Texts/Plural Authors: Perspectives on Collaborative Writing* (1990), *The New St. Martin's Handbook* (1999), *The Everyday Writer* (1997), *Easy Writer* (1998), *Four Worlds of Writing* (1991), and *Preface to Critical Reading* (1984). She is coeditor of *Essays on Classical Rhetoric and Modern Discourse* (1984), *The Right to Literacy* (1990), *The Future of Doctoral Studies in English* (1989), *The 1987 Coalition Conference: Democracy through Language* (1989), *Reclaiming Rhetorica: Women in the Rhetorical Tradition* (1995), and *The Presence of Others* (1997).

Mary Ellen Malloy received her master's degree in English from the University of Iowa and her doctorate in foreign and second language education from Ohio State University, where she received the university's Graduate Teaching Associate Award and Provost's Fellowship. Her article "'*Ein Riessen-SpaB!*' ('Great Fun!'): Using Authentic Picture Books to Teach a Foreign Language" appeared in *The New Advocate* (1999). She has taught both Spanish and German and is presently the German teacher at Central High School in Champaign, Illinois.

Paul Kei Matsuda is assistant professor of English at Miami University (Ohio). He received his doctorate in English from Purdue University, where he taught the graduate practicum in teaching ESL writing as well as undergraduate and graduate writing courses for both native and nonnative speakers of English. He has coedited two books, *Landmark Essays on ESL Writing* (forthcoming) and *On Second Language Writing* (forthcoming), and he cochaired the Symposium on Second Language Writing at Purdue University in 1998. His articles have appeared in *College Composition and Communication, Composition Studies, Journal of Second Language Writing,* and *Written Communication.*

George Newell is professor of English education at Ohio State University. His recent publications include "How Much Are We the Wiser? Continuity and Change in Writing and Learning in the Content Areas," in *The Reading-Writing Connection,* ed. N. Nelson and R. C. Calfee (1998); "Reader-Based and Teacher-Centered Instructional Tasks," *Journal of Literacy Research* (1996); and, with coauthor P. Winograd, "Writing about and Learning from History Texts: The Effects of Task and Academic Ability," *Research in the Teaching of English* (1995). Since 1994, he has been actively involved in developing the Professional Development Schools network to encourage collaboration between intern teachers and experienced teachers in urban high school settings.

Terence Odlin is associate professor of English at Ohio State University. He is the author of *Language Transfer* (1989) and editor of *Perspectives on Pedagogical Grammar* (1994).

Diane Pecorari is a doctoral student at the University of Birmingham in England. Her paper "International Contact and Academic Values: The Example of Plagiarism" will appear in the proceedings of the 1998 SIETAR (Society for International Education, Training, and Research) Europa Congress. Her doctoral dissertation focuses on institutional responses to plagiarism.

Susan S. Peterson obtained her doctorate in foreign and second language education from Ohio State University. She has taught Spanish and English for several years at the college level and is currently teaching at Veritas Christian School in Columbus, Ohio.

John M. Swales is professor of linguistics and director of the English Language Institute at the University of Michigan, positions he has held since 1987. His recent book-length publications include *Genre Analysis: English in Academic and Research Settings* (1990); *Academic Writing for Graduate Students: Essential Tasks and Skills,* coauthored with Christine Feak (1994); and *Other Floors, Other Voices: A Textography of a Small Academic Building* (1998). He is editor emeritus of *English for Specific Purposes—an International Journal.*

Patricia Watts holds a master's degree in TESL from the University of Illinois. She currently serves as the associate director of the ESL Service Courses at the University of Illinois at Urbana-Champaign.

Author Index

Subject Index